eBay®
FOR
DUMMIES®
6TH EDITION

by Marsha Collier

WILEY

Wiley Publishing, Inc.

eBay® For Dummies®, 6th Edition

Published by
Wiley Publishing, Inc.
111 River Street
Hoboken, NJ 07030-5774
www.wiley.com

Copyright © 2009 by Wiley Publishing, Inc., Indianapolis, Indiana

Published by Wiley Publishing, Inc., Indianapolis, Indiana

Published simultaneously in Canada

No part of this publication may be reproduced, stored in a retrieval system or transmitted in any form or by any means, electronic, mechanical, photocopying, recording, scanning or otherwise, except as permitted under Sections 107 or 108 of the 1976 United States Copyright Act, without either the prior written permission of the Publisher, or authorization through payment of the appropriate per-copy fee to the Copyright Clearance Center, 222 Rosewood Drive, Danvers, MA 01923, (978) 750-8400, fax (978) 646-8600. Requests to the Publisher for permission should be addressed to the Permissions Department, John Wiley & Sons, Inc., 111 River Street, Hoboken, NJ 07030, (201) 748-6011, fax (201) 748-6008, or online at http://www.wiley.com/go/permissions.

Trademarks: Wiley, the Wiley Publishing logo, For Dummies, the Dummies Man logo, A Reference for the Rest of Us!, The Dummies Way, Dummies Daily, The Fun and Easy Way, Dummies.com, Making Everything Easier, and related trade dress are trademarks or registered trademarks of John Wiley & Sons, Inc. and/or its affiliates in the United States and other countries, and may not be used without written permission. eBay is a registered trademark of eBay, Inc. All other trademarks are the property of their respective owners. Wiley Publishing, Inc., is not associated with any product or vendor mentioned in this book.

For general information on our other products and services, please contact our Customer Care Department within the U.S. at 877-762-2974, outside the U.S. at 317-572-3993, or fax 317-572-4002.

For technical support, please visit www.wiley.com/techsupport.

Wiley also publishes its books in a variety of electronic formats. Some content that appears in print may not be available in electronic books.

Library of Congress Control Number: 2009928738

ISBN: 978-0-470-49741-8

Manufactured in the United States of America

10 9 8 7 6 5 4 3

WILEY

About the Author

Marsha Collier spends a good deal of time on eBay. She loves buying and selling (she's a PowerSeller with her own eBay store) as well as meeting eBay users from around the world. As a columnist, an author of three bestselling books on eBay, and an invited lecturer at eBay Live, she shares her knowledge of eBay with millions of online sellers. *eBay For Dummies* is published in special versions for the United Kingdom, Canada, Germany, and Australia. Currently, she has 15 books in print on her favorite subject — eBay.

Before her eBay career took off, Marsha owned and operated her own marketing and advertising firm, a company that won numerous awards and earned her "Small Business of the Year" accolades from several organizations. She got started with eBay during the site's early years and quickly mastered the art of buying and reselling for profit.

Marsha is one of the foremost eBay experts and educators in the world and the top-selling eBay author. In 1999 Marsha created the first edition of *eBay For Dummies*, the bestselling book for eBay beginners. She followed up the success of the first book with *Starting an eBay Business For Dummies,* a book targeting individuals interested in making e-commerce their full-time profession. That book became an instant nationwide hit, making several notable bestseller lists. These books are updated regularly to keep up with site and market changes.

Marsha's books have sold over 1,000,000 copies (including the special editions in foreign countries — two in Australia, two in Canada, and two in the United Kingdom — as well as translations in Spanish, French, Italian, Chinese and German).

Along with her writing, Marsha is an experienced e-commerce educator. She was the lead instructor at eBay University (teaching seminars all over the United States), as well as a regular presenter at the eBay Live national convention since its inception. Marsha also hosted "Make Your Fortune Online," a PBS special on online business that premiered in 2005. The show was the basis for her PBS premium five DVD set, "Your Online Business Plan." In 2006, she was invited to address the Innovations Conference in Singapore to present the ideas of e-commerce to a new market. In 2008, she was dubbed one of twenty influential iCitizens in Kelly Mooney's *The Open Brand: When Push Comes to Pull in a Web Made World*, and was invited to speak at a leading e-commerce conference attended by Coca-Cola, Hewlett Packard, Procter & Gamble, Victoria's Secret, and leading e-commerce leaders.

During the holiday season, she does several national satellite media tours to explain the safety of shopping online. She hosts Computer & Technology Radio on KTRB 860 AM in San Francisco as well as on the Web at www.computerandtechnologyradio.com. She also makes regular appearances on television, radio, and in print to discuss customer needs and online commerce.

Marsha currently resides in Los Angeles, CA. She can be reached via her Web site, www.coolebaytools.com or her blog at http://mcollier.blogspot.com.

Dedication

To all the future eBay buyers and sellers who have purchased this book to get a taste of how much fun online buying and selling can be. I look forward to seeing your auctions and hearing your stories.

I dedicate this book also to all the employees at eBay, who work very hard and don't always get noticed or appreciated by the community. I want to thank all of you for your endeavors; you make eBay a fun and profitable site to visit for millions of people. Keep on doing what you're doing.

Author's Acknowledgments

This book couldn't have been written without the input from thousands of eBay sellers and buyers that I've spoken to from all over the country. You inspire me to work harder and do my best to help all of you.

I've made so many friends along my eBay travels: if it wasn't for them, this book wouldn't be here. Thanks to the rest of my eBay buddies — who always seem to have a moment when I call.

I particularly want to thank my editors at Wiley Publishing, Inc.: my really fun and smart project editor Susan Pink; my super tech editor Louise (aunt*patti); Ruby (who, by the way, was one of the very first eBay employees) — she's always there for me!; Steven Hayes, who is always there for supports and ideas; and Andy Cummings, my publisher, who, lucky for me — still takes my calls!

Thank you all!

Publisher's Acknowledgments

We're proud of this book; please send us your comments through our online registration form located at http://dummies.custhelp.com. For other comments, please contact our Customer Care Department within the U.S. at 877-762-2974, outside the U.S. at 317-572-3993, or fax 317-572-4002.

Some of the people who helped bring this book to market include the following:

Acquisitions and Editorial

Project Editor: Susan Pink

(Previous Edition: Nicole Haims)

Acquisitions Editor: Steve Hayes

Copy Editor: Susan Pink

Technical Editor: Patti Louise Ruby

Editorial Manager: Jodi Jensen

Editorial Assistant: Amanda Foxworth

Sr. Editorial Assistant: Cherie Case

Cartoons: Rich Tennant
(www.the5thwave.com)

Composition Services

Project Coordinator: Lynsey Stanford

Layout and Graphics: Reuben W. Davis, Andrea Hornberger, Christine Williams

Proofreaders: Cynthia Fields, Amanda Graham

Indexer: Glassman Indexing Services

Publishing and Editorial for Technology Dummies

Richard Swadley, Vice President and Executive Group Publisher

Andy Cummings, Vice President and Publisher

Mary Bednarek, Executive Acquisitions Director

Mary C. Corder, Editorial Director

Publishing for Consumer Dummies

Diane Graves Steele, Vice President and Publisher

Composition Services

Debbie Stailey, Director of Composition Services

Table of Contents

Introduction

Welcome to *eBay For Dummies,* 6th Edition! Thanks for opening up this book. This is the newly updated version of the original best-selling eBay how-to guide, first published in 1999. Heed my words and you may soon be joining the millions of people interested in learning the no-nonsense facts about eBay from an active user. I'm a longtime eBay shopper and PowerSeller. My original career was in retail marketing and for over 10 years I've been making money on the site. (I even put my daughter through college on my profits!) I work from home and apply my background successfully to all facets of the site.

I can't begin to tell you how excited I am that my enthusiasm and excitement for shopping and selling on eBay has spread to so many corners of the world. eBay users (like you and I) total close to 200 million — that's quite a community. It's a community of buyers who don't feel the need to scour the streets for items to buy and of sellers who forage wholesale items to sell online and make a few dollars (or a full-time living). This makes eBay the new international marketplace, and the best part is that eBay is available to anyone who wants to take the time to figure out how it works.

My books are written sequentially, and this is the one to start with if you're a beginner. *eBay For Dummies* will give you the solid foundation you need to go on to my other, more advanced books on eBay selling.

eBay is a constantly evolving Web site. It isn't too hard to master, but just as with any tool, when you know the ins and outs, you're ahead of the game. You can get the deals when you shop, and you can make the most money when you sell. You've come to the right place to find out all about eBay. This book is designed to help you understand the basics about buying and selling on eBay, the most successful person-to-person trading community. Without the basics, you can't be successful in any endeavor. You get all the tools you need to get moving on eBay, whether you're new to the Internet or a Webaholic. You see how to turn your everyday household clutter into cold, hard cash — and how to look for items that you can sell on eBay. If you're an online shopper (or you'd like to be), I show you how to figure out how much you should spend, how to make smart bids, and how to win the auctions. How much money you earn (or spend) depends entirely on how *often* and how *smartly* you conduct your eBay transactions. *You* decide how often you want to run auctions and place bids; I'm here to help with the *smart* part by sharing tips I've learned over my past ten years on eBay.

A Web site as complex as eBay has many nooks and crannies that may confuse users. Think of this book as a detailed road map that can help you navigate eBay, getting just as much or as little as you want from it. Unlike an actual road map, however, you won't get frustrated folding it back to its original shape. Just close the book and come back anytime you need a question answered.

After you figure out the nuts and bolts of eBay, you can start buying and selling stuff. I have a ton of terrific buying and selling strategies that help you get the most out of your auctions. With this book and a little elbow grease, you can join the ranks of the millions of people who use their home computers to make friends, find great deals, have a lot of fun, and make a profit. When you've got the hang of eBay and feel that it's time to graduate from this book, look for my *Starting an eBay Business For Dummies,* 3rd Edition (Wiley) — it'll take you to the next plateau.

About This Book

Remember those open-book tests that teachers sprang on you in high school? Well, sometimes you may feel like eBay pop-quizzes you while you're online. Think of *eBay For Dummies,* 6th Edition, as your open-book-test cheat sheet with all the answers. You don't have to memorize anything; just keep this book handy to help you get over the confusing parts of eBay. Over the years, some of the top sellers and buyers on the eBay site have visited with me when I'm at a book signing or teaching at eBay University just to show me their dog-eared, highlighted, marred copy of an earlier edition of *eBay For Dummies* that got them started. This book will do the same for you.

With all that in mind, I've divided this book into pertinent sections to help you find your answers fast. I'll show you how to

- Get online and register on eBay.
- Navigate eBay to do just about anything you can think of — search for items for sale, set up auctions, monitor your transactions, and join the community circuit.
- Bid on and *win* eBay auctions.
- Choose an item to sell, pick the right time for your listing, market it so that a bunch of bidders see it, and make a nice profit.
- Communicate well and close deals without problems, whether you're a buyer or a seller.
- Handle problems with finesse, should they crop up.
- Become a part of a unique community of people who like to collect, buy, and sell items of just about every type!

Do not adjust your eyes. To protect the privacy of eBay users, screen images (commonly called *screen shots*) in this book blur user IDs to protect the innocent (or not so . . .).

Foolish Assumptions

You may have picked up this book because you heard that people are making huge money selling on eBay and you want to find out what's going on. Or you heard about the bargains and wacky stuff you can find in the world's largest shopping emporium. If either of these assumptions is true, this is the right book for you.

Here are some other foolish assumptions I've made about you:

- ✔ You have, or would like to have, access to a computer, a modem, and the Internet so that you can do business on eBay.

- ✔ You have an interest in collecting stuff, selling stuff, or buying stuff, and you want to find out more about doing that stuff online.

- ✔ You want tips and strategies that can save you money when you bid or buy and make you money when you sell. (You too? I can relate. We already have a lot in common.)

- ✔ You're concerned about maintaining your privacy and staying away from people who try to ruin everyone's good time with negligent (and sometimes illegal) activity.

How This Book Is Organized

This book has five parts. The chapters stand on their own, which means that you can read Chapter 5 after you read Chapter 10 or skip Chapter 3 altogether. It's all up to you. I do think that you should at least dip into Chapter 1 and Chapter 2 to get an overview on what eBay is all about and find out how to become a registered user.

If you're already conducting transactions on eBay, you certainly can jump ahead to get good tips on advanced strategies to enhance your sales. Don't wait for permission from me — just go for it. I won't argue with you that well-written listings equal higher profits!

Part I: Getting a Feel for eBay

In Part I, I tell you what eBay is and how you use it. I take you through the registration process, help you organize your eBay transactions and interactions using the My eBay page, and get you comfortable navigating the site from the home page.

Part II: Buying Like an Expert

If you're pretty sure you want to start making bids on items, check out Part II, which gives you the lowdown on searching, grading a collectible item's value, researching, bidding, and winning auctions.

That old cliché, "Let the buyer beware," (*caveat emptor* for the literati in the audience) became a cliché because even today (maybe especially today) it's sound advice. Use my friendly, sugar-free tips to help you decide when to bid and when to take a pass.

Part III: Making Money the eBay Way

Part III gets you up-to-speed on how to sell your items on eBay. Think of it as an eBay course in marketing. Here you find important information on how to conduct your auctions, what to do after you sell an item, how to ship the item, and how to keep track of all the money you make. Even Uncle Sam gets to chime in on his favorite topic: taxes. Know the rules so your friendly local tax office doesn't invite you over for a cup of coffee and a little audit.

I also show you how to gussy up your auctions by adding pictures and how to use basic HTML to add a little extra "sell" like they do in infomercials. You can make your digital images look like high art with my tips, hints, and strategies.

Part IV: Even More of eBay's Special Features

Check out Part IV to discover how to handle privacy concerns relating to eBay and how you can resolve buying and selling issues with the help of Trust & Safety, eBay's problem-solving clearinghouse. Also included are ways to have fun with the eBay community and using charity auctions to bid on great items for a good cause.

Part V: The Part of Tens

In keeping with a long *For Dummies* tradition, Part V is a compendium of short chapters that give you ready references and useful facts. I share more terrific tips for buying and selling items, as well as descriptions of my favorite software programs that can help lighten your auction load.

In addition to all these parts, you also get an appendix. It gives some insider information on how to spot a trend before the rest of the world catches on and how to acquire items cheaply that others may spend a bundle on. After you've read this book and you're ready to go to the next level, take a look at my other book, *Starting an eBay Business For Dummies.* It takes off where this book ends.

Icons Used in This Book

These are facts that you just *have* to know! Time is money on eBay. When you see this shortcut or time-saver come your way, read the information and think about all the greenbacks you just saved.

Think of this icon as a sticky note for your brain. If you forget one of the pearls of wisdom revealed to you, you can go back and reread it. If you *still* can't remember something here, go ahead, dog-ear the page — I won't tell. Even better: Use a yellow highlighter.

Don't feel my pain. I've done plenty of things wrong on eBay before and really want to save you from my mistakes. I put these warnings out there bright and bold so that you don't have a bad experience. Don't skip these warnings unless you're enthusiastic about masochism.

When you see this icon, you know you're in for the real deal. I created this icon especially for you to give you war stories and success stories from eBay veterans that can help you strategize, make money, and spare you from the perils of a poorly written auction item description. ("Learn from their experiences" is my motto.) You can skip these icons if you want to, but you may get burned if you do.

You'll also see a sidebar now and then. They contain text on a gray background to make them stand out. Sometimes they have an important short fact that I want you to know or contain some useful technical stuff.

What Now?

Like everything else in the world, eBay changes. Some of the eBay screens in this book may look slightly different than the ones you see on your home computer display. That's just eBay tweaking and improving things on the site. My job is to arm you with everything you need to know to join the eBay community and begin conducting transactions. If you hit rough waters, just look up the problem in the table of contents or index in this book. I either help you solve it or let you know where to go on eBay for some expert advice.

Although eBay makes its complex Web site as easy to navigate as possible, you may still need to refer to this book for help. Don't get frustrated if you have to keep reviewing topics before you feel completely comfortable trading on eBay.

After all, Albert Einstein once said, "Don't commit to memory something you can look up." (Although I forget when he said that. . . .)

Feedback, Please

Communication makes the world go round, and I'd love to hear from you. Contact me at talk2marsha@coolebaytools.com. Please know that I can't answer each and every question you send. There isn't enough time in the day — between writing, teaching, and, oh yes, my personal life! Do know that I will read each e-mail.

Check out my Web site at www.coolebaytools.com. And follow me on Twitter.com for my seller tips and comments; http://twitter.com/marshacollier.

You can also call in and speak to me live on my radio show on 877-474-3302. Every Saturday from noon to 2 p.m. Pacific Time, I co-host the *Computer and Technology Show* with Marc Cohen. We can even help you with your computer problems. The show is also archived online at www.computerand technolgyradio.com and on iTunes.

 eBay is always working to make the site even more new and exciting — that means switching things around to see if you notice. You may click a link on the home page that's there today but replaced with something else tomorrow. When in doubt, use the main navigation bar as your own personal breadcrumb trail.

Part I
Getting a Feel for eBay

The 5th Wave   By Rich Tennant

"Oh, that there's just something I picked up as a grab bag special from the 'Everything Else' category."

In this part . . .

New technology can be intimidating for anyone. You've wanted to visit eBay, maybe make a few dollars selling or getting in on some of the great bargains, but to some, eBay feels kind of big and scary. What you need is someone to point out the most useful tools you need to get around, help you find out how eBay works, and start showing you how to do your own transactions. That's what I do in Part I.

In this part, you find out how to become a registered user, maneuver the eBay home page, and customize your very own private My eBay page. You can also find out about the all-important feedback profile that follows every eBay user around like a shadow.

Chapter 1

Why You're Going to Love Your Time on eBay

*e*Bay has emerged as *the* marketplace of the twenty-first century. Way back in 2003, *Wired* magazine predicted that eBay's promise is that "retailing will become the national pastime." The founders had a pretty great idea back in 1995 (read about some eBay history in the "eBay's humble beginnings" sidebar later in this chapter), and the world has taken to shopping and selling online. eBay is a safe and fun place to shop for everything from collectibles to brand-new clothing, all from the comfort of your home.

eBay is now also a marketplace for new merchandise. It's no longer just the destination for collectibles and old china patterns. These days you can purchase new and useful items, such as alarm systems, fancy electronic toothbrushes, lightbulbs, clothing, cars, homes — just about anything you can think of.

Take a look around your house. Nice Manolos. Spiffy microwave. Great-looking clock. Not to mention all the other cool stuff you own. All these great fashions, household appliances, and collectibles are fabulous to own, but when was the last time your clock turned a profit? When you connect to eBay, your PC or Mac can magically turn into a money machine. Just visit eBay and marvel at all the items that are just a few mouse clicks away from being bought and sold.

In this chapter, I tell you what eBay is and how it works. eBay is the perfect alternative to spending hours wandering through boutiques, antiques shops, or outlet malls looking for the perfect doohickey. It can also be your personal shopper for gifts and day-to-day items. (For more information on how to match the perfect eBay gift with one of your friends, check out my book, *Santa Shops on eBay*, also published by Wiley.)

Not only can you buy and sell stuff in the privacy of your home, but you can also meet people who share your interests. Those who use the eBay site are a friendly bunch, and soon you'll be buying, selling, swapping stories, and trading advice with the best of them.

To get to eBay, you need to access the Internet. To access the Internet, you need a PC or a Mac with an Internet connection. (Inexpensive laptops are available for as little as $299.) If you're not ready to take the high-tech plunge, this book shows you how to start operating on eBay (and earning money) without owning a single cyber thing.

What Is eBay, and How Does It Work?

The Internet is spawning all kinds of businesses (known as *e-commerce* to Wall Street types), and eBay is the superstar. The reason is simple: It's the place where buyers and sellers can meet, do business, share stories and tips, and have fun. It's like one giant online potluck party — but instead of bringing a dish, you sell it!

eBay *doesn't* sell a thing. Instead, the site does what all good hosts do: It creates a comfy environment that brings together people with common interests. You can think of eBay as the person who set you up on your last blind date — except the results are often a lot better. Your matchmaking friend doesn't perform a marriage ceremony but does get you in the same room with your potential soul mate. eBay puts buyers and sellers in a virtual store and lets them conduct their business safely within the rules that eBay has established.

All you need to do to join eBay is fill out a few forms online and click. Congratulations — you're a member with no big fees or secret handshakes. After you register, you can buy and sell anything that falls within the eBay rules and regulations. (Chapter 2 eases you through the registration process.)

The eBay home page, shown in Figure 1-1, is your first step to finding all the cool stuff you can see and do on eBay. You can conduct searches, find out what's happening, and get an instant link to the My eBay page, which helps you keep track of every item you have up for sale or have a bid on. You can read more about the eBay home page in Chapter 3 and find out more about My eBay in Chapter 4.

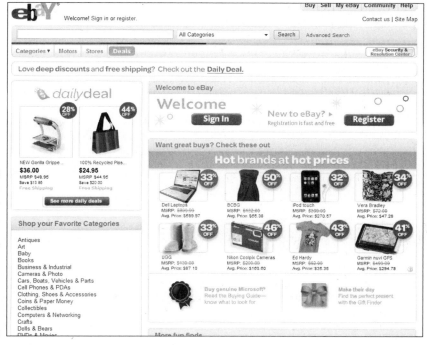

Figure 1-1:
The eBay home page, your starting point for bargains and for making some serious cash.

Yikes! What happened? The eBay home page on your computer looks nothing like the one in Figure 1-1? Don't rub your eyes — even squinting hard won't help; eBay has a different version of the home page for those who have never registered on eBay. Even if *you* have never registered, someone else who uses the computer may already have. Know that whatever version of the eBay home page you view, it has the same basic elements.

eBay's humble beginnings

The long-standing urban legend says eBay all started with a Pez dispenser. But as romantic as the story is (of the young man who designed the site for his fiancé to trade Pez dispensers), the story is, sadly, public relations spin. The founder, Pierre Omidyar, had the right vision at the right time, and the first item he sold on the site, originally named AuctionWeb, was a broken laser pointer. Day by day, new people (including me in 1996) were drawn to the site from Internet chatter. The site eventually grew to the point where it began to strain Pierre's ISP.

The ISP charged him more, so he started charging a small listing fee for sellers, just so he could break even. Legend has it that the day $10,000 in fees arrived in Pierre's mailbox, he quit his day job. (I hope that's not apocryphal too!)

eBay was born on Labor Day 1995. The name eBay is taken from Echo Bay, the name Pierre originally wanted for his company. Upon checking with the State of California, he found that the name was taken by another company, so he shortened the name to eBay — and the rest, as they say, is history.

All about Auctions

The value of an item is determined by how much someone is willing to spend to buy it. That's what makes auctions exciting. eBay offers several kinds of auctions, but for the most part, they all work the same way. An *auction* is a unique sales event where the exact value of the item for sale is not known. As a result, an element of surprise is involved — not only for the bidder (who may end up with a great deal) but also for the seller (who may end up making a killing). Here's how an auction works from a seller's perspective and a bidder's perspective:

- ✔ **Seller:** A seller pays a fee, fills out an electronic form, and sets up the auction, listing a *minimum bid* he or she is willing to accept for the item. Think of an auctioneer at Sotheby's saying, "The bidding for this diamond necklace begins at $5,000." You might *want* to bid $4,000, but the bid won't be accepted. Sellers can also set a *reserve price* — sort of a financial safety net that protects them from losing money on the deal. I explain how this stuff works later in this section.

- ✔ **Bidder:** Bidders in auctions duke it out over a period of time (the minimum is one day, but most auctions last a week or even longer) until one comes out victorious. Usually, the highest bidder wins. The tricky thing about participating in an auction (and the most exciting aspect) is that no one knows the final price an item goes for until the last second of the auction.

eBay auctions

Unlike "traditional" live auctions that end with the familiar phrase "Going once, going twice, sold!" eBay auctions are controlled by the clock. The seller pays a fee and lists the item on the site for a predetermined period of time; the highest bidder when the clock runs out takes home the prize.

Reserve-price auctions

Unlike a minimum bid, which is required in any eBay auction, a *reserve price* protects sellers from having to sell an item for less than the minimum amount they want for it. You may be surprised to see a 1968 Jaguar XKE sports car up for auction on eBay with a minimum bid of only a dollar. It's a fair bet that the seller has put a reserve price on this car to protect himself from losing money. The reserve price allows sellers to set lower minimum bids, and lower minimum bids attract bidders. Unfortunately, if a seller makes the reserve price too high and it isn't met by the end of the auction, no one wins.

eBay charges a fee for sellers to run these auctions. Nobody knows (except the seller and the eBay computer system) what the reserve price is until the auction is over (assuming that the reserve price is met and that someone wins the auction), but you can tell from the auction page whether you're dealing with a reserve-price auction. Reserve-price auctions are in the listings alongside the other items, so you have to click to find out whether it has a reserve. If bids have been made on an item, a message also appears on the page telling you if the reserve price hasn't been met. You can find out more about bidding on reserve-price auctions in Chapter 6 and setting up a reserve-price auction in Chapter 9.

Restricted-access auctions

If you're over 18 years of age and interested in bidding on items of an adult nature, eBay has an Adults Only category, which has restricted access. Although you can peruse the other eBay categories without having to submit credit card information, you must have a credit card number on file on eBay to view and bid on items in this category. Restricted-access auctions are run like the typical timed auctions. To bid on adult items, you first need to agree to a terms of use page after entering your user ID and password. This page pops up automatically when you attempt to access this category.

If you aren't interested in seeing or bidding on items of an adult nature, or if you're worried that your children may be able to gain access to graphic adult material, eBay has solved that problem by excluding adult-content items from easily accessible areas such as the Featured Items page. And children under the age of 18 aren't allowed to register on eBay and should be under an adult's supervision if they do wander onto the site.

Charity auctions: All for a good cause

A *charity auction* is a high-profile fund-raising auction run by eBay Giving Works where the proceeds go to a selected charity. Most people don't wake up in the morning wanting to own the shoes that Ron Howard wore when he put his footprints in cement at Mann's Chinese Theater in Hollywood, but one-of-a-kind items like that often are auctioned off in charity auctions. (In fact, someone did want those shoes badly enough to buy them for a lot of money on eBay.) Charity auctions became popular after the NBC *Today Show* sold an autographed jacket on eBay for over $11,000 with the proceeds going to Toys for Tots. Charity auctions

are run like most other auctions on eBay, but because they're immensely popular, bidding can be fierce, and the dollar amounts can go sky high. Many famous celebrities use eBay to help out their favorite charities. Billionaire Warren Buffet auctions a private lunch each year to support one of his favorite charities — in 2008 lunch for 8 with Warren went for over $2,110,100. I suggest that you visit these auctions and bid whenever you can. Charity auctions are a win-win situation for everyone. You can read more about celebrity auctions in Chapter 18.

Private (shhh-it's-a-secret) listings

Some sellers choose to hold *private listings* because they know that some buyers may be embarrassed to be seen bidding on a box of racy neckties in front of the rest of the eBay community. Others may go the private route because they are selling big-ticket items and don't want to disclose their bidder's financial status.

Private auctions are run like the typical timed auctions except that each bidder's identity is kept secret. At the end of the auction, eBay provides contact info to the seller and to the high bidder, and that's it.

You can send e-mail questions to the seller in a private auction, but you can't check out your competition because the item page will never show the high bidder's user ID.

Buying It Now on eBay

You don't have to participate in an auction on eBay to buy something. If you want to make a purchase — if it's something you *must* have — you can usually find the item and buy it immediately. Of course, using Buy It Now (*BIN* in eBay speak) doesn't come with the thrill of an auction, but purchasing an item at a fraction of the retail price without leaving your chair or waiting for an auction to end has its own warm and fuzzy kind of excitement. If you seek this kind of instant gratification on eBay, visit eBay Stores. Or you can isolate these items by clicking the Buy It Now tab when browsing categories or performing searches.

eBay Stores

Visiting eBay Stores is as easy as clicking the eBay Stores link from the home page. Thousands of eBay sellers have set up stores with merchandise meant for you to Buy It Now. eBay Stores are classified just like eBay, and you can buy anything from socks to jewelry to appliances.

Sellers who open an eBay Store have to meet a certain level of experience on eBay, and when you buy from an eBay Store, you're protected by the same fraud protection policy that covers you in an eBay auction.

Buy It Now and fixed-price sales

More and more sellers are selling items with a *Buy It Now* option or at a fixed price. These features enable you to buy an item as soon as you see one at a price that suits you. For more on how these sales work, check out Chapter 6.

So You Wanna Sell Stuff

If you're a seller, creating an auction page on eBay is as simple as filling out an online form. You type the name of your item and a short description, add a crisp digital picture, set your price, and voilà — it's auction time. (Okay, it's a tad more involved than that, but not much). eBay charges a small fee ($0.05 (during promotions) to $4.00) for the privilege. When you list your item, millions of people (eBay has over 100 million registered users) from all over the world can take a gander at it and place bids. With a little luck, a bidding war may break out and drive the bids up high enough for you to turn a nice profit. After the auction, you deal directly with the buyer, who sends you the payment either through a payment service or through the mail. Then you ship the item. Abracadabra — you just turned your item (everyday clutter, perhaps) into cash. You can run as many auctions as you want, all at the same time. To get info on deciding what to sell, leaf through Chapter 9; to find out how to set up an auction, jump to Chapter 10; and to get the scoop on advanced selling techniques, visit Chapter 14. When you're ready to go pro, check out the appendix.

So You Wanna Buy Stuff

If you're a collector or you just like to shop for bargains on everyday goods, you can browse 24 hours a day through the items up for auction in eBay's tens of thousands of categories, which range from Antiques to Writing Instruments. Find the item you want, do a little research on what you're buying and who's selling it, place your bid, and keep an eye on it until the auction closes. When I wrote *Santa Shops on eBay* (Wiley), I had a great time visiting the different categories and buying a little something here and there — it's amazing just how varied the selection is. I even bought some parts for my pool cleaner!

Take a look at Chapter 5 for info on searching for items to bid on. When you see an item you like, you can set up a bidding strategy and let the games begin. Chapter 6 gives you bidding strategies that can make you the winner. After you win your first auction, look for expert advice about completing the transaction in Chapter 8.

You can bid as many times as you want on an item, and you can bid on as many auctions as you want. Just keep in mind that each bid is a binding contract that you are required to pay should you win.

Research for Fun and Profit

eBay's awesome search engine allows you to browse through countless *categories* of items up for sale. As a buyer, you can do lots of comparison shopping on that special something you just can't live without or just browse around until something catches your eye. If you're a seller, the search engine allows you to keep your eye on the competition and get an idea of how hot your item is. That way, you can set a competitive price. To find out more about using search options and categories, check out Chapters 3 and 5.

The search engine also lets you find out what other people are bidding on. From there, you can read up on a seller's *feedback ratings* (eBay's ingenious honor system) to get a sense of the seller's reputations — *before* you deal with them.

eBay's Role in the Action

Throughout the auction process, eBay's computers keep tabs on what's going on. When the auction or sale is over, eBay takes a small percentage of the final selling price and instructs the seller and buyer to contact each other through e-mail. At this point, eBay's job is pretty much over, and eBay steps aside.

Most of the time, everything works great, everybody's happy, and eBay never has to step back into the picture. But if you happen to run into trouble in paradise, eBay can help you settle the problem, whether you're the buyer or the seller.

eBay regulates members with a detailed system of checks and balances known as *feedback,* which is described in Chapter 4. The grand plan is that the community polices itself. Don't get me wrong — eBay does jump in when shady activity comes to light. But the people who keep eBay most safe are the community members, the buyers and sellers who have a common stake in conducting business honestly and fairly. Every time you sell something or win an auction, eBay members have a chance to leave a comment about you. You should do the same for them. If they're happy, the feedback is positive; otherwise, the feedback is negative. Either way, your feedback sticks to you like glue.

Building a great reputation with positive feedback ensures a long and profitable eBay career. Negative feedback, like multiple convictions for grand-theft auto, is a real turnoff to most folks and can make it hard to do future business on eBay.

If your feedback rating becomes a –4 (negative 4), eBay suspends your buying and selling privileges. You can find out more about how eBay protects you as a buyer or a seller in Chapter 16.

Features and Fun Stuff

So eBay is all about making money, right? Not exactly. The folks at eBay aren't kidding when they call it a community — a place where people with similar interests can compare notes, argue, buy, sell, and meet each other. Yes, people have married after meeting on eBay. (Take a guess how friends bought them wedding gifts!)

Chatting it up

eBay has dozens of specific chat rooms and discussion boards (even a Night Owl's Nest — for those who can't sleep) whose topics range from advertising to trading cards. So if you have no idea what that old Mobil gas station sign you found in your grandfather's barn is worth, just post a message on the Advertising chat board. Somewhere out there is an expert with an answer for you. Your biggest problem is deciding whether to keep the sign or put it up for auction. Those are good problems to have! For more about posting messages and chat rooms, visit Chapters 5 and 17.

Trust & Safety

Trust & Safety is the catchall resource for information and services about making deals on eBay safer — and for information on what to do if deals go sour. I don't like to think about it, but sometimes — despite your best efforts to be a good eBay user — buyers or sellers don't keep their word. In a small percentage of cases, unscrupulous louts invade the site and try to pull scams. You may buy an item that isn't as it was described, or the winner of your auction doesn't send payment. Sometimes even honest members get into disputes. Trust & Safety is an excellent resource when you need questions answered or you need a professional to come in and handle an out-of-hand situation. Chapter 16 tells you all about Trust & Safety.

Extra Gizmos You're Gonna Want

At some point in your eBay career, you'll become comfortable with all the computer-related hoops you have to jump through to make the eBay magic happen. At that time, you may be ready to invest in a few extra devices that can make your eBay experiences even better. Digital cameras and scanners can help make your time on eBay a more lucrative and fun adventure. You find out how to use digital technology in your auctions in more detail in Chapter 14.

Chapter 2

Ready, Set, Go: Signing Up on eBay

In This Chapter

▶ Using eBay's easy forms

▶ Getting up close and personal about your privacy

▶ Identifying with user IDs and passwords

▶ Learning the ropes (eBay rules and regs)

You've probably figured out that you sign on to eBay electronically, which means you don't *really* sign on the dotted line as folks did in days of old. Nowadays, the art of scrawling your signature has become as outdated as vinyl records (although you can still get very collectible vinyl records on eBay if you're feeling nostalgic).

Compared to finding a parking space at a shopping center during the holidays, signing up for eBay is a snap. The toughest thing you have to do is type your e-mail address correctly (and, if you're like me, that's often a challenge).

In this chapter, you find out everything you need to know about registering on eBay. You get tips on what information you have to disclose and what you should keep to yourself. Don't worry — this is an open-book test. You don't need to memorize state capitals, the periodic table, or even multiplication tables. (Whew.)

Registering on eBay

You don't have to wear one of those icky "Hello, My Name Is" stickers on your shirt after you sign on, but eBay needs to know some things about you before it grants you membership. You and millions of other folks will be roaming around eBay's online treasure trove; eBay needs to know who's who. So, keeping that in mind, sign in, please!

You don't have to be a rocket scientist to register on eBay, but you can buy a model rocket or something bigger after you do. The only hard-and-fast rule on eBay is that you must be 18 years of age or older. Don't worry, the Age Police won't come to your house to card you; they have other ways to discreetly ensure that you're at least 18 years old. (**Hint:** Credit cards do more than satisfy account charges.) If you're having a momentary brain cramp and you've forgotten your age, but you can hum the theme to *Speed Racer* when you gun your car engine — you're in. Or if you can remember watching the original episodes of that favorite show of the '90s, you're in. Head to the eBay home page and register. The entire process takes only a few minutes.

Registering Is Free, Fun, and Fast

Before you can sign up for some fun on eBay, you have to be connected to the Web. This is the time to fire up your computer and connect to the Internet. After you open your Internet browser, you're ready to sign up.

Just type **www.ebay.com** in the address box of your browser and press Enter. Your next stop is the eBay home page. Right there, where you can't miss it, is the Register button (look for the big red button, as you can see in Figure 2-1). Click the button and let the sign-up process begin. See Chapter 3 for details.

The eBay home page changes all the time. If you don't see a Register button, look around the page — a Register button or link is there somewhere.

Here's an overview of how easy it is to register:

1. **Enter the basic required info.**

2. **Read and accept the User Agreement.**

3. **Confirm your e-mail address.**

4. **Breeze through (or past) the optional information.**

The following sections fill you in on all the details.

The Registration pages on eBay are through a secure SSL connection. *SSL* (Secure Sockets Layer) enables you to have an encrypted connection to eBay because a bunch of really smart techie types made it that way. You can tell you're on an SSL connection because the normal *http* at the beginning of the Web address (also called the URL) is now *https*. Also, you'll see a small closed lock at the bottom-left (or bottom-right) corner of your screen. I could tell you how SSL works, but instead I'll just give you the bottom line: It *does* work, so trust me and use it. The more precautions eBay (and you) take, the harder it is for some hypercaffeinated high-school kid to get into your files.

When you're at the Registration form, you go through a four-step process.

Like, what's your sign? Filling in required information

After you click the Register button, you're taken to the heart of the eBay Registration pages. You may register as a business or as an individual; I registered as an individual (even though I run a business on eBay). So if you don't quite have a business up and running, register simply as an individual. To get started, follow these steps:

1. **At the top of the first registration page, after eBay shows the steps of the registration process, fill in some required information.**

   Here's what eBay wants to know about you:

   - Your full name, address, and primary telephone number. eBay keeps this information on file in case the company (or a member who is a transaction partner) needs to contact you.

   - Your e-mail address (`yourname@myISP.com`).

If you register with an anonymous e-mail service such as Yahoo! Mail, Gmail, or Hotmail, you're taken to a page that requires additional information for authentication. It wouldn't surprise me if eBay will be randomly authorizing all new members by requiring a credit card. (This is for your safety.) You must provide valid credit card information for identification purposes. Your information is protected by eBay's privacy policy, and your credit card won't be charged.

After you input your personal information, you're ready to create your eBay persona.

2. Scroll down the page to select your new eBay user ID.

See "A Not-So-Quick Word about Choosing a User ID," later in this chapter, for some tips on selecting your user ID.

Because many of the "good" user IDs are taken, eBay supplies a link on the registration form to check on the availability of your preferred ID. (I found a pretty good one in Figure 2-2. If your chosen name is taken, try again. (Lather, rinse, repeat). Finding an awesome user ID can be as difficult as finding an untaken vanity plate at the California DMV.

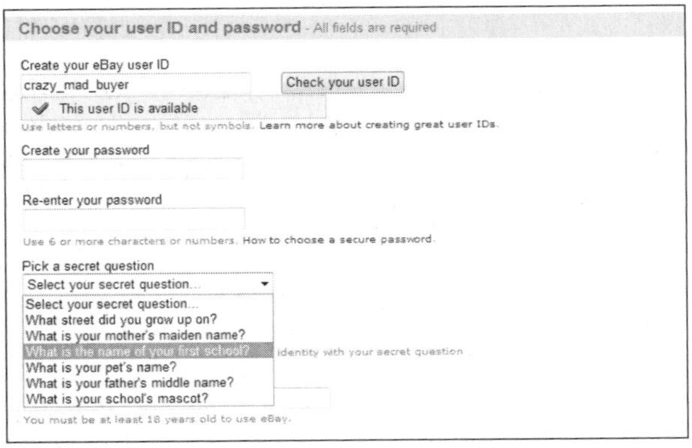

Choose your user ID and password · All fields are required

Create your eBay user ID

crazy_mad_buyer   [Check your user ID]

✔ This user ID is available

Use letters or numbers, but not symbols. Learn more about creating great user IDs.

Create your password

Re-enter your password

Use 6 or more characters or numbers. How to choose a secure password.

Pick a secret question

Select your secret question... ▾

Select your secret question...
What street did you grow up on?
What is your mother's maiden name?
What is the name of your first school?
What is your pet's name?
What is your father's middle name?
What is your school's mascot?

...identity with your secret question

You must be at least 18 years old to use eBay.

Figure 2-2:
Type your proposed user ID and check if it's available.

3. Choose a password, enter it in the Create Your Password box, and then type it a second time in the Re-enter Your Password box to confirm it.

For more information on choosing a password, see "A Quick Word about Passwords," later in this chapter.

4. Create your unique secret question and input the answer.

The secret question you select here is used by eBay to identify you if you ever have problems signing in.

5. **If eBay requires your credit card information (for identification that you're a real person), it will ask on the next screen.**

6. **Type your date of birth and fill in the Verification code.**

7. **Make sure all the info you entered is correct.**

   Think back to your second-grade teacher, who kept saying, "Class, check your work." Remember that? She's still right! Review your answers.

8. **Indicate that you agree to eBay's Terms and Policies.**

   You can find more information on this agreement later in the chapter.

9. **Click the Register button to move on to the next screen.**

   (If you've made a mistake, eBay gives you the opportunity to correct the information by using the Edit Information button).

   If eBay finds a glitch in your registration, such as an incorrect area or zip code, you see a warning message. This is part of eBay's security system to ward off fraudulent registrations. Use the Back button to correct the information — if you put in a wrong e-mail address, for example, eBay has no way of contacting you, so you don't hear a peep from eBay regarding your registration until you go through the entire process all over again.

If you registered with an anonymous e-mail service, such as Yahoo! Mail or Hotmail, you must enter your credit card information, as I mentioned earlier, before you see the license agreement, which I cover in the next section. If, when you look at it, your eyes start glazing over at all the legalese, the next section can help you make sense of it.

Do you solemnly swear to . . . ?

During the registration you'll be asked to check the boxes that say you agree to the eBay User Agreement and Privacy Policy. At this point, you take an oath to keep eBay safe for democracy and commerce. You promise to play well with others, not to cheat, and to follow the Golden Rule. No, you're not auditioning for a superhero club, but don't ever forget that eBay takes this stuff very seriously. You can be kicked off eBay or worse. (Can you say "federal investigation"?)

Be sure to read the User Agreement thoroughly when you register. So that you don't have to put down this riveting book to read the legalese right this minute, I provide the nuts and bolts here:

✔ You understand that every transaction is a legally binding contract. (Click the User Agreement link at the bottom of any eBay page for the current eBay Rules and Regulations.)

✔ You agree that you can pay for the items you buy and the eBay fees that you incur. (Chapter 8 fills you in on how eBay takes its cut of the auction action.)

✔ You understand that you're responsible for paying any taxes.

✔ You're aware that if you sell prohibited items, eBay can forward your personal information to law enforcement for further investigation. (Chapter 9 explains what you can and can't sell on eBay — and what eBay does to sellers of prohibited items.)

✔ eBay makes clear that it is just a *venue,* which means it's a place where people with similar interests can meet, greet, and do business.

When everything goes well, the eBay Web site is like a school gym that opens for Saturday swap meets. At the gym, if you don't play by the rules, you can get tossed out. But if you don't play by the rules on eBay, the venue gets un-gymlike in a hurry. eBay has the right to get state and federal officials to track you down and prosecute you. But fair's fair; if you click the appropriate box on this page, eBay keeps you posted by e-mail of any updates in the User Agreement.

If you're a stickler for fine print, click the links provided on the registration page for all the *Ps* and *Qs* of the latest policies. The User Agreement is vital to your success on eBay.

Before you can proceed, you must click the two check boxes, indicating that you really, *really* understand what it means to be an eBay user. Because I know that you, as a law-abiding eBay member, will have no problem following the rules, go ahead and click the I Agree to These Terms button at the bottom of the page. You're transported to a screen stating that eBay is sending you an e-mail. You're almost done.

The next step is confirming your e-mail address, which I cover in the next section.

It must be true if you have it in writing

After you accept the User Agreement and Privacy Policy, eBay takes less than a minute to e-mail you an activation notice. When you receive the eBay registration activation e-mail, be sure to print it, and don't delete the e-mail — save it somewhere special.

With your confirmation number in hand, head back to the eBay Registration page by clicking the link supplied in your e-mail. If your e-mail doesn't support links, go to this address:

```
cgi4.ebay.com/ws/eBayISAPI.dll?RegisterConfirmCode
```

After you reconnect with eBay and it knows your e-mail address is genuine, you'll be heartily congratulated with an eBay e-mail. It's time to start shopping!

If you don't receive your eBay registration confirmation e-mail within 24 hours, there was most likely an error in your e-mail address. At this point, the customer-support folks can help you complete the registration process. Try visiting the Contact Us link on the eBay home page. They are always happy to help.

If for some reason (even a late night watching the *24* marathon is a perfectly acceptable excuse) you incorrectly type the wrong e-mail address, you have to start the registration process all over again with a different user ID (eBay holds the previous ID for 30 days). If you run into a snag, you can click the Contact Us button to reach Live Help. See Figure 2-3 for one of my previous Live Help discussions.

Figure 2-3: Within minutes of clicking Live Help, I was online with a real person.

Getting to know you: Optional information

When you're a full-fledged, officially registered member of the eBay community, you may see an eBay pop-up window, giving you the option to provide more information about yourself. These optional questions allow you to fill in your self-portrait for your new pals from eBay.

Although eBay doesn't share member information with anyone, you don't have to answer the optional questions if you don't want to.

The following points show you the optional questions eBay asks. You decide what you feel comfortable divulging and what you want to keep personal. eBay asks for this information because the company wants a better picture of who is using its Web site. In marketing mumbo-jumbo, this stuff is called *demographics* — statistics that characterize a group of people who make up a community. In this case, it's the eBay community. Here is the optional information you can provide:

- **Gender:** This first choice gets right down to the basics; some people find it a good test of whether the requests for information seem too personal. (eBay will no doubt figure it out anyway when they see what items you search the site for!)

- **Annual household income:** Fill this in if you want to (eBay states that this info is kept anonymous), but I think this information is too personal. If you're not comfortable with providing it, skip it.

- **Your highest completed education level:** Again if this is too personal, leave this area blank.

After selecting your responses from the drop-down box, you can click Submit. If you're not in the mood right now, you can click the Answer Later link. (This pop-up box reappears for your response later in your eBay dealings.) If you don't want to answer any demographic queries, click the Please Don't Ask Me Again link at the bottom of the pop-up window.

If somebody you're in a transaction with requests your info, you get an e-mail from eBay giving you the name, phone number, city, and state of the person making the request. Keep your information up-to-date. If you don't, you risk being ejected from the site. See Chapter 15 for details.

A Quick Word about Passwords

Choosing a good password is not as easy (but is twice as important) as it may seem. Whoever has your password can (in effect) "be you" on eBay — running sales, bidding on auctions, and leaving possibly litigious feedback for others. Basically, such an impostor can ruin your eBay career and possibly cause you serious financial grief.

As with any online password, you should follow these rules to protect your privacy:

✔ Don't choose an obvious password, such as your birthday, your first name, or (especially!) your Social Security number. (***Hint:*** If it's too easy to remember, it's probably too easy to crack.)

✔ Make things tough on the bad guys — combine numbers and letters (use uppercase and lowercase) or create nonsensical words.

✔ Don't give out your password to anyone — it's like giving away the keys to the front door of your house.

✔ If you ever suspect that someone has your password, immediately change it by going to the following address:

```
https://scgi.ebay.com/ws/eBayISAPI.dll?ForgotYourPasswordShow
```

✔ Change your password every few months just to be on the safe side.

✔ Don't use the same password for eBay and PayPal.

A Not-So-Quick Word about Choosing a User ID

eBay gives you the option of picking your user ID. Making up a user ID is my favorite part. If you've never liked your real name (or never had a nickname), here's your chance to correct that situation. Have fun. Consider choosing an ID that tells a little about you. Of course, if your interests change, you may regret having too narrow a user ID.

You can call yourself just about anything; you can be silly or creative or boring. But remember, this ID is how other eBay users will know you. So here are some commonsense rules:

✔ Don't use a name that would embarrass your mother.

✔ Don't use a name with a negative connotation, such as *scam-guy*.

✔ Don't use a name that's too weird. If people don't trust you, they won't buy from you.

✔ eBay doesn't allow spaces in user IDs, so make sure that the ID makes sense when putting two or more words together.

If you're dying to have several short words as your user ID, you can use under-scores or hyphens to separate them, as in *super-shop-a-holic*. If you sign in to eBay once a day on your computer, typing underscores or dashes won't slow you down.

You can change your user ID once every 30 days if you want to, but I don't recommend it. People come to know you by your user ID. If you change your ID, your past does play tagalong and attaches itself to the new ID. But if you change your user ID too many times, people may think you're trying to hide something.

Nevertheless, to change your user ID, click the My eBay link at the top of most eBay pages. From your My eBay login page, click the Preferences/Set-up tab and scroll to the Change My User ID link, fill in the boxes, and click the Change User ID button. You now have a new eBay identity.

eBay also has some user ID rules to live by:

- ✔ No offensive names (like &*#@@guy).

- ✔ No names with *eBay* in them. (It makes you look like you work for eBay, and eBay takes a dim view of that.)

- ✔ No names with & (even if you *do* have both looks&brains).

- ✔ No names with @ (like @Aboy).

- ✔ No symbols such as the greater than or less than symbols (> <) or consecutive underscores _ _.

- ✔ No IDs that begin with an *e* followed by numbers, an underscore, a dash, a period, or a dot.

- ✔ No names of one letter (such as Q).

When you choose your user ID, make sure that it isn't a good clue for your password. For example, if you use *Natasha* as your user ID, don't choose *Boris* as your password. Even Bullwinkle could figure that one out.

Hey, AOL users, this one's for you: Make sure that your Mail Controls are set to receive e-mails from eBay. If you have Internet e-mail blocked, you need to update your AOL Mail Controls. To do so, enter the AOL keyword **Mail Controls**.

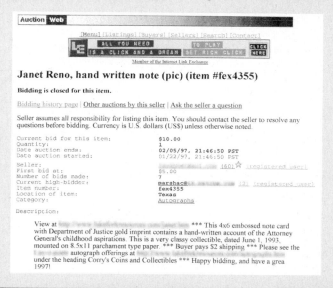

The craze that began with AW

Back in 1994, when eBay founder Pierre Omidyar had the idea to start a Web auction, he named his first venture Auction Web. The following figure shows a vintage Auction Web Internet auction that I won in February 1997. There were some great deals even in those days!

Your License to Deal (Almost)

You are now officially a *newbie,* or eBay rookie. The only problem is that you're still at the window-shopping level. If you're ready to go from window-shopper to item seller, just zip through a few more forms, and before you know it, you can start running your own auctions on eBay.

Until you've been a member of eBay for 30 days, a picture of a beaming golden cartoonlike icon shows up next to your user ID wherever it appears on the site. This doesn't mean that you have been converted into a golden robot; the icon merely indicates to other eBay users that you are new to eBay.

Chapter 3

You *Can* Go Home — Again and Again!

I hate to say it, but the famous writer Thomas Wolfe was wrong; the title of this chapter is true! You *can* go home again. At least on eBay! I visit the eBay home page on a regular basis; it's a place where I can keep up with eBay's newest offerings. Month after month, millions of people (just like us) land on eBay's home page without wearing out the welcome mat (probably because they are wearing their bunny slippers). The eBay home page is the front door to the most popular auction site on the Internet.

Everything you need to know about navigating eBay begins right here. In this chapter, I give you the grand tour of the areas you can reach right from the home page with the help of links.

What Is the Home Page?

The eBay *home page* is shown in Figure 3-1 and includes the following key areas:

✔ A navigation bar at the top of the page with five eBay links that can zip you straight to any of the many eBay areas, as well as two additional — and powerful — links right below the navigation bar.

✔ A search box that helps you find items by title keywords as well as a link to eBay's Advanced Search page.

✔ A list of links to the most popular auction categories.

✔ A link box that takes you directly to a drop-down menu of a complete listing of top-level categories, a direct link to eBay Motors and eBay Stores.

✔ Links to eBay's Deals of the Day, featured items, fun stuff such as charity auctions, and information about what else is moving on eBay.

Figure 3-1:
The home page, your jumping-off point for fun, profit, and values.

Do not adjust your computer monitor. You're not going crazy. Today you may notice that a link that was on the eBay home page a minute ago is gone. That's normal. The links on the eBay home page change often to reflect what's going on — not just on the site, but in the world as well.

Sign In, Please

Sign In is possibly the most powerful of all the links on the eBay pages, and it should be your first stop if you plan on doing any business on the site (see Figure 3-2).

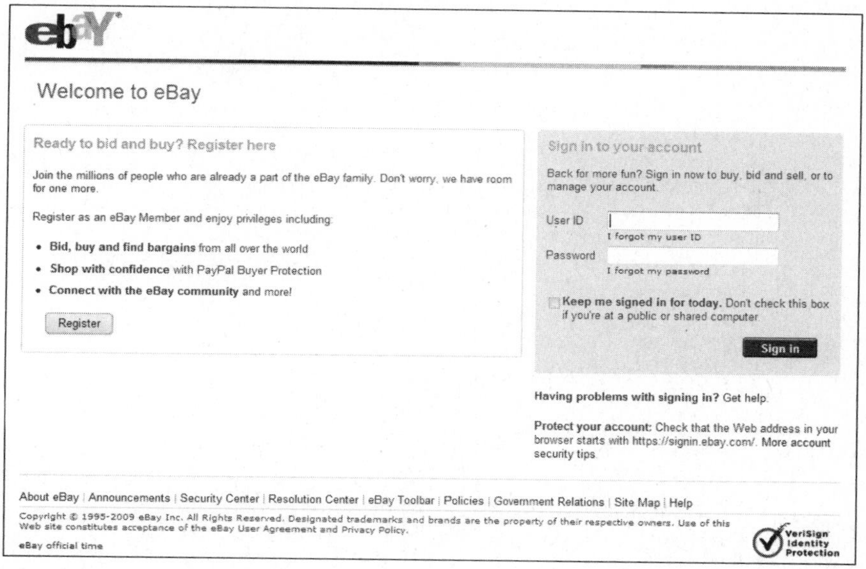

Figure 3-2:
The eBay
Sign In
page.

Welcome to eBay

Ready to bid and buy? Register here

Join the millions of people who are already a part of the eBay family. Don't worry, we have room for one more.

Register as an eBay Member and enjoy privileges including:

- **Bid, buy and find bargains** from all over the world
- **Shop with confidence** with PayPal Buyer Protection
- **Connect with the eBay community** and more!

Register

Sign in to your account

Back for more fun? Sign in now to buy, bid and sell, or to manage your account.

User ID
I forgot my user ID

Password
I forgot my password

☐ **Keep me signed in for today.** Don't check this box if you're at a public or shared computer.

Sign In

Having problems with signing in? Get help.

Protect your account: Check that the Web address in your browser starts with https://signin.ebay.com/. More account security tips.

About eBay | Announcements | Security Center | Resolution Center | eBay Toolbar | Policies | Government Relations | Site Map | Help

Copyright © 1995-2009 eBay Inc. All Rights Reserved. Designated trademarks and brands are the property of their respective owners. Use of this Web site constitutes acceptance of the eBay User Agreement and Privacy Policy.

eBay official time

VeriSign Identity Protection

If you use the link to go to the Sign In page and then sign in, you don't have to enter your user ID again that day. You can set your preferences to take you directly to your My eBay page after Sign In; It's essential for every eBay user. (See Chapter 4 for info on My eBay.)

You can search for items on eBay without signing in, but what fun is that? If you haven't registered with eBay, you're pretty much out of luck if you find a great deal on a lamp that's just what you've been looking for — and the auction closes in 5 minutes!

If you're the only one who uses your computer, be sure to select the box that says Keep Me Signed in For Today. This way, you're always signed in to eBay every time you go to the site during the next 24 hours. The Sign In process places a _cookie_ (a technical thingy — see Chapter 15 for details) on your computer that remains a part of your computer for the rest of the day.

If you don't select the box, you will be signed in only while your browser is open. After you close your browser the cookie expires, and you have to sign in again.

Here's how to get to the eBay Sign In page and sign in:

1. **Click the Sign In link at the top of any eBay page.**

   At the bottom of the new page that appears is a Secure Sign In page. The logo indicates that your personal information is even more secure than usual. (See Chapter 2 for details about SSL.)

2. **Enter your user ID and password.**

3. **Select the Sign Me In for Today box if you're not at a public computer.**

You're now signed in to eBay and can travel and transact on the site with ease. You can enter your My eBay page by clicking the My eBay link that appears in the navigation bar. (See Chapter 4 for more on My eBay.)

This Bar Never Closes

As mentioned, the *navigation bar* is at the top of the eBay home page and lists five eBay links that take you directly to different eBay areas. Using the navigation bar is kind of like doing one-stop clicking. You can find this bar at the top of every page you visit on eBay. No matter where you are on the site, when you click one of the five links you go straight to a related page.

Below the navigation bar is the Sign In/Sign Out link. This link, which toggles between Sign In and Sign Out depending on your sign-in status, is important, and I remind you about it throughout this book.

Think of links as expressways to specific destinations. Click a link just once, and the next thing you know, you're right where you want to be. You don't even have to answer that proverbial annoying question, "When are we gonna get there?" from the noisy kids in the backseat.

Here, without further ado, are the five navigation-bar boxes and where they take you:

- **Buy:** Takes you to the page that lists Featured Items (see Chapter 6), all the main eBay categories, as well as links to popular stores and eBay promotions that vary from time to time. If you're signed in, there is also a link to your favorite searches and sellers. From this page, you can link to any one of the millions of items up for auction on eBay.

On the Buy page, you find links to browse by categories, keywords, or stores. If you scroll to the very bottom of the page, you find the Artist Pages. There you can click the Music, Movies, or Books links to search for your favorite artists' items quickly (see Figure 3-3). If you want to find your favorite artists' pages even more quickly, go to `http://artist-index.ebay.com`. On this page, they're ranked by their standing in eBay's Top Sellers.

Figure 3-3:
Nice to see that Beatles (The) are still in the #5 slot on the eBay Bestselling Artists page.

When you click a link to browse a category (for example, Books: Antiquarian & Collectible), you see some tabs above the listings. These tabs offer you ways to search, and each tab gives you a different viewing option to browse:

- **All Items** is the default setting for the page. This option delivers on its promise — you see all items, including those up for auction and Buy It Now items.

- Click **Auctions Only** in the tabs area to be taken to eBay's version of an auction catalog.

- Click the **Buy It Now Only** tab to see all items in the category that you can buy immediately if you don't want to wait for an auction to end.

Note that not all sellers list their items in the Auctions area (at this moment only 55,000 of the 120,000 items in this category are auctions), so by not browsing All Items, you may be missing out on some special items or deals.

Browse Categories. Clicking takes you to a list of all categories and the first level subcategories. What's even more fun is that you get to see the listing counts, as shown in Figure 3-4.

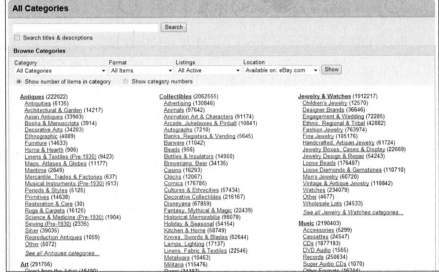

All Categories

[Search]

☐ Search titles & descriptions

Browse Categories

Category	Format	Listings	Location	
All Categories ▼	All Items ▼	All Active ▼	Available on: eBay.com ▼	[Show]

◉ Show number of items in category   ○ Show category numbers

Antiques (222022)
Antiquities (6135)
Architectural & Garden (14217)
Asian Antiques (33903)
Books & Manuscripts (3914)
Decorative Arts (34203)
Ethnographic (4089)
Furniture (14633)
Home & Hearth (906)
Linens & Textiles (Pre-1930) (9423)
Maps, Atlases & Globes (11177)
Maritime (2849)
Mercantile, Trades & Factories (637)
Musical Instruments (Pre-1930) (613)
Periods & Styles (5125)
Primitives (14638)
Restoration & Care (30)
Rugs & Carpets (16125)
Science & Medicine (Pre-1930) (1904)
Sewing (Pre-1930) (2335)
Silver (39035)
Reproduction Antiques (1059)
Other (5072)
See all Antiques categories...

Art (291756)
Direct from the Artist (45490)

Collectibles (2062555)
Advertising (130846)
Animals (97642)
Animation Art & Characters (91174)
Arcade, Jukeboxes & Pinball (10841)
Autographs (7210)
Banks, Registers & Vending (5645)
Barware (11042)
Beads (956)
Bottles & Insulators (14950)
Breweriana, Beer (34135)
Casino (16293)
Clocks (12067)
Comics (176785)
Cultures & Ethnicities (57434)
Decorative Collectibles (216167)
Disneyana (67859)
Fantasy, Mythical & Magic (22439)
Historical Memorabilia (98078)
Holiday & Seasonal (54154)
Kitchen & Home (58749)
Knives, Swords & Blades (62644)
Lamps, Lighting (17137)
Linens, Fabric & Textiles (22546)
Metalware (10463)
Militaria (115476)
Paper (34187)

Jewelry & Watches (1912217)
Children's Jewelry (12570)
Designer Brands (36646)
Engagement & Wedding (72285)
Ethnic, Regional & Tribal (42882)
Fashion Jewelry (763974)
Fine Jewelry (105176)
Handcrafted, Artisan Jewelry (61724)
Jewelry Boxes, Cases & Display (22669)
Jewelry Design & Repair (54243)
Loose Beads (176487)
Loose Diamonds & Gemstones (110710)
Men's Jewelry (60720)
Vintage & Antique Jewelry (118842)
Watches (234079)
Other (4677)
Wholesale Lots (34533)
See all Jewelry & Watches categories...

Music (2190403)
Accessories (5299)
Cassettes (24547)
CDs (1877183)
DVD Audio (1565)
Records (250634)
Super Audio CDs (1070)
Other Formats (16244)

Figure 3-4:
Who'd have thought there are over *two million* items for sale in the collectibles category!

- **Help with Buying and Bidding:** What can I say, you bought this book and I can guarantee that I've bought more on eBay than almost any eBay employee. Just jump over to Chapter 6 for the lowdown.

- **Buyer Tools:** Hmmm, the only buyer tools I'm interested in are a credit card and my PayPal account. Keep in mind that anything you download to your computer will track you. Free tools are not written out of the goodness of a company's heart; they're written to sign people up, get data, and then sell such data at a profit. Get it?

- **Reviews & Guides:** Here's where you can participate in the eBay community by writing guides and reviewing products. If you're here to make money, perhaps you might be better spending your time honing your sales skills and selling items. There's more on this area of eBay in Chapter 17.

- **eBay Mobile:** You want eBay to call you on your cell phone? They will do it for a fee. It's free to check your eBay listings on a Web-enabled cell phone by going to m.ebay.com.

Keep in mind that all informational links provided to you by eBay in these drop-down menus are just that: from eBay. They may be influenced by advertising deals, alliances with providers . . . get the drift? Do not ever consider the information you get as unbiased. This book is unbiased — I have no sponsors or advertisers to please.

The drop-down menus are often more helpful in getting you where you want to go. The drop-down menu that appears as you mouse over the Buy button gives you these offerings:

Sell: Takes you to the start of the Sell Your Item form, which you must fill out to start your sale. I explain how to navigate this form in Chapter 9. The links at the bottom of the page direct you to various Seller Guides. The Sell drop-down menu also gives you these options through convenient links:

- **Sell an Item:** Here's your direct link to the Sell Item form. Try to remember to click here directly when you want to list an item for sale — one step is easier than two, especially when the first step has promotional information.

- **Selling Tips:** Let's just say that whoever wrote these tips read an earlier edition of this book.

- **What's Hot:** This connects you to eBay Pulse (pulse.ebay.com), shown in Figure 3-5. It's a fun area that lets you view (by category if you want) the most popular searches on eBay. One caveat: Just because an item is hot doesn't mean you can get your hands on it or even want to sell that particular item. (I know a high-level eBay seller who sells brake pads, which are not my cup of tea.) Use this information as a market gauge rather than the gospel.

- **Seller Tools & eBay Stores:** Here's a quick link to the tools eBay offers, such as Selling Manager (more on that in Chapter 4). Take my advice and follow my lead in this book; don't subscribe to any of these tools until you're ready. They will just drain your wallet.

- **Shipping Center:** This link takes you to eBay's Shipping Center, which is a handy way to get to the Shipping Calculator. There are plenty of other links, and because UPS and the USPS are "partners" with eBay, you won't find info on my favorite ground shipper, FedEx Ground. See the chapter on shipping to get the full picture of who you should ship with.

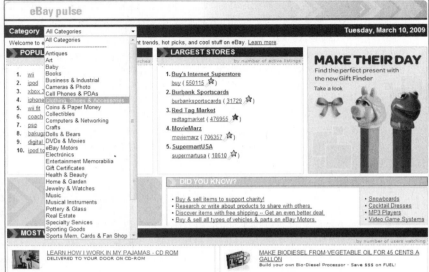

Figure 3-5:
eBay Pulse
gives you
and idea of
what's hot
on the site.

✔ **My eBay:** Takes you to your personal My eBay page, where you keep track of all your buying and selling activities, account information, and favorite categories (there's more about My eBay in Chapter 4). A drop-down menu takes you to the various areas on your My eBay page. Chapter 4 gives you information on all these links.

✔ **Community:** Takes you to a page where you can find the latest news and announcements, chat with fellow traders in the eBay community, find charity auctions, and find out more about eBay. (Chapters 17 and 18 tell you how to use these resources.)

✔ **Help:** Takes you to one of the most valuable areas of the eBay site. The Help area can give you answers to many of your questions, as well as keep you apprised of eBay's rules and regulations regarding trading on the site. The eBay Help Center overview page consists of a search box, where you can type your query, links for help topics, an A–Z index, and a list of the top five questions on eBay. The page offers links to the answers to the questions most frequently asked by eBay users and to the Security & Resolution Center.

At the top of the eBay home page, below the navigation bar, you find several powerful links that are just as important as the links on the navigation bar:

✔ **eBay Logo:** Click the eBay logo and it takes you right back to the home page. Use this link from any other page when you need to get back to the home page right away.

✔ **Contact Us:** Clicking here, you'll have to sign in (which is not helpful when you have a problem such as a hijacked account), but the resulting page lets you into eBay through a bold link that says I'm a Guest. Click there. You will then be taken to the Contact Us page. (For more on contacting eBay, see Chapter 16.)

✔ **Register:** Click here to become a member of the eBay community. If you haven't registered, turn to Chapter 2 to get the quick and painless facts about the easy eBay registration process. (If you're signed in, the Register link isn't visible.)

✔ **Site Map:** Provides you with a bird's-eye view of the eBay world. Every *top-level* (that is, main) link available on eBay is listed here. If you're ever confused about finding a specific area, try the Site Map first. If a top-level link isn't listed here, it's not on eBay — yet.

Exploring Your Home Page Search Options

An old Chinese expression says, "Every journey begins with the first eBay search." Okay, I updated the quote, but wise words nonetheless. You can start a search from the home page in one of two ways:

✔ **Use the search text box:** It's right there at the top of the home page, with the Search button next to it. It's a fast way of finding item listings.

✔ **Use the Advanced Search link next to the search box on the home page:** These links take you to the Advanced Search page, where you can do all kinds of specialized searches.

Both options can give you the same results. The instructions I offer in the next two sections about using these search methods are just the tip of the eBay iceberg. For the inside track on how to finesse the eBay search engine to root out just what you're looking for, visit Chapter 5.

Peering through the home page search box

To launch a title search from the home page, follow these steps:

1. **In the search box, type no more than a few keywords that describe the item you're looking for.**

   Refer to Figure 3-1 to see the search box.

2. **Click the Search button.**

   The results of your search appear on-screen in a matter of seconds.

You can type just about anything in this box and get some information. Say you're looking for *Star Trek* memorabilia. If so, you're not alone. The television show premiered on September 8, 1966, and even though it was canceled in 1969 because of low ratings, *Star Trek* became one of the most successful science-fiction franchises in history. A new Star Trek film came out this year! If you like *Star Trek* as much as I do, you can use the search box on the eBay home page to find all sorts of *Star Trek* stuff. I just ran a search and found 18,047 items — in hundreds of categories — with *Star Trek* in their titles (your results will probably vary).

Try the Advanced Search link next to the search box to narrow your search. This link takes you to the Advanced Search: Find Items page, which is explained in the following section.

When you search for popular items on eBay (and a classic example is *Star Trek* memorabilia), you may get inundated with thousands of listings that match your search criteria. Even if you're traveling at warp speed, you could spend hours checking each auction individually. ("Scotty, we need more power *now!*") If you're pressed for time like the rest of us, eBay has not-so-mysterious ways to narrow your search so finding a specific item is much more manageable. Turn to Chapter 5 for insider techniques that can help you slim those searches and beef up those results.

Going where the Advanced Search link takes you

One of the most important buttons on the eBay page is the Advanced Search link. When you click this link, you're whisked away to the Advanced Search page, which promptly presents you with several search options. Each option enables you to search for information in a different way. Here's how the search options on the menu can work for you:

✔ **Find Items:** Search by keywords, item number, in eBay Motors, or by an individual seller or bidder. Type the keywords that describe an item (for example, **Superman lunchbox** or **antique pocket watch**) and click Search, and you can see how many are available on eBay. The site gives you the option to search by one of the main categories — but to get the largest number of items, use All Categories and narrow your search from the results.

Another handy way to search is by item number. Every item that's up for sale on eBay is assigned an item number, which is displayed next to the item name on its page. To find an item by number, just type the number in the box, click Search, and away you go. (To find out more about how individual sales pages work on eBay, spin through Chapter 6.)

You can also find items by number if you type the item number into any of the small search boxes that appear on eBay pages.

✔ **Sort Your Searches:** Here you can sort your searches in three ways.

✔ **Advanced Search drop-down menu:** By clicking this link, you can define your search without using a bunch of code. It works pretty much the same as the basic Search method, but you can exclude more features from your search. You can also take advantage of eBay's regional trading and find items for sale in your neighborhood. Figure 3-6 shows the Advanced Search options.

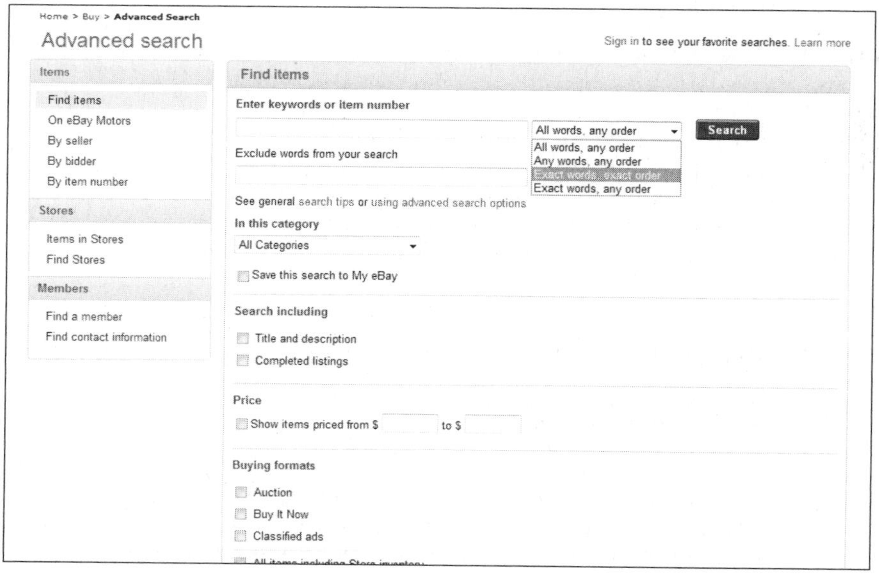

Figure 3-6:
The
Advanced
Search
page and its
options.

Home > Buy > **Advanced Search**

Advanced search   Sign in to see your favorite searches. Learn more

Items

Find items
On eBay Motors
By seller
By bidder
By item number

Stores

Items in Stores
Find Stores

Members

Find a member
Find contact information

Find items

Enter keywords or item number

[   ]   All words, any order ▾   **Search**
                                            All words, any order
Exclude words from your search   Any words, any order
                                            Exact words, exact order
[   ]   Exact words, any order

See general search tips or using advanced search options

In this category

All Categories   ▾

☐ Save this search to My eBay

Search including

☐ Title and description
☐ Completed listings

Price

☐ Show items priced from $ [   ] to $ [   ]

Buying formats

☐ Auction
☐ Buy It Now
☐ Classified ads
☐ All items including Store inventory

The search by category filter is a snappy search function that helps you figure out which subcategories have the item you want — or, if you want to sell, helps you decide where to list your item for sale. It produces a regular search in a selected category but also has a column on the left side of the page that lets you know which subcategories your item is listed in — and how many of the item you'll see listed in each category.

To find an item that sold on eBay in the past, indicate that you want to use the Completed Listings search. Then type the keywords of an item, and you get a list of items of this type that have been sold in the last 14 (or so) days, as well as what they sold for. You can use this type of search to strategize your asking price before you put an item up for auction (or to determine how much you'll have to bid to win an item).

Although Chapter 5 tells you all you need to know about searching eBay, the following list explains some other searches you can perform from the Search page. In a nutshell, here's what they do:

- **Items By Seller:** Every person on eBay has a personal user ID (the name you use to conduct transactions). Use a By Seller search if you liked the merchandise from a seller's auction and want to see what else the seller has for sale. Type the seller's user ID, and you get a list of every auction that person is running.

- **Items By Bidder:** For the sake of practicality and convenience, user IDs help eBay keep track of every move a user makes on eBay. If you want to see what a particular user (say, a fellow *Star Trek* fan) is bidding on, use the Items By Bidder search. Type a user ID in the Items By Bidder search box, and you get a list of everything the user is currently bidding on, as well as how much he or she is bidding. (I show you how to use this search option as a strategic buying tool in Chapter 6.)

- **Stores Search:** Here's something I bet you didn't know. When you use eBay's search engine, it searches eBay Stores for matching items but only secondarily. (I think that's a bunch of malarkey, but who am I?) If you search for your item here, you'll see whether any matching items are available in eBay Stores (perhaps even at lower prices).

  If you're looking for a particular eBay store, eBay provides a search box that allows you to search for a store by name (or part of the name).

Home Links, the Next Generation

If you look carefully, you can see that the home page has several other links that give you express service to key parts of the site. Here are the highlights:

✔ **My Recent Activities:** If you've been browsing around the site and then return to the home page, you see a box with images of items you've looked at in past history. (See? I told you your travels on the site are tracked.)

✔ **From Our Sellers:** Visit the featured items. (Translation: Sellers paid more to have them featured in this section.)

✔ **More eBay Sites:** This box is full of links that take you to more eBay-owned sites, such as Half.com, Kijiji, PayPal, ProStores, Rent.com, Shopping.com, Skype, StubHub, and StumbleUpon. (More on these sites throughout the book.)

✔ **Global Sites:** Use these links to visit eBay's international auction sites. A quick and easy way to shop the world.

You may notice that the graphic links on the home page change from day to day — even hour to hour. If you're interested in the featured areas of the site, visit this page several times a day to see the entire array of special happenings on eBay.

Maneuvering through Categories

So how does eBay keep track of the millions of items that are up for sale at any given moment? The brilliant minds at eBay decided to group items into a nice, neat little storage system called *categories*. The home page lists most of the main categories, but currently eBay lists tens of thousands of subcategories — ranging from Antiques to Writing Instruments. And don't ask how many subsubcategories (categories within categories) eBay has — I can't count that high.

Well, okay, I *could* list all the categories and subcategories currently available on eBay — if you wouldn't mind squinting at a dozen pages of really small, eye-burning text. But a category browse is an adventure that's unique for each individual, and I wouldn't think of depriving you of it. Suffice it to say that if you like to hunt for that perfect something, you're in browsing heaven now.

Here's how to navigate around the categories:

1. **Click the category that interests you, such as Books or DVDs & Movies.**

   You're transported to the category's page. You see categories and subcategories listed next to each heading. Happy hunting.

If you don't find a category that interests you among those on the home page, simply click the Buy button on the navigation bar, and you're off to the main categories page. Not only do you get a pretty impressive page of main categories and subcategories, but you also get a short list of featured auctions and a link to them all.

If you really and truly want to see a list of all the categories and subcategories, click the Categories on the Home page (rather than using the drop-down menu). Alternatively you can go to listings.ebay.com/ListingCategoryList.

2. **After the category page appears, find a subcategory below the main category title that interests you. Click the subcategory, and keep digging through the subsubcategories until you find what you want.**

   For example, if you're looking for items honoring your favorite television show, click the Entertainment Memorabilia category. The page that comes up includes the subcategories of the category. You'll notice that the Entertainment Memorabilia category has many links, including the Television Memorabilia subcategory. If you look under the TV Memorabilia subcategory head, you'll see links to various subsubcategories that include Ads, Flyers, Clippings, Photos, Pins, Buttons, Posters, Press Kits, Props, Scripts, Wardrobe, and Other. At the bottom of that page, below the links, you also find a link to See all featured items. Click any link to see the listings in the categories. Little *icons* (pictures) next to the listings tell you more about each item — whether it's pictured (the camera) and whether it's a new item (the sunrise). You can also click the tabs to isolate Auctions only or Buy It Now items.

   By the way, I have lots more to say about featured items in Chapter 10.

3. **When you find an item that interests you, click the item, and the full Auction page pops up on your screen.**

   Congratulations — you've just navigated through several million items to find that one TV-collectible item that caught your attention. (Pardon me while I bid on that Lily Munster/Yvonne DeCarlo–signed picture.) You can instantly return to the home page by clicking its link at the top of the page (or return to the Listings page by repeatedly clicking the Back button at the top of your browser).

Near the bottom of every subcategory page, you can see a link list of numbers. The numbers are page numbers, and you can use them to fast-forward through all the items in that subcategory. So, if you feel like browsing around page 8, without going through 8 pages individually, just click number 8; you're presented with the items on that page (their listings, actually). Happy browsing.

If you're a bargain hunter by habit, you may find some pretty weird stuff while browsing the categories and subcategories of items on eBay — some of it super-cheap and some of it (maybe) just cheap. (There's even a Weird Stuff category — no kidding!) Remember that (as with any marketplace) you're responsible for finding out as much as possible about an item before you buy and definitely before you bid. So, if you're the type who sometimes can't resist a good deal, ask yourself what you plan to *do* with the pile of garbage you can get for 15 cents — and ask yourself *now,* before it arrives on your doorstep. Chapters 6 and 7 offer more information on savvy bidding.

Going Global

Listed below the Categories list are links to eBay's international auction sites. You may enter eBay Argentina, Australia, Austria, Belgium, Brazil, Canada, China, France, Germany, Hong Kong, India, Ireland, Italy, Korea, Malaysia, Mexico, Netherlands, New Zealand, Philippines, Poland, Singapore, Spain, Sweden, Switzerland, Taiwan, Thailand, Turkey, the United Kingdom, and (whew) Vietnam. Click one of these links and you jet off (virtually) to eBay sites in these countries. The international sites are in the countries' native languages. It might be a good place to practice your third-year French — or maybe not! Remember that after you leave eBay USA, you're subject to the contractual and privacy laws of the country you're visiting.

Using the Seller's Items Links

Here on eBay, money talks pretty loudly. In the center of the home page, you see a list of the auctions eBay is featuring at the moment. eBay usually posts six featured items at any given time and rotates items throughout the day so that as many sellers as possible get a shot at being in the spotlight. When you click the featured listings link, you're instantly beamed to eBay's Home Page Featured Items section.

You can find everything from Las Vegas vacations to Model-T Fords to diet products in the Home Page Featured Items. Home Page Featured Items are not for mere mortals with small wallets. They've been lifted to the exalted *featured* status because sellers shelled out lots of money to get them noticed. All you need to get your auction featured is $39.95 ($79.95 for Multiple Item listings), plus a second or two to click Home Page Featured Item on the Sell Your Item form. (See Chapter 10 if you have an item that all eyes must see.)

Note that bidding on these items works the same way as bidding on regular items.

The Home Page Featured Items page contains many expensive items. Sellers who put up high-priced items have been around the block a few times and make it clear that they will verify each bid on the item. That means if you place a bid on one of Jay Leno's autographed Harley-Davidsons (auctioned in 2005 to benefit tsunami relief and Hurricane Katrina relief), be prepared to get a phone call from the seller. The seller may ask you to prove that you can actually *pay* for the motorcycle. Nothing personal; it's strictly business.

Charities

Click the Giving Works (or Charity) link on the home page to see eBay charity auctions. Winning bids contribute to programs that help charities. Charity auctions are a great way for memorabilia collectors to find one-of-a-kind (and authentic) items. (Chapter 18 tells you more about what charity items you can bid on — and the good you can do with your checkbook.)

Promotion du Jour

The eBay community is constantly changing. To help you get into the swing of things right away, eBay provides a special box with links that take you right to the current word on the latest eBay special events.

Even if the main promotion box doesn't appeal to you, usually you can find some interesting links dotted around the home page without a headline. You can find links to eBay's special promotions for the day (or is it the hour? — it can change every 15 minutes)

You *can* get there from here — lots of places, in fact:

- ✔ A rotating list of special-interest links changes at least once a day. (Half the fun is getting a closer look at pages you haven't seen.)

- ✔ Special money-saving offers from third-party vendors can be a boon if you're on the lookout for a bargain.

Bottoming Out

At the very bottom of the home page is an unassuming group of links that provide more ways to get to some seriously handy pages. I've listed some important ones in this section:

- ✔ **Feedback Forum:** This link takes you to one of the most important spots on eBay. The Feedback Forum is where you can find out whether you've forgotten to place feedback on a transaction. You can also place feedback and respond to feedback left for you — all in one friendly location.

- ✔ **Downloads:** Here's a place where you can download some of eBay's handy software. It's a link to eBay-supplied selling-assistance software. (See Chapter 20 for more on these programs.)

- ✔ **Gift Certificates & Gift Cards:** Send someone an eBay gift certificate for any special occasion. You can print it yourself, or eBay will send it to any e-mail address you provide. The gift certificate is good for any item on the site for the value you specify, and you can pay for it immediately with PayPal. If the person you give the gift certificate to bids higher than the value of the gift certificate, he or she can make up the difference using another payment option.

- ✔ **Jobs:** Click here if you want to work *for* eBay instead of *through* eBay.

- ✔ **Affiliates:** If you have your own Web site and want to make a few bucks, click this link. If you sign up for the program and put a link to eBay on your Web page, eBay pays you money for any new user who signs up directly from your Web site (plus other bonuses).

- ✔ **Developers:** So are you a geek too? If you are, you can enter eBay's Developer program and get access to the eBay API for fun and profit.

- ✔ **The eBay Shop:** This link enables you to browse and buy eBay merchandise from the eBay company store.

- ✔ **eBay Mobile:** They're really pushing using a cell phone for eBay. Trust me. A computer works a lot better.

- ✔ **About eBay:** Click this link to find out about eBay the company and to get its press releases, company overview, and stock information. You can also find out about eBay community activities and charities — and even apply for a job at eBay.

- ✔ **Announcements:** Visit the General Announcements Board when you want to know about any late-breaking news.

- ✔ **Learning Center:** Click here to see eBay's featured educational tools.

✔ **Security Center:** This link takes you to a page where concerns about fraud and safety are addressed. It's such an important eBay tool that I dedicate an entire chapter to this program. Before buying or selling, it's a good idea to check out Chapter 16.

✔ **Resolution Center:** When you have an issue with another person on the site, click here to get some action.

✔ **Policies:** This is a good place to visit to brush up on the site's policies and guidelines.

✔ **Government Relations:** Here's where your eBay membership can make a real difference. Join eBay's Main Street Member Program and become involved with important legislation that may affect your online future. If you sign up, you will receive important updates.

✔ **Site Map.** Another way to reach eBay's very handy road map of links.

On other eBay pages, the bottom navigation bar looks a little different. It often includes even more links so you can cruise the site quickly without necessarily having to use the top navigation bar.

Chapter 4

My Very Own, Private eBay

I know eBay is a sensitive, touchie-feelie kind of company because it gives all users plenty of personal space. Long preceding Facebook.com, eBay's My eBay page is your private space for all your activities on eBay — sort of a "This is your eBay life." I think it's the greatest organizational tool around, and I want to talk to somebody about getting one for organizing my life outside eBay.

In this chapter, you find out how you can use the My eBay page to keep tabs on what you're buying and selling, find out how much money you've spent, and add categories to your personalized list so that you can get to any favorite eBay place with just a click of your mouse. You gain knowledge of the ins and outs of feedback — what it is, why it can give you that warm, fuzzy feeling, and how to manage it so all that cyber-positive reinforcement doesn't go to your head.

I do want to preface this chapter by warning you that the My eBay page has become the hub for the zillions of features that eBay offers. As a beginner on the site, you'll be doing yourself a favor if you stick to the basics of the buying, selling, feedback, and account settings. eBay's offerings are fun, but they do a heck of a job confusing you when you're just starting out. Ease into the extras slowly.

Getting to Your My eBay Page

Using your My eBay page makes keeping track of your eBay life a whole lot easier. And getting there is easy enough. After you enter eBay, sign in through the Sign In link (described in Chapter 3). After you sign in to eBay, you can access your My eBay page by clicking the My eBay link in the navigation bar (see Figure 4-1) at the top of almost every eBay page.

Figure 4-1:
The My
eBay link in
the naviga-
tion bar.

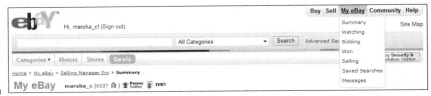

If you've forgotten your eBay user ID or password, click the Forgot Your User ID or Forgot Your Password link. For your user ID, you can then type your e-mail address, and eBay will send you an e-mail with your user ID. Your user ID appears in any search results, posts, or pages. For the password, you have to answer your secret question (the one you filled in when you registered). If you don't remember that, eBay will send you a password-reset e-mail if you input your correct contact information with telephone number.

After you click the My eBay link, you arrive at your My eBay Summary page. As you can see by my absolutely busy Summary page in Figure 4-2, you can access just about anything you need right here. You find some handy reminders on the center of this page. Useful buying and selling reminders also show up here, although when you're involved in a large number of eBay transactions, they may seem like the whining of a nagging spouse. Bottom line? These reminders help keep your business under control.

The My eBay drop-down menu in the navigation bar takes you to the main areas of My eBay. Also, look at the left side of the main My eBay page in Figure 4-2. Under the Summary heading are many handy links that take you to different areas of your eBay business. Table 4-1 gives you the scoop on the major links on the page.

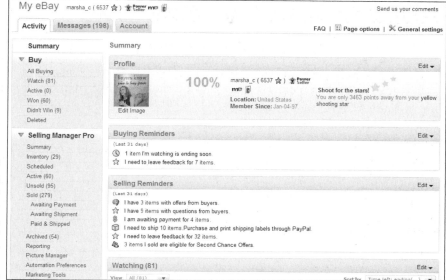

Figure 4-2:
Your My
eBay sum-
mary page,
the hub for
your eBay
activities.

Table 4-1	The Major Links on Your My eBay Page
Click Here	*To See This on Your My eBay Page*
Buy	Every listing that you're currently bidding on, have marked to watch, and made a Best Offer on, and the items you've won or didn't win.
Sell	Every listing for items you're currently selling. Also, there are links to any listings you've scheduled to start at a later date. Most importantly, you have links to lists of items you've sold (and not sold).
Messages	This tab links to your My Messages area, eBay's private e-mail service for members. My Messages is the best and safest way to communicate with other eBay members.
Organize	This area links to your collections of Saved Searches, Saved Sellers, and your lists.
Account	This tab lets you select the activities for which you want eBay to remember your password so that you don't have to type it every time. (I like to have eBay remember my password when I'm selling, bidding, managing items, and so on.) You also have the option to change your personal information on eBay. You can see what you currently owe eBay. The tab also links to your PayPal and Half. com accounts.

Houston, we don't have a problem

Here's an item I wish I'd bought: a very clean 8-x-10-inch color Neil Armstrong–signed official NASA portrait w/COA (Certificate of Authenticity). In recent years, Armstrong, the first human on the moon, has been reclusive, and his autographs are difficult to obtain in any form. Many forgeries and reproductions are being offered, so buyer beware. This portrait came with a lifetime COA. The starting price was $10, and the portrait sold on eBay in 1999 for $520!

Many believe that Neil Armstrong's autograph will be among the most important of the twentieth century. Just think about it. He was the first human to step onto another celestial body. This feat may never happen again, and certainly not in our lifetimes. When I updated this book for the third edition, this same portrait was selling for $650. When I checked this out for the 4th edition in 2004, the picture sold for $1,925. A quick scan in 2005 showed that such a signed picture just closed at $2,025.

The economy being what it is, Armstrong original signed photos aren't selling, but you'll not find one up for sale for less than $3,500. He did sign an Apollo 11 capsule model, and that sold for $1,412. Why didn't I follow my own advice and buy one in 1999?

At the bottom of left side section, under the Shortcuts heading, are important links to activities and information.

Don't confuse the My eBay page with the About Me page. The About Me page is a personal Web page that you can create to let the world know about you and your eBay dealings. (You don't have to have an About Me page if you don't want to — but they are free for the taking and are fun to share.) I tell you how to get your own About Me page in Chapter 14.

Keeping Track of Your Personal Business

Your My eBay page has three tabs: Activity, Messages, and Account. They're on the top side of the page below the My eBay heading. If you mouse over the Account tab, you see a drop-down menu like the one in Figure 4-3. Clicking Account brings you to a summary page that has snippets of each topic in the My Account section. It's really better to click the individual menu options so that you can go directly to the place you want to explore.

Figure 4-3:
Access individual areas of your account in this menu.

Checking your account information

The Account drop-down menu has options to take you to two very important areas of My eBay: Personal Information and Addresses. This is where you update your contact information. Initially, all this data comes from your registration. But it's policy on eBay that every user files his or her current contact information — so if you move or change phone numbers, e-mail addresses, or banks, you need to input that information here.

It's also where you can change your user ID (if you ever decide that Charlie18907 doesn't properly reflect your personality). Also, your instant messenger name can be inserted here so that you can get IM alerts at Yahoo! Messenger, AIM, or whatever messenger program you use; add wireless numbers for auctions about which you want to be notified. You can also change your password and all your other registered information here.

On eBay you can change your user ID at any time (every 30 days), and your feedback rating will follow.

What's that thingy?

For the first 30 days after you register or change your user ID (which you can do anytime, as Chapter 2 explains) — eBay gives you an icon that stays next to your user ID every time it appears on eBay (when you bid, run an auction, or post a message on any of the chat boards).

So why the icon? eBay calls the graphic of a beaming robot-like critter the "new ID" icon. It's sort of a friendly heads-up to others that you are a new user. (If you've changed your user ID, the icon consists of two of the little guys with an arrow connecting them.) You still have all the privileges that everybody else has on eBay while you're breaking in your new identity. The icons are nothing personal, just business as usual.

Choosing your notification preferences

Because we live in a world where everyone has his or her own way of doing things, eBay allows you to set all kinds of preferences for your eBay account. One of the links leads to the Preferences page. The Preferences settings are all important to your eBay tasks. You have to decide which activities you want activated for your eBay account (you can always change these later). The most convenient thing is to select all the options that make sense to you. You can set many Notification preferences:

✔ **Notification Delivery:** This is where you let eBay know which method of notification works best for you. You can also indicate whether you want HTML or text-based e-mails.

✔ **Buying Notifications:** Be careful here. If you indicate that you want all this e-mail and you plan to be active on the site, prepare to be deluged. Select wisely! But remember, you can always make changes. You can get real-time notifications on your shopping for the following:

- Watched Item (also daily, weekly or monthly) e-mail
- Watched Items that were relisted by the seller
- Confirmations for your bids
- E-mails when you're outbid in an auction
- Winning buyer e-mails
- Losing bidder e-mails

As you can see, this is way too many e-mails, especially if you do a lot of buying and selling. They will send you e-mails for even more than I mention here. For sanity's sake, narrow your selections to the minimum.

✔ **Selling Notifications:** If you're selling on the site, most of these notifications will be useful. You can indicate you want to receive the following e-mails:

- Notification that you've saved a draft on the Sell Your Item Form

- E-mail confirmation each time you list an item for sale

- Yay! The end-of-listing e-mail when your item has sold

- Boo. The e-mail you get when your item doesn't sell

- Notification when your buyer performs Checkout

These are all important, especially when you're a new seller. When you become more active as a seller, you might want to whittle these down a bit — but not too much! Information is power.

✔ **Other Transactions and Notices:** Again, up to you. These can be overwhelming. eBay gives you the option to receive e-mails in the following areas:

- Member-to-member communications

- Indicate whether you choose to receive Second Chance Offers

- Reminders to leave feedback

- Account preference changes

Without enumerating everything else (I can see you're about to doze off), you can also opt in (or opt out) of eBay surveys, promotions, telephone update, and direct USPS mail from eBay.

Next on the Preferences hit parade are your *actual* site preferences — how you'd like to conduct business on the site. These are settings for the more advanced seller. You can make most of these decisions on the Sell Item Page. If you have time, though, click through each of the individual links to show the options and be sure the default settings work for you.

When you finally get your My eBay page set up the way you like it, save yourself a lot of work and time by using your browser to bookmark your My eBay page as a favorite. Doing so saves you a lot of keystrokes later. If you want to send a shortcut to your desktop, in Internet Explorer choose File⇨Send⇨ Shortcut to Desktop. This way, you can open your browser directly onto your My eBay page. Some eBay members make their My eBay page their browser home page so that their My eBay page appears the minute they log on. That's true dedication.

Your Feedback link

Next (after the Seller Dashboard which I explain further on) comes the Feedback option. In the Feedback area, you see all the items that need your feedback attention, and you can see the recent feedback that has been left for you. Save yourself a trip; you can more conveniently leave feedback from the item page, your Sell page, or your Buy page.

Account links

Not surprisingly, the My Account option leads you to more links for your PayPal and eBay Seller accounts. After you start selling, your Accounts pages become powerful. Figure 4-4 shows you the Seller Accounts summary section of my My eBay page. There's also a drop-down menu so that you can view past or current invoices. You can look up every detail of your account history, as well as make changes to your personal preferences (such as how and when you want to pay fees).

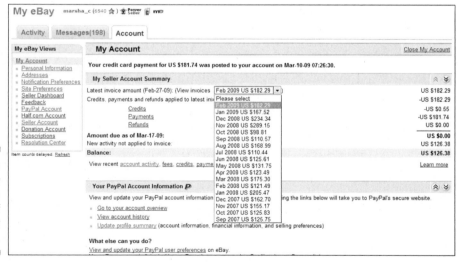

Figure 4-4: The Seller Accounts section of my My eBay page.

Before you jump into the money game, you may want to review the links that eBay gives you to manage your money:

✔ **View Account Status:** Click here to get a complete explanation of your eBay account — charges, credits, and your current balance since your last invoice.

✔ **View Invoices:** Click the drop-down menu to see your most recent invoice and details of the transactions.

✔ **PayPal:** A quick click here, and you're taken to the PayPal home page. Check out Chapter 6 for more on the PayPal payment service.

When you give eBay your credit card information, eBay attempts to authorize your card immediately. Your credit card company's response, either Declined or Approved, appears on your View Account Status page.

✔ **Payment Terms:** Although you need to post a credit card for ID purposes to sell on eBay, you can pay your eBay bill in one of three ways. They like to deduct it directly from your registered checking account, but I prefer the ways listed next. You can change your method of payment at any time. See Table 4-2 to find out when the different payments are charged to your account.

- **Credit Card on File:** You can place your credit card on file with eBay so that each month eBay can place your selling charges on your credit card. I've been using this format since I became an eBay user and find that it works out very well.

- **PayPal:** You can make single payments directly through your PayPal account. If you have a cash balance in your account, you can have it applied to your eBay bill; if not, you can pay the amount through the credit card you've registered on PayPal.

Table 4-2	eBay's Automatic Payments		
Billing Cycle	*Invoice*	*Deducted from Checking Account*	*Credit Card Charged*
15th of month	Between 16th and 20th	5th of the next month	5–7 days after receipt of invoice
Last day of month	Between 1st and 5th of next month	20th of next month	5–7 days after receipt of invoice

Understanding Your Seller Dashboard

If you look at the links in the box on the left of your Account Summary page, you see a group of links to quickly zip to specific areas as well as navigating by using the tab with its drop-down menu. One of the most important is the link to the Seller Dashboard, which is the place where eBay calculates your ratings on the site. An explanation of the Detailed Seller Ratings (DSRs) is in Chapter 8. Figure 4-5 shows you a shot of my Seller Dashboard.

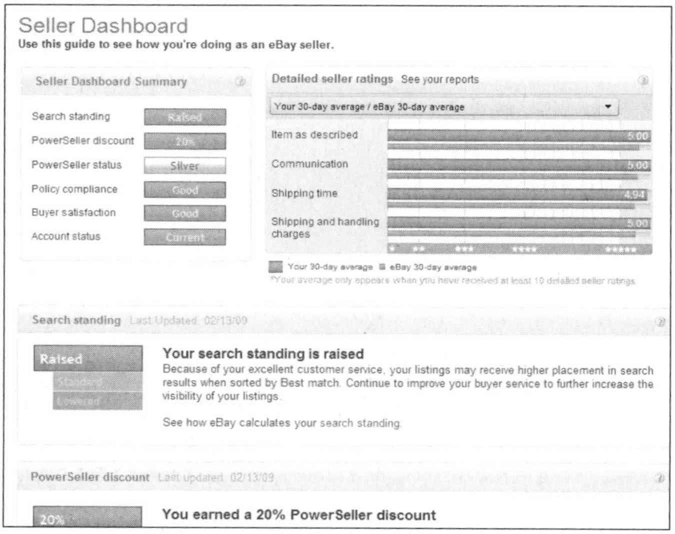

Figure 4-5: Viewing my current Seller Dashboard.

This is an important place to go on a regular basis because eBay evaluates your status on the site daily. Your status affects your placement in searches and whether you get a discount on your fees (based on your customer satisfaction ratings) if you're a PowerSeller.

Using the Resolution Center

If you sell an item and the buyer backs out (a rare but disheartening situation), you can at least get a refund on some of the fees that eBay charges you as a seller. These are the final value fees, and they're based on the selling price of the item. In the Resolution Center you can keep track of the disputes in progress and send or receive messages from the other party regarding payment.

Before you can collect a final value fee refund, the following conditions must apply:

- After your listing is over, you have to allow buyers at least three business days to respond to you. If they don't respond, you can send them an e-mail politely reminding them of their commitment to buy.

- If at least seven days have elapsed since the end of the transaction and you have the feeling that you're not going to see your money, you *must* open an Unpaid Item Alert. After you file this notice, eBay sends you a copy and the bidder gets an ominous e-mail with a reminder to complete the transaction or to respond with a reason.

  You have up to 45 days from the end of the auction to file an Unpaid Item Alert — and you can't get a final value fee credit without filing this alert.

- The next ten days after you file the Unpaid Item Alert are your "work out" days — the period where you and the bidder hopefully complete your transaction. You may try to give the bidder a call or send an e-mail through the Dispute Console to resolve the situation during this time.

- After the ten days have passed but no more than 60 days have elapsed since the end of the auction, you may file for a final value fee credit.

If you have begin the process and file for a final value fee credit but then manage to work things out with the buyer, eBay removes the complaint from the buyer's account after the buyer pays through PayPal. Buyers with too many of these warnings can be suspended from using the eBay site. You can automatically file to have this alert removed through the Dispute Console.

Organizing in the Organize Area

Part of the fun of eBay is searching for stuff that you'd never in a million years think of looking for. Wacky stuff aside, most eBay users spend their time hunting for specific items — say, Barbie dolls, designer dresses, plumbing supplies, or U.S. stamps. That's why eBay came up with the Organize area of your My eBay page. Whenever you view your My eBay Organize links, you see a list of your favorite searches and sellers. But because eBay isn't psychic, you have to tell it what you want listed.

If you shop eBay at all like I do, you'll be looking for similar things and sellers over and over. The My eBay Organize area allows you to make note of your favorite searches and sellers. You can perform these searches and visit these stores with a click of your mouse.

Saved searches

You have the opportunity to list a maximum of 100 searches here. When you want to repeat one of these searches, just click the Search name to search for the item. eBay will even e-mail you up to 20 of your searches when new items are listed. (For more on that advanced function, check out Chapter 18.)

To add a search to your favorites, first perform the search. (For details on how to perform a search, see Chapter 5.) When the search appears on your screen, click the Save This Search link, shown at the top of the search results in Figure 4-6.

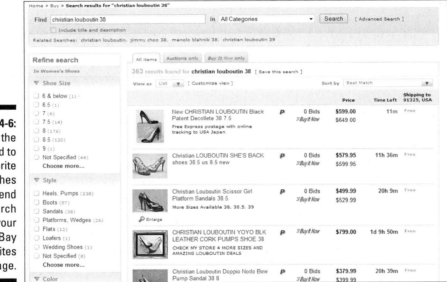

Figure 4-6: Click the Add to Favorite Searches link to send a search to your My eBay Favorites page.

The search is now transported to your My eBay Favorite Searches area for that particular search, as shown in Figure 4-7. If you want to be notified by e-mail when new items are listed, select the check box and the time frame in the drop-down menu.

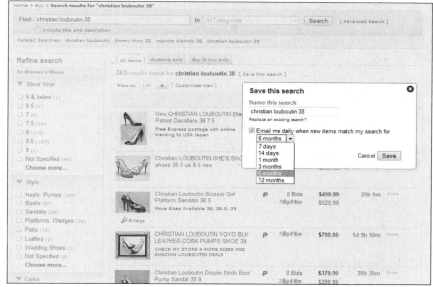

Figure 4-7:
The Adding
a Favorite
Search
details
page.

Saved sellers

When you find a seller whose merchandise and prices are right up your alley and you'd like to occasionally check out the seller's auctions, you can list the seller in the Favorite Sellers area:

1. **When you've shopped eBay and found a seller that you're happy with, click the link on the listing page to view the seller's other items.**

   You see a search page listing all the items for sale by that seller.

2. **Scroll down the page, and on the left side, click the Add to saved sellers link.**

   The seller is saved to your Saved sellers (favorites) page.

If you find seller that you'd like to make favorites while you're browsing or buying in their eBay stores, click the Add to Saved Sellers link at the top of the store's home page.

Got the time? eBay does. Click the eBay Official Time link, which is at the bottom of virtually every eBay page. The eBay clock is so accurate that you can set your watch by it. And you may want to, especially if you want to place a last-second bid before an auction closes. After all, eBay's official time is, um, *official.*

Following the Action on Your Buying and Watching Pages

I have the most fun on eBay when I'm shopping. Shopping on eBay is exciting, and I can find a zillion great bargains. Fortunately, eBay gives us a place to keep all our shopping information together: the Buying area.

Seeing the Items I'm Buying

When you bid on an item, eBay automatically lists the item in the Buying area of your My eBay Page. If you're winning an auction, the price appears in green; if you're losing, it appears in red. After the auction's over, the listing moves to Won (yea!) or Didn't Win (boo!). You can watch the progress of the auction from here and see the number of bids on the item, the high bid, and how much time is left until the end of the auction. All this information can help you decide whether you want to jump back in and make a bid.

eBay also keeps a total of all your active bids and buys to the left your data in the Totals: Buying Total box — which I hope helps you stay within your spending limits.

Keeping track of Items I've Won

When you've won an auction or purchased an item in a store, it appears in the Won area. From this area, you can visit the auction to print the auction page or double-check it. From the links in the Action column, you can also pay for your item through PayPal; if you've already paid, you can view the PayPal payment details. You can also click a Leave Feedback link here from the drop-down menu — after you've received the item and are satisfied with your purchase — to leave feedback.

Sleuthing with Items I'm Watching

Items I'm Watching is the most active area of my My eBay page (see Figure 4-8). This is the place for you to work on your strategy for getting bargains without showing your hand by bidding. In this area, you can watch the auction evolve and decide if you want to bid on it. You can list several auctions for the same item and watch them develop and then bid on the one that can give you the best deal. You can track the progress of up to 100 auctions in your Items I'm Watching area.

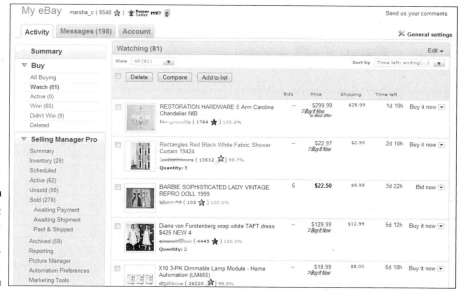

Figure 4-8: The Watch area of the My eBay page.

Moving auctions into the Item's I'm Watching area is easy. When you've found an item that you want to keep track of, look for the Watch This Item (Track It in My eBay) link, which is located just below the price on the listing page. Just click this link to transport the item to your Items I'm Watching area.

Surveying Your Sales on Your My eBay Selling Page

Your My eBay page supplies you with the tools to keep track of items you're selling on eBay. The My eBay Selling page works much the same as the Bidding page, but this time you're making the money — not spending it! Your current auction sales are listed in the Items I'm Selling area. The items with bids on them appear in green, and the ones without bids (or where the reserve hasn't been met) are in red. At the bottom, you have a dollar total of the current bids on your auctions.

Your Sell page

Similar to the Buy section of the All Buying section, the Sell area keeps track of your ongoing listings on eBay. You can observe the auction action in real time (or at least every time you refresh the page). You can see how many bids have been placed, when the auction closes, and the time left in the auction. If you want more information about what's going on, click the handy All Item Details link, which gives you a miniversion of each auction (without the description).

Your Sold page

When the sale is final, the items go into the Sold area (shown in Figure 4-9). Here's where you can keep track of the sale. You can check whether the buyer has paid with PayPal as well as the transaction status. If the buyer has completed checkout, you can get his or her information by clicking the Next Steps/Status link. If the buyer hasn't completed checkout, you can click the Send Invoice button to send the buyer an invoice. Very handy!

If you haven't heard from the buyer after three days (the prescribed eBay deadline for contact), you may need to resend your invoice or send another e-mail. See Chapter 12 for more information on post-sale correspondence.

After the transaction is complete (which means the item has arrived and the buyer is happy with his or her purchase), you can click the handy Leave Feedback link to leave feedback about the buyer.

You can also relist the item from a quick link or place a Second Chance offer to an underbidder if you have more than one of the item. See the nearby sidebar for more on the Second Chance feature.

Your secret seller tool — Second Chance!

Those cagey minds at eBay have come up with another great selling implement. Say you have multiples of a single item (you *did* sell that set of Minton china one piece at a time, didn't you?) or the winning bidder backs out of the transaction without paying. Second Chance offer gives you the opportunity to offer the item to one of the underbidders (okay, the losers) at their high bid price. You can also create a Second Chance if you set a reserve that wasn't met before the auction ended. The Second Chance opportunity is available for up to 60 days after the sale ends.

You can offer the item to as many of the underbidders (as you have merchandise to cover) at a time and make this personal offer good for one to seven days. The bidder receives an e-mail regarding the offer and can access it on the site through a special link. It is visible to only you and the other bidder for the duration of the offer. The best part is that eBay doesn't charge any additional listing fees for this feature, but you are charged the final value fee after the transaction is complete.

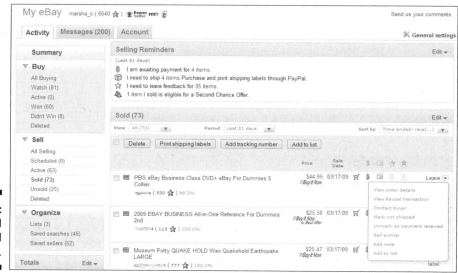

Figure 4-9: The Sold area and all its options.

eBay's Selling Manager/Selling Manager Pro

If you're at the point where you're selling bunches of items on the site, you may want to subscribe to one of eBay's Selling Manager tools. These tools make your Selling area look completely different and give you the opportunity to handle more sales in a compact and convenient design. See Chapter 20 for detailed information.

Keeping Track of Your Transactions

Yes, I bug you about printing stuff at the outset of your selling career — not because I'm in cahoots with the paper industry but because I care. The eBay transaction process can be daunting, and beginners can easily lose track. The best way to protect yourself is to keep good records on your own. Don't depend on eBay to cover you — not that eBay doesn't care. But this is your money, so keep a close eye on it.

Now don't become a pack rat and overdo it. To help point you in the right direction, here's a list of important documents I think you should print and file whether you're a buyer or a seller:

✔ Auction pages as they appear when they close

✔ PayPal statements indicating any payment you receive that doesn't clear

✔ Insurance or escrow forms

✔ Refund and credit requests

✔ Receipts from purchases you make for items to sell on eBay

 Always, always, *always* save every e-mail message you receive about a transaction, whether you buy or sell until the transaction is over and feedback is left. Also save your EOAs (End of Auction e-mails) that eBay sends. For more information about EOAs and correspondence etiquette after the auction is over, see Chapters 8 and 12.

Why should you save all this stuff? Here are some reasons:

✔ Even if you're buying and selling just a few items a month on eBay, you need to keep track of who you owe and who owes you money.

✔ Good e-mail correspondence is a learned art, but if you reference item numbers, your e-mail is an instant record. If you put your dates in writing — and follow up — you have a nice, neat paper trail.

✔ Documenting the transaction through e-mail will come in handy if you ever end up in a dispute over the terms of the sale.

✔ If you sell specialized items, you can keep track of trends and your frequent buyers.

✔ Some day the IRS may come knocking on your door, especially if you buy stuff for the purpose of selling it on eBay. Scary, but true. For more on where you can get tax information, take a look at Chapter 9.

When it comes to keeping records via e-mail and documents about transactions, I say that after you've received your feedback (positive, of course), you can dump it. If you get negative feedback (how could you?), hang on to your paperwork for a little longer. Use your discretion, but generally you can toss the paperwork from a bad transaction after it has reached some sort of resolution. (You can find out more about feedback in the next section.)

Once a month, do a seller search on yourself and print your latest eBay history. Chapter 5 tells you more about doing seller searches, organizing your searches, and starting files on items you want to track.

Getting and Giving Feedback

You know how they say you are what you eat? On eBay, you are only as good as your feedback says you are. Your feedback is made up of comments — good, bad, or neutral — that people leave about you (and you leave about others). In effect, people are commenting on your overall professionalism. (Even if you're an eBay hobbyist with no thought of using it professionally, a little businesslike courtesy can ease your transactions with everyone.) These comments are the basis for your eBay reputation.

Because feedback is so important to your reputation on eBay, you don't want others leaving feedback or making bad transactions under your name. The only way to ensure this doesn't happen is to always keep your password a secret. If you suspect somebody may know your password, change it before that person has a chance to sign in as you and ruin your reputation. (For more on selecting and protecting your level of privacy, see Chapters 1 and 15.)

When you get your first feedback, the number that appears next to your user ID is your feedback rating, which follows you everywhere you go on eBay, even if you change your user ID or e-mail address. It sticks to you like glue. Click the number next to any user ID and get a complete look at the user's feedback profile. The thinking behind the feedback concept is that you wouldn't be caught dead in a store that has a lousy reputation, so why on earth would you want to do business on the Internet with someone who has a lousy reputation?

You're not required to leave feedback, but because it's the benchmark by which all eBay users are judged, whether you're buying or selling, you should *always* leave feedback comments. Get in the frame of mind that every time you complete a transaction — the minute the package arrives safely if you're a seller or an item you've bid on and won arrives — you should go to eBay and post your feedback.

Every time you get a positive comment from a user who hasn't commented on you before within the past week, you get a point. Every time you get a negative rating, this negative cancels out one of your positives. Neutral comments rate a 0 — they have no impact either way. eBay even has what it calls the Star Chart, shown in Figure 4-10, which rewards those with good-and-getting-higher feedback ratings.

Here's what the different stars mean:
Yellow star ( ) = 10 to 49 ratings
Blue star ( ) = 50 to 99 ratings
Turquoise star ( ) = 100 to 499 ratings
Purple star ( ) = 500 to 999 ratings
Red star ( ) = 1,000 to 4,999 ratings
Green star ( ) = 5,000 to 9,999 ratings
Yellow shooting star ( ) = 10,000 to 24,999 ratings
Turquoise shooting star ( ) = 25,000 to 49,999 ratings
Purple shooting star ( ) = 50,000 to 99,999 ratings
Red shooting star ( ) = 100,000 to 499,000 ratings
Green shooting star ( ) = 500,000 to 999,999 ratings
Silver shooting star ( ) = 1,000,000 ratings or more

Figure 4-10: The eBay feedback achievement Star rating.

The flip side (or Dark Side to you *Star Wars* fans) of the star system is negative numbers. Negative comments deduct from your total of positive comments, thereby lowering the number beside your user ID. *eBay riddle:* When is more than one still one? Gotcha, huh? The answer is, when you get more than one feedback message from the same person in the same week. Confused? This should help: You can sell one person 100 different items, but even if the buyer gives you a glowing review 100 times in the same week, your feedback rating doesn't increase by 100. In this case, the other 99 feedback comments appear in your feedback profile, but your rating increases only by 1.

Sellers are only allowed to leave positive feedback for buyers — I know this may not make sense, but that's the way it is. You can leave a "positive," but still be honest about your transaction in your words. eBay made this rule so sellers wouldn't leave retaliatory feedback to buyers who left them negative feedback.

Should a buyer who hasn't paid leave you a negative, eBay cooperates and removes the feedback, provided you've filed an Unpaid Item report.

If feedback is left individually and stretched out over several weeks (only one per week), the person on the other end of the transaction will get a single feedback point each time you leave a positive. I do this for my buyers who buy multiple items from me (it's easy from the My eBay page). But, grrrrrr, they don't seem to know this rule so I'll get several positives — one after another — netting me only one positive. *Sigh*

Anyone with a –4 rating has his or her eBay membership terminated. Remember, just because a user may have a 750 feedback rating, it doesn't hurt to click the number after the name to double-check the person's eBay ID card. Even if someone has a total of 1,000 feedback messages, 250 of them *could* be negative.

You can get to your personal feedback profile page right from your My eBay page by clicking the number next to your user ID.

Feedback comes in three exciting flavors:

- ✔ **Positive feedback:** Someone once said, "All you have is your reputation." Reputation is what makes eBay function. If the transaction works well, you get positive feedback; whenever it's warranted, you should give it right back.

- ✔ **Negative feedback:** If there's a glitch (for instance, it takes six months to get your *Charlie's Angels* lunchbox or the seller substitutes a rusty thermos for the one you bid on or you never get the item), you have the right — some would say *obligation* — to leave negative feedback.

- ✔ **Neutral feedback:** You can leave neutral feedback if you feel so-so about a specific transaction. It's the middle-of-the-road comment. Say you bought an item that had a little more wear and tear on it than the seller indicated, but you still like it and want to keep it.

How to get positive feedback

If you're selling, here's how to get a good reputation:

- ✔ Establish contact with the buyer (pronto!) after the listing ends (see Chapter 12).
- ✔ After you've received payment, send the item quickly (see Chapter 12).

- Make sure that your item is exactly the way you described it (see Chapter 10).
- Package the item well and ship it with care (see Chapter 12).
- React quickly and appropriately to problems — for example, the item's lost or damaged in the mail, or the buyer is slow in paying (see Chapter 12).

If you're buying, try these good-rep tips:

- Send your payment fast (see Chapter 8).
- Keep in touch through e-mail with the seller (see Chapter 8).
- Work with the seller to resolve any problems in a courteous manner (see Chapters 8 and 12).

How to get negative feedback

If you're selling, here's what to do to tarnish your name big-time:

- Tell a major fib in the item description. (Defend truth, justice, and legitimate creative writing — see Chapter 10.)
- Take the money but "forget" to ship the item. (Who did you say you are? See Chapter 16.)
- Package the item poorly so that it ends up smashed, squashed, or vaporized during shipping. (To avoid this pathetic fate, see Chapter 12.)

If you're buying, you can't get official negative feedback, but the seller still has their "say." Here's how to make your feedback comment a serious mess:

- Bid on an item, win the auction, and never respond to the seller. (Remember your manners and see Chapter 6.)
- Send a personal check that bounces and never make good on the payment. (See Chapter 16 — and don't pass Go.)
- Ask the seller for a refund because you just don't like the item. (Remember how to play fair and see Chapter 8.)

Extra, extra, read all about it

Normally, I believe in the adage, "Keep your business private." But not when it comes to feedback. The default setting is for public viewing of your feedback. This way, everyone on eBay can read all about you. If you want to make your feedback a private matter, you need to go to the Feedback Forum. Click the Feedback link under the My Account heading of the My eBay page. Then click the Go to Feedback Forum link. The link you need to click from there is the Hide my Feedback link.

However, hiding your feedback is a very bad idea. You want people to know that you're trustworthy; being honest and upfront is the way to go. If you hide your feedback profile, people may suspect that you're covering up bad things and eBay takes away your selling privileges. It's in your best interest to let the spotlight shine on your feedback history. It's your reputation, your money, and your experience as an eBay member. Keep in mind that all three are always linked.

The Feedback page

When you click the Feedback number next to a member's user ID, you'll see all the tools you need to gauge the member. Think of your feedback profile as your eBay report card. Your goal is to get straight *A*s — in this case, all positive feedback. Unlike a real report card, you don't have to bring it home to be signed.

When someone clicks the feedback number next to your user ID, they see the following information (see Figure 4-11):

- ✔ **Your user ID:** Your eBay nickname appears, followed by a number in parentheses — the net number of the positive feedback comments you've received, minus any negative feedback comments you may have (but that wouldn't happen to you).

- ✔ **Your membership information:** Listed here is the date you first signed up as a member of the eBay community. Below that is the country from which you're registered, your star rating (refer to Figure 4-11), and any icons leading to more areas related to you on eBay, such as your About Me page (see Chapter 14). This area also notes whether you are a PowerSeller (see Chapter 20) and whether you have an eBay Store.

- ✔ **Detailed Seller Ratings:** This area sums up the ratings, from one to five, that buyers have left for you.

✔ **Your Recent Feedback Ratings:** This area is a scorecard of your feedback for the last 12 months. At the bottom of the feedback tote board is a summary of your bid retractions in the past six months — the times you have retracted bids during an auction.

Figure 4-11:
The feedback Member Profile — there's one on every member.

Be careful when you retract a bid. All bids on eBay are binding, but under what eBay calls "exceptional circumstances," you may retract bids — very sparingly. Here are the circumstances in which it's okay to retract a bid:

✔ If you've mistakenly put in the wrong bid amount — say, $100 instead of $10

✔ If the seller adds to his or her description after you've placed your bid, and the change considerably affects the item

✔ If you can't contact the seller (your e-mail continuously bounces back and the phone number doesn't work)

You can't retract a bid just because you found the item elsewhere cheaper or you changed your mind or you decided that you really can't afford the item. If that's the case, e-mail the seller and ask *them* to please remove your bid. See Chapter 6 for more information on retracting bids.

Reading your feedback

Your eBay reputation is at the mercy of the one-liners that buyers and sellers leave for you in the form of feedback comments. Each feedback box contains these reputation-building (or reputation-trashing) ingredients:

- The user ID of the person who sent the feedback. The number in paren-theses next to the person's name is his or her own feedback rating.

- The date and time the feedback was posted.

- The item number of the transaction that the feedback refers to. If the item has closed in the past 30 days, you can click the transaction number to see what the buyer purchased.

- Seller or Buyer — indicating whether you were the seller or the buyer in the transaction.

- Feedback bullets in different colors: praise (in green with a plus mark), negative (in red with a minus mark), or neutral (in grey with a white dot).

- The feedback the person left about you.

You have the last word — responding to feedback

After reading feedback you've received from others, you may feel compelled to respond. If the feedback is negative, you may want to defend yourself. If it's positive, you may want to say thank you.

To respond to feedback, follow these steps:

1. **Click the Feedback link in the drop-down menu under the Account tab on your My eBay page, and then click the Go to Feedback Forum link at the top of the page.**

   You're transported to the Feedback Forum, where you can reply to feed-back comments left for you.

2. **Find the feedback you want to respond to and click the Reply link.**

3. **Type your response.**

If you want to follow up to a feedback you've already left for someone, follow the preceding steps, but in Step 2, click the Follow Up to Feedback Left link on the Feedback Forum page.

Do not confuse *replying* to feedback with *leaving* feedback. Replying does not change the other user's feedback rating; it merely adds a line below the feedback with your response.

Leaving feedback with finesse

Writing feedback well takes some practice. It isn't a matter of saying things; it's a matter of saying *only the appropriate things.* Think carefully about what you want to say because once you submit feedback, it stays with the person for the duration of his or her eBay career. I think you should always leave feedback, especially at the end of a transaction, although doing so isn't mandatory. Think of leaving feedback as voting in an election: If you don't leave feedback, you can't complain about lousy service.

eBay says to make feedback "factual and emotionless." You won't go wrong if you comment on the details (either good or bad) of the transaction. If you have any questions about what eBay says about feedback, click the Feedback link on your My eBay page and then click the Go to Feedback Forum link.

In the Feedback Forum, you can perform six feedback-related tasks:

- **See feedback about an eBay user.**

- **Leave feedback for many auctions at once.** Here, you see all pending feedback for all transactions within the past 90 days. You are presented with a page of all your transactions for which you haven't left feedback. Fill them in, one at a time, and with one click you can leave as many as 25 feedback comments at once.

- **Review and respond to existing feedback about you.**

- **Review the feedback you have left for others.** Here, you may also leave follow-up feedback after the initial feedback, should situations change.

- **Make your feedback profile public or private.** Remember, if you make your feedback profile private, you may hinder your future business on eBay. See the sidebar "Extra, extra, read all about it," elsewhere in this chapter.

- **Check the Feedback FAQ to review any changes in the feedback system.**

In the real world (at least in the modern American version of it), anybody can sue anybody else for slander or libel; this fact holds true on the Internet, too. It's a good idea to be careful not to make any comments that could be libelous or slanderous. eBay is not responsible for your actions, so if you're sued because of negative feedback (or anything else you've written), you're on your own. The best way to keep yourself safe is to stick to the facts and to not get personal.

Mincing words: The at-a-glance guide to keeping feedback short

eBay likes to keep things simple. If you want to compliment, complain, or take the middle road, you have to do it in 80 characters or less. That means your comment needs to be short and sweet (or short and sour if it's negative, or sweet and sour if you're mixing drinks or ordering Chinese food). If you have a lot to say but you're stumped about how to say it, here are a few examples for any occasion. String them together or mix and match!

Positive feedback:

✔ Very professional

✔ Quick e-mail response

✔ Fast service

✔ A+++

✔ Good communication

✔ Exactly as described

✔ Highly recommended

✔ Smooth transaction

✔ Would deal with again

✔ An asset to eBay

✔ I'll be back!

Negative feedback:

✔ Never responded

✔ Never sent item

✔ Desperately slow shipping

✔ Beware track record

✔ Not as described

Neutral feedback:

✔ Slow to ship but item as described

✔ Item not as described but seller made good

✔ Poor communication but item came OK

If you're angry, take a breather *before* you type your complaints and click the Leave Comment button. If you're convinced that negative feedback is necessary, try a cooling-off period before you send a comment. Wait an hour or a day and then see whether you feel the same. Nasty feedback based on emotion can make you look vindictive (even if what you're saying is true).

Safety tips for giving feedback

And speaking of safety features you should know about feedback, you may want to study up on these:

✔ Remember that feedback, whether good or bad, is *sticky*. eBay won't remove your feedback comment if you change your mind later. Be sure of your facts and carefully consider what you want to say.

✔ Before you leave feedback, see what other people had to say about that person. Is your thinking in line with the comments others have left?

- Your feedback comment can be left as long as the transaction remains on the eBay server. This is usually within 90 days of the end of the listing. After 90 days have passed, you must have the transaction number to leave feedback.

- Your comment can be a maximum of only 80 letters long, which is really short when you have a lot to say. Before you start typing, organize your thoughts and use common abbreviations to save precious space.

- Before posting negative feedback, try to resolve the problem by e-mail or telephone. You may discover that your reaction to the transaction is based on a misunderstanding that can be easily resolved.

- eBay users generally want to make each other happy, so use negative feedback *only as a last resort*. See Chapters 8 and 10 for more details on how to avoid negative feedback.

If you do leave a negative comment that you later regret, you can't remove it. You can go back to follow up and leave an explanation or a more positive comment (but it won't change the initial feedback or rating), so think twice before you blast.

The ways to leave feedback

Several ways are available to leave feedback comments:

- If you're on the user's Feedback page, click the Leave Feedback link; the Leave Feedback page appears.

- In the Won area of your My eBay page, click the Leave Feedback link next to the listing.

- Go to your auction and click the Leave Feedback icon.

- In the Feedback Forum, click the Leave Feedback link to see a list of all your completed items from the last 90 days for which you haven't yet left feedback.

To leave feedback for a buyer, follow these steps:

1. **Enter the required information.**

   Note that your item number is usually filled in, but if you're placing feedback from the user's Feedback page, you need to have the number at hand.

2. **Type your comment.**

   Only positive feedback can be left for a buyer, so choose your words carefully.

3. **Click the Leave Feedback button.**

Part II
Buying Like an Expert

The 5th Wave   By Rich Tennant

"Guess who found a Kiss merchandise blowout on eBay while you were gone?"

In this part . . .

After you have an idea how to get around the eBay site, no doubt you'll want to get started buying. You've come to the right place. Here you can find all the information you need to start bidding and winning items at the lowest possible prices.

Although eBay is a lot more fun than school, you still have to do your homework. After you've registered to become an eBay member (in Part I), you can place a bid on (or outright buy) any item you see. But first you have to find the item that's right for you . . . and then maybe find out what it's worth. And what happens when you win?!

In this part, I show you how to find the items you want without sifting through every single one of eBay's millions of listings. I also give you an insider's look at determining the value of a collectible, deciding how much you're willing to spend, and using the right strategy to win the item at just the right price. When the listing is over, follow my advice to make closing the deal go as smooth as silk. Watch the positive feedback come pouring in.

Chapter 5

Seek and You Shall Find: Research

· ·

In This Chapter

▶ Getting real-world buying advice on collectibles

▶ Obtaining solid online buying advice

▶ Checking out information sources for savvy buyers

▶ Conducting a special item search on eBay

· ·

*P*icture all the stores you've ever seen in your life, located in one giant mall. You walk in and try to find the single item you're looking for. Man, that's tough! Consider also walking into a store with thousands of aisles of shelves with tens of millions of items on them. Browsing the categories of listings on eBay can be just as pleasantly boggling, without the prospect of sore feet. Start surfing around the site and you instantly understand the size and scope of what's for sale there. Everything. Without question, you'll feel overwhelmed at first, but the eBay staff has come up with lots of ways to help you find exactly what you're looking for. As soon as you figure out how to find the items you want to bid or buy on eBay, you can protect your investment-to-be by making sure that what you find is actually what you seek.

Of course, searching is easier if you have an idea of what you're looking for. In this chapter for collectors, I offer the first-time buyer some expert tips and tell you how to get expert advice from eBay and other sources. I also give you tips for using the eBay search engine from a buyer's perspective.

The best advice you can follow as you explore any free-market system is *caveat emptor* — let the buyer beware. Although nobody can guarantee that every one of your transactions will be perfect, research items thoroughly before you bid so that you don't lose too much of your hard-earned money — or too much sleep.

General Online Tips for Collectors

If you're just starting out on eBay, chances are you like to shop and you also collect items that interest you. You'll find out pretty early in your eBay adventures that a lot of people online know as much about collecting as they do about bidding — and some are serious contenders.

How can you compete? Well, in addition to having a well-planned buying strategy (covered in Chapter 7), knowing your stuff gives you a winning edge. I've gathered the opinions of two collecting experts to get the info you need about online collecting basics. (If you're already an expert collector but want help finding that perfect something on eBay so you can get ready to bid, you've got it. See "Looking to Find an Item? Start Your eBay Search Engine," later in this chapter.) I also show you how one of those experts puts the information into practice, and I give you a crash course on how items for sale are (or should be) graded.

Although these tips from the experts are targeted for collectors, much of the information is sound advice for those involved in any transaction online.

The experts speak out

Bill Swoger closed his collectibles store in Burbank, California and sold the balance of his G.I. Joe and Superman items on eBay. And Lee Bernstein, a columnist and collectibles dealer who operates Lee Bernstein Books and Collectibles from her home base in Schererville, Indiana, authors a monthly column for the *New England Antiques Journal*. She also is the author of eBay's Collectibles original "Inside Scoop." Bill and Lee offer these tips to collectors new to eBay:

- **Get all the facts before you put your money down.** Study the description carefully. It's your job to analyze the description and make your bidding decisions accordingly. Find out whether all original parts are included and whether the item has any flaws. If the description says that the Fred Flintstone figurine has a cracked back, e-mail the seller for more information on just how cracked Fred really is.

- **Don't get caught up in the emotional thrill of bidding.** First-time buyers (known as *Under-10s* or *newbies* because they have fewer than ten transactions under their belts) tend to bid wildly, using emotions instead of brains. If you're new to eBay, you can get burned if you just bid for the thrill of victory without thinking about what you're doing.

I can't stress how important it is to determine an item's value, whether collectible or new. But because values are such flighty things (values depend on supply and demand, market trends, and all sorts of other variables), I recommend that you get a general idea of the item's value and use this ballpark figure to set a maximum amount of money you're willing to bid for that item. Then *stick to* your maximum and don't even think about bidding past it. If the bidding gets too hot, there's always another auction. To find out more about bidding strategies, Chapter 7 is just the ticket.

✔ **Know what the item should cost.** Buyers used to depend on *price guides* — books on collectibles and their values — to help them bid. Bill says that price guides are becoming a thing of the past. Sure, you can find a guide that says an original *Lion King* Broadway poster in excellent condition has a book price of $150, but if you do a search on eBay, you'll see that they're actually selling for $65 to $75.

When your search on eBay turns up what you're looking for, average the current prices you find. Also check the completed listings. Doing so gives you a much better idea of what you need to spend than any price guide can.

✔ **Timing is everything, and being first costs.** If you're into movie posters, for example, consider this: If you can wait three to six months after a movie is released, you can get the poster for 40 to 50 percent less. The same goes for many new releases of collectibles. Sometimes you're wiser to wait and save money.

✔ **Be careful of presale items.** Sometimes you may run across vendors selling items that they don't have in stock but that they'll ship to you later. For example, before *Star Wars Episode I: The Phantom Menace* came out, some vendors ran auctions on movie posters they didn't have yet. If you had bid and won, and for some reason the vendor had a problem getting the poster, you'd have been out of luck. Don't bid on anything that can't be delivered as soon as you pay for the item. See some of eBay's presale rules later in this chapter.

✔ **Being too late can also cost.** Many collectibles become more difficult to find as time goes by. Generally, as scarcity increases, so does desirability and value. Common sense tells you that if two original and identical collectibles are offered side by side, with one in like-new condition and the other in used condition, the like-new item will have the higher value.

✔ **Check out the seller.** Check the feedback rating (the number in parentheses next to the person's user ID) a seller has before you buy. If the seller has many comments with a minute number of negative ones, chances are good that this is a reputable seller. For more on feedback, see Chapter 4.

Although eBay forbids side deals, an unsuccessful bidder may (at his or her own risk) contact a seller after an auction is over to see if the seller has more of the item in stock. If the seller is an experienced eBay user (a high feedback rating is usually a tip-off) and has more of the item in stock, he or she may consider making a perfectly eBay-legal Second Chance offer. Don't ask to buy the item off-site. eBay strictly prohibits selling items off the site. If you conduct a side deal and are reported to eBay, you can be suspended. Not only that, but buyers who are ripped off by sellers in away-from-eBay transactions shouldn't look to eBay to bail them out; you're on your own. The way to purchase these items is by asking the seller to post another of the item for you — or if you were an underbidder in the auction, send you a Second Chance offer. That way, you're also protected by PayPal buyer protections.

✔ **If an item comes to you broken in the mail, contact the seller to work it out.** The best bet is to request shipping insurance (you pay for it) before the seller ships the item. But if you didn't ask for insurance, it never hurts to ask for a discount (or a replacement item, if available) if you're not satisfied. Chapter 12 offers the lowdown on buying shipping insurance, and Chapter 16 provides pointers on dealing with transactions that go sour.

Go, Joe: Following an expert on the hunt

I know that not many of us collect G.I. Joes, but by studying what an expert looks for in this specialty collectible, we can get a good idea of what we should be looking for when purchasing whatever it is that we collect.

Bill looks for specific traits when he buys his very collectible G.I. Joe figures. Although his checklist is specific to the G.I. Joe from 1964 to 1969, the information here can help you determine your maximum bid on other collectibles (or whether an item is even *worth* bidding on) before an auction begins. As you find out in Chapter 7, the more you know before you place a bid, the happier you're likely to be when you win. Bill's checklist can save you considerable hassle:

✔ **Find out the item's overall condition.** For G.I. Joe, look at the painted hair and eyebrows. Expect some wear, but overall, a collectible worth bidding on should look good.

✔ **Be sure the item's working parts are indeed working.** Most G.I. Joe action figures from this period have cracks on the legs and arms, but the joints should move, and any cracks should not be so deep that the legs and arms fall apart easily.

✔ **Ask if the item has its original parts.** Because you can't really examine items in detail before buying, e-mail the seller with specific questions relating to original or replacement parts. Many G.I. Joe action figures are rebuilt from parts that are not from 1964 to 1969. Sometimes the figures even have two left or right hands or feet! If you make it clear to the seller before you buy that you want a toy with only original parts, you'll be able to make a good case for a refund if the item arrives rebuilt as the Six Million Dollar Man. Chapter 7 has plenty of tips on how to protect yourself before you bid, and Chapter 16 has tips on what to do if the deal goes bad.

✔ **Ask if the item has original accessories.** A G.I. Joe from 1964 to 1969 should have his original dog tags, boots, and uniform. If any of these items are missing, you will have to pay around $25 to replace each missing item. If you're looking to bid on any other collectible, know in advance what accessories came as standard equipment with the item, or you'll be paying extra just to bring it back to its original version.

✔ **Know an item's value before you bid.** A 1964 to 1969 vintage G.I. Joe in decent shape, with all its parts, sells for $300 to $400 without its original box. (Mint-in-box Joes can sell for thousands of dollars.) If you're bidding on a G.I. Joe action figure on eBay and you're in this price range, you're okay. If you get the item for less than $300, congratulations — you've nabbed a bargain.

✔ **If you have any questions, ask them *before* you bid.** Check collectors' guides, research similar auctions on eBay, and visit one of eBay's category chat rooms.

Making the grade

Welcome to my version of grade school without the bad lunch. One of the keys to establishing value is knowing an item's condition, typically referred to as an item's *grade*. Table 5-1 lists the most common grading categories that collectors use. The information in this table is used with permission from (and appreciation to) Lee Bernstein.

Grading is subjective. Mint to one person may be Very Good to another. Always ask a seller to define the meaning of the terms used. Also, be aware that many amateur sellers may not really know the different definitions of grading and may arbitrarily add Mint or Excellent to their item descriptions.

Table 5-1	Collectibles Grading Categories	
Category (Also Known As)	**Description**	**Example**
Mint (M, Fine, Mint-In-Box [MIB], 10)	A never-used collectible in perfect condition with complete packaging (including instructions, original attachments, tags, and so on) identical to how it appeared on the shelf in the original box.	Grandma got a soup tureen as a wedding present, never opened it, and stuck it in her closet for the next 50 years.
Near Mint (NM, Near Fine, Like-New, 9)	The collectible is perfect but no longer has the original packaging or the original packaging is less than perfect. Possibly used but must appear to be new.	Grandma used the soup tureen on her 25th anniversary, washed it gently, and then put it back in the closet.
Excellent (EX, 8)	Used, but barely. Excellent is just a small step under Near Mint, and many sellers mistakenly interchange the two, but "excellent" can have very minor signs of wear. The wear must be a normal, desirable part of aging or so minor that it's barely noticeable and visible only upon close inspection. Damage of any sort is not "very minor." Wear or minor normal factory flaws should be noted. (Factory flaws are small blemishes common at the time of manufacture — a tiny air bubble under paint, for example.)	Grandma liked to ring in the New Year with a cup of soup for everyone.
Very Good (VG, 7)	Looks very good but has defects, such as a minor chip or light color fading.	If you weren't looking for it, you might miss that Grandma's tureen survived the '64 earthquake, as well as Uncle Bob's infamous ladle episode.
Good (G, 6)	Used with defects. More than a small amount of color loss, chips, cracks, tears, dents, abrasions, missing parts, and so on.	Grandma had the ladies in the neighborhood over for soup and bingo every month.
Poor (P or G-, 5)	Barely collectible, if at all. Severe damage or heavy use. Beyond repair.	Grandma ran a soup kitchen.

Finding More Research Information

Experts have been buying, selling, and trading collectible items for years. But just because you're new to eBay doesn't mean you have to be a newbie for decades before you can start bartering with the collecting gods. I wouldn't leave you in the cold like that — and neither would eBay. You can get information on items you're interested in, as well as good collecting tips, right at the eBay Web site. Visit the Category-Specific Discussion Boards in the Community area. You can also search the rest of the Web or go the old-fashioned route and check the library (yes, libraries are still around).

Keep in mind that there are truly several prices for an item. The retail (or manufacturer's suggested retail price — MSRP) price, the book value, the secondary market price (the price charged by resellers when an item is unavailable on the primary retail market), and the eBay selling price. The only way to ascertain the price an item will go for on eBay is to research completed auctions. Later in this chapter, I give you the skinny on how to research a completed auction.

Searching sites online

If you don't find the information you need on eBay, don't go ballistic — just go elsewhere. Even a site as vast as eBay doesn't have a monopoly on information. The Internet is filled with Web sites and Internet auction sites that can give you price comparisons and information about cyberclubs.

Getting professional info from Terapeak Research

If you become an eBay fanatic someday, you may find yourself praising the genius of an amazing service offered by eBay and Terapeak. Terapeak Research allows you to research pricing further back than the 14 days of completed listings that the normal eBay search allows. If you come across a special or very old item, and there are not many on the site, you can use this tool to find how much the item has sold for in the past few months.

As with most of eBay's special features, there is a charge to use the service. But the price is right, and you only have to pay for the service as long as you need it. They have several levels of search: from 7 to 90 days. I recommend using the 30-day search because in my (not so) humble opinion, 90 days is an eternity in Internet time — what sold well three months ago may be worth bupkis now.

Your home computer can connect to powerful outside servers (really big computers on the Internet) that have their own fast-searching systems called *search engines*. Remember, if something is out there and you need it, you can find it right from your home PC in a matter of seconds. Here are the addresses of some of the Web's most highly regarded search engines or multi-search-engine sites:

- ✔ Google (www.google.com)
- ✔ Live Search (www.live.com)
- ✔ Shopzilla (www.shopzilla.com)
- ✔ Yahoo! (www.yahoo.com)

The basic process of getting information from an Internet search engine is pretty simple:

1. **Type the address of the search-engine site in the Address box of your Web browser.**

   You're taken to the Web site's home page.

2. **Find the text box next to the button labeled Search or something similar.**

3. **In the text box, type a few words indicating what interests you.**

   Be specific when typing search text. The more precise your entry, the better your chances of finding what you want. Look for tips, an advanced search option, or help pages on your search engine of choice for more information about how to narrow your search.

4. **Click the Search (or similar) button or press Enter on your keyboard.**

   The search engine presents you with a list of how many Internet pages have the requested information. The list includes brief descriptions and links to the first group of pages. You'll find links to additional listings at the bottom if your search finds more listings than can fit on one page. (And if you ask for something popular, like *Harry Potter,* don't be surprised to get millions of hits.)

Always approach information on the Web with caution. Not everyone is the expert he or she would like to be. Your best bet is to get lots of different opinions and then boil 'em down to what makes sense to you. And remember — *caveat emptor.* (Is there an echo in here?)

Many people out here on the West Coast buy cars on eBay. (Could it be because cars are way more expensive here? Maybe.) If you're researching prices to buy a car on eBay, look in your local newspaper to get a good idea of prices in your community. Several good sites are on the Internet. My personal favorite is www.nadaguides.com. I've had many of my friends (and editors) visit the various sites, and we've settled on this one because it seems to give the most accurate and unbiased information.

Finding other sources of information

If you're interested in collecting a particular item, you can get a lot of insider collecting information without digging too deep:

- ✔ **Go to other places on eBay.** eBay's chat rooms and message boards (covered in detail in Chapter 17) are full of insider info. The eBay community is always willing to educate a newbie. Remember to take advice with caution, however, because sometimes the "competition" likes to keep the good nuggets of info for themselves.

- ✔ **Go to the library.** Books and magazines are great sources of info. At least one book or one magazine probably specializes in your chosen item. For example, if old furniture is your thing, *Antiquing For Dummies,* by Ron Zoglin and Deborah Shouse (Wiley Publishing, Inc.), can clue you in to what antiques collectors look for.

  If you find an interesting specialty magazine at the library, try entering the title in your search engine of choice. You may just find that the magazine has also gone paperless and you can read it online.

- ✔ **Go to someone else in-the-know.** Friends, clubs, and organizations in your area can give you a lot of info. Ask your local antiques dealer about clubs you can join and see how much info you end up with.

Looking to Find an Item? Start Your eBay Search Engine

The best part about shopping on eBay is that, aside from collectibles, you can find just about everything from that esoteric lithium battery to new designer dresses (with matching shoes) to pneumatic jackhammers. New or used, it's all here — if you can find it hiding in the (get this!) 6 million new daily listings. (According to eBay, 89 million listings are on the site worldwide at any given time. That's a lot of gavels being banged!)

Finding the nuggets (deals) can be like searching for the proverbial needle in the haystack. The search secrets in this chapter will put you head and shoulders above your competition for the deals.

eBay has lots of cool ways for you to search for items (sample 'em in Chapter 3). Although eBay allows you to search by item number, let's be realistic here. Do you remember what I said a few paragraphs back about the number of active listings? I can't remember my own phone number, let alone an item number (and I never write them down correctly). Look for those numbers to get longer and longer as eBay continues to grow in popularity. Four main options are the most useful for researching:

- ✔ Search Title (or Search Title and Description)
- ✔ Search Items by Seller
- ✔ Search Items by Bidder
- ✔ Search Items in eBay Stores

You can access the four search options by clicking the Advanced Search link to the right of the Search box at the top of any eBay page. Each search option can provide a different piece of information to help you find the right item from the right seller at the right price.

If you plan to repeat specific eBay searches, I recommend that you conduct searches often by saving them in your My eBay Saved Searches area (see Chapter 18 to find out how). And when you find a particularly juicy item or subcategory, bookmark it, or if it's an item, click Watch This Item (a link on the auction page just under the price), or use your My eBay page. (See Chapter 18 for more on eBay's personal shopper.)

Testing, testing . . . how long does a search take on eBay?

Having a massive search engine is a matter of necessity on eBay — millions of items are up for auction at any given time — and often, an easy, fast search makes all the difference between getting and not getting. After all, time is money, and eBay members tend to be movers and shakers who don't like standing still.

So how long do searches really take on eBay? I put it to the test. In the Search window of the eBay home page, I typed **1933 World's Fair Pennant** and let 'er rip.

The search engine went through about 89 million general items and World's Fair items (860 of them in 1999, 1,200 items in 2003 and over 2,100 in 2006!) and gave me my one specific item in just 4 seconds. (Now, if the wizards at eBay could only figure out a way to find that sock that always escapes from clothes dryers, they'd really be on to something.)

By the way, in 1999 that slightly wrinkled felt pennant got four bids and sold for $17.50; in 2003, the aging pennant sold for $43.88 with eight bids. And today? In 2009, one just went for $14.99. Humph, must be the economy.

Using the Search page

When you click the Advanced Search link to the right of the Search box, the Search page appears. It's the most basic of searches (with a few options) and the one you'll be using the most. (To get the really advanced features, you must click the Advanced Search link at the very bottom of the page.)

When you use any of the Search options on eBay, the search engine looks for every listing (auction or fixed price) that has the words you're looking for in the title or the description (if you specify so). The title (as you may expect) is just another word or group of words for what you call the item. For example, if you're looking for an antique sterling iced tea spoon, just type **sterling iced tea spoon** into the search window (see Figure 5-1). If someone is selling a sterling iced-teaspoon and used exactly those words in his or her title or description, you're in Fat City.

Figure 5-1: Using Search to find sterling iced tea spoons.

Before you click the Search button, know you can narrow your search further. If you go to Advanced Search, you have the option of choosing how you want the search engine to interpret your search entry. You can have the search engine search the title and description for

- ✔ All the words you type
- ✔ Some of the words you type
- ✔ The exact phrase in the order you've written it

When you're familiar with the tricks listed later in this chapter, you'll be able to get most of these fancy Search results in one of the many search boxes you see littered around the eBay site.

In addition to the following, you can find other useful criteria on the Advanced Search page (more on this further on):

- **What price range you want to see:** Type the price range you're looking for, and eBay searches the specific range between that low and high price. If money is no object, leave this box blank.

- **Words to exclude:** If you want to find a sterling iced tea spoon, but you don't want it to be plated silver, exclude the word *plated* from the drop-down menu.

- **From sellers:** You can exclude (or include) particular sellers. If you'd like, you can just search sellers from your Favorite Sellers list. (But why?)

- **The payment:** You may restrict your search to items that accept PayPal.

- **Within a category:** Use this option if you want to limit your search to a particular main (or *top-level*) category, for example, instead of searching all eBay categories. But why? eBay sellers are notorious for making listing mistakes and selecting wrong categories. Wait till you see your results, and then decide whether you want to narrow things.

- **The item location:** You can narrow your search to the United States only, North America, or worldwide. Depending on your item, this search criterion can help weed out the most esoteric items. If you're looking for hefty items (like an elliptical exercise machine that will probably end up as a place to hang clothes) that would cost much too much to ship, you can specify how many miles from your zip code (or any zip) you will allow the search to extend.

- **The order in which you want your results to appear:** If you indicate *Time: Ending Soonest*, the search engine gives you the results so that auctions closing soon appear first on the list. *Best Match* is the eBay default, and I recommend you select a sort that better fits your needs. *Time: Newly Listed* lists all the newly listed auctions. *Price: Lowest First* and *Price: Highest First* list them just that way.

- **Whether you want the search engine to check through item titles alone or check both item titles *and* item descriptions:** You will get more hits on your search if you select the Search Title and Description check box, but you may also get too many items that are out of your search range. See "Shortcuts for a quick eBay search," later in this chapter, for some solid advice.

Okay, *now* click the Search button (see Figure 5-2). In a few seconds, you see the fruits of all the work you've been doing. (Wow, you're not even perspiring.)

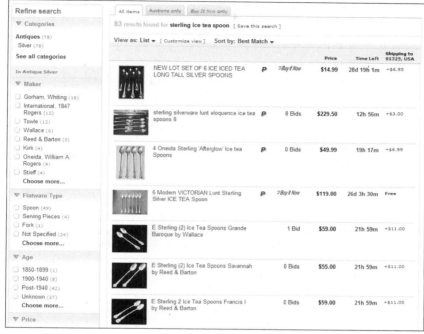

Figure 5-2: Use eBay's handy Refine Search to ferret out even more related listings.

You may notice that eBay has a Refine Search box to the left of your results. Be sure to click the select related specifics here, because eBay's search functions can often be a bit temperamental — and you don't want to miss any great deals.

Next to item listings you often see pictures, or *icons*. A golden yellow rising sun picture means the listing is brand new (this icon stays on for the first 24 hours an item is listed.

An easy way to keep track of an item you're interested in is to click the Watch This Item link just below the current bid amount of an item page. The listing then appears on your My eBay Watch page, and you can keep your eyes on the action.

On the left side of the results page there may a list of categories that your search term is listed under, which is a great reference. Next to each category is a number in parentheses that tells you how many times your search item appears in that category. Figure 5-3 shows a sample of the category spread. To view the items appearing only in a particular category, click that category (or subcategory) title.

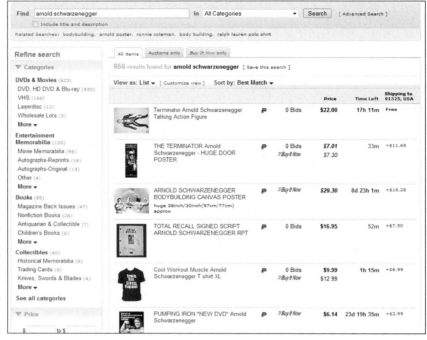

Figure 5-3:
Search
results
within the
category
listings.

Using the Advanced Search page

The Advanced Search page of the search area throws quite a few more options into the package. Don't be intimidated by this area; you need to understand just a few important bells and whistles.

A Completed Items search

A Completed Items search returns results of items that have already ended. This is my favorite search option on eBay because you can use it as a strategic bidding tool. How? If you're bidding on an item and want to know if the prices are likely to go too high for your pocketbook, you can use this search option to compare the current price of the item to the selling price of similar items from auctions that have already ended.

You can use this tool also if you want to sell an item and are trying to determine what it's worth, the demand, and whether this is the right time to list the item. (Chapter 10 offers the nuts, bolts, and monkey wrenches you need to set up your auction.)

Type your keyword criteria and scroll down the page to the Completed Items Only box. Step by step, here's how to do a Completed Items Only search:

1. **In the title search field, type the title name or the keywords of the item you want to find.**

2. **Select the Search Including Completed Listings check box to see completed listings as far back as the eBay search engine will permit.**

   Currently, you can go back about two weeks.

3. **Tell eBay how you want the results sorted.**

   In the Sort By area, choose one of the following options:

   - **Best Match:** This is eBay's magical sort formula that weighs all sorts of things, including how a seller lists an item, the seller's feedback, and whether eBay feels the shipping price is appropriate. eBay's judgment is iffy, at best. (Once eBay suggested I charge $5 to ship an item that cost $18 to ship because most sellers sold a tiny item from the same manufacturer.)

   - **Time: Ending Soonest:** Includes completed listings starting with the oldest available (about two weeks).

   - **Time: Newly Listed:** Lists the most recently posted listings first.

   - **Distance: Nearest First:** Unless you're looking to see how many of your item sold close to you, this is a pretty useless sort. You want pricing info!

   - **Price: Lowest First:** Lists items from the lowest price attained to the highest price paid for an item.

   - **Price: Highest First:** Lists completed items from highest to lowest. (This is a very useful option when you're searching for a 1967 Camaro and you want to buy a car and not a Hot Wheels toy.)

4. **Click Search.**

   The search results appear in just a few seconds.

 An alternate way to find completed items is to run a current auction search from any of the little search boxes on almost any eBay page. When the results of your auction show up, scroll down to the Preferences box, and below Search Options in the left column, click the Completed Items link, as shown in Figure 5-4. That way, you can scout out the active auction competition quickly before moving on to the completed sales.

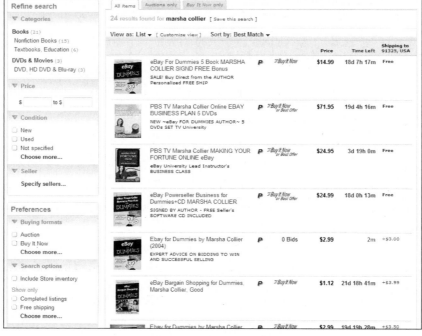

Figure 5-4:
The
convenient
Show Only
Completed
Listings
box in the
Display
box of the
search
results
page.

An international search

You can select any country (from Afghanistan to Zimbabwe, no kidding!) or narrow your search to the United States or Canada, as shown in Figure 5-5. Don't forget that you have to pay for shipping, so if you don't want to pay to ship a heavy Victorian-style fainting sofa from Hungary to Hoboken, New Jersey, stick close to home. Also, I'll bet Egyptian cotton is even better when it comes from Egypt. (It is — I've bought from an Egyptian seller!)

The Location Search option is pretty much an international version of Search, and it's done the same way. You have the choice of narrowing your country search to countries that offer an item, and to which countries they ship to. (Most eBay sellers will ship to the United States).

A seller search

The By Seller link in the search area, shown in Figure 5-6, gives you a list of all the items a seller is selling, and it's a great way for you to keep tabs on people you have successfully done business with in the past. The By Seller page is also a strategy that eBay users use to assess the reputation of a seller. You can find out more about selling strategies in Chapter 9.

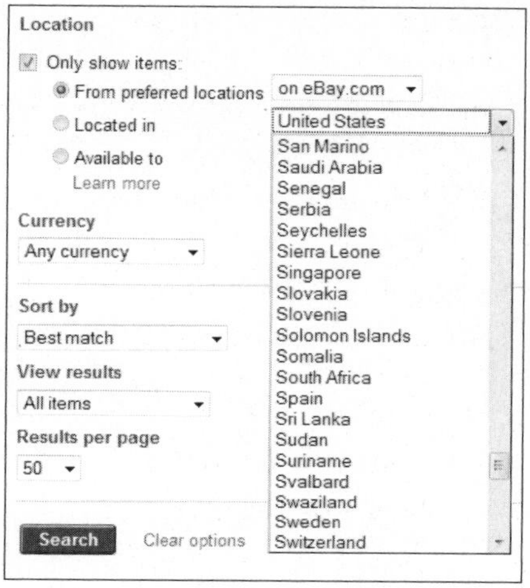

Figure 5-5:
The Inter
national
search
product
selector.

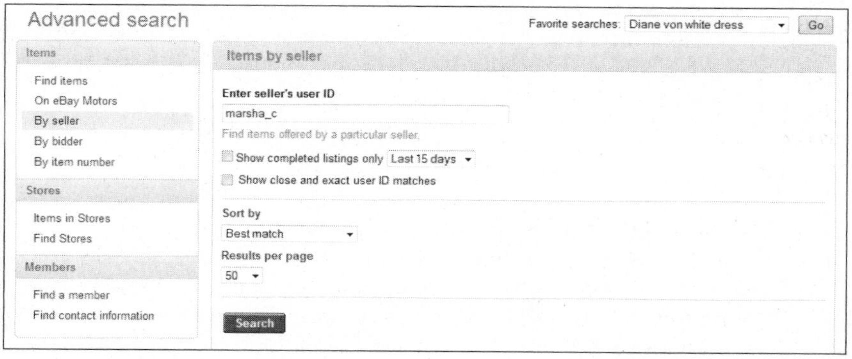

Figure 5-6:
You can
search for
all auc-
tions by an
individual
or search
for one item
from many
sellers.

View all items by a single seller

Select the By Seller option in the left side Items search area in Advanced Search. This way you can see all of a single seller's items. Follow these steps:

1. **In the By Seller search field, type the eBay user ID of the person you want to learn more about.**

2. **If you want to see auctions that this seller has conducted in the past, select the Show Completed Listings box.**

   You can choose to see all current and previous auctions, as well as auctions that have ended in the last day, last two days, last week, or last two weeks.

eBay keeps past item results active for only 30 days; if you're looking for something auctioned 31 days ago (or longer), sorry — no dice.

3. **In the Sort By drop-down box, select how you want the results of your search to appear on-screen.**

   If you want to see the items that are closing right away, select Time: Ending Soonest.

4. **Choose the number of results you want to see per page.**

   If the person you're looking up has 200 auctions running, for example, you can limit the number of results to a manageable 50 listings on four separate pages.

5. **Click the Search button at the bottom of the form.**

   Figure 5-7 shows the results page of a By Seller search.

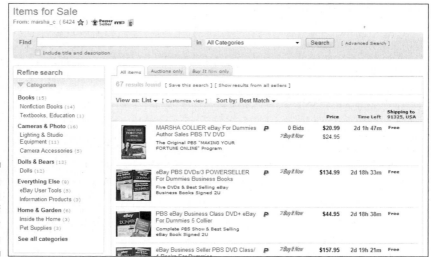

Figure 5-7:
The results of a By Seller search.

Finding items by keywords for multiple sellers

If you're looking for a specific item from a group of sellers, you can enter the search information in the bottom half of the By Seller Advanced Search page. You may need to perform this type of search after you settle into shopping on eBay and have several sellers that you like doing business with (or alternatively, you can exclude sellers you prefer not to do business with). With this method, you can limit the search for a particular item to just the sellers you want, rather than tens of thousands of sellers.

Free hanging chads . . .

eBay gives you the opportunity to have the same fine museum-quality items as the Smithsonian Institution. In November 2001, the Palm Beach County Board of County Commissioners found themselves in a bit of a pickle. Due to the infamous Presidential election of November 7, 2000 — fraught with hanging, pregnant, and dimpled chads — the announcement of the election winner was delayed for an unprecedented 37 days. As a result of this election, the Florida legislature outlawed the future use of punch-card voting systems — all Florida counties had to move to more stable, state-approved voting machines.

Palm Beach County chose to move to a touch-screen type of voting device, which cost its residents over $14 million. What to do with the old historic punch-card voting machines? Yep, donate one to the Smithsonian — and auction the rest off on eBay. Palm Beach County donated machine #1 to the Auction for America; it netted $4,550.01 for the Twin Towers fund.

The rest? Well, the Palm Beach County folks should have read this book. They ran a Dutch auction for 3,055 of the basic voting packages, with a starting bid of $300. Included with the voting machine was the iniquitous "butterfly ballot" with official stylus; a brass plaque certifying that it was used in the November 7 election; a Certificate of Authenticity signed by

Theresa LePore, Palm Beach County Supervisor of Elections; 25 demonstrator punch cards for playing polling place at home; a signed photograph of the folks in charge of recounting the ballots: Palm Beach County Supervisor of Elections Theresa LePore, Palm Beach County Commissioner Carol Roberts, and Judge Charles Burton; and "any chads which are in the machine from previous elections." What a package! There also were 569 Premier packages, which included an Official Ballot box, starting at $600.

In the 10-day auctions (run at the same time!), Palm Beach County sold 78 of the Premier packages and 389 of the Basic voting-machine packages. I called the County Commissioner's office to find out why my voting machine hadn't arrived and asked when the rest would be auctioned. I was assured they would be put back up on eBay auction, but at a higher starting bid.

Palm Beach County should have followed the strategies in this book, like some smart eBay sellers did. Soon after, one of the basic packages sold after a 7-day auction for $670. Other entrepreneurial sellers have been selling voting machines from counties other than Palm Beach on eBay. Unfortunately for those who purchase them, only the Palm Beach County machines had the infamous, butterfly ballot.

When you find a seller who you want to continue doing business with, you can add his or her link to your My eBay Saved Sellers area. Just click a link to Watch This Item on the item page. It will then appear on your My eBay page, in the Organize, Saved Sellers area. You can add up to 100 sellers in this area, and can search their sales with a click of your mouse!

A bidder search

The Bidder search option is unique because sellers and buyers alike use it when an auction is going on to figure out their best strategies. After all, money is the name of the game. For information on conducting a Bidder search, take a look at Chapter 7.

Shortcuts for a Quick eBay search

After you become familiar with each of eBay's search options, you need a crash course in what words to type into those nice little boxes. Too little information and you may not find your item. Too much and you're overwhelmed with information. If you're really into bean-bag toys, for example, you may be looking for Ty's Tabasco the Bull. But if you just search for *Tabasco,* you'll get swamped with results ranging from hot sauce to advertisements.

Some simple tricks can help narrow your eBay search results when you're searching from pages other than the main Search page (where you don't find all the searching bells and whistles). Table 5-2 has the details.

Table 5-2	Symbols and Keywords for Conducting Searches with the eBay Search Engine	
Symbol	*Effect on Search*	*Example*
No symbol, multiple words	Returns auctions with all included words in the title.	**reagan letter** might return an auction for a mailed message from the former U.S. president, or it might return an auction for a mailed message from Boris Yeltsin to Ronald Reagan.
Quotes ""	Limits the search to items with the exact phrase inside the quotes.	**"Wonder Woman"** returns items about the comic book/TV heroine. Quotes don't make the search term case sensitive. Using either uppercase or lowercase in *any* eBay search gets you the same results.
Asterisk *	Serves as a wild card.	**budd*** returns items that start with *budd,* such as Beanie Buddy, Beanie Buddies, or Buddy Holly.

Symbol	Effect on Search	Example
Separating comma without spaces (a,b)	Finds items related to either the item before or after the comma.	**(gi joe,g.i. joe)** returns all G.I. Joe items no matter which way the seller listed them.
Minus sign –	Excludes results with the word after the –.	Type **box –lunch**, and you'd better not be hungry because you may find the box, but lunch won't be included.
Minus symbol and parentheses	Searches for auctions with words before the parentheses but excludes words inside the parentheses.	**midge –(skipper,barbie)** means that auctions with the Midge doll won't have to compete for Ken's attention.
Parentheses	Searches for both versions of the word in parentheses.	**political (pin,pins)** searches for political pin and political pins.

Here are additional tips to help you narrow any eBay search:

- ✔ **Don't worry about capitalization:** You can capitalize proper names or leave them lowercase; the search engine doesn't care.

- ✔ **Don't use *and, a, an, or,* or *the*:** Called *noise words* in search lingo, these words are interpreted as part of your search. So if you want to find something from *The Sound of Music* and you type **the sound of music**, you may not get any results. Most sellers drop noise words from the beginning of an item title when they list it, just as libraries drop noise words when they alphabetize books. So make your search for **sound music**. An even more precise search would be **"sound of music"** (in quotes).

- ✔ **Search within specific categories:** This type of search narrows your results because you search only one niche of eBay — just the specific area you want. For example, if you want to find Tabasco the Bull, start at the home page and, under the Categories heading, click Toys and Bean Bag. The only problem with searching in a specific category is that sometimes an item can be in more than one place. For example, if you're searching for a Mickey Mouse infant snuggly in the Disney category, you may miss it because the item might be listed in infant wear. It's best not to limit yourself to a category because some of the best deals are miscategorized by sellers. What makes them such a good deal is that not everyone can find them. But you know better.

Use the asterisk symbol often to locate misspellings. I've often found some great deals by finding items incorrectly posted by the sellers. Here are a few examples:

- **Rodri*** In this search I look for items by the famous Cajun artist *George Rodrigue*. His Blue Dog paintings are world-renowned and very valuable. By using this search, I managed to purchase a signed Blue Dog lithograph for under $200. (I resold it on eBay later that year for $900!)

- **Alumi* tree** Remember the old aluminum Christmas trees from the '60s? They've had quite a resurgence in popularity these days. You can buy these "antiques" in stores for hundreds of dollars . . . or you can buy one on eBay for half the price. You can find them even cheaper if the seller can't spell *aluminum*. . . .

- **Cemet* plot** If you're looking for that final place to retire, eBay has some great deals. Unfortunately, sellers haven't narrowed down whether they want to spell it *cemetery* or *cemetary*. This search will find both.

After studying these examples, I'm sure you can think of many more instances in which your use of the asterisk can help you find the deals. Be sure to e-mail me and let me know when you find something special in this way!

Finding eBay Members: The Gang's All Here

With millions of eBay users on the loose, you may think tracking folks down is hard. Nope. eBay's powerful search engine kicks into high gear to help you find other eBay members in seconds.

Here's how to find people or get info on them from eBay:

1. **From the top of most eBay pages, click the Advanced Search link.**

   This action takes you to the main Search page, where two links appear on the left side of the page, under Members.

2. **In the box on the left side of the page, click the Find a Member link.**

   This link takes you to the main Find Members page, where you can search for other members of the community. When you find the member, you can see his or her About Me page (see Chapter 14 to find out how to create your own personal eBay Web page). You can also get a look at the feedback profile of a user (see Chapter 4 for details about feedback), find user ID histories of fellow eBay members (which comes in handy when you're bidding on items, as Chapter 7 avows), or get contact information when you're involved in a transaction.

If you're involved in a transaction with another eBay member and feel that you need to contact the individual by phone, click the Find Contact Information link, which is under the Members heading on the left side of the screen. On that page you'll need to type the transaction number along with the other person's user ID. eBay compares this data with yours, and if you are indeed involved in a transaction with each other, eBay e-mails you the other person's phone number (along with the person's full name, city, and state). Your contact information is, in turn, sent to the other party.

Clicking the arrow in the Favorite Searches drop-down box at the top right of the page allows you to scroll through your My eBay Favorite Searches. You can tell eBay about the items you're looking for, and it does automatic searches for you. You can also have eBay e-mail you when auctions that match your descriptions crop up. (Chapter 18 gives you more info on how this works.)

Chapter 6

Shopping eBay: The Basics

Browsing different categories of eBay, looking for nothing in particular, you spot that must-have item lurking among other Elvis paraphernalia in the Collectibles category. Sure, you *could* live without that faux gold Elvis pocket watch, but life would be so much sweeter *with* it. And even if it doesn't keep good time, at least it'll be right twice a day.

When you bid for items on eBay, you can get that same thrill that you would get at Sotheby's or Christie's for a lot less money, and the items you win are likely to be *slightly* more practical than an old Dutch masterpiece you're afraid to leave at the framer's. (Hey, you have to have a watch, and Elvis is — er, *was* — the King.)

In this chapter, I give you the lowdown about the types of auctions and fixed-price listings available on eBay and a rundown of the nuts and bolts of bidding strategies. I also share some tried-and-true tips that'll give you a leg up on the competition. Hey, I buy *almost* everything on eBay.

The Item Listing Page

At any given point, you have more than a million pages of items that you can look at on eBay, making item pages the heart (better yet, the skeleton) of eBay listings. All item pages on eBay — whether auctions, fixed-price items, or Buy It Now items — look about the same. For example, Figure 6-1 shows a conventional listing page with a Buy It Now option; Figure 6-2 shows a fixed-price sale; and Figure 6-3 shows a fixed-price sale with a twist — the Make Offer option. All item pages show the listing title at the top, bidding or buying info in the middle, and seller info below that. Below all this is a tabbed area that displays the complete description of the item, along with a tab for shipping and payment information.

Figure 6-1: Here's one of my typical auctions, featuring the Buy It Now button, the Place Bid button, and PayPal payment options.

Figure 6-2: In a fixed-price sale, you see the Buy It Now button and info about buying through PayPal, but no Place Bid button.

Figure 6-3:
Some
sellers
offer a
Make Offer
option on
their fixed-
price sales.

The listing types have some subtle differences. Some auctions feature multiple pictures at the top left of the page, and others don't, depending on how the seller sets up the sale page. (Some sellers insert pictures within the item description to save money on listing fees.) Some listings have set item specifics in the description (as shown in Figure 6-4). This area is set up by eBay and filled in by the seller to give you a snapshot description of the item for sale. If you search for an item and end up finding it available in a fixed-price sale, you won't see the Place Bid button (as shown in Figure 6-1). But overall, the look and feel of these pages is the same.

Item specifics - Nonfiction Books

Author:	--	Publisher: --
ISBN-10:	--	Category: Business & Economics
ISBN-13:	9780470168424	--
Format:	Softcover	
Publication Year:	2008	Condition: Brand New
Special Attributes:	Signed, 1st Edition	
See reviews		

Detailed item info

Details
Series: For Dummies (Business & Personal Finance)

Size
Length: 430 pages
Height: 9.3 in.
Width: 7.3 in.
Thickness: 1.2 in.
Weight: 24.0 oz.

Figure 6-4:
Item
specifics
are filled in
by the seller
according
to the
parameters
eBay sets
up for them.

When you come to a fixed-price listing with the Make Offer option, you have the ability to make your own offer on the item. I talk about the best ways to make your offer later in this chapter.

Here's a list of stuff you see as you scroll down on a typical item page:

- ✔ **Item title and number:** The title and number identify the item. Keep track of this info for inquiries later. You find the item number in the box under the Seller Info area on the right.

  If you're interested in a particular type of item, note the key words used in the title (you're likely to see them again in future titles). Doing so helps you narrow future searches.

- ✔ **Item category:** Located just above the item, you can click the category listing and do some comparison shopping. (Chapter 5 gives more searching strategies.)

- ✔ **Current bid:** This field in an auction indicates the dollar amount the bidding has reached, which changes throughout the auction as people place bids. If no bids have been placed on the item, this field is called Starting bid.

  Sometimes, next to the current dollar amount in an auction, you see *(Reserve not met)*. This statement means that the seller has set a *reserve price* for the item — a secret price that must be reached before the seller will sell the item. If you don't see this note on a listing item page, don't be alarmed. Most auctions don't have reserve prices. Also, the moment a reserve is met, the indicator disappears.

- ✔ **Buy It Now price:** If you want the item immediately and the price quoted in this area is okay with you, click the Buy It Now link, which takes you to a page where you can complete your purchase. This is also an option in an auction listing, as in Figure 6-1. In this case you can still place a bid for the lower bid price and the listing will convert to an auction format.

- ✔ **Quantity:** This field appears only in a multiple item fixed-price sale. It tells you how many items are available. If you see a number other than 1 in this field, it means that there is only one of the item left for sale (the others have been sold). You can be sure it's a fixed-price sale because you have no opportunity to bid; you can just use the Buy It Now option for whatever quantity of the item you desire. You'll be prompted for a quantity when you buy. But if a seller is selling two Elvis watches for the price of one, the item quantity still shows up as 1 (as in 1 set of 2 watches).

- ✔ **Time left:** The official clock keeps ticking down as time passes. When the item gets down to the last hour of the auction, eBay automatically starts an interactive clock that counts the minutes and seconds. This field tells you the time remaining in this particular auction.

Timing is the key in an eBay bidding strategy (covered in Chapter 7). Because eBay's world headquarters is in California, eBay uses Pacific Standard Time or Pacific Daylight Time as the standard, depending on the season. Not a major deal if you live on the West Coast like I do, but it can be an issue if you live anywhere else.

✔ **Bid history:** This field (below the item title) tells you how many bids have been placed. To use the number of bids to your advantage, you have to read between the lines. You can determine just how "hot" an item is by comparing the number of bids the item has received over time. Based on the amount of interest in an item, you can create a time strategy (which I talk about later in this chapter). If you want to see the starting bid, you have to click the See History link next to the number of bids (refer to Figure 6-1). By clicking there you can also find out who is bidding and what date and time bids were placed. The dollar amount of each bid is shown in the bidding history, but bidders' maximum bids are kept secret.

Bidding is more an art than a science. Sometimes an item gets no bids because everyone's waiting until the last second to bid. You see a flurry of activity as bidders all try to outbid each other (called *sniping,* which Chapter 7 explains). But that's all part of the fun of eBay.

✔ **Item location:** This field tells you at the very least the country where the seller is located, and you may also see more specific info, such as the city and geographic area where the seller is. (What you see depends on how detailed the seller wants to be.)

Factor in the geographic location of a seller when you consider bidding on an item. Knowing the exact location of an item can help you quickly calculate approximately how long it will take for the item to get to you. (Chapter 10 tackles that subject.) Also, if you buy from someone in your own state, you may also have to pay sales tax on your purchase. If the item is in Australia, for example, and you're in Vermont, you may decide that you don't really need that wrought-iron doorstop. (Remember, *you* pay the shipping charges.)

✔ **Watch This Item:** Click this link to magically add the item to the Watch section of your My eBay page. From there, you can keep an eye on the progress of the auction — without bidding. If you haven't signed in, you have to type your user ID and password before you can save the auction to your My eBay page.

Be sure to use the Watch This Item feature. Organization is the name of the game on eBay, especially if you plan to bid on multiple auctions while you're running auctions of your own. I figure you're in the bidding game to win, so start keeping track of items now.

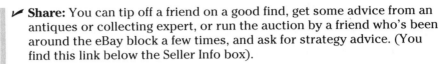

✔ **Share:** You can tip off a friend on a good find, get some advice from an antiques or collecting expert, or run the auction by a friend who's been around the eBay block a few times, and ask for strategy advice. (You find this link below the Seller Info box).

✔ **Print:** If you'd like to print a copy of the listing for reference, click here to get an abbreviated version of the page.

If you want a complete printout of a listing, use the print feature of your Internet browser. That way you will get the entire description for your records.

✔ **Get alerts:** Using a sniping service is more my style, but Get alerts is great for those do-it-yourselfers out there. If you really enjoy the thrill of the bid, the Get alerts option enables you to receive a notification if you're outbid and (or) when the auction is about to end. You will see this option on a page only after you've placed a bid. There are three versions of notices:

- **Text messages:** You can get a text message directly to your cellphone. You will be charged $0.25 for up to ten messages per item. After ten messages for an item, the charges increase another $0.25 for the next ten messages. The charges appear on your mobile phone bill as eBay services.

  Keep in mind that unless you have unlimited text messaging service on your cellphone, you can also be charged for receiving a text message.

- **Instant messages:** You can opt to receive an IM on your own account from AIM (AOL Instant Messenger), Yahoo! Messenger, MSN Messenger, or Skype. You're not charged for the IM service, so if you have a Blackberry or a Sidekick and you don't want to miss any bidding action, this could be a great option for you. Also, with the IM service, you can bid again from a link that comes along with the Outbid alert.

- **E-mails:** Yes, Good old fashioned e-mails can be sent to you for these notifications as well!

To let eBay know how you'd like to receive your notifications, go to your My eBay page. Select My Account and Notification Preferences. Fill in your preferences there.

✔ **Seller Info:** This area gives you links to information about the seller. *Know thy seller* ranks right after *caveat emptor* as a phrase that pays on eBay. As I tell you nearly a million times in this book, *read the feedback rating!* (Okay, maybe not a million — it would drive the editors bonkers.) Human beings come in all shapes, sizes, and levels of honesty, and like any community, eBay has its share of good folks and bad folks. Your best defense is to read the seller's feedback. You'll see several things in the Seller Info box (as shown in Figure 6-5).

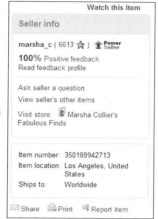

Figure 6-5:
Lots of data
on the seller
can be
accessed
from here.

✔ **Feedback rating:** This is the number next to the seller's ID. Click the number to view his or her eBay ID card and entire feedback history. Read, read, and reread all the feedback (hey, I'm one feedback reference closer to a million!) to make sure you feel comfortable doing business with this person. Clicking the link (or the Read Feedback Profile link) will allow you to view the following information:

- **Positive feedback percentage:** The eBay computers cipher this figure. It's derived from all the positive and negative feedback that a user receives.

- **Read Feedback Profile:** Clicking here will do the same thing as clicking the number next to the seller's ID.

- **Ask seller a question:** Clicking this link hooks you up with eBay's e-mail system. You can ask the seller a question regarding the item here. Clicking the tiny telephone receiver icon (if available) will begin a Skype voice call to the seller. Clicking the tiny Chat icon will open a chat window with the seller if he or she is online.

- **View seller's other items:** This link takes you to a page that lists all the seller's current auctions and fixed-price sales.

  If the seller has an eBay store, a link to it appears next. I give you a step-by-step guide on how these links work later in this chapter.

✔ **Description tab:** You see a tabbed bar of one to three tabs. The opening (default) is the Description tab. The other two tabs are the Shipping and Payments tab and, in some cases, the Related Items and Services tab. Scroll down and always read the entire item description information carefully *before* bidding.

✔ **Shipping and Payments tab:** Click this tab, shown in Figure 6-6, to see the details on shipping. You see

- Who pays (remember that on eBay, it's usually the buyer).

- Whether insurance is offered.

- Which states have to pay sales tax (if any).

- Whether the seller is willing to ship to your area. (Sometimes sellers won't ship internationally, and they'll let you know here.)

Also, always check the item description for other shipping information and terms.

Figure 6-6: Check the shipping and payment boxes below the item description to find out about additional costs, shipping, and taxes that may apply when you buy.

If the item doesn't have flat price shipping, the seller may have conveniently included eBay's shipping calculator in this area. eBay knows your zip code, so you're presented with the shipping cost to your location.

The Payment details area tells you the payment methods that the seller accepts: PayPal, Moneybookers, Paymate, Propay, or their own merchant credit card service. Often, you are directed to read the item description for more details. I explain how to read item descriptions later in this chapter.

✔ **Related Items and Services:** Click this tab and eBay may list similar items to the item you're viewing. Or they may not; it's catch as catch can.

Beating the Devil in the Details

As with any sale — whether you find it at Joe's Hardware, Bloomingdale's, or Target — carefully check out what you're buying. The item page gives you links to help you know what you're bidding on — and who you're potentially buying from. If you take advantage of these features, you won't have many problems. But if you ignore these essential tips, you may end up unhappy with what you buy, who you buy it from, and how much you spent.

Read the item description carefully

The *item description* is the most critical item on the auction item page. This is where the seller lists the details about the item being sold. Read this page carefully and pay very close attention to what is, and *isn't,* written.

Don't judge a book by its cover — but do judge a seller by his or her item description. If the sentences are succinct, detailed, and well structured, you're most likely dealing with an individual who planned and executed the listing with care. It takes time and effort to post a good listing. If you see huge lapses in grammar, convoluted sentences, and misspellings, *you may be gonna get burnt!* Make sure that you feel comfortable dealing with this person; decide for yourself whether he or she is out to sell junk for a quick buck or is selling on eBay for the long term.

If additional pictures are available, take a good look. The majority of eBay sellers jazz up their auctions with several photos of their items. The seller should answer a few general questions in the item description. If these questions aren't answered, that doesn't necessarily mean that the seller's disreputable — only that if you're really interested, you should e-mail the seller and get those answers before you bid. In particular, ask questions like these:

- ✔ Is the item new or used?

- ✔ Is the item a first edition or a reprint? New or used? An original or a reissue? (See Chapter 5 for tips on how to assess what you're buying.)

- ✔ Is the item in its original packaging? Does it still have the original tags?

- ✔ Is the item under warranty?

Most sellers spell out in their item descriptions exactly how the item should be paid for and shipped. Check the Shipping and Payments tab, which is next to the Description tab, to see whether an actual shipping charge applies — and if so, how much it'll cost you. Some sellers use eBay's incredibly convenient shipping calculator. Here are a few other things to consider regarding your item:

✔ If you're in a hurry to get the item, are delays likely? If so, what sort and how long?

✔ Can the seller guarantee you a refund if the item is broken or doesn't work upon delivery?

✔ What condition is the item in? Is it broken, scratched, flawed, or mint?

Most experienced eBay buyers know that, depending on the item, a tiny scratch here or there may be worth the risk of making a bid. But a scratch or two may affect your bidding price. (Look at Chapter 5 for more expert advice for buying collectibles.)

✔ Is this item the genuine article or a reproduction, and if it's the real deal, does the seller have papers or labels certifying its authenticity?

✔ What size is the item, and how much does it weigh? (That life-size fiberglass whale may not *fit* in your garage. That baby grand piano might cost a lot to ship from Anchorage, so you need to factor in the cost of shipping when you consider how much you're willing to bid.)

If you win the item and find out the seller lied in the description, you have the right to request to return the item. But, if you win the item and discover that *you* overlooked a detail in the description, the seller isn't obligated to take the item back. If the seller won't take the item back, you may be able to apply for a refund through PayPal's Buyer Protection.

The seller is obligated to describe the item honestly and in detail, so if your questions aren't answered in the item description, for goodness' sake, e-mail the seller for the facts. If a picture is available, is it clear enough that you can see any flaws? You can always ask the seller to e-mail you a picture taken from another angle.

Get the scoop on the seller

I can't tell you enough that the single most important way you can make an auction go well is to *know who you're dealing with*. Apparently, the eBay folks agree; they enable you to get info on the seller right from the auction item page. I recommend that you take advantage of the links offered there. (Chapter 5 demonstrates how to conduct a thorough By Seller search.) To get the full scoop on a seller, here's what you need to do:

✔ Click the number beside the seller's user ID to get his or her feedback history. Click the Me link (if there is one) next to the seller to view the seller's About Me page. This page frequently gives you a good deal more information about the seller. (To set up your own free About Me page on eBay, check out Chapter 14.)

> ✔ Make note if you see the PowerSeller icon next to the seller's name. This icon means he or she is an eBay seller who has met certain stringent certifications. (For more on PowerSellers, see Chapter 20.)

> ✔ Click the View seller's other items link to take a look at what else that person is selling. (If you win more than one auction from a seller, he or she will often combine the shipping costs.) Check the seller's feedback (message sound familiar?).

Check the seller's Feedback Profile. All together, now — *check the feedback*. (Is there an echo in here?) What you will find are (for the most part) the honest thoughts and comments of buyers from previous transactions. No eBay user has control over the comments that others make, and feedback sticks to you like your permanent record from high school.

Read the feedback — the good, the bad, and the neutral — and unless you're prepared to kiss your money goodbye, I've found it safer not to buy from a seller who has a large percentage of negative comments — and eBay won't allow them to sell on the site for long.

eBay, like life, is full of shades of gray. Some sellers are unfairly hit with negative comments for something that wasn't their fault. If you suspect that a seller has received a bum rap (after you've read all his or her positive feedback), be sure to read the seller's response. (Look at Chapter 4 for more on reading and leaving feedback.)

Although scoping out an eBay Feedback Profile is *just that fast, just that simple,* you still need to take the time to read the feedback. (There's that echo again. Good thing it's a wise echo.) Someone with 500 positive feedback messages may look like a good seller, but if you take a closer look, you may find that his or her ten most-recent feedback messages are negative.

View the seller's other items

To find out what other sales the seller has going on eBay, all you have to do is click the corresponding link on the item page; you're whisked away to a list of the other item pies the seller has a finger in. If the seller has no other items going and has no current feedback, you may want to do a more thorough investigation and conduct a By Seller search that will show you all that person's completed listings in the last 30 days. (See Chapter 5 for details.)

Ask seller a question

If anything about the auction is unclear to you, remember this one word: *ask.* Find out all the details about that item before you bid. If you wait until you've won the item before you ask questions, you may get stuck with something you don't want. Double-checking may save you woe and hassle later.

How Swede it is!

A savvy eBay user I know benefited from a major seller error. The seller titled his auction "Swede Star Trek Cast Jacket." My friend checked out the item description and found that it was written with bad spelling and incoherent grammar, so she e-mailed the seller for more information. The seller explained that the jacket was a suede cast jacket given as a wrap gift to the cast and crew of the movie *Star Trek: Generations.* He had won it in a local radio contest, and it was brand new. Because of the seller's mistake, only one bidder bid on this lovely green suede (silk-lined!) jacket, which my friend picked up for $150. Because of its *Star Trek* connection, the jacket is worth upwards of $400 to collectors. So study the item page carefully. You may get lucky and find that errors can work to your benefit. (And a word to the wise: Check your own spelling and grammar carefully when you put an item up for sale.)

You can find out more about payment options, shipping charges, insurance, and other fun stuff in Chapters 8 and 12.

If you're bidding on a reserve-price auction, don't be afraid to e-mail the seller and ask what the reserve is. Yeah, reserves are mostly kept secret, but there's no harm in asking — and many sellers gladly tell you.

To ask a seller a question, follow these steps:

1. **Click the Ask Seller a Question link on the item page.**

   You're presented with the Ask the Seller a Question form.

2. **Fill in the message area and politely fire off your questions; then click Send Message.**

   Expect to hear back from the seller within a day. If it takes the seller more than a day or two to respond (unless it's over the weekend — eBay sellers are entitled to a little rest), and you get no explanation for the delay, think twice before shelling out your cash.

You can always change your user ID, but your past life (in the form of feedback messages) stays with you on eBay. Along with your feedback from your previous user ID, all your previous user IDs are listed as well in a user ID history search from the eBay Search page.

Factoring in the Extras

Before you think about placing a bid on an item, you should consider the financial obligation you have to make. In every case, the maximum bid you place won't be all you spend on an item. I recommend that you look closely at the payment methods that the seller is willing to accept and also factor in shipping, insurance, and escrow costs (if any). If you have only $50 to spend, you shouldn't place a $50 bid on a fragile item that will be shipped a long distance because often the buyer (that would be you) pays for shipping and insurance. In addition, if you live in the same state as the seller, you may have to pay sales tax if the seller is running an official business.

Payment methods

Several payment options are available, but eBay only allows sellers to show electronic payment methods. If you want to make a payment in the form of a check or money order, use the Ask the seller a question link — and ask! The seller is not required to accept any other form of payment but PayPal or one of the other electronic payment options (ProPay, Paymate, Moneybookers or a merchant account). These are the forms of payment available to you:

- ✔ **Credit card:** Paying with a credit card is a favorite payment option for many buyers, one that's offered mainly by businesses and dealers. I like paying with credit cards because they're fast and efficient. In addition, using a credit card offers you another ally, your credit card company, if you're not completely satisfied with the transaction. Credit cards can also be used for payment through the other electronic payment options a seller may offer. I still prefer PayPal.

  Sometimes sellers use a friend's company to run credit card payments for eBay auctions. So don't be surprised if you buy a vintage Tonka bulldozer and your credit card is billed from Holly's Hair-o-Rama.

- ✔ **PayPal:** I pay for all my eBay purchases through PayPal. Owned by eBay, PayPal is the largest Internet-wide payment network. Sellers who accept PayPal are identified with a special icon in the Seller Information box (as well as a large PayPal logo in the Payment method area below the description) and accept MasterCard, Visa, American Express, and Discover as well as electronic checks and debits. The service is integrated directly into eBay auctions, so paying is a mouse click away.

After you register with PayPal to pay for an item, PayPal debits your credit card or your bank checking account (or your account — if you have earned some money from sales) and sends the payment to the seller's account. PayPal does not charge buyers to use the service. Buyers can use PayPal to pay any seller within the United States (and around the world in over 55 countries). Some international bidders can pay for their eBay auctions from sellers in the United States. To see a current list of PayPal's international services, go to

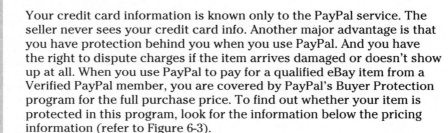

```
www.paypal.com/cgi-bin/webscr?cmd=p/gen/approved_countries-outside
```

PayPal deposits the money directly into the seller's checking or savings account. The service charges the seller a small transaction fee, so the seller absorbs the cost.

Your credit card information is known only to the PayPal service. The seller never sees your credit card info. Another major advantage is that you have protection behind you when you use PayPal. And you have the right to dispute charges if the item arrives damaged or doesn't show up at all. When you use PayPal to pay for a qualified eBay item from a Verified PayPal member, you are covered by PayPal's Buyer Protection program for the full purchase price. To find out whether your item is protected in this program, look for the information below the pricing information (refer to Figure 6-3).

For more details, check out the PayPal Web site (www.paypal.com).

✔ **Money order:** My second-favorite method of receiving payment is the money order. Sellers love money orders because they don't have to wait for a check to clear. When you ask to pay with a money order, they will almost always say yes.

Money orders are the same as cash. As soon as the seller gets your money order, he or she has no reason to wait to send the item. You can buy money orders at banks, supermarkets, convenience stores, and your local post office. The average cost is about a dollar. If you're purchasing an item that's being shipped internationally, you can pay with an international money order from the U.S. Postal Service, which costs about $3.00.

✔ **Personal or cashier's check:** Again, you have to ask. Paying by check is convenient but has its drawbacks. Most sellers won't ship you the goods until after your check clears, which means a lag time of a couple of weeks or more. Unfortunately, that means that while the seller is waiting for your check to clear, your merchandise is collecting dust in a box somewhere. This is no fun for you or for the seller. If a seller takes personal checks, you'll have to e-mail the seller and ask. Cashier's checks are available at your bank but often cost much more than a money order. It's not worth the extra money — have fun and buy more eBay items instead.

Before you send a personal check, make sure that you have enough money to cover your purchase. A bounced check can earn you negative feedback — too many negative transactions will bounce you off eBay.

The good news about checks is that you can track whether or not they've been cashed. Personal checks leave a paper trail that you can follow if a problem occurs later on. The bad news about checks is that you're revealing personal information, such as your bank account number, to a stranger.

✔ **C.O.D.:** I know of no eBay seller who will accept your request for an item to be mailed via cash on delivery.

Most business on eBay is conducted in U.S. dollars. If you happen to buy an item from an international seller, you may need to convert American dollars into another currency. eBay has a currency converter, located at the following URL:

```
pages.ebay.com/services/buyandsell/currencyconverter.html
```

Just select your choice of currency, type the amount, and click Perform Currency Conversion.

Never use a form of payment that doesn't let you keep a paper trail. **Don't wire money, and never send cash in the mail!** If a seller asks for cash, quote Nancy Reagan and just say no. Occasionally, I hear of international buyers sending U.S. greenbacks in the mail. But if a seller asks for cash, chances are that you may never see the item or your money again. Oh, yeah, here's something else — if a seller asks you to send your payment to a post office box, get a phone number. Many legitimate sellers use post office boxes, but so do the bad guys.

Using an escrow service

Even though most sales on eBay are for items that cost $100 or less, using an escrow service comes in handy on occasion — such as when you buy a big-ticket item or something extremely rare. *Escrow* is a service that allows a buyer and seller to protect a transaction by placing the money in the hands of a neutral third party until a specified set of conditions are met. Sellers note in their item descriptions if they're willing to accept escrow. If you're nervous about sending a lot of money to someone you don't really know (like a user named Clumsy who has only two feedback comments and is shipping you bone china from Broken Hill, Australia), consider using an escrow company.

Using an escrow company is worthwhile only if the item you're bidding on is expensive, rare, fragile, or traveling a long distance. If you're spending less than $300.00 for the item, I recommend that you purchase insurance from your shipper instead — just in case. eBay has a partnership with Escrow.com to handle eBay auction escrow sales in Canada and the United States. After an auction closes, the buyer sends the payment to the escrow company. After the escrow company receives the money, it e-mails the seller to ship the merchandise. After the buyer receives the item, he or she has an agreed-on period of time to look it over. If everything's okay, the escrow service sends the payment to the seller. If the buyer is unhappy with the item, he or she must ship it back to the seller. When the escrow service receives word from the seller that the item has been returned, the service returns the payment to the buyer (minus the escrow company's handling fee, of course).

Before you start an escrow transaction, make sure that you and the seller agree on these terms (use e-mail to sort it out). Here are three questions about escrow that you should know the answers to before you bid:

- ✔ Who pays the escrow fee? (Normally, the buyer does, though sometimes the buyer and seller split the cost.)

- ✔ How long is the inspection period? (Routinely, it's two business days after receipt of the merchandise.)

- ✔ Who pays for return shipping if the item is rejected? (The buyer usually pays.)

Shipping and insurance costs

Don't let the sale go down with the shipping. If the item is not an odd shape, excessively large, or fragile, experienced sellers calculate the shipping based on Priority Mail at the U.S. Postal Service, which is the unofficial eBay standard. Expect to pay a minimum of $5.00 for the first pound and another $0.50 for tracking the item.

Some sellers smartly use First Class Mail for items that weigh less than 13 ounces once packed, and sellers of media will often use the slower delivery Media Mail for their items. These forms of shipping will save you big bucks!

It has also become somewhat routine for the seller to add a dollar or so for packing materials such as paper, bubble wrap, tape, and such. This is a fair and reasonable handling charge because the cost of these items can add up over time.

You may come across sellers trying to nickel-and-dime their way to a fortune by jacking up the prices on shipping to ridiculous proportions. If you have a question about shipping costs, ask before you bid on the item.

Before bidding on big stuff, like a barber's chair or a sofa, check for something in the item description that says "Buyer Pays Actual Shipping Charges." When you see that, always e-mail the seller prior to your bid to find out what those shipping charges would be to your home. On larger items, you may need to factor in packing and crating charges. The seller may also suggest a specific shipping company.

As the bumper sticker says, (ahem) *stuff* happens — sometimes to the stuff you buy. But before you give up and just stuff it, consider insuring it. eBay transactions sometimes involve two types of insurance that may have an effect on your pocketbook:

✔ **Shipping insurance:** This insurance covers your item as it travels through the U.S. Postal Service, UPS, FedEx, or any of the other carriers.

Some savvy sellers have signed up with a company called Package In-Transit Coverage (U-PIC) (www.u-pic.com). This company insures all the packages of its clients using an annual policy. This way, the seller doesn't have to stand in line at the post office to get an insurance stamp from a clerk. The seller simply logs the packages and reports on them on a monthly basis. Sellers will let you know that they use this service when they ship your item.

Although many sellers offer shipping insurance as an option, others don't bother because if the price of the item is low, they'd rather refund your money and keep you happy than go through all that insurance paperwork. Don't forget that if you want shipping insurance, you pay for it. (See Chapter 12 for details on shipping insurance.)

✔ **Buyer protection:** Paying through PayPal provides excellent protection against all kinds of seller shenanigans. Depending on the seller's status with PayPal, your items are covered for the full purchase price. (The details of this type of protection are covered in Chapter 16.).

Placing Your Bid on an Auction

Okay, so you've found the perfect item to track (say a really classy Elvis Presley wristwatch), and it's in your price range. You're more than interested — you're ready to bid. If this were a live auction, some stodgy-looking guy in a gray suit would see you nod your head and start the bidding at, say, $2. Then some woman with a fierce hairdo would yank on her ear, and the Elvis watch would jump to $3.

eBay reality is more like this: You're sitting at home in your fuzzy slippers, sipping coffee in front of the computer; all the other bidders are cruising cyberspace in their pajamas, too. You just can't see 'em. (Be really thankful for the small things.)

When you're ready to jump into the eBay fray, you can find the bidding box at the top of the auction item page. If the item includes a Buy It Now option, you see that next to the bidding form.

To fill out the bidding form and place a bid, first make sure that you're registered (see Chapter 2 for details) and then follow these steps. After you make your first bid on an item, you can instantly get to auctions you're bidding on from your My eBay page. (If you need some tips on how to set up My eBay, see Chapter 4.)

1. **Enter your maximum bid in the appropriate box.**

   The bid needs to be an increment or more higher than the current minimum bid. The lowest amount you can bid is displayed to the right of the bidding box. (See "Bidding to the Max: Proxy Bidding" for more information about bidding increments.)

   You don't need to put in the dollar sign but *do* use a decimal point — unless you really *want* to pay $1,049.00 instead of $10.49. If you make a mistake with an incorrect decimal point, you can retract your bid (see "Retracting your bid" later in this chapter).

2. **Click Place Bid.**

   The Review Bid page appears on your screen, filled with a wealth of legalese. This is your last chance to change your mind: Do you really want the item, and can you really buy it? The bottom line is this: If you bid on it and you win, you buy it. eBay really means it.

3. **At this point, you have to sign in if you haven't already. If you're signed in, skip to Step 5.**

4. **If you agree to the terms, click Confirm Bid.**

   After you agree, the Bid Confirmation screen appears.

When you first start out on eBay, I suggest that you start with a *token bid* — a small bid that won't win you the auction but can help you keep tabs on the auction's progress.

After you bid on an item, the item number and title appear on your My eBay page, listed under (big surprise) Bidding, as shown in Figure 6-7. (See Chapter 4 for more information on My eBay.) The Bidding list makes tracking your auction (or auctions, if you're bidding on multiple items) easy.

eBay considers a bid on an item to be a binding contract. You can save yourself a lot of heartache if you make a promise to *never bid on an item you don't intend to buy.* Don't make practice bids, assuming that because you're new to eBay, you can't win; if you do that, you'll probably win simply because you've left yourself open to Murphy's Law. Therefore, before you go to the bidding form, be sure that you're in this auction for the long haul and make yourself another promise: *Figure out the maximum you're willing to spend.* (Read the section "The Agony (?) of Buyer's Remorse," later in this chapter, for doleful accounts of what can happen if you bid idly or get buyer's remorse.)

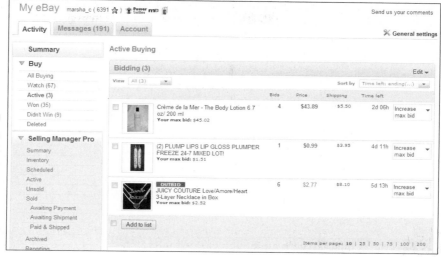

Figure 6-7: Keep track of items you're bidding on right from your My eBay page.

Bidding to the Max: Proxy Bidding

When you make a maximum bid on the bidding form, you actually make several small bids — again and again — until the bidding reaches where you told it to stop. For example, if the current bid is up to $19.99 and you put in a maximum of $45.02, your bid automatically increases incrementally so that you're ahead of the competition — at least until someone else's maximum bid exceeds yours. Basically, you bid by *proxy,* which means that your bid rises incrementally in response to other bidders' bids.

No one else knows for sure whether you're bidding by proxy, and no one knows your maximum bid. And the best part is that you can be out having a life of your own while the proxy bid happens automatically. Buyers and sellers have no control over the increments (appropriately called *bid increments*) that eBay sets. The bid increment is the amount of money by which a bid is raised, and eBay's system can work in mysterious ways.

The current maximum bid can jump up a nickel or a quarter or even an Andrew Jackson, but there is a method to the madness, even though you may not think so. eBay uses a *bid-increment formula* (see Table 6-1) that uses the current high bid to determine how much to increase the bid increment. As you can see, the proxy bidding amounts become larger the higher you bid. For example:

✔ A 5-quart bottle of cold cream has a current high bid of $14.95. The bid increment is $0.50 — meaning that if you bid by proxy, your proxy will bid $15.45.

✔ But a 5-ounce can of top-notch caviar has a high bid of $200. The bid increment is $2.50. If you choose to bid by proxy, your proxy will bid $202.50.

Table 6-1	eBay's Proxy Bid Increments
Current Bid	**Your Bid Increment**
$0.01–$0.99	$0.05
$1.00–$4.99	$0.25
$5.00–$24.99	$0.50
$25.00–$99.99	$1.00
$100.00–$249.99	$2.50
$250.00–$499.99	$5.00
$500.00–$999.99	$10.00
$1000.00–$2499.99	$25.00
$2500.00–$4999.99	$50.00
$5000.00 and up	$100.00

Table 6-2 shows you what kind of magic happens when you put the proxy system and a bid-increment formula together in the same cyberroom.

Table 6-2		Proxy Bidding and Bid Increments		
Current Bid	**Bid Increment**	**Minimum Bid**	**eBay Auctioneer**	**Bidders**
$2.50	$0.25	$2.75	"Do I hear $2.75?"	Joe Bidder tells his proxy that his maximum bid is $8.00. He's the current high bidder at $2.75.
$2.75	$0.25	$3.00	"Do I hear $3?"	You tell your proxy your maximum bid is $25.00 and take a nice, relaxing bath while your proxy calls out your $3.00 bid, making you the current high bidder.

Current Bid	Bid Increment	Minimum Bid	eBay Auctioneer	Bidders
$3.00	$0.25	$3.25	"I hear $3.00 from proxy. Do I proxy hear $3.25?"	Joe Bidder's proxy bids $3.25, and while Joe Bidder is out walking his dog, he becomes the high bidder.
A heated bidding war ensues between Joe Bidder's proxy and your proxy while the two of you go on with your lives. The bid increment inches from $0.25 to $0.50 as the current high bid increases.				
$7.50	$0.50	$8.00	"Do I hear $8.00?"	Joe Bidder's proxy calls out $8.00, his final offer.
$8.00	$0.50	$8.50	"The bid is at $8.00. Do I hear $8.50?"	Your proxy calls out $8.50 on your behalf, and having outbid your opponent, you win the auction.

Specialized Auction Categories

After you get the hang of bidding on eBay, you may venture to the specialized auction areas. You can purchase a car or car parts and accessories from eBay Motors, or your own piece of land or a new home in the Real Estate category. eBay is always adding new specialty areas, so be sure to check the announcements as well as the home page.

Should you reach the big-time bidding, be aware that if you bid over $15,000 in an auction, you *must* register a credit card with eBay. All items in the special categories are searchable in eBay's search engine, so don't worry about missing your dream Corvette when you use the Search page.

eBay Motors

Visiting the automotive area of eBay is an auto enthusiast's dream. You can also find some great deals in used cars, and eBay offers creative ways to make buying vehicles of all shapes and sizes (as well as the largest array of parts you'll find anywhere on the planet) easy. Visit eBay Motors by clicking the eBay Motors link on the home page or by going to www.ebaymotors.com.

- ✔ **Search engine:** If you want to search for cars without coming up with hundreds of die-cast vehicles, eBay Motors has its own search available from the eBay Motors home page.

- ✔ **Vehicle shipping:** If you don't want to drive across the country to pick up your new vehicle, you can have it shipped through Dependable Auto Shippers. Check online for a free quote.

- ✔ **Inspections:** Many used-car sellers take advantage of inspection service vendors. These companies offer a comprehensive inspection covering the mechanical condition and cosmetic appearance and they supply a detailed inspection report. Car auctions from sellers who have their cars inspected have their auctions listed with an Inspection icon.

- ✔ **Lemon Check:** With the vehicle's VIN (Vehicle Identification Number), you can run a lemon check on the car through CARFAX.com.

- ✔ **Escrow:** Escrow.com is one of the safest ways to purchase a vehicle online. Escrow.com verifies and secures the buyer's payment and releases payment to the seller only after the buyer inspects and is completely satisfied with the vehicle.

eBay Stores

The eBay Stores are a quick, easy, and convenient way to find items for sale that you can buy now. A large number of eBay sellers have opened eBay Stores for a monthly fee as an inexpensive way to display a large amount of items for sale. They're offered a much lower listing fee for their items, as low as 3 cents, and the items stay in their stores for as long as they want. The lower listing fees are quite a savings over the fees for listing an item for auction, and sellers often pass the savings onto you.

When you're perusing the auctions on eBay, look for the little red door icon next to a seller's user ID. If you click the door, you're magically transported to the seller's virtual eBay storefront. Figure 6-8 shows you the eBay Stores hub. You get there by clicking the eBay Stores link on the upper-left of the home page.

eBay Stores have a separate search engine than the eBay core search engine. If you don't find the item you're looking for on eBay auctions, look at the column on the left side of the page. Under the Related Stores heading is a list of eBay stores that may contain the item you're looking for and a Search Stores link. Click the link, and eBay performs the same search for you in all eBay Stores.

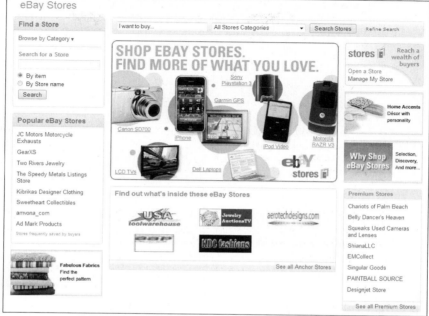

Figure 6-8:
The eBay
Stores
hub — from
here, you
can browse
categories,
visit stores,
or search
all items
in all eBay
Stores.

The Agony (?) of Buyer's Remorse

Maybe you're used to going into a shopping mall and purchasing something that you're not sure you like. What's the worst that could happen? You end up back at the mall, receipt in hand, returning the item. Not so on eBay. Even if you realize you already have a purple feather boa in your closet that's just like the one you won yesterday on eBay, deciding that you don't want to go through with a transaction *is* a big deal. Not only can it earn you some nasty feedback, but it can also give you the reputation of a deadbeat.

Buyer's remorse can pay off

Sometimes buyer's remorse does pay off. I know one eBay buyer who got a serious case of remorse after winning an auction. She decided to do the right thing and pay for the item even though she didn't want it. After receiving the item, she turned around and *sold* it on eBay for triple what she paid. If you really don't want the item, think like a seller — see whether you can turn a horrible mistake into a profitable venture. For more information on the benefits of selling, take a look at Chapter 9.

It would be a shame to float around eBay with the equivalent of a scarlet *D* (for *deadbeat*) above your user ID. Okay, eBay uses a kinder term — *non-paying bidder* — but for many members, it boils down to the same thing. If you win an auction and have to back out of your obligation as the winner — even through no fault of your own — you need some info that can keep you in good (well, okay, *better*) standing. Look no further; you've found it.

Retracting your bid

Remember, many states consider your bid a binding contract, just like any other contract. You can't retract your bid unless one of these three outstandingly unusual circumstances applies:

- ✔ If your bid is clearly a typographical error (you submitted a bid for $4,567 when you really meant $45.67), you may retract your bid. If this occurs, you should reenter the correct bid amount immediately. You won't get any sympathy if you try to retract an $18.25 bid by saying you meant to bid $15.25, so review your bid before you send it.

- ✔ You have tried to contact the seller to answer questions on the item, and he or she doesn't reply in a timely fashion.

- ✔ If the seller substantially changes the description of an item after you place a bid (the description of the item changes from "can of tennis balls" to "a tennis ball," for example), you may retract your bid.

If you simply must retract a bid, try to do so long before the auction ends — and have a good reason for your retraction. eBay users are understanding, up to a point. If you have a good explanation, you should come out of the situation all right. So admit you've made a mistake.

If you've made an error, you must retract your bid prior to the last 12 hours of the auction. At this point, a retraction removes all bids you have placed in the auction. Mistakes or not, when you retract a bid that was placed within the last 12 hours of the listing, only the most recent bid you made is retracted — your bids placed prior to the last 12 hours are still active.

Here's how to retract a bid while the auction's still going on:

1. **Go to http://offer.ebay.com/ws/eBayISAPI.dll?RetractBidShow.**

2. **Read the legalese and scroll down the page. Enter the item number of the auction you're retracting your bid from. Then open the drop-down menu and select one of the three legitimate reasons for retracting your bid.**

3. **Click the Retract Bid button.**

   You receive a confirmation of your bid retraction via e-mail. Keep a copy of it until the auction is completed.

If you've made a mistake when making a Best Offer, go to the following:

```
http://offer.ebay.com/ws/eBayISAPI.dll?RetractBestOfferShow&guest=1
```

The seller may send you an e-mail to ask for a more lengthy explanation of your retraction, especially if the item was a hot seller that received a lot of bids. You may also get e-mails from other bidders. Keep your replies courteous. After you retract one bid on an item, all your lower bids on that item are also retracted (unless the retraction is done within the last 12 hours), and your retraction goes into the bidding history — another good reason to have a really good reason for the retraction. The number of bids you've retracted also goes on your feedback rating scorecard.

After the auction: Side deals or personal offers?

If a bidder is outbid on an item that he or she really wants or if the auction's reserve price isn't met, the bidder may send an e-mail to the seller and see whether the seller is willing to make another deal. Maybe the seller has another similar item or is willing to sell the item directly rather than run a whole new auction. You need to know that this could happen — but eBay doesn't sanction this outside activity.

If the seller has more than one of the item, or the original auction winner doesn't go through with the deal, the seller can make a Second Chance offer. This is a legal eBay-sanctioned second chance for *underbidders* (unsuccessful bidders) who participated in the auction. Second Chance offers can also be made in reserve auctions if the reserve price wasn't met.

Any side deals other than Second Chance offers are unprotected. My friend Jack collects autographed final scripts from hit television sitcoms. So when the curtain fell on *Seinfeld,* he had to have a script. Not surprisingly, he found one on eBay with a final price tag that was way out of his league. But he knew that by placing a bid, someone else with a signed script to sell might see his name and try to make a deal. And he was right.

After the auction closed, he received an e-mail from a guy who worked on the final show and had a script signed by all the actors. He offered it to Jack for $1,000 less than the final auction price on eBay. Tempted as he was to take the offer, Jack understood that eBay's rules and regulations wouldn't help him out if the deal turned sour. He was also aware that he wouldn't receive the benefit of feedback (which is the pillar of the eBay community) or any eBay Standard Purchase Protection insurance for the transaction.

If you even *think about* making a side deal, remember that not only does eBay *strictly* prohibit this activity, but eBay can also suspend you if you are reported for making a side deal. And if you're the victim of a side-deal scam, eBay's rules and regulations don't offer you any protection. My advice? Watch out!

Avoiding deadbeat (non-paying bidder) status

Some bidders are more like kidders — they bid even though they have no intention of buying a thing. But those folks don't last long on eBay because of all the negative feedback they get. In fact, when honest eBay members spot these ne'er-do-wells, they often post the deadbeats' user IDs on eBay's message boards. Some eBay members have created entire Web sites to warn others about dealing with the deadbeats . . . ahem . . . *non-paying bidders*. (Civilized but chilly, isn't it?)

Exceptions to the deadbeat (er, sorry, *non-paying bidder*) rule may include the following human mishaps:

- A death in the family
- Computer failure
- A huge misunderstanding

If you have a good reason to call off your purchase, make sure that the seller knows about it. The seller is the only one who can excuse you from the sale.

If you receive a non-paying bidder warning but you've paid for the item, eBay requires proof of payment. That would include a copy of the check (front and back) or money order, a copy of the payment confirmation from PayPal (or other online payment service), or an e-mail from the seller acknowledging receipt of payment. If the seller excused you from the auction, you need to forward the e-mail with all headers.

- Fax hard copies to eBay at 888-379-6251.
- Send the e-mail via an online form. Go to `pages.ebay.com/help/buy/appeal-unpaid-item.html`, click the link to the online form, and plead your case.

There's no guarantee that your non-paying bidder appeal will be accepted. eBay will contact you after an investigation and let you know whether your appeal was successful.

eBay has a message for non-paying bidders: The policy is *three strikes and you're out*. After the first complaint about a non-paying (deadbeat) bidder, eBay gives the bad guy or gal a warning. After the third offense, the non-paying bidder is suspended from eBay for good and becomes *NARU* (Not A Registered User). Nobody's tarred and feathered, but you probably won't see hide nor hair of that user again on eBay.

Chapter 7

Power-Buying Strategies

When I travel the country talking about eBay, I speak to so many people who find an item on eBay, bid on it, and at the last minute — the last hour, or the last day — are outbid. Sad and dejected, they find losing often cuts to the core and makes them feel like losers.

You're not a loser when you lose an auction on eBay. You just may not know the fine art of sneaky bidding (my way of saying *educated* bidding).

When the stakes are high and you really, really want the item, you have to resort to a higher form of strategy. Sports teams study their rivals, and political candidates scout out what the opposition is doing. Bidding in competition against other bidders is just as serious an enterprise. Follow the tips in this chapter and see if you can come up with a strong bidding strategy of your own. (Feel free to e-mail me with any scathingly brilliant plans; I'm always open to new theories.)

Make an Offer!

If you come across a fixed-price listing and you're in the mood to negotiate, why not make an offer? A seller on eBay can use the Make Offer option anytime they list a fixed-price item. It should indicate to you that you're dealing with a seller who's motivated to sell. The eBay Make an Offer option is a great way to get bargains. You make an offer on the item and the seller will either accept your offer or send you a counteroffer.

Making an offer to buy an item has a drawback; the seller has 48 hours to respond to you and you may find the same item from another seller at a better price before then. By making an offer, you guarantee that you will buy the item at the price of your offer if the seller agrees to it. If they don't you're off the hook and can find another of the item elsewhere.

To make an offer, click the Make Offer button (instead of Buy It Now button); see Figure 7-1.

Figure 7-1:
Use the
Make Offer
option
anytime
you're not
in a rush
and want
to wangle a
good deal.

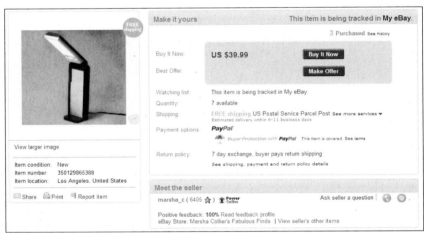

When making an offer, you might want to put in a really, really low offer. But be sensible; if the item is new, the seller may have only a little wiggle room on the price. Also, putting in a low offer (say $10 on a $25 item) may just annoy the seller and he or she may turn you down without giving you an opportunity to negotiate.

Find Out an Item's Bidding History

You can access the bidding history by clicking the History link, which appears after the number of bids on the item page. The bidding history lists everyone who is bidding on the item. You can see how often and at what time bids are placed, but you can't see the bidder's real eBay username because (to protect the innocent) eBay changes user IDs to a gibberish of asterisks and numbers. Each bidder is assigned a faux bidder ID in the history. Look at Figure 7-2 to see the bidding history on an auction where I'm no longer the highest bidder.

Bidders: **6**   Bids: **9**   Time left: **2 days 19 hours 59 mins**

You've been outbid. Bid again before it's too late!

Only actual bids (not automatic bids generated up to a bidder's maximum) are shown. Automatic bids may be placed days or hours before a listing ends. Learn more about bidding.

Show automatic bids

Bidder ⓘ	Bid Amount	Bid Time
s***p (2015 ⭐)	US $6.80	Feb-03-09 23:45:35 PST
c***s (441 ⭐)	US $6.30	Feb-03-09 23:20:42 PST
c***m (20 ⭐)	US $5.00	Feb-01-09 16:32:03 PST
***** (47 ⭐)	US $3.99	Feb-02-09 22:00:36 PST
marsha_c (6413 ⭐) me 📱	US $2.52	Feb-01-09 21:59:46 PST
***** (47 ⭐)	US $2.02	Jan-31-09 21:35:51 PST
***** (47 ⭐)	US $1.99	Jan-31-09 20:45:32 PST
c***m (20 ⭐)	US $1.50	Feb-01-09 16:31:54 PST
n***1 (14 ⭐)	US $1.00	Jan-31-09 17:57:38 PST
Starting Price	US $0.99	Jan-31-09 11:41:35 PST

Figure 7-2: The bidding history tells you the date and time of day at which the bidders placed their bids as well as the amount.

Pay attention to the times at which bidders are placing their bids; you may find that, like many eBay users, the people bidding in this auction seem to be creatures of habit — making their bids about once a day and at a particular time of day. They may be logging on before work, during lunch, or after work. Whatever their schedules, you have great info at your disposal in the event that a bidding war breaks out: Just bid after your competition traditionally logs out, and you increase your odds of winning the auction.

Early in an auction, there may not be much of a bidding history for an item, but that doesn't mean you can't still check out the dates and times a bidder places bids. You can also tell that a bidder practices *sniping* (discussed later in this chapter) if his or her bid zips in during the last few minutes (or even seconds!) of the auction. You may have a fight on your hands if the bidder does practice sniping.

Get to Know the Other Bidders

It used to be an easy task to study up on your competition, but the brains at eBay got smart and made it all but impossible. That is, all but impossible to me! In this section I show you how I figured out the now-circuitous route you can use to research your competition.

The concatenated ID of the person the item would belong to if the auction ended right now is listed on the auction item page. You can tell if the auction has bidders because the number of bidders appears on the listing page.

Take a look at this ID because you may see this bidder again later in this auction. By clicking the ID, you are presented with a page like the one shown in Figure 7-3, which shows just what that bidder has been up to — bidding wise.

Figure 7-3: Clicking on an ID in the bid history reveals a lot about the competition. In this sample, this person is clearly *highly interested* in the Jewelry category. Are they a dealer?

Bidding Details				
Bidder Information		**30-Day Summary**		
Bidder:	***** (46 ☆)	Total bids:	480	
Feedback:	100% Positive	Items bid on:	332	
Item description:	JUICY COUTURE Love/Amore/Heart 3-Layer Necklace in Box	Bid activity (%) with this seller:	6%	
Bids on this item:	3	Bid retractions:	9	
		Bid retractions (6 months):	24	

30-Day Bid History			
Category	**No. of Bids**	**Seller**	**Last Bid**
Jewelry & Watches > Fine Bracelets	4	Seller 1	4d 5h
Jewelry & Watches > Mixed Jewelry Lots	6	Seller 2	4d 5h
Jewelry & Watches > Necklaces & Pendants	2	Seller 2	5d 15h
Jewelry & Watches > Fine Earrings	2	Seller 3	3d 19h
Jewelry & Watches > Juicy Couture	3	Seller 4	4d 13h
Jewelry & Watches > Fine Rings	1	Seller 4	6d 20h
Jewelry & Watches > Fine Rings	1	Seller 4	6d 20h
Jewelry & Watches > Pocket Watches	1	Seller 4	6d 20h
Jewelry & Watches > Fine Rings	1	Seller 4	6d 20h
Jewelry & Watches > Other	4	Seller 4	1d 20h
Jewelry & Watches > Fine Necklaces & Pendants	1	Seller 5	4d 21h
Collectibles > Perfumes	1	Seller 6	1h
Collectibles > Pill Boxes	1	Seller 6	2d 1h
Jewelry & Watches > Necklaces & Pendants	1	Seller 7	17h
Jewelry & Watches > Necklaces & Pendants	1	Seller 8	16h
Jewelry & Watches > Necklaces & Pendants	1	Seller 9	14h
Jewelry & Watches > Necklaces & Pendants	1	Seller 9	14h
Jewelry & Watches > Necklaces & Pendants	1	Seller 10	2d 17h
Jewelry & Watches > Necklaces & Pendants	1	Seller 10	2d 17h
Jewelry & Watches > Necklaces & Pendants	1	Seller 10	1h
Jewelry & Watches > Necklaces & Pendants	1	Seller 10	6h
Jewelry & Watches > Necklaces & Pendants	1	Seller 11	4h

Now, how do you find out more? After you've lost an auction or two, go to eBay's Advanced Search, use the Items By Bidder search option, and run a search as described next

To get the skinny on a competitor, here's the move:

1. **Type your user ID.**

2. **Click the option button on the Include Completed Listings line.**

   Keep in mind that eBay has a 30-day limit on the auction information it returns, so don't expect to see results from a year ago.

3. **Choose the number of items you want to see per page.**

4. **Click Search.**

On the resulting page you will see a list of all the items you've bid on. The ones that you've won are marked with your user ID and an asterisk (*) indicating you are the winner. You will also see the listings that you've lost, and the user ID of the person that won!

The tale of the 3-plus-negative seller

A friend of mine took a risk and bid on an old Winchester rifle (now a banned item — see Chapter 9 for a rundown of what you're allowed and not allowed to sell on eBay) without reading the seller's feedback. The seller had a (+3) next to his user ID, which is a somewhat okay rating. Good thing my friend lost the auction. It turned out that the seller had a whopping 20 negative feedback messages. He had 23 positives, mostly posted by suspicious-looking names. Repeat after me: *Always read the feedback comments!*

Now, run the same search with that person's user ID and you'll get an idea of how much they bid in similar auctions to win. I think you should check all of the bidder's auctions to see how aggressively he or she bids on items. You can also get a pretty good handle on how badly a bidder wants specific items — and how high that person will bid before dropping out.

If the bidder was bidding on the same item in the past that you're both interested in now, you can also get a fairly good idea of how high that person is willing to go for the item.

You may be tempted to try to contact a bidder you're competing with so you can get information about the person more easily. This is not only bad form but could also get you suspended. Don't do it.

Strategies to Help You Outsmart the Competition

Your 2 cents do matter — at least on eBay. Here's why: Many eBay members tend to round off their bids to the nearest dollar figure. Some choose nice, familiar coin increments such as 25, 50, or 75 cents. But the most successful eBay bidders have found that adding 2 or 3 cents to a routine bid can mean the difference between winning and losing. So I recommend that you make your bids in oddish figures (such as $15.02 or $45.57) as an inexpensive way to edge out your competition. If you have a proxy bid in, say for $22.57, and a sniper jumps in at the last second and places a bid for $22.50 — you still win! The highest bid placed always wins. For the first time ever, your 2 cents (or in this case 7 cents) may actually pay off!

That's just one of the many strategies to get you ahead of the rest of the bidding pack without paying more than you should. *Note:* The strategies in this section are for bidders who are tracking an item over the course of a week or so, so be sure you have time to track the item and plan your next moves. Also, get a few auctions under your belt before you throw yourself into the middle of a bidding war.

Here's a list of do's and don'ts that can help you win your item. Of course, some of these tips *are* eBay-endorsed, but I had to get you to notice what I have to say somehow:

- **Don't bid early and high.** Bidding early *and* high shows that you have a clear interest in the item. It also shows that you're a rookie, apt to make mistakes. If you bid early and high, you may give away just how much you want the item.

  Of course, a higher bid does mean more bucks for the seller and a healthy cut for the middleman. So it's no big mystery that many sellers recommend it. In fact, when you sell an item, you may want to encourage it too.

  If you must bid early and can't follow the auction action (you mean you have a life?), use software or an online sniping service. Then feel free to place your highest possible bid! You can find out more about that in Chapter 20.

- **Do wait and watch your auction.** If you're interested in an item and you have the time to watch it from beginning to end, I say that the best strategy is to wait. Mark the auction to Watch This Item on your My eBay page and remember to check it daily. But if you don't have the time, go ahead — put in your maximum bid early and cross your fingers.

- **Don't freak out if you find yourself in a bidding war.** Don't keel over if, at the split second you're convinced that you're the high bidder with your $45.02, someone beats you out at $45.50.

  You can increase your maximum bid to $46.02, but if your bidding foe also has a maximum of $46.02, the tie goes to the person who put in the highest bid first. Bid as high as you're willing to go, but bid at the very end of the auction.

- **Do check the item's bidding history.** If you find yourself in a bidding war and want an item badly enough, check the bidding history and identify your fiercest competitor; then refer to the previous section "Get to Know the Other Bidders" for a pre-auction briefing.

  To get a pretty exact picture of your opponent's bidding habits, make special note of the times of day when he or she has bid on other auctions. You can adjust your bidding times accordingly.

- **Do remember that most deals go through without a problem.** The overwhelming majority of deals on eBay are closed with no trouble, which means that if the auction you're bidding in is typical and you come in second place, you've lost. Or maybe not . . .

Pirates of the Caribbean . . . or Carribean?

Just before the movie *Pirates of the Caribbean* premiered; Disneyland gave out exclusive movie posters to its visitors. My then college student daughter, savvy eBayer that she is, snagged several copies to sell on the site. She listed them (one at a time) when the movie opened and couldn't get more than the starting bid of $9.99 for each of them.

When we searched eBay for *pirates poster*, we found that the very same posters listed with a misspelled title, "Pirates of the Carribean,"

were selling for as high as $30 each. After selling out her initial stock, my daughter found another seller who had ten for sale — in one auction — with the proper spelling. She bought those as well (for $5.00 each) and sold them with misspelled titles on the site for between $15 and $27!

The moral of this story is always to search alternate spellings of your item; you might possibly eke out a gem without any competition.

If the winning bidder backs out of the auction or the seller has more than one of the item, the seller *could* (but isn't obligated to) come to another bidder and offer to sell the item at the second bidder's price through eBay's Second Chance option. (See Chapter 13 for more details on this feature.)

Time Is Money: Auction Strategy by the Clock

You can use different bidding strategies depending on how much time is left in an auction. By paying attention to the clock, you can learn about your competition, beat them out, and end up paying less for your item.

Most auctions on eBay run for a week; the auction item page always lists how much time is left. However, sellers can run auctions for as short as one day or as long as ten days. So synchronize your computer clock with eBay's master time and become the most precise eBay bidder around. Figure 7-4 shows eBay's Official Time page (which you can find at the very bottom of almost every eBay page).

To synchronize your clock, make sure that you're logged on to the Internet and can easily access the eBay Web site. Then follow these steps:

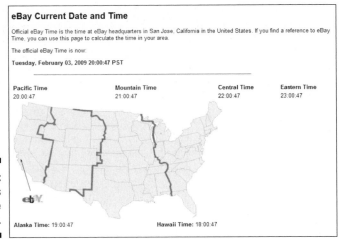

eBay Current Date and Time

Official eBay Time is the time at eBay headquarters in San Jose, California in the United States. If you find a reference to eBay Time, you can use this page to calculate the time in your area.

The official eBay Time is now:

Tuesday, February 03, 2009 20:00:47 PST

Pacific Time	Mountain Time	Central Time	Eastern Time
20:00:47	21:00:47	22:00:47	23:00:47

Alaska Time: 19:00:47   Hawaii Time: 18:00:47

Figure 7-4:
eBay's
Official Time
page.

1. **Go into your computer's Control Panel and double-click the icon that represents your system's date and time functions.**

2. **On the eBay Web site, click the Site Map link, which is above the navigation bar on the top of every eBay page.**

3. **Click the eBay Official Time link.**

   This link is located at the bottom of the Browse column on the left side of the page.

4. **Check your computer's time against eBay's current time.**

5. **Click the minutes in your computer's clock and then click the Reload button (sometimes it's called Refresh) on your browser.**

   Clicking Reload ensures that you see the latest, correct time from eBay.

6. **Type the minutes displayed on the eBay Official Time page as soon as the newly reloaded page appears.**

7. **Repeat Steps 5 and 6 to synchronize your computer's seconds display with eBay's.**

This process takes a little practice, but it can mean the difference between winning and losing an auction.

You don't need to worry about the hour display unless you don't mind your system clock displaying Pacific Time.

Most bidding on eBay goes on during East Coast work time and early evening hours, which gives you a leg up if you live out West. Night-owl bidders will find that after 10 p.m. Pacific Time (about 1:00 a.m. Eastern Time), lots of bargains are to be had. And believe it or not, lots of auctions end in the wee hours of the morning. Monday holidays are also great for bargains, as are Thanksgiving and the day after. While everyone is in the living room digesting and arguing about what to watch on TV (or getting up at 5:00 a.m. to buy the big discount deal at Wal-Mart), fire up eBay and be thankful for the great bargains you can win.

For simplicity's sake, go over to my Web site and print my quick and easy eBay time-conversion chart. It's located at

```
www.coolebaytools.com/usa_time_zones.html
```

Using a laid-back strategy

Sometimes the best strategy at the beginning of an auction is to do nothing at all. That's right; relax, take off your shoes, and loaf. Go ahead. You may want to make a *token bid* (the very lowest you are allowed) or mark the page to watch in your My eBay area. I generally take this attitude through the first six days of a week-long auction I want to bid on, and it works pretty well. Of course, I check in every day just to keep tabs on the items I'm watching on my My eBay page, and revise my strategy as time goes by.

The seller has the right to up his minimum bid — if his auction has received no bids — up to 12 hours before the auction ends. If the seller has set a ridiculously low minimum bid and then sees that the auction is getting no action, the seller may choose to up the minimum bid to protect his investment in the item that's up for sale. By placing the minimum token bid when you first see the auction, you can foil a Buy It Now from another bidder (because Buy It Now is disabled after a bid has been placed unless there is a Reserve on the listing) or prevent the seller from upping the minimum. If it's important enough, you can see whether the seller has done this in the past, by searching the Seller's completed auctions (see "Get to Know the Other Bidders" previously in this chapter to find out how to do this search). All preclosing changes are available for public view; just click View All Revisions just above the words Seller's Description on the item page. See Figure 7-5 for a sample.

If you see an item that you *absolutely must* have, mark it to watch on your My eBay page (or make that token bid) and plan and revise your maximum bid as the auction goes on. I can't stress enough how important this is.

Item Revisions summary for item #220255908883		
The seller has revised the following item information:		
Date	**Time**	**Revised Information**
Jul-14-08	10:58:44 PDT	Description
Sep-16-08	15:31:01 PDT	Title Description
Sep-16-08	18:55:25 PDT	Description
Oct-13-08	17:56:03 PDT	Description
Oct-13-08	18:03:32 PDT	Description
Oct-27-08	11:50:51 PDT	Description
Oct-30-08	11:52:54 PDT	Description
Nov-25-08	16:34:20 PST	Description

Figure 7-5:
This page
shows the
revisions
made by the
seller during
this auction.

As you check back each day, take a look at the other bids and the high bidder. Is someone starting a bidding war? Look at the time that the competition is bidding and note patterns. Maybe at noon Eastern Time? During lunch? If you know what time your major competition is bidding, when the time is right you can safely bid after he or she does (preferably when your foe is stuck in rush-hour traffic).

If you play the waiting game, you can decide if you really want to increase your bid or wait around for the item to show up again sometime. You may decide you really don't want this particular item after all. Or you may feel no rush because many sellers who offer multiple items put them up one at a time.

Using the beat-the-clock strategy

You should rev up your bidding strategy during the final 24 hours of an auction and decide, once and for all, whether you really *have* to have the item you've been eyeing. Maybe you put in a maximum bid of $45.02 earlier in the week. Now's the time to decide whether you're willing to go as high as $50.02. Maybe $56.03?

No one wants to spend the day in front of the computer (ask almost anyone who does). You can camp out by the refrigerator or at your desk or wherever you want to be. Just place a sticky note where you're likely to see it, reminding you of the exact time the auction ends. If you're not going to be near a computer when the auction closes, you can also use an automatic bidding site to bid for you; see Chapter 20 for details.

The story of the Snipe sisters

Cory and Bonnie are sisters and avid eBay buyers. Bonnie collects vases. She had her eye on a Fenton Dragonfly Ruby Verdena vase, but the auction closed while she was at work and didn't have access to a computer. Knowing that, her sister Cory decided to snipe for it. With 37 seconds to go, she inserted the high bid on behalf of her sister. Bang, she was high bidder at $63. But, with 17 seconds left, another bidder sniped back and raised the price to $73. It was, of course, Bonnie, who had found a way to get access to a computer from where she was. Bonnie got the vase, and they both had a good laugh.

In the last half hour

With a half hour left before the auction becomes ancient history, head for the computer and dig in for the last battle of the bidding war. I recommend that you log on to eBay about 5 to 10 minutes before the auction ends. The last thing you want to have happen is to get caught in Internet gridlock and not get access to the Web site. Go to the item you're watching and click the auction title.

With 15 minutes to go, if your auction has a lot of action, eBay reloads the bidding action every second so you can get the most current info on what people are bidding.

Sniping to the finish: The final minutes

The rapid-fire, final flurry of bidding is called sniping. *Sniping* is the fine art of waiting until the very last seconds of an eBay auction and then outbidding the current high bidder just in time. Of course, you have to expect that the current high bidder is probably sniping back.

With a hot item, open a second window on your browser (in Internet Explorer or Firefox, you do that by pressing the Ctrl key and the N key together); keep one open for bidding and the other open to watch eBay's constant reloading during the final few minutes. With the countdown at 60 seconds or less, make your final bid at the absolute highest amount you will pay for the item. The longer you can hold off — I'm talking down to around 15 seconds — the better. It all depends on the speed of your Internet connection (and how strong your stomach is), so practice on some small auctions so you know how much time to allow when you're bidding on your prize item. Keep watching the time tick to the end of the auction, as in Figure 7-6.

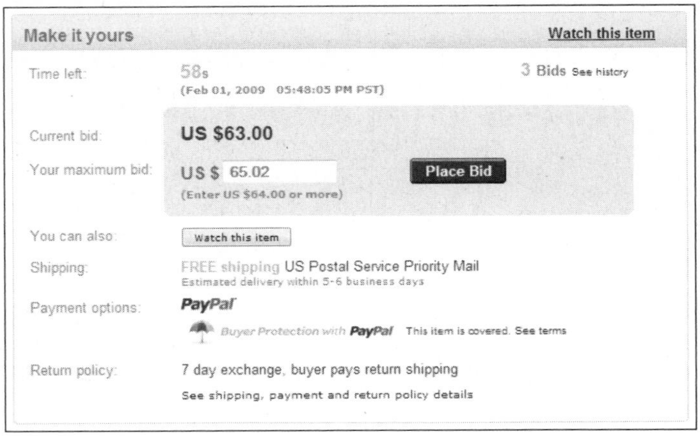

Make it yours		Watch this item

Time left: 58s
(Feb 01, 2009 05:48:05 PM PST)

3 Bids See history

Current bid: US $63.00

Your maximum bid: US $ 65.02
(Enter US $64.00 or more)

Place Bid

You can also: Watch this item

Shipping: FREE shipping US Postal Service Priority Mail
Estimated delivery within 5-6 business days

Payment options: *PayPal*

🌂 *Buyer Protection with PayPal* This item is covered. See terms

Return policy: 7 day exchange, buyer pays return shipping

See shipping, payment and return policy details

Figure 7-6:
Watching
the seconds
count down

If you want to be truly fancy, you can open a third window for bidding and have a back-up high bid in case you catch another sniper swooping in on your item immediately after your first snipe. (I recently received an e-mail from one of my readers who used my somewhat paranoid method — which she learned from a previous edition of this book — and by using the second snipe, she won her item!) You can avoid the third-window routine if you've bid your highest bid with the first snipe. Then, if you're outbid, you know the item went for more than you were willing to pay. (I know; it's some consolation, but not much.)

Some eBay members consider the practice of sniping highly unseemly and uncivilized — it's like when dozens of parents used to mob the department store clerks to get to the handful of Beanie Babies that were just delivered. (Come to think of it, whatever happened to *those* collectibles?) Of course, sometimes a little uncivilized behavior can be a hoot.

I say that sniping is an addictive, fun part of life on eBay auctions. And it's a blast. So my recommendation is that you try sniping. You're likely to benefit from the results and enjoy your eBay experience even more — especially if you're an adrenaline junkie.

Here's a list of things to keep in mind when you get ready to place your last bid:

✔ **Know how high you're willing to go.** If you know you're facing a lot of competition, figure out your highest bid to the penny. You should have already researched the item and know its value at this point. Raise your bid only to the level where you're sure you're getting a good return on your investment; don't go overboard. Certainly, if the item has some emotional value to you and you just have to have it, bid as high as you want (and can afford — but you knew that). But remember, you'll have to pay the piper later. You win it, you own it!

> ✔ Know the speed of your Internet connection.
>
> ✔ Remember, this is a game, and sometimes it's a game of chance, so don't lose heart if you lose the auction.

Although sellers love sniping because it drives up prices and bidders love it because it's fun, a sniper can ruin a week's careful work on an auction strategy. The most skillful snipers sneak in a bid so close to the end of the auction that you have no chance to counterbid, which means you lose. Losing too often, especially to the same sniper, can be a drag.

If your Internet connection is slower than most, and you want to do some sniping, make your final bid *2 minutes before the auction ends* — and adjust the amount of the bid as high as you feel comfortable with so you can beat out the competition.

If you can make the highest bid with less than 20 seconds left, you most likely will win. With so many bids coming in the final seconds, your bid might be the last one that eBay records.

This stuff is supposed to be fun, so don't lose perspective. If you can't afford an item, don't get caught up in a bidding war. Otherwise, the only person who wins is the seller. If you're losing sleep, barking at your cat, or biting your nails over an item, it's time to rethink what you're doing. Shopping on eBay is like being in a long line in a busy department store. If it's taking too much of your life or an item costs too much, be willing to walk away — or log off — and live to bid (or shop) another day.

Chapter 8

After You Win the Item

*T*he thrill of the chase is over, and you've won your first eBay item. Congratulations — now what do you do? You have to follow up on your victory and keep a sharp eye on what you're doing. The post-sale process can be loaded with pitfalls and potential headaches if you don't watch out. Remember, sometimes money, like a full moon, does strange things to people.

In this chapter, you can get a handle on what's in store for you after you win your item. I clue you in on what the seller is supposed to do to make the transaction go smoothly and show you how to grab hold of your responsibilities as a buyer. I give you info here about following proper post-auction etiquette, including the best way to get organized, communicate with the seller professionally, and send your payment without hazards. I also brief you on how to handle an imperfect transaction.

eBay Calling: You're a Winner

The All Buying section of your My eBay page highlights the titles of auctions you've won and indicates the amount of your winning bid. If you think you may have won the auction and don't want to wait around for eBay to contact you, check out the All Buying section for yourself and find out whether you're a winner.

Throughout the bidding process, dollar amounts of items that you're winning appear in green on your My eBay Active page. If you've been outbid, they appear in red. After the auction ends, there's no marching band, no visit from Ed McMahon and his camera crew, no armful of roses, and no oversized check to duck behind. In fact, you're more likely to find out that you've won the auction from either the seller or the Won section of your My eBay page than you are to hear it right away from eBay. eBay tries to get its End of Sale e-mails out pronto, but sometimes there's a bit of lag time. For a look at all the contact information in the winner's e-mail, see Figure 8-1.

Figure 8-1:
Everything
you need to
know about
contacting
your buyer
or seller is
included in
eBay's
winner's
e-mail.

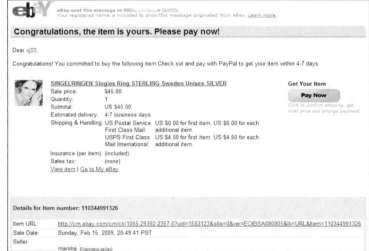

If you can receive text messages on your cellphone, eBay will send EOA notices to your mobile. (See Chapter 6 for more information on the types of eBay alerts available.) Go to your My eBay: My Account: Preferences page and click the Show link. (The link appears next to Notification Delivery.) You can indicate just how you want to receive the various notifications from eBay here.

Getting Your Paperwork Together

Yeah, I know that PCs were supposed to create a paperless society, but cars were supposed to fly by the year 2000, too. Maybe it's just as well that some predictions don't come true (think of the way some people drive or steer shopping carts). Paper still has its uses; printing copies of your purchase records can help you keep your transactions straight.

An order of fries with a menu on the side

In 1999, one seller auctioned an old menu from Howard Johnson's, estimating its era as the 1950s based on the cars pictured on the cover — and the prices (fried clams were $1.25). Also included was a separate menu card that listed fresh seafood and had a liquor menu (with Pieman logo) on the back — plus a list of locations in the New York City area. Except for a couple of staple holes at the top of the front cover (maybe evidence of daily specials past), the menu was in very good condition. The starting bid was $5; the item sold for $64. These menus are even harder to come by now but are selling in the $25 range. (I wonder how much they want for fried clams in New York City these days. . . .)

The item page shows the amount of your winning bid, the item's description, and other relevant information. The second you find out you've won the item, click the Print link below the Gallery photo in the listing and print a copy of the item page for your files.

eBay displays listings for only 30 days in the Bidder search, so don't put off printing out that final item page for your records. If you save your End of Sale e-mails that you get from eBay, you can access the listing for up to 90 days if you use the link in the e-mail.

Many sellers have multiple listings going at the same time, so the more organized you are, the more likely you will receive the correct item (and quick feedback) from the seller. Here's a list of the items you should keep in your item purchases file:

- ✔ A copy of your e-mail from eBay. *Don't* delete the e-mail — at least not until you print a copy and keep it for your records. You may need to refer to the e-mail later, and there's no way to get another copy.

- ✔ Printed copies of any e-mail correspondence between you and the seller that details specific information about the item or special payment and shipping arrangements.

- ✔ A printed copy of the final auction page.

Sellers can edit and update their auctions even while they're in progress, so keep your eyes peeled for changes in the listing as you monitor it. If the seller makes major changes, you are within your rights to withdraw your bid. (Check out Chapter 6 for more on the bidding process.)

Getting Contact Information

The eBay rules and regulations say that buyers and sellers must contact each other within three business days of the listing's end. So, if an item closes on a Saturday, you need to make contact by Wednesday.

If you've won an item and intend to pay through PayPal, it's de rigueur for you to go to the item as soon as possible after you've won and use the Pay Now link on the item page as soon as possible.

So, What's Your Number?

If something comes up between buying and receiving an item you've won and an e-mail you're sending gets no response, you need to get more contact information. Remember back when you registered and eBay asked for a phone number? eBay keeps this information for times like this.

To get an eBay member's phone number, click the Advanced Search link next to the Search box and then click the Members: Find Contact Information link on the left side of the screen. You need to enter the seller's user ID and the number of the item that you're trading with the other member; then click the Submit button.

eBay automatically generates an e-mail to both you and the other user.

eBay's e-mail includes the seller's user ID, name, e-mail address, company, city, state, and country of residence, as well as the seller's phone number and date of initial registration. eBay sends this same information about you to the user you want to get in touch with.

Often, sellers jump to attention when they receive this e-mail from eBay and get the ball rolling to complete the transaction.

eBay doesn't tolerate any abuses of its contact system. Make sure that you use this resource only to communicate with another user about a specific transaction. To use contact information to complete a deal outside eBay is an infringement of the rules. If you abuse the contact system, eBay can investigate you and kick you off the site.

If the seller doesn't contact you within three business days, you may have to do some nudging to complete the transaction. (See "Keeping in Touch: Dealing with an AWOL Seller," later in this chapter, and take a look at Chapter 13.)

Checking Out

When you buy something in a store, you need to check out to pay. eBay isn't much different. eBay's Checkout is a convenient way to pay for your completed auctions, fixed-price sales, and Buy it Now sales with a credit card or eCheck through PayPal. You may also use Checkout to exchange your information with the seller and pay for your item at a place other than PayPal (such as by money order, check, or another payment service that the seller accepts).

Checkout is integrated directly onto the item page so that you can win and pay for an item in less than a minute. Some sellers indicate, in their description, that they will send you a link to their private checkout page. When the sale is over, the item page will have checkout information, as shown in Figure 8-2.

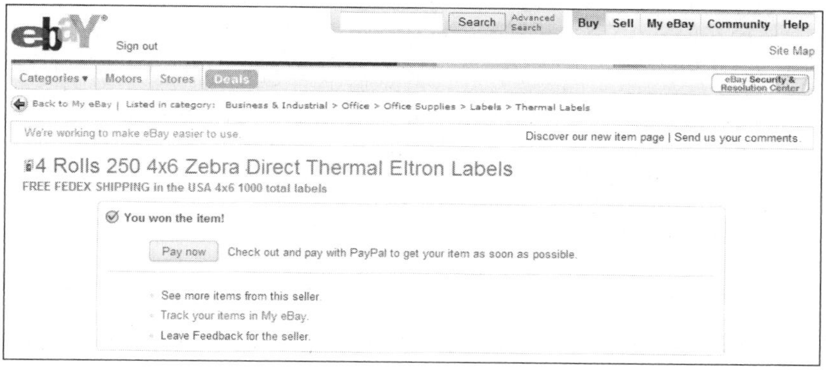

Figure 8-2:
Click the
Pay Now
button to
pay for
the item
immediately
through
PayPal.

When you click the Pay Now button, you're taken step-by-step through the checkout process. You pay for the item, and the seller is notified. You also get an e-mail confirming your payment, along with the seller's e-mail address.

If you're dealing with a Buy It Now or fixed-price listing, you don't have to wait and go back to the listing once you've purchased the item. After you confirm to eBay that you want to make a purchase, you're taken immediately to a page with a Pay Now button, as in Figure 8-3.

Figure 8-3:
Once you
commit to
buy, you
can pay
via PayPal
immediately.

Communicating with the Seller

Top-notch sellers know that communication is the absolute key to a successful transaction, and they do everything they can to set a positive tone for the entire process with speedy and courteous e-mails (or, at the very least, invoices).

Contact from a professional eBay seller should include the following information:

✔ Confirmation of the winning price

✔ The link for paying with PayPal or a secure Web site for credit card processing

✔ A review of the shipping options and price (the fee you pay)

✔ Confirmation of escrow (if offered in the listing)

✔ The date the item will be shipped

When you read the seller's e-mail, be sure to compare the terms the seller laid out in his or her e-mail with the terms on the auction page. And make sure that the form of payment and where it should be sent are clear.

You should pay immediately upon receipt of the invoice. If you have a question before paying, contact the seller immediately — he or she will be expecting your payment.

If you see significant differences between what the e-mail you receive from the seller after the sale and what is on your printout of the item page, address them immediately with the seller before you proceed with the transaction. For more on clarifying payment options during the buying process, see Chapter 6.

Sending the Payment Promptly and Securely

So how many times have you heard the saying "The check is in the mail"? Yeah, I've heard it about a thousand times, too. If you're on the selling end of a transaction, hearing this line from the buyer but not getting the money is frustrating. If you're on the buying end, it's very bad form and may also lead to bad feedback for you.

Being the good buyer that you are (you're here finding out how to do the right thing, right?), you'll get your payment out pronto via PayPal. Do it immediately — why wait? (The sooner you pay, the sooner you get that charming Flying Monkey decanter you won!)

Most sellers expect to get paid within three business days after the close of the listing. Although this timeline isn't mandatory, it makes good sense to let the seller know if there will be any delay in payment.

Send your payment promptly. If you have to delay payment for any reason (you have to go out of town, you are over your credit card limit, you broke your leg), let the seller know as soon as possible. Most sellers understand if you send them a kind and honest e-mail. Let the seller know what's up, give him or her a date by which the money can be expected, and then meet that deadline. If the wait is unreasonably long, the seller may cancel the transaction. In that case, you can kiss your positive feedback goodbye.

If the seller acknowledges through e-mail that they will accept other forms of payment, here are some tips on how to make sure that your payment reaches the seller promptly and safely:

✔ Have your name and address printed on your checks. A check without a printed name or address sends up a big red flag to sellers that the check may not clear. For privacy and safety reasons, though, *never* put your driver's license number or Social Security number on your check.

✔ Always write the item title and your user ID on a check or money order and enclose a printout of the final auction page in the envelope. The Number 1 pet peeve of most eBay sellers is that they get a payment but don't know what it's for — that is, buyers send checks without any auction information.

✔ If you're paying with a credit card without using a payment service and you want to give the seller the number over the telephone, be sure to request the seller's phone number in your reply to the seller's initial e-mail and explain why you want it.

> ✔ You can safely e-mail your credit card information over the course of several e-mails, each containing four numbers from your credit card. Stagger your e-mails so that they're about 20 minutes apart and don't forget to let the seller know what kind of credit card you're using. Also, give the card's expiration date.

Buyers routinely send out payments without their name, their address, or a clue as to what they've purchased. No matter how you pay, be sure to include a copy of the eBay confirmation letter, a printout of the auction page, or a copy of the e-mail the seller sent you. If you pay with a credit card via e-mail or over the phone, you should still send this info through the mail just to be on the safe side.

Using PayPal, a person-to-person payment service

Chapter 6 covers the pros and cons of using PayPal to pay for your auctions, but the bottom line is that every eBay seller accepts it as the main payment option. Let me make you feel more comfortable about why PayPal is the safest way to pay on eBay. eBay sees to it that PayPal is incredibly easy to use because PayPal is the official payment service on eBay. After the auction is over, a link to pay appears. If you'd prefer, wait until you hear from the seller. You can make your payment in three ways:

> ✔ **Credit Card:** You can use your American Express, Discover, Visa, or MasterCard to make your payment through PayPal. The cost of the item is charged to your card, and your statement will reflect a PayPal payment with the seller's ID.

> ✔ **eCheck:** Sending money with an eCheck is easy. It debits your checking account just like a paper check. It does not clear immediately, and the seller probably won't ship until PayPal tells him or her that the eCheck has cleared your bank.

> ✔ **Instant Transfer:** An instant transfer is just like an eCheck, except that it clears immediately and the money is directly posted to the seller's account. To send an instant transfer, you must have a credit card on file with PayPal as a backup (should the payment from your bank be denied).

PayPal is my favorite payment service for another reason. PayPal has a buyer protection program, which covers your purchases against fraud or if your item arrives not as described. Read more about that in Chapter 16.

When the auction is over, you can click the Pay Now button to check out and enter the PayPal site. If you don't pay immediately from the item page or seller's invoice, click the Pay link on the drop-down menu to the left of your item on your My eBay Won area. Once you click, just follow these steps:

1. **If this is your first visit to the PayPal site, register.**

2. **If you're already a registered user, go ahead and log in by following the steps on-screen.**

3. **Your transaction appears and you decide how to pay.**

If you're new to PayPal, they take you step-by-step through the process of filling out a payment form to identify the auction you're paying for as well as your shipping information. You're all done. Your credit card information is held safely with PayPal, and the payment is deposited into the seller's PayPal account. The seller receives notice of your payment and notifies you about how quickly he or she will ship your item.

By paying with PayPal, you can instantly pay for an auction without hassle. Your credit card information is kept private, and your payment is deposited into the seller's PayPal account.

You can always view your checkout status by going to your My eBay: Won area. Click the drop-down menu in the Action column for the item in question.

Keeping in Touch: Dealing with an AWOL Seller

The eBay community, like local towns and cities, is not without its problems. With the millions of transactions that go on every week, transactional difficulties do pop up now and then.

The most common problem is the AWOL seller — the kind of person who pesters you for payment and then disappears. Just as you're expected to hustle and get your payment off to the seller within a day or so, the seller has an obligation to notify you within a few days of receiving your payment with an e-mail that says the item has been shipped. If you sent the payment but you haven't heard a peep in a while, *don't* jump the gun and assume the person is trying to cheat you, but *do* follow up.

Follow this week-by-week approach if you've already paid for the item but haven't heard from the seller:

- ✔ **Week one, the gentle-nudge approach:** Remind the seller with an e-mail about the auction item, its number, and the closing date. "Perhaps this slipped your mind and got lost in the shuffle of your other auctions" is a good way to broach the subject. Chances are good that you'll get an apologetic e-mail about some family emergency or last-minute business trip. You'll find that the old saying "You can attract a lot more bees with honey than with vinegar" works great on eBay.

- ✔ **Week two, the civil-but-firm approach:** Send an e-mail again. Be civil but firm. Set a date for when you expect to be contacted. Meanwhile, tap into some of eBay's resources. See the section "Getting Contact Information," earlier in this chapter, to find out how to get an eBay user's phone number. After you have this information, you can send a follow-up letter or make direct contact and set a deadline for some sort of action.

- ✔ **Week three, take-action time:** If you still haven't heard from the seller, e-mail the seller once more and let him or her know that you're filing a complaint. Then go to your My eBay Won area, and in the drop-down menu next to the item in question, choose Resolve a problem. You will then be able to open a case for an Item Not Received or for one stating that the item is Not as Described. Next, you will be taken to PayPal. See "Filing for a Refund" later in the chapter to see how the process will go. Also, turn to Chapter 16 to find out more about filing complaints and using other tools to resolve problems.

You Get the Item . . . Uh-Oh What's This?

The vast majority of eBay transactions go without a hitch. You win, you send your payment, you get the item, you check it out, you're happy. If that's the case — a happy result for your auction — skip this section and go leave some positive feedback for the seller!

On the other hand, if you're not happy with the item you receive, the seller may have some 'splaining to do. E-mail or call the seller immediately and politely ask for an explanation if the item isn't as described. Some indications of a foul-up are pretty obvious:

- ✔ The item's color, shape, or size doesn't match the description.

- ✔ The item's scratched, broken, or dented in ways that don't match the description (the description said the doll was new, but the box is tattered and the doll has seen more than its share of action).

▮ ✔ You won an auction for a set of candlesticks and received a vase instead.

A snag in the transaction is annoying, but don't get steamed right away. Contact the seller and see whether you can work things out. Keep the conversation civilized. The majority of sellers want a clean track record and good feedback, so they'll respond to your concerns and make things right. Assume the best about the seller's honesty, unless you have a real reason to suspect foul play. Remember, you take some risks whenever you buy something that you can't touch. If the item has a slight problem that you can live with, leave it alone and don't go to the trouble of leaving negative feedback about an otherwise pleasant, honest eBay seller.

Of course, while I can give you advice on what you *deserve* from a seller, you're the one who has to live with the item. If you and the seller can't reach a compromise and you really think you deserve a refund, ask for one.

If you paid the U.S. Postal Service to insure the item, and it arrives at your home pretty well pulverized, call the seller to alert him or her about the problem. Find out the details of the insurance purchased by the seller. After you have all the details, follow the seller's instructions on how to make a claim. If the item was shipped through the post office, take the whole mangled shebang back to the post office and talk to the good folks there about filing a claim. Check out Chapter 12 for more tips on how to deal with a shipping catastrophe. And jump over to Chapter 16 to find out how to file your eBay and/or PayPal insurance claim.

Filing to Get a Refund through PayPal

If you're item never arrives or (as described in the preceding section) isn't what you expected based on the description, you are able to get a refund on tangible goods through PayPal. (This comes under the PayPal Buyer Protection plan.) To do so, follow these steps:

1. **Go to your My eBay Won area, and in the drop-down menu next to the item in question, choose Resolve a problem.**

2. **Verify that this is the item in question.**

3. **Click Continue.**

4. **Click the Resolution Center tab and then the Resolution Center link to report your case.**

   You will be able to negotiate with the seller. If the case can't be resolved, you will be able to file a buyer protection claim.

Don't Forget to Leave Feedback

Good sellers should be rewarded, and potential buyers should be informed. That's why no eBay transaction is complete until the buyer fills out the feedback form. Before leaving any feedback, though, always remember that sometimes no one's really at fault when transactions get fouled up; communication meltdowns can happen to anyone. (For more info on leaving feedback, see Chapter 4.) Here are some scenarios that give you an idea on what kind of feedback to leave for a seller:

- ✔ **Positive:** If the transaction could have been a nightmare, but the seller really tried to make it right and meet you halfway, that's an easy call — give the seller the benefit of the doubt and leave positive feedback.

- ✔ **Positive:** Whenever possible, reward someone who seems honest or tried to fix a bad situation. For example, if the seller worked at a snail's pace but you eventually got your item and you're thrilled with it, you may want to leave positive feedback with a caveat. Something like "Item as described, good seller, but very slow to deliver" sends the right feedback message.

- ✔ **Neutral:** If the seller worked at a snail's pace and did adequate packaging and the item was kinda-sorta what you thought, you may want to leave neutral feedback; the transaction wasn't bad enough for negative feedback but doesn't deserve praise, either. Here's an example of what you might say: "Really slow to deliver, didn't say item condition was good not excellent, but did deliver." Wishy-washy is okay as a response to so-so; at least the next buyer will know to ask very specific questions.

- ✔ **Negative:** If the seller never shipped your item or the item didn't match the description when it arrived, *and* the seller won't make things right, you need to leave negative feedback. Make sure that both conditions apply. Never write negative feedback in the heat of the moment and never make it personal. Keep it mellow and just state the facts. Do expect a response but don't get into a negative feedback war. Life's interesting enough without taking on extra hassles.

The Accidental Deadbeat might be an intriguing title for a movie someday, but being a deadbeat isn't much fun in real life. See Chapter 6 for details on buyer's remorse and retracting a bid *before* the end of an auction.

Properly Giving the Seller's Detailed Star Rating (DSRs)

In addition to a feedback comment and rating (positive, negative, or neutral), buyers should leave detailed seller ratings, too. The DSR part of the feedback system asks you to rate sellers by filling in one to five stars. A 5-star rating doesn't cost you anything as the buyer, and if the seller is a PowerSeller, it can affect a discount they receive on their eBay fees. Table 8-1 outlines what the stars mean to me when I leave a rating.

Table 8-1	What the DSR Stars Mean	
Rating Question	*# of Stars = Meaning*	*In the Real World*
How accurate was the item's description?	1 = Very inaccurate 2 = Inaccurate 3 = Neither inaccurate nor accurate 4 = Accurate 5 = Very accurate	In my world, the item was either described right or wrong — to me, there is no in-between. So when I rate a seller, either the item is as advertised or it isn't.
How satisfied were you with the seller's communication?	1 = Very unsatisfied 2 = Unsatisfied 3 = Neither unsatisfied nor satisfied 4 = Satisfied 5 = Very satisfied	As I buyer, I lean more with being very satisfied that I got enough communication from the seller, or not. If I get one e-mail, I'm usually satisfied. But if I haven't heard from a seller until the item reaches my door, I'm definitely rating in the 2-star range.
How quickly did the seller ship the item?	1 = Very slowly 2 = Slowly 3 = Neither slowly nor quickly 4 = Quickly 5 = Very quickly	Now, here I have another issue: As a buyer, you need to check the postmark on the package you receive. If the seller ships the next day or the next day after — you have to click 5 (Very Quickly), no matter how long the postal service took to get it there.
How reasonable were the shipping and handling charges?	1 = Very unreasonable 2 = Unreasonable 3 = Neither unreasonable nor reasonable 4 = Reasonable 5 = Very reasonable	When I purchase an item, I know what the shipping cost will be. The only surprise here is when you get an item in a small envelope and you've paid $9.00 for shipping — or if you paid for Priority Mail and it comes in another class of service. This is, to me, pretty black-and-white. The shipping and handling charges are either reasonable or unreasonable.

Here are some other items to keep in mind when you're deciding on what Detailed Star Rating to leave for a seller:

- **Shipping takes time:** You have to realize that Ground shipping can take up to 10 days. This isn't the seller's fault. So before leaving this rating, make sure to check the postmark or the date on the shipping label.

- **Shipping costs money:** Sellers have to add a little to cover the costs of tape, boxes, and packing materials. As a buyer, you have to keep that in mind. If you are unfamiliar with postage rates, you should also know that a package costs a lot more to ship across the country than to ship to the next state. So do a little homework and evaluate shipping costs *before* you buy. If the shipping is too high, go to another seller.

If your seller is a PowerSeller, you should also know that your star ratings affect the fees he or she pays to eBay. Being a good seller (with high DSRs) can save as much as 20 percent on final value fees, so your rating is a very serious matter.

Part III
Making Money the eBay Way

The 5th Wave   By Rich Tennant

"Oh, we're doing just great. Philip and I
are selling decorative jelly jars on eBay.
I manage the listings and Philip sort of
controls the inventory."

In this part . . .

A lot of different factors are at work when a seller makes a nice profit on an item he or she has put up for sale.

If you're new to online selling, you can find out all the benefits and get pointed in the right direction to find items that could make you a tidy profit. In fact, you may be sitting on major profits hiding in your own home! eBay has its rules, though, so when you assess an item's value to prepare for your listing, you need to make sure the item isn't prohibited from being sold at the eBay site.

In this part, I walk you through the paperwork you need to fill out to list an item for selling, and I show you how to close the deal and ship the item without any hassles. But even though I'm good, I can't stop problems from occurring, which is why I try to walk you through (almost) every conceivable mishap. There's also a chapter for those eBay newbies out there who already know that a picture's worth a thousand words. That's right — if you really want to make money on eBay, you can't miss the advanced strategies.

Chapter 9

Selling in Your Bunny Slippers for Fun and Profit

In This Chapter

▶ Discovering the benefits of selling

▶ Looking for inventory in your own backyard

▶ Knowing what to sell, when to sell, and how much to ask

▶ Staying out of trouble — what you can't sell on eBay

▶ Paying the piper with eBay fees

▶ Keeping the taxman happy (or at least off your back)

*F*inding items to sell can be as easy as opening up your closet (kitchen cupboard? car trunk?) or as challenging as acquiring antiques overseas (I even took the leap and imported custom items from Taiwan to sell on eBay). Either way, establishing yourself as an eBay seller isn't as difficult as it seems when you know the ropes. In this chapter, you find out how to look for items under your own roof, figure out what they're worth, and turn them into ready cash. But before you pick your house clean (I know eBay can be habit-forming, but please keep a *few* things for yourself!), read up on the eBay rules of the road — such as how to sell, when to sell, and what *not* to sell. If you're interested in finding out how to set up your auction page, get acquainted with Chapter 10; if you want to read up on advanced selling strategies, the Appendix is where to find them.

Why Should You Sell Stuff on eBay?

Whether you need to clear out 35 years of odd and wacky knickknacks cluttering your basement or you seriously want to earn extra money, the benefits of selling on eBay are as diverse as the people doing the selling. The biggest plus to selling on eBay is wheeling and dealing from your home in pajamas and bunny slippers (every day is Casual Friday in my office — see Figure 9-1). But no matter where you conduct your business or how you dress, many more important big-time rewards exist for selling on eBay.

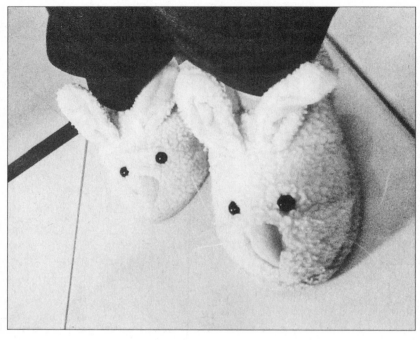

Figure 9-1:
My bunny
slippers at
work, listing
items on
eBay.

Most people starting a business have to worry about rounding up investment capital (start-up money they may lose), building inventory (buying stuff to sell), and finding a selling location such as a booth at a swap meet or even a small store. Today, even a little Mom-and-Pop start-up operation requires a major investment. eBay has helped to level the playing field a bit; everybody can get an equal chance to start a small business with just a little money. Anyone who wants to take a stab at doing business can get started with just enough money to cover the Insertion Fee.

Get a few transactions under your belt. Sell your old collection of postcards. See how you like the responsibilities of marketing, collecting money, shipping, and customer service. Grow a bit more, and you'll find yourself spotting trends, acquiring inventory, and marketing your items for maximum profit. In no time, you'll be making items disappear faster than David Copperfield (though you may have a little trouble with the Statue of Liberty — how'd he *do* that, anyway?). If you think you're ready to make eBay a full- or part-time business, take a look at the Appendix. If you still want to go long on eBay, please take a look at my book, *Starting an eBay Business For Dummies* (Wiley Publishing, Inc). It gives you just what you need to ramp up from hobbyist to big-time eBay tycoon making a few hundred (or even thousand) dollars a month!

Life lessons learned on eBay

If you have kids, get them involved with your eBay selling. They'll get real-life lessons they can't learn in school. Give them a feel for meeting deadlines and fulfilling promises. Get them writing e-mails (if they aren't already) and helping to pack the items. eBay is a great place to learn basic economics and how to handle money. When I first started on eBay, I taught my preteen daughter about geography by using eBay. Every time I completed a transaction, she used a search engine to look up the city in which the buyer (or seller) lived — and then marked the city by placing a pin on a huge map of the United States. She graduated from college, having majored in business and marketing. (Thank you, eBay!)

Get creative and make eBay a profitable learning experience, too. Remember, however, that eBay doesn't let anyone under the age of 18 register, buy, or sell — so make sure you're in charge of handling all transactions. Your kids can help out, but they need to be under your supervision at all times.

A fun way to get your feet wet on eBay is to buy some small items. When I say small, I mean it. Some of the least expensive items you can buy on eBay are recipes. Type **recipe** in the search box and sort the results by Lowest Prices First. You'll find recipes for a dollar and under. You don't have to pay a shipping charge, either. The sellers usually e-mail the recipe direct to you after the auction. You can also begin selling your very own secret recipes. This is a great way to become familiar with how eBay works, and you'll be gaining experience with feedback — as well as building yours!

Finding Stuff to Sell

Finding merchandise to sell on eBay is as easy as checking your garage and as tough as climbing up to the attic. Just about anything you bought and stashed away (because you didn't want it, forgot about it, or it didn't fit) is fair game. Think about all those awful birthday and holiday presents (hey, it was the thought that counted — and the givers may have forgotten about them, too). Now you have a place you can try to unload them for cash. They could even make somebody happy.

In your closet, find what's just hanging around:

 ✔ Clothing that no longer fits or is out of fashion. (Do you really want to keep it if you wouldn't be caught dead in it or you know it will never fit?) Don't forget the pair of shoes you wore once and put away.

- Any item with a brand-name label that's in new or almost-new condition.

- Kids' clothes. (Kids outgrow things fast. Use profits from the old items to buy new clothes they can grow into. Now that's recycling.)

 Have the articles of clothing in the best condition possible before you put them up for sale. For example, shoes can be cleaned and buffed till they're like new. According to eBay's policies, clothing *must* be cleaned before shipping.

And consider what's parked in your basement, garage, or attic:

- **Old radios, stereo and video equipment, and 8-track systems:** Watch these items fly out of your house — especially the 8-track players (believe it or not, people love 'em).

- **Books you finished reading long ago and don't want to read again:** Some books with early copyright dates or first editions by famous authors earn big money on eBay.

- **Leftovers from an abandoned hobby:** Who knew that building miniature dollhouses was so much work?

- **Unwanted gifts:** Have a decade's worth of birthday, graduation, or holiday gifts collecting dust? Put them up on eBay and hope Grandma or Grandpa doesn't bid on them because they think you need another mustache spoon!

Saleable stuff may even be lounging around in your living room or bedroom:

- **Home décor you want to change:** Lamps, chairs, and rugs (especially if they're antiques) sell quickly. If you think an item is valuable but you're not sure, get it appraised first.

- **Exercise equipment:** If you're like most people, you bought this stuff with every intention of getting in shape, but now all that's building up is dust. Get some exercise carrying all that equipment to the post office after you've sold it on eBay.

- **Records, videotapes, and laser discs:** Sell them after you've upgraded to new audio and video formats such as DVD (Digital Versatile Disc) or DAT (Digital Audio Tape). (Think Betamax is dead? You may be surprised.)

- **Autographs:** All types of autographs — from sports figures, celebrities, and world leaders — are popular on eBay. A word of caution, though: A lot of fakes are on the market, so make sure that what you're selling (or buying) is the real thing. If you're planning on selling autographs on eBay, be sure to review the special rules that apply to these items. Here's where to find them:

```
pages.ebay.com/help/policies/autographs.html
```

Know When to Sell

Warning . . . warning . . . I'm about to hit you with some of my clichés: *Timing is everything. Sell what you know and know when to sell. Buy low and sell high. Fast quarters are better than slow dollars.*

Okay, granted, clichés may be painful to hear over and over, but they do contain nuggets of good information. (Perhaps they're well known for a reason?)

Experienced eBay sellers know that when planning a sale, timing is almost everything. Fur coats don't sell well in July, and as a collectible seller you don't want to be caught with 200 Nintendo games during a run on Xbox. (Hold on to them; vintage games still sell well.) Star Wars action figures are traditionally good sellers unless a new Star Trek movie is coming out.

Some items — such as good antiques, rugs, baseball cards, and sports cars — are timeless. But timing still counts. Don't put your rare, antique paper cutter up for auction if someone else is selling one at the same time. I guarantee that will cut into your profits.

Snapping up profits

Way back in 1980, when Pac-Man ruled, my friend Ric decided to try his hand at photography. Hoping to be the next Ansel Adams — or to at least snap something in focus — he bought a 1/4 Kowa 66, one of those cameras you hold in front of your belt buckle while you look down into the viewfinder. Soon after he bought the camera, Ric's focus shifted. The camera sat in its box, instructions and all, for over 15 years until he threw a garage sale.

Ric and his wife didn't know much about his Kowa, but they knew that it was worth something. When he got an offer of $80 for it at the garage sale, his wife whispered "eBay!" in his ear, and he turned down the offer.

Ric and his wife posted the camera on eBay with the little information they had about its size and color, and the couple was flooded with questions and information about the camera

from knowledgeable bidders. One bidder said that the silver-toned lens made it more valuable. Another gave them the camera's history.

Ric and his wife added each new bit of information to their description and watched as the bids increased with their every addition — until that unused camera went for more than $400 in a flurry of last-minute sniping in 1999. These days, when Ric posts an auction, he always asks for additional information and adds it to the auction page.

What difference does a year make? You'll learn that the values of all items on eBay trend up and down. In 2000, this camera sold on eBay for over $600; in late 2001, it sold for $455. In the winter of 2003, interest in it was waning; it sold in the $375 to $400 range. In 2009, one sold for $390. Not bad considering everyone is saying film cameras are dead merchandise.

Timing is hardly an exact science. Rather, timing is a little bit of common sense, a dash of marketing, and a fair amount of information gathering. Do a little research among your friends. What are they interested in? Would they buy your item? Use eBay itself as a research tool. Search to see whether anyone's making money on the same type of item. If people are crazed for some fad item and you have a bunch, *yesterday* was the time to sell. (In other words, if you want your money out of 'em, get crackin' and get packin'.)

If the eBay market is already flooded with dozens of an item and no one is making money on them, you can afford to wait before you plan your auction.

Know Thy Stuff

At least that's what Socrates would have said if he'd been an eBay seller. Haven't had to do a homework assignment in a while? Time to dust off those old skills. Before selling your merchandise, do some digging to find out as much as you can about it.

Getting the goods on your goods

Here are some ideas to help you flesh out your knowledge of what you have to sell:

✔ **Hit the books.** Check your local library for books about the item. Study historic guides and collector magazines.

Even though collectors still use published price guides when they put a value on an item, so much fast-moving e-commerce is on the Internet that price guides often lag behind the markets they cover. Take their prices with a grain of salt.

✔ **Go surfin'.** Conduct a Web search and look for info on the item on other auction sites. If you find a print magazine that strikes your fancy, check to see whether the magazine is available on the Web by typing the title of the magazine into your browser's search window. (For detailed information on using search engines to conduct a more thorough online search, check out Chapter 5.)

✔ **When the going gets tough, go shopping.** Browse local stores that specialize in your item. Price the item at several locations.

When you understand the demand for your product (whether it's a collectible or a commodity) and how much you can realistically ask for it, you're on the right track to a successful auction.

✓ **Call in the pros.** Need a quick way to find the value of an item you want to sell? Call a dealer or a collector and say you want to *buy* one. A merchant who smells a sale will give you a current selling price.

✓ **eBay to the rescue.** eBay members often offer guidance for your research on the Community Boards and Chats. eBay has category-specific chat rooms, where you can read what other collectors are writing about items in a particular category. (See Chapter 17 for more on eBay's Chat area.)

For information on how items are graded and valued by professional collectors, jump to Chapter 5, where I discuss grading your items.

Be certain you know what you have — not only what it is and what it's for, but also *whether it's genuine.* Make sure it's the real McCoy. You are responsible for your item's authenticity; counterfeits and knock-offs are not welcome on eBay. In addition, manufacturers' legal beagles are on the hunt for counterfeit and stolen goods circulating on eBay — and they *will* tip off law enforcement.

Spy versus spy: Comparison selling

Back in the old days, successful retailers like Gimbel and Macy spied on each other to figure out ways to get a leg up on the competition. Today, in the bustling world of e-commerce, the spying continues, and dipping into the intrigue of surveilling the competition is as easy as clicking your mouse.

Say that you're the biggest *Dukes of Hazzard* fan ever and you collect *Dukes of Hazzard* stuff, such as VHS tapes from the show, movie memorabilia, General Lee models, and lunchboxes. Well, good news: That piece of tin that holds your lunchtime PB&J may very well fetch a nice sum of money. To find out for sure, you can do some research on eBay. To find out the current market price for a *Dukes of Hazzard* lunchbox, you can conduct a Completed Items search on the Search page (as described in Chapter 5) and find out exactly how many *Dukes of Hazzard* lunchboxes have been sold in the past few weeks. You can also find out their high selling prices and how many bids the lunchboxes received by the time the auctions were over. And repeating a completed search in a week or two is not a bad idea — you can get at least a month's worth of data to price your item. Figure 9-2 shows the results of a Completed Items search sorted by highest prices first.

You can easily save your searches on eBay. Just click the Save This Search link in the top-right corner (refer to Figure 9-2) to add a search to your favorite searches. Then it's on your My eBay Favorites page, and you can repeat the search with a click of your mouse.

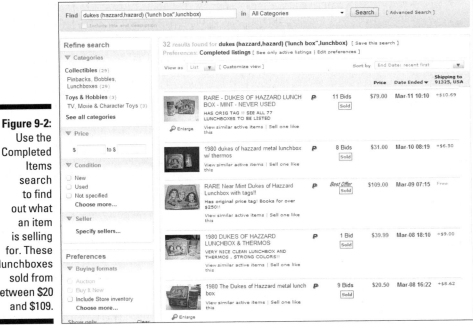

Figure 9-2:
Use the
Completed
Items
search
to find
out what
an item
is selling
for. These
lunchboxes
sold from
between $20
and $109.

Sometimes sellers make spelling errors when they write item titles. In the case of a *Dukes of Hazzard* lunchbox, when you conduct a search for such an item, I suggest that you use one of my favorite search tricks, which I featured in Chapter 5. The eBay search engine accommodates for one correction (as in *hazard* and *hazzard*) but when you want to check for two variations, you must input both. Type your search this way: **dukes (hazzard,hazard) ("lunch box",lunchbox)**. (Be sure that you drop the noise word *of*.) This way, you find all instances of *dukes hazzard lunchbox* and *dukes hazard lunchbox*.

Sure enough, when I tried this tactic, I found a considerable number of additional listings for a *Dukes of Hazzard Lunchbox*. Coincidentally, when I changed my search (remember, sellers *do* make mistakes) to **dukes (hazzard,hazard) ("lunch box",lunchbox)**, my search results went from 28 lunchboxes to 32! The best deals for buyers (and for sellers to resell) are always when the seller misspells a name or brand in the title.

Always search for the same item with different word variations or spellings. This is about the only time "creative" spelling can help you.

Look at the pictures on individual auction item pages for each item that your Completed Items search turns up. That way, you can confirm that the items (lunchboxes, for example) are identical to the one you want to sell. And when you do your research, factor in your item's condition. Read the individual item descriptions. If your item is in better condition, expect (and ask for) more money for it; if your item is in worse condition, expect (and ask for) less. Also, note the categories the items are listed under; they may give you a clue about where eBay members are looking for items just like yours.

If you want to be extremely thorough in your comparison selling, go to a search engine to see whether the results of your eBay search mesh with what's going on elsewhere. If you find that no items like yours are for sale anywhere else online and are pretty sure people are looking for what you have, you may just find yourself in Fat City.

Don't forget to factor in the history of an item when you assess its value. Getting an idea of what people are watching, listening to, and collecting can help you assess trends and figure out what's hot. For more about using trend-spotting skills to sniff out potential profits, take a look at the Appendix.

Know What You Can (and Can't) Sell

The majority of items sold on eBay are aboveboard. But sometimes eBay finds out about listings that are either illegal (in the eyes of the state or federal government) or prohibited by eBay's rules and regulations. In either case, eBay steps in, calls a foul, and makes the item invalid.

eBay doesn't have rules and regulations just for the heck of it. eBay wants to keep you educated so you won't unwittingly bid on, buy — or sell — an item that has been misrepresented. eBay also wants you to know what's okay and what's prohibited so that if you run across an item that looks fishy, you'll help out your fellow eBay members by reporting it. And eBay wants you to know that getting your listing shut down is the least of your worries: You can be suspended if you knowingly list prohibited items. And I won't even talk about criminal prosecution.

You need to know about these three categories:

- ✔ **Prohibited** lists the items that may *not* be sold on eBay under any circumstances.
- ✔ **Questionable** lists the items that may be sold under certain conditions.
- ✔ **Potentially Infringing** lists the types of items that may be in violation of copyrights, trademarks, or other rights.

You may not even offer to give away for free a prohibited or an infringing item, nor can you give away a questionable item that eBay disallows; giving it away doesn't relieve you of potential liability.

The items that you absolutely *cannot* sell on eBay can fit into *all three* categories. Those items can be legally ambiguous at best — not to mention potentially risky and all kinds of sticky. To find a detailed description of which items are prohibited on the eBay Web site, follow these steps:

1. **Click the Policies link, which is on the bottom of all eBay pages.**

   You arrive at the friendly eBay Policies page.

2. **Scroll to the Prohibited and Restricted items link and click.**

   Ta-da! You are presented with the lists and links that will help you decipher whether selling your item falls within eBay's policy boundaries.

   Or, if you don't mind typing, you can go directly to `pages.ebay.com/help/policies/items-ov.html`.

Sometimes an item is okay to own but not to sell. Other times the item is prohibited from being *sold and possessed.* To complicate matters even more, some items may be legal in one part of the United States but not in others. Or an item may be illegal in the United States but legal in other countries.

Because eBay's base of operations is in California, United States law is enforced — even if both the buyer and seller are from other countries. Cuban cigars, for example, are legal to buy and sell in Canada, but even if the buyer *and* the seller are from Canada, eBay says *"No permiso"* and shuts down auctions of Havanas fast. Figure 9-3 shows an auction that was shut down soon after I found it.

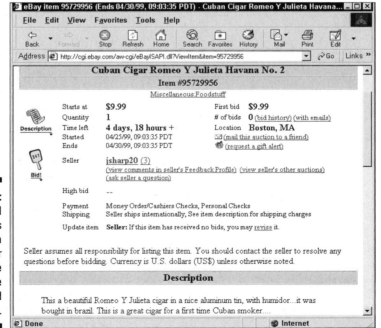

Figure 9-3:
In 1999, I found this auction for a Cuban cigar before the eBay police found it (and cancelled it).

Prohibited items

Even though possessing (and selling) many of the items in the following list is legal in the United States and elsewhere, you are absolutely, positively *prohibited* from buying and selling the following on eBay:

- **Firearms of all types:** This also means firearm accessories — including antique, collectible, sport, or hunting guns; air guns; BB guns; silencers; converters; kits for creating guns; gunpowder; high-capacity ammunition magazines (receptacles designed to feed ten rounds or more into a gun, not the publications about ammo); and armor-piercing bullets. You can't even sell a gun that *doesn't* work.

  You *can* buy and sell single bullets, shells, and even antique bombs and musket balls — as long as they have nothing explosive in them.

- **Firearms and military weapons:** No way can you sell any type of firearm that is designed to propel a metal (or similar) projectile, regardless of whether it works. Military weapons? Items included are bazookas, grenades, and mortars.

- **Police and other law-enforcement badges and IDs:** Stop in the name of the law if you're thinking about buying or selling any of these items, including actual United States federal badges or imitation badges. In fact, selling just about any U.S. government badge can get you in hot water.

  You also can't own or sell those agencies' identification cards or credential cases or those really cool jackets they use in raids. Selling a copy or reproduction of any of these items is prohibited, too, because these items are copyrighted (see the section on infringing items in this chapter).

  If you find a badge that's legal to sell and own, you need to provide a letter of authorization from the agency. The same letter of authorization is required for fake badges, such as reproductions or movie props.

- **Replicas of official government identification documents or licenses:** Birth certificates, drivers' licenses, and passports fall into this category.

- **Current vehicle license plates or plates that claim to resemble current ones:** Note that expired license plates (at least 5 years old) are considered collectible — as long as they are no longer valid for use on a vehicle.

- **Locksmithing devices:** These items can be sold only to authorized recipients. Federal law prohibits the mailing of such devices.

- **Human parts and remains:** Hey, we all have two kidneys, but if you get the urge to sell one to pay your bills, eBay is not the place to sell it. You can't sell your sperm, eggs, blood, or anything else you manage to extricate from your body. What's more, you can't even *give* away any of these items as a free bonus with one of your auctions.

✔ **Drugs or drug paraphernalia:** Narcotics, steroids, or other controlled substances may not be listed, as well as gamma hydroxybutyrate (GHB). Drug paraphernalia includes all items that are primarily intended or designed for use in manufacturing, concealing, or using a controlled substance, including 1960s-vintage cigarette papers, bongs, and water pipes.

✔ **Anything that requires a prescription from a doctor, a dentist, or an optometrist to dispense:** Listen, just because it's legal to use doesn't mean it doesn't require special permission to get. For example, even though penicillin is legal to buy in the United States, only a doctor can prescribe it — which is why, when you get sick, you have to stand in that *loooong* line at the pharmacy sneezing on all the other sick people. And if you're looking for Viagra auctions on eBay, don't even *go* there.

✔ **Stocks, bonds, or negotiable securities:** Nope, you can't sell stock in your new pie baking company or an investment in property you may own. And if you're thinking of offering credit to someone, you can't do that either. (Note that antiques and collectible items are permitted.)

✔ **Bulk e-mail lists:** No bulk e-mail or mailing lists that contain personal identifying information. You may not even sell tools or software designed to send unsolicited commercial e-mail.

✔ **Pets and wildlife, including animal parts from endangered species:** If you've had it with Buster, your pet ferret, don't look to eBay for help in finding him a new home. And you can't sell your stuffed spotted owls or rhino-horn love potions, either. If you're in the animal business — *any* animal business — eBay is not the place for you.

✔ **Child pornography:** Note that this material is strictly prohibited on eBay, but you can sell other forms of erotica. (See the section later in this chapter about questionable items.)

✔ **Forged items:** Autographs from celebrities and sports figures are big business — and a big opportunity for forgers. Selling a forgery is a criminal act. The state of New York is taking the lead on this issue, investigating at least two dozen suspected forgery cases linked with online auctions.

If you're in the market for an autograph, don't even consider bidding on one unless it comes with a *Certificate of Authenticity* (COA). Many sellers take authenticity so seriously that they give buyers the right to a full refund if any doubt about authenticity crops ups. Figure 9-4 shows an item that comes with a COA from an auction on eBay. Find out more about authentication services in Chapter 16.

✔ **Items that infringe on someone else's copyright or trademark:** Take a look at the very next section for details on infringing items.

✔ **Satellite and cable TV descramblers:** Although the Internet is loaded with hardware and instructions on how to get around cable TV scrambling, eBay prohibits the sales of anything in this arena. After all, it is illegal to get around these technologies.

✔ **Stolen items:** Need I say more? (Seems obvious, but you'd be surprised.) If what you're thinking about selling came to you by way of a five-finger discount, fell off a truck, or is hot, don't sell it on eBay.

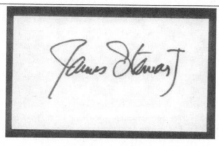

Figure 9-4:
When bidding on an item with a COA, be sure that the seller is reputable (hint, hint, check the feedback).

The item you are bidding on is a 3x5 Card , Autographed by the late James Stewart ....

The card is white and in mint condition... Signed bold and clear , in black felt tip pen ...

This Autograph is 100% Genuine , and I will provide my COA that Guarantees it for life...

Ignorance is no excuse. If you list an item that's in any way prohibited on eBay, eBay will end your auction. If you have any questions, always check eBay's Trust & Safety department at `pages.ebay.com/help/policies/items-ov.html`.

Infringing items

In school, if you copied someone's work, you were busted for plagiarism. Even if you've been out of school for a while, you can get busted for copying someone else's work. Profiting from a copy of someone else's legally owned *intellectual property* is an *infringement* violation. Infringement, also known as *piracy,* is the encroachment on another person's legal ownership rights on an item, a trademark, or a copyright. eBay prohibits the selling of infringing items at its site.

All the legal mumbo-jumbo, translated to English, comes down to this: Profiting from someone else's idea, original work, or patented invention is very bad and can get you in hot water.

Here's a checklist of no-no items commonly found at the center of infringement violations:

- Music that's been recorded from an original compact disc, cassette tape, or record.

- Movies that have been recorded from an original DVD, laser disc, or commercial VHS tape.

- Television shows that have been recorded off the air, off cable, or from a satellite service.

Selling a used original CD, tape, commercial VHS movie cassette, DVD, or CD-ROM is perfectly legal. Some television shows have sold episodes on tape; you can sell those originals as well. But if you're tempted to sell a personal copy that you made of an original, you are committing an infringing violation.

- Software and computer games that have been copied from CD-ROMs or disks (and that includes hard drives — anybody's).

- Counterfeit items (also called *knock-offs*), such as clothes and jewelry, that have been produced, copied, or imitated without the permission of the manufacturer. (Bart Simpson knock-off T-shirts abounded in the early '90s.)

If you pick up a brand-name item dirt cheap from a discount store, you can check to see whether it's counterfeit by taking a look at the label or comparing it on the Web with like items. If something isn't quite right, the item is probably a knock-off.

Trademark and copyright protection don't just cover software, music, and movies. Clothing, toys, sunglasses, and books are among the items covered by law.

Intellectual property owners actively defend their rights and, along with help from average eBay users, continually tip off eBay to fraudulent and infringing auctions. Rights owners can use eBay's Verified Rights Owner (VeRO) program, as well as law-enforcement agencies. (See "VeRO to the Rescue," later in this chapter, for info about the VeRO program.)

Hot property busted

In 1961, a young jockey named John Sellers won his first Kentucky Derby on a horse named Carry Back. He was so emotional about the victory that he was crying as he crossed the finish line. Seventeen years later, someone broke into his California home and stole his priceless trophy. But today, more than two decades after it was stolen, it's back in his possession — thanks to an observant eBay member. The prized trophy was put up for auction in 1999 by a seller who had bought it legitimately. An eBay member who knows the history of the trophy saw that it was for sale and alerted the seller. The seller stopped the auction immediately, contacted the former jockey, and personally returned the trophy to him. Now that's a great finish!

Questionable items: Know the laws

Because some items are prohibited in one place and not another, eBay lists a few items that you can trade but that are restricted and regulated. As a member of eBay, you're responsible for knowing the restrictions in your area — as well as those on the eBay Web site.

Certain items are illegal in one geographic area and not another. This list mentions a few of the major questionables:

✔ **Event tickets:** Laws regarding the sale of event tickets vary from state to state, even city to city. Some laws prohibit reselling the ticket for a price higher than the amount printed on the face of the ticket. Some states limit the amount you can add to the ticket's face value.

If you're planning to sell event tickets, visit `pages.ebay.com/help/policies/event-tickets.html` for details. This page has details featuring the various states' legal requirements. Be sure to double-check this page to be certain you're following the appropriate laws for your area.

✔ **Wine and alcohol:** Selling wine and alcohol on eBay — and anywhere else, for that matter — is tricky business. For starters, you have no business in this business unless you're at least 21 years old. eBay does not permit sales of any alcohol products unless they are sold for their "collectible" containers. You may sell alcoholic beverages for consumption if you have a liquor license and are preapproved by eBay. In the case of collectible bottles, some strict rules apply:

- The value must be in the collectible container, not in its contents. You can't auction off your uncle's Chateaux Margaux because the value is in the wine — not the bottle.

- The bottle must be unopened, and your auction must state that the contents are not meant for consumption.

- The container's value must substantially exceed the price of the alcohol in the container, and it must not be available at a retail outlet.

- You must be sure that the buyer is at least 21 years old.

- You must be sure that the sale complies with all laws and shipping rules. Every state has its own laws about shipping alcohol and wine. Some states require licenses to transport it; some limit the amount you can ship. You're responsible for knowing what your state laws are (and you're expected to conduct your auctions accordingly).

For the latest news and all the clickable links you need to keep your wine-shipping business on the good side of the law, visit `www.wine institute.org/programs/shipwine/current_events/current_ events.htm` or check with the Alcoholic Beverage Control (ABC) agency of your state. The Wine Institute page also gives the latest info on the status of shipping wine in the United States.

✔ **Erotica:** Some forms of erotica are allowed on eBay. To see what eBay allows and what it prohibits, type `pages.ebay.com/help/policies/ adult-only.html` into your browser.

One thing that's definitely illegal, wrong, and criminal is child pornography. If someone reports that you're selling child pornography, eBay forwards your registration information to law enforcement for criminal prosecution.

Forbidden items

The folks on eBay didn't just fall off the turnip truck. eBay staffers have seen just about every scam to get around paying fees or following policy guidelines. Chances are good that if you try one of these scams, you'll get caught. Then eBay cancels the listing. Do it once, and shame on you (don't count on getting the listing fee credited back to you). Do it a lot, and you're no longer welcome on eBay.

The following items are definitely forbidden:

✔ **Raffles and prizes:** You need to sell something in your auction; you can't offer tickets or chances for a giveaway.

✔ **Want ads:** If you want something, you have to search for it. Don't try to run your needs as an ad thinly disguised as an auction. Visit eBay's Want-It-Now (`pages.ebay.com/wantitnow/`) section and legally post your wants and needs there.

✔ **Advertisements:** An eBay auction is not the place to make a sales pitch (other than attractive copy describing your item, that is). Some eBay bad guys list an auction name and then use the auction to send bidders to some other auction or Web site. The Real Estate category is one exception. You can run an ad there for your property. Look out for eBay to expand its ads in the future.

✔ **Bait-and-switch tactics:** These are a variation on the ugly old sales technique of pretending to sell what you're not really selling. Some eBay users who are selling an unfamiliar brand of item try to snag bidders by putting a more familiar brand in the title. For instance, writing *Designer Chanel purse — not really, but a lot like it!* is a fake-out. eBay calls it *keyword spamming.* I call it lousy.

- ✔ **Choice listings:** You cannot offer your bidder a choice of significantly different items. But you can, if you're selling a particular T-shirt, list small, medium, and large sizes.

- ✔ **Mixing apples with oranges:** This gambit tries to attract more bidders to view an item by putting it in a high-traffic category where it doesn't belong. Forget it. eBay will move it for you if necessary, but keeping that rutabaga recipe book *away* from the list of automotive repair manuals is more considerate.

- ✔ **Catalogs:** "Buy my catalog so you can buy more stuff from me!" Uh-huh. I don't know why anyone would put a *bid* on a catalog (unless it's a Sears-Roebuck antique). If it's only a booklet that shows off all the cool junk you're selling, you can't offer it as an auction item.

Reporting a Problem Listing

You probably don't think that eBay can monitor millions of items for sale on a daily basis. You're right; it can't. eBay relies on eBay members like you to let it know when a shady listing is afoot. If you ever smell something fishy, for goodness' sake, report it to eBay. Sometimes eBay takes a few days to cancel a listing, but rest assured that eBay invests a lot of time protecting its users from fraudulent auctions.

If you see something that just doesn't look right, you should report the auction using an online form by clicking the Report Item link, which is below the Seller info box on every eBay item listing page.

eBay doesn't personally prosecute its users. However, eBay does have a stake in protecting its honest users — and will act as an intermediary between honest eBay users and law-enforcement agencies.

VeRO to the Rescue

If you own intellectual property that you think is being infringed upon on the eBay site, you should take advantage of the eBay *Verified Rights Owner* (VeRO) program. Owners of trademarked or copyrighted items and logos, as well as other forms of intellectual property, can become members of this program for free.

You can find out more about the VeRO program by clicking the Help link above the main navigation bar. To get eBay's current VeRO policy, go to `pages.ebay.com/help/tp/vero-rights-owner.html`. Read the information, and if you qualify, click to download the form, fill it out, and fax it to eBay. Then you're on your way to protecting your intellectual property from being auctioned to the highest bidder. Remember, only *you* can stop the infringement madness. If eBay agrees with you that your intellectual property is being infringed upon, it invalidates the auction and informs the seller by e-mail that the auction "is not authorized." The high bidders in the auction are also notified and warned that they may be breaking the law if they continue the transaction.

I am a member of the Vero program. Should someone think it's a good idea to scan and sell pirate copies of my books, I file my VeRO notice and the listing is removed within hours.

eBay understands that sometimes people don't know that they're selling infringing items, but it draws a hard line on repeat offenders. eBay not only shuts down the offenders' auctions but also suspends repeat offenders of this ilk. Also, eBay cooperates with the proper authorities on behalf of its VeRO program members.

If eBay deems your auction invalid because the item doesn't meet eBay's policies and guidelines, you can find out why by checking the page at pages. ebay.com/help/sell/questions/listing-ended.html. If you still feel you're in the right, scroll down the page to the Contact Us link. Click there to plead your case.

eBay Fees? What eBay Fees? Oops . . .

The Cliché Police are going to raid me sooner or later, but here's one I'm poking a few holes in this time around: *You gotta spend it to make it.* This old-time business chestnut means that you need to invest a fair amount of money before you can turn a profit. Although the principle still holds true in the real world (at least most of the time), on eBay you don't have to spend much to run your business. This is one reason why eBay has become one of the most successful e-commerce companies on the Internet and a darling of Wall Street. eBay keeps fees low and volume high.

eBay charges the following types of fees for listing on the site:

- **Regular auction insertion fees:** $0.10 to $4.00.

- **Fixed-price listing fees:** Either $0.15 for media, such as books or DVDs, or $0.35.

- **Real estate listing fees:** Vary because you have the choice of listing your property as an ad rather than an auction. Because eBay real estate auctions are *non-binding* (due to legalities), you may be better off running an ad. eBay charges different prices for different types of real estate:

- **Timeshares, manufactured homes, and land**

   Auctions: 1-, 3-, 5-, 7-, or 10-day listing ($35.00); 30-day listing ($50.00)

   Ad format: 30-day listing ($150.00); 90-day listing ($300.00)

- **Residential, commercial, and other real estate**

   Auctions: 1-, 3-, 5-, 7-, or 10-day listing ($100.00); 30-day listing ($150.00)

   Ad format: 30-day listing ($150.00), 90-day listing ($300.00)

✔ **Automotive fees:** The first four listings are free, with subsequent listings $20.00; motorcycles are only $15.00.

✔ **Additional reserve-auction fees:** $2.00; auctions with reserves over $200.00 are 1 percent of the reserve with a maximum of $50.00.

✔ **Final value fees:** A percentage of the sales price.

✔ **Optional fees:** Vary.

Insertion fees

Every item listed on eBay is charged an insertion fee. There's no way around it. The insertion fee is calculated on a sliding scale based on the *minimum bid* (your starting price), your fixed-sale price, or the *reserve price* (the secret lowest price that you're willing to sell your item for) for your item. (Later in this chapter, I explain how the reserve price affects what you eventually have to pay.)

eBay understands that there's not as much profit margin when you're selling a media item, so they have a lower listing fee to encourage you. What's a media item? New or used books, music, DVDs, movies, and video games. Take a look at Table 9-1 for eBay's insertion fee structure.

Table 9-1	Auction Insertion Fees	
Starting or Reserve Price	*Insertion Fee*	*Insertion Fee for Media*
$0.01–$0.99	$0.15	$0.10
$1.00–$9.99	$0.35	$0.25
$10.00–$24.99	$0.55	$0.35
$25.00–$49.99	$1.00	$1.00
$50.00–$199.99	$2.00	$2.00
$200.00–$499.99	$3.00	$3.00
$500–gazillions	$4.00	$4.00

If you're running a reserve-price auction (explained in detail in Chapter 10), eBay bases its insertion fee on the reserve price, not the starting bid. eBay also charges a fee to run a reserve-price auction.

eBay has a different fee structure for items that are listed as fixed-price sales. They are quite the bargain, so if you have multiples of a single item and know what you need to get for them, a fixed-price sale is a great way to go! Do know that there is a slightly higher final value fee for fixed-price listings, but more on that later. Table 9-2 shows you the insertion charges for a fixed-price listing that can stay on the site for as long as 30 days!

Table 9-2	Fixed-Price Insertion Fee	
Fixed Price	**Insertion Fee**	**Insertion Fee for Media**
$1.00 and more	$0.35	$0.15

Here's a snapshot of how a reserve price affects your insertion fee. If you set a starting bid of $1.00 for a gold Rolex watch (say what?) but your reserve price is $5,000.00 (that's more like it), you're charged a $4.00 insertion fee based on the $5,000.00 reserve price plus a $50.00 reserve fee (1 percent of the reserve price). (See Table 9-5, later in this chapter, for the reserve auction fees.)

So what does the insertion fee buy you on eBay?

- A really snazzy-looking display page for your item that millions of eBay members can see, admire, and breathlessly respond to. (Well, we can only hope.)
- The use of eBay services, such as the Trust & Safety program, which protects your selling experience. (Chapter 16 tells you how to use Trust & Safety during and after your sale.)

Final value fees

If you follow the movie business, you hear about some big A-list stars who take a relatively small fee for making a film but negotiate a big percentage of the gross profits. This is known as a *back-end deal* — in effect, a commission based on how much the movie brings in. eBay does the same thing, taking a small insertion Fee when you list your item and then a commission on the back end when you sell your item. This commission is called the *final value fee* (FVF) and is based on the final selling price of your item.

eBay doesn't charge a final value fee on an auction in the Real Estate/ Timeshares category as they do in other categories; instead, they charge a flat *notice fee* of $35.00. There's no FVF fee for Timeshares, Manufactured Homes, and Land or Commercial or Residential. But in the Automotive category, you pay a flat transaction services fee of $40.00 for passenger vehicles and $30.00 for motorcycles if your auction ends with a winning bidder (and the reserve has been met).

In real life, when you pay sales commissions on a big purchase such as a house, you usually pay a fixed percentage. eBay's final value fee structure is different: It's set up as a three-tiered system. Table 9-3 covers the calculation of final value fees for auctions.

Table 9-3	Auction Final Value Fees
Closing Bid	**To Find Your Final Value Fee**
$0.01–$25.00	Multiply the final sale price by **8.75 percent.** If the final sale price is $25.00, multiply 25 by 8.75 percent. You owe eBay $2.19.
$25.01–$1,000.00	You pay $2.19 for the first $25.00 of the final sale price (which is 8.75 percent). Subtract $25.00 from your final closing bid and then multiply this amount by **3.5 percent.** Add this total to the $2.19 you owe for the first $25.00. The sum is what you owe eBay. If the final sale price is $1,000.00, multiply 975 by 0.035. (**Hint:** The answer is $34.13.) *Now,* add $34.13 and $1.31. You owe eBay $36.32.
$1,000.01 and over	You owe $2.18 for the first $25.00 of the final sale price (which is 8.75 percent). But you also have to pay $34.13 for the remainder of the price between $25.01 through $1,000 (which is 3.5 percent). This amount is $36.32. ***Now,*** subtract $1,000.00 from the final sale price (you've already calculated those fees) and multiply the final sale amount that is over $1,000.00 by 1. 5 percent. Add this amount to $36.32. The sum is the amount you owe eBay. If the final sales price is $3,000.00, multiply $2,000.00 by **1.5 percent.** (**Hint:** The answer is $30.) Add $36.32 to $30. The sum, $66.32, is what you owe eBay. (You won't be graded on this.)

Table 9-3 shows where things get tricky. There are different final value fees (FVFs) for fixed-price items in different categories. Checking out the costs involved in the individual categories may help you decide which type of items you choose to sell. Table 9-4 is an attempt to clarify the tiers.

Table 9-4	Fixed-Price Final Value Fees	
eBay Category	**Closing Price**	**To Find Your Final Value Fee**
Consumer Electronics, Video Game Systems, Cameras & Photo	$0.01–$50.00	**8%** of the final value
	$50.01–$1,000.00	**8%** of the first $50.00, plus **4.5%** of the remaining final value balance ($50.01–$1,000.00)
	$1,000.01 and over	**8%** of the first $50.00, plus **4.5%** of the amount up to $1,000.00 and then **1%** of the remaining final value ($1000.01 to the final sale amount)
Computers & Networking	$0.01–$50.00.00	**6%** of the final value
	$50.01–$1,000.00	**6%** of the first $50.00, plus **3.75%** of the remaining final value balance ($50.01–$1,000.00)
	$1,000.01 and over	**6%** of the first $50.00, plus **3.75%** of the amount up to $1,000 and then **1%** of the remaining final value ($1000.01 to the final sale amount)
Clothing, Shoes & Accessories	$0.01–$50.00	**12%** of the final value
	$50.01–$1,000.00	**12%** of the first $50.00, plus **9%** of the remaining final value balance ($50.01–$1,000.00)
	$1,000.01 and over	**12%** of the first $50.00, plus **9%** of the amount up to $1,000.00 and then **2%** of the remaining final value ($1000.01 to the final sale amount)
Media (Books, Music, DVDs & Movies, Video Games)	$0.01–$50.00	**15%** of the final value
	$50.01–$1,000.00	**15.00%** of the first $50.00, plus **5%** of the remaining final value balance ($50.01–$1,000.00)
	$1,000.01 and over	**15.00%** of the first $50.00, plus **5%** of the amount up to $1,000.00 and then **2%** of the remaining final value ($1000.01 to the final sale amount)
All Other Categories	$0.01–$50.00	**12%** of the final value
	$50.01–$1,000.00	**12.00%** of the first $50.00, plus **6%** of the remaining final value balance ($50.01–$1,000.00)
	$1,000.01 and over	**12.00%** of the first $50.00, plus **6%** of the amount up to $1,000.00 and then **2%** of the remaining final value ($1000.01 to the final sale amount)

If you try to work out your own final value fees, you may get an extreme headache — and come up with fractional cents. Know that eBay rounds up fees of $0.005 and more and drops fees below $0.005. These roundings are done on a per-transaction basis, and generally even out over time.

Always keep track of the exact amount. Here's why (you're gonna love this): An item that is sold for $37.89 will show a final value fee of $1.67 on the View Account Status page (and in other areas where final value fees are displayed), although the exact amount of the final value fee is $1.670275. For display purposes the additional digits are rounded to the closest cent on invoices and other pages. However, the *exact* amount ($1.670275) — *not the displayed amount* — is used to calculate the total amount due on your invoice. Therefore, if several items have been sold, multiple line items showing final account fees that have been rounded to the nearest cent will appear on invoices and other pages, and the correctly calculated total balance will appear to be off by one or a few cents. (In other words, eBay charges you those fractions of a cent.) Here's where you can get further details:

```
http:// pages.ebay.com/help/sell/invoice.html
```

Because of the sliding percentages, the higher the final selling price, the lower the commission eBay charges. (I guess math can be a beautiful thing, when applied for my benefit.)

Optional fees

You don't have to pay a license fee and destination charge, but setting up your auction can be like buying a car. eBay has all sorts of options to jazz up your auction. (Sorry, eBay is fresh out of two-tone metallic paint — but how about a nice pair of fuzzy dice for your mirror?) I explain how all these bells, whistles, and white sidewalls dress up your auction in Chapter 10.

As a hint of things to come, Table 9-5 lists the eBay listing options and what they'll cost you.

Table 9-5	eBay Optional-Feature Fees	
Option	*Fee (Auction or Fixed Price, 3, 5, 7, 10 Days)*	*Fixed-Price Fee (per 30 Days)*
Value Pack (Gallery Plus, Subtitle, and Listing Designer)	$0.65	$2.00
Boldface title	$2.00	$4.00
Border	$4.00	$8.00

(continued)

Table 9-5 *(continued)*

Option	Fee (Auction or Fixed Price, 3, 5, 7, 10 Days)	Fixed-Price Fee (per 30 Days)
Home page Featured	$59.95	$179.95
Featured First	$24.95	$74.95
Featured Plus	$0.01–$24.99 $9.95 $25.00–$199.99 $14.95 $200.00 or more $19.95	3-, 5-, 7-, or 10-day duration $14.95 30-day, good until cancelled $39.95 Classified Ad $39.95
List in two categories	Double-listing and upgrade fees	Double-listing and upgrade fees
10-day auction	$0.40	n/a
Highlight	$5.00	$10.00
Listing Designer	$0.10	$0.30
Scheduled listings	$0.10	$0.10
Gift services	$0.25	$0.75
Subtitle	$0.50	$1.50
Picture hosting	First picture free, each additional $0.15	
Auction BIN (Buy It Now) fee	(See Table 9-6)	
eBay Motors vehicle BIN fee	$1.00 for vehicles, $0.50 for motorcycles	
Passenger vehicle reserve fee		$5.00

eBay also charges an upgrade fee when you use the Buy-It-Now option on your listings. Table 9-6 shows how Buy-It-Now upgrade fees break down.

Table 9-6	Buy-It-Now Fees
Buy-It-Now Price	*Fee*
$0.01–$9.99	$0.05
$10.00–$24.99	$0.10
$25.00–$49.99	$0.20
$50.00 or more	$0.25

Keep current on your profits

When you've finished all the legwork needed to make some money, do some brain-work to keep track of your results. The best place to keep watch on your eBay sales is on your My eBay page, a great place to stay organized while you're conducting all your eBay business. (I describe all the functions of the page in Chapter 4.) When it comes to calculating your bottom line, it's best to get used to using a program like QuickBooks.

Here's a checklist of what to watch out for after the auction closes:

- ✓ **Keep an eye on how much you're spending to place items up for sale on eBay.** You don't want any nasty surprises, and you don't want to find out that you spent more money to set up your listing than you received selling your item.

- ✓ **If you decide to turn your eBay selling into a business, keep track of your expenses for your taxes.** (I explain Uncle Sam's tax position on eBay next. Stay tuned.)

- ✓ **Make sure that you get refunds and credits when they're due.**

- ✓ **Double-check your figures to make certain eBay hasn't made mistakes.** If you have any questions about the accounting, let eBay know.

Find an error or something that isn't quite right with your account? Use the form at `pages.ebay.com/help/contact_us/_base/index_selection.html` to get your questions answered.

Uncle Sam Wants You — to Pay Your Taxes

What would a chapter about money be without a discussion of taxes? As Ben Franklin knew (and we've all found out since), you can't escape death and taxes. (C'mon, it's not a cliché; it's traditional wisdom.) Whether in cyberspace or face-to-face life, never forget that Uncle Sam is always your business partner.

If you live outside the United States, check the tax laws in that country so you don't end up with a headache down the road.

As with offline transactions, knowledge is power. The more you know about buying and selling on eBay before you actually start doing it, the more savvy the impression you make — and the more satisfying your experience.

For more details on taxes and bookkeeping, check out my book, *Starting an eBay Business For Dummies* (Wiley).

Two wild rumors about federal taxes

I've heard some rumors about not having to pay taxes on eBay profits. If you hear any variation on this theme, smile politely and don't believe a word of it. I discuss two of the more popular (and seriously mistaken) tax notions running around the eBay community these days.

The U.S. government uses two laws on the books to go after eBay outlaws. One is the Federal Trade Commission (FTC) Act, which prohibits deceptive or misleading transactions in commerce. The other is the Mail or Telephone Order Merchandise Rule, which requires sellers to ship merchandise in a timely manner or offer to refund a consumer's money. The FTC is in charge of pursuing these violations. If you have a question about federal laws, you can find a lot of information online. For example, I found these three Web sites that keep fairly current lists of U.S. law and federal codes:

```
www4.law.cornell.edu/uscode
www.ftc.gov
www.fourmilab.ch/ustax/ustax.html
```

Rumor #1: E-commerce isn't taxed

One story claims that "there will be no taxes on e-commerce sales (sales conducted online) for three years." No one ever seems to know when those three years start or end.

Some people confuse state sales tax issues with income tax issues. You don't pay Internet sales taxes, but that's not the same as not reporting income from the Internet or selling within your home state.

Congress's Internet Tax Freedom Act stated that until October 2001, Congress and state legislatures couldn't institute *new* taxes on Internet transactions. President Bush signed a unanimously approved law that extended (through November 1, 2003) a ban on multiple and discriminatory Internet taxes and Internet-access taxes. (The moratorium did not apply to sales taxes or federal taxes.) The legislation also lengthened the "Sense of the Congress" resolution that there should be no federal taxes on Internet access or electronic commerce, and that the United States should work aggressively through the EU (European Union) and WTO (World Trade Organization) to keep electronic commerce free from tariffs and discriminatory taxes.

Even though November 1, 2003, has passed, there's still discussion about the law. Some people want to exempt online merchants if they bring in less than $25,000 per year. Others say no taxes should be imposed unless the merchant has sales of $5 million a year.

Something new is on the horizon: the *Streamlined Sales Tax Project* (SSTA). Although the name of this government project may make it sound like the states will be charging state sales tax on all e-commerce purchases, the reality isn't that simple. The battle is ongoing — and though I don't feel that eBay sellers with sales under $100,000 a year have much to fear, I still recommend that you do a Google search on the SSTA every once in a while to keep up-to-date.

As of this writing, the rules are up in the air. Please continue to check my Web site, www.coolebaytools.com, for news on the SSTA when it applies.

Rumor #2: Profits from garage sales are tax-exempt

"eBay is like a garage sale, and you don't have to pay taxes on garage sales." (Uh-huh. And the calories in ice cream don't count if you eat it out of the carton. Who comes up with this stuff anyway?)

This notion is just an urban (or shall I say *suburban*) legend — somebody's wishful thinking that's become folklore. If you make money on a garage sale, you have to declare it as income — just like anything else you make money on. Most people never make any money on garage sales because they usually sell things for far less than they bought them for. However, the opposite is often true of an eBay transaction.

Even if you lose money, you may have to prove it to the government, especially if you're running a small business. You most definitely should have a heart-to-heart talk with your accountant or tax professional as to how to file your taxes. If something might look bad in an audit if you *don't* declare it, consider that a big hint.

To get the reliable word, I checked with the IRS's e-commerce office. The good folks there told me that even if you make as little as a buck on any eBay sale after all your expenses (the cost of the item, eBay fees, shipping charges), you still have to declare it as income on your federal tax return.

If you have questions about eBay sales and your taxes, check with your personal accountant, call the IRS Help Line at 800-829-1040, or visit the IRS Web site at www.irs.ustreas.gov. And be friendly. (Just in case.)

State sales tax

If your state has sales tax, a *sales tax number* is required before you *officially* sell something. If sales tax applies, you may have to collect the appropriate sales tax for every sale that falls within the state that your business is in. A 1992 U.S. Supreme Court decision said that states can only require sellers that have a physical presence in the same state as the consumer to collect so-called use taxes.

To find the regulations for your state, visit one of the following sites, which supply links to every state's tax board. The tax board should have the answers to your questions.

```
www.taxsites.com/agencies.html
www.aicpa.org/yellow/yptstax.htm
```

State income taxes

Yes, it's true. Not only is Uncle Sam in Washington, D.C., looking for his slice of your eBay profits, but your state government may be hankering to join the feast.

If you have a good accountant, give that esteemed individual a call. If you don't have one, find a tax professional in your area. Tax professionals actually do more than just process your income tax returns once a year; they can help you avoid major pitfalls even before April 15.

Here's how to find out what your responsibilities are in your home state:

- ✔ You may need to collect and pay state sales taxes, but only if you sell to someone in your state.
- ✔ You can get tax information online at this Web site:

  ```
  www.taxadmin.org/fta/rate/tax_stru.html
  ```

  The site has links to tax information for all 50 states.

- ✔ You can also call your state tax office and let the good folks there explain the requirements. The state tax office should be listed in the government section of your phone book.

Chapter 10

Time to Sell: Completing the Cyber Paperwork

It's time to make some money? Are you ready? Yes? (Call it an inspired guess.) You're on the threshold of adding your items to the hundreds of thousands that go up for sale on eBay every day (and perhaps also shedding from your home some of the valuable things you haven't touched in years). Some listings are so hot that the sellers quadruple their investments. Other items, unfortunately, are so stone cold that they may not even register a single bid.

In this chapter, I explain all the facets of the Sell an Item page — the page you fill out to get your auction going on eBay. You get some advice that can increase your odds of making money, and you find out the best way to position your item so buyers can see it and bid on it. I also show you how to modify, relist, or end your auction whenever you need to.

A caveat here: To keep the marketplace vibrant, eBay's programmers are constantly working to improve the site, and improvement means change. The listing form (as I describe in this chapter) can change from time to time, but the basic decisions you need to make will not. The selling philosophy laid out in this chapter should help you ride the waves of change on eBay — whatever they may be.

Getting Ready to List Your Item

After you decide what you want to sell, find out as much as you can about it and conduct a little market research. Then you should have a good idea of the item's popularity and value. To get this info, check out Chapter 9.

Before you list your item, make sure that you have these bases covered:

✔ **The specific category under which you want the item listed:** Ask your friends or family where they'd look for such an item and remember the categories you saw most frequently when you conducted your market research with the eBay search function.

To find out which category will pay off best for your item, run a search and then check Completed Listings. See how many of this type of item are selling now (and if people are actually bidding on it). Scroll down to the left of the page and click the Show Only Completed Listings box. Then sort your results by highest prices first and look over the sales to see which categories they're listed in. For more information on how to get ahead of the crowd through eBay's search, visit Chapter 5.

✔ **What you want to say in your item description:** Jot down your ideas. Take a good look at your item and make a list of keywords that describe your item. Keywords are single descriptive words that can include the following (this is hardly a complete list):

- Brand name
- Size of the item (citing measurements if appropriate)
- Age or date of manufacture
- Condition
- Rarity
- Color
- Size
- Material

I know all about writer's block. If you're daunted by the Sell an Item page, struggle through it anyway. This way you've finished the hard work before you even begin.

✔ **Whether you want to attach a picture (or pictures) to your description via a Uniform Resource Locator (URL):** Pictures help sell items, but you don't have to use them. (This information won't be on the test, but if you want to know more about using pictures in your auctions, see Chapter 14.)

✔ **The price at which you think you can sell the item.** Be as realistic as you can. (That's where your market research comes in.)

Examining the Sell an Item Page

The Sell an Item form is where your listing is born. Filling out your virtual paperwork requires a few minutes of clicking, typing, and answering all kinds of questions. The good news is that when you're finished, your listing is up and running and (I hope) starting to earn you money.

Before you begin, you have to be a registered eBay user. If you still need to register, go to Chapter 2 and fill out the preliminary online paperwork. If you've registered but haven't provided eBay with your financial information (credit card or checking account), you'll be asked for this information to set up your seller account before you proceed. Fill in the data on the secure form. Then you're ready to roll.

Just like the dizzying menu in a Chinese restaurant, you have four ways to sell an item on eBay. Four ways may not seem to be very dizzying, unless you're trying to psychically decide which format is the best for you. Here's what you need to know about each type:

✔ **Online auction:** This is the tried-and-true traditional sale format on eBay. This is what the newbies look for, and you can combine this with a Buy It Now for those who want the item immediately. Often, if you're selling a collectible item, letting it go to auction may net you a much higher profit — remember to do your research before listing.

✔ **Fixed price:** Just like shopping at the corner store, a fixed-price sale is easy for the buyer to comprehend and complete. The only problem is that many potential buyers may lean toward an auction because of the perception that they *may* get a better deal.

A variation on a fixed-price listing is to add the *Make an offer* option. This enables buyers to think they can get a great deal — but you have the opportunity to accept the offer or make a counteroffer. Cultural leanings toward bargaining mean some buyers prefer this method. You may not. It can be fun and is just another way to spur sales in a slow retail environment.

✔ **Sell in your eBay store:** Chapter 11 covers eBay Stores — a convenient place to sell more items to your auctions or fixed-price sales.

✔ **Classified ad:** If you don't want to put your property or other valuable item up for auction and you'd like to correspond with the prospective buyer, this is the option for you. Although this option originated with real estate, the ad format is available in many categories. The cost of your ad is $9.95 for a 30-day listing. If you're interested in finding out which type of items you can sell with a classified ad, check out this URL:

```
pages.ebay.com/help/sell/adformatfees.html
```

Say, for example, that you want to list a good, old-fashioned eBay auction. You want to sell an item for a fixed price but are willing to let it go to auction.

To find eBay's Sell an Item form from the eBay Home page, you can use either of these methods:

- ✔ Click the Sell link on the navigation bar at the top of the page. eBay allows you to select your category and download the Sell an Item page in seconds.

- ✔ Start your listing from your My eBay page. Just click the Sell Similar link (on the All Selling page) next to one of your existing items. Using the form that appears, you can change the item data.

When listing your item, here's the info you're asked to fill out (each of these items is discussed in detail later in this chapter):

- ✔ **Category:** The category where you've decided to list your item (required).

- ✔ **Title:** The name of your item (required).

- ✔ **Description:** What you want to tell eBay buyers about your item (required).

- ✔ **eBay Picture Services or Image URL:** The Web address of any pictures you want to add (optional). To add the URL of image on the Sell an Item form, you must click the Customize Form link at the top of the page and add the option to include a URL (versus using eBay picture services). Note that you get a free Preview picture at the top of your auction. Chapter 14 has more information on using images in your auction.

- ✔ **The Gallery:** By adding a picture, you can add your item's picture to eBay's photo Gallery (optional). There is no extra charge to add the item to the Gallery, but it will set you back $0.75 to have a Gallery image that gets larger when a user drags his or her mouse over it, and $19.95 to make your item a featured auction in the Gallery. (You can find more on the Gallery later in this chapter.)

- ✔ **Gallery image URL:** If you want to include a hosted image, you must include the Web address of the JPEG image you want to place in the Gallery (optional). (If you're using eBay Picture Services, the first photo you upload is resized for the Gallery.) See Chapter 14.

- ✔ **Item location:** The region, city, and country from which the item will be shipped (required).

- ✔ **Quantity:** The number of items you're offering in this auction is always one (required).

- ✔ **Starting price:** The starting price (sometimes called a *minimum bid*) you set (required).

- ✔ **Selling price:** If this is a fixed-price listing, you have to post your selling price.

✔ **Duration:** The number of days you want the auction to run (required).

✔ **Reserve price:** The hidden target price you set. This is the price that must be met before this item can be sold (optional). eBay charges you a fee for this feature.

✔ **Private auction:** You can keep the identity of all bidders secret with this option (optional). This type of auction is used only in special circumstances.

✔ **Buy It Now:** You can sell your item directly to the first buyer who meets this price (optional).

✔ **List item in two categories:** If you want to double your exposure, you can list your item in two categories. Note that double exposure equals double listing fees (optional).

✔ **Home page featured:** You can place your auction in a premium viewing section and have the possibility that your listing will cycle through the direct links from the front page (optional). eBay charges $59.95 for auction or fixed-price listings from 1 to 10 days and $179.95 extra for fixed-price items that stay on the site for 30 days.

✔ **Featured First:** You can have your auction appear at the top of the category in which you list it (optional). eBay charges $24.95 extra for this feature; $74.95 for listings that last 30 days.

✔ **Highlight:** Your item title is highlighted in the auction listings and search listings with a lilac-colored band, which may draw eBay members' eyes right to your auction (optional). eBay charges $5.00 extra for this feature and $10.00 for the 30-day listings.

✔ **Boldface title:** A selling option to make your item listing stand out. eBay charges $2.00 ($4.00 for 30 days) extra for this feature (optional).

✔ **Free counter:** If you want to avail yourself of a free counter, indicate so here (optional).

✔ **Ship-to locations:** Here's where you can indicate where you're willing to ship an item. If you don't want the hassle of shipping out of the United States, check that option only. You can individually select different countries as well (optional).

You may want to consider whether you *really* want to be in the international shipping business. Buyers pick up the tab, but you have to deal with customs forms and post office paperwork. If time is money, you may want to skip it entirely — or at least have all the forms filled out before you get in line at the post office. (Better yet, print your customs forms along with your postage from your computer — see Chapter 12). But remember that if you don't ship internationally, you're blocking a bunch of possible high bidders. Depending on what you're selling, shipping internationally may or may not be worth the investment in extra time.

- **Shipping and handling charges:** eBay requires you to show your shipping charge in the listing. Buyers are more likely to bid or buy right then and there if they feel your shipping costs are reasonable. If they have to e-mail you with questions, they may find another listing for the same item — with clear shipping — and bid or buy that one. Also, when you list a flat shipping charge on your listing, eBay will take that into account when deciding how your item shows up in Search. For larger items, see information on eBay's handy shipping calculator, later in this chapter.

- **Payment instructions:** Here's the place you put any after-sale information. You are required to accept PayPal or at least one electronic payment or Internet merchant credit card option for your items. (These are the safest options anyway.) If you want to offer the option to pay with a different electronic payment service, mention that as well. This information appears at the top of your sale when the sale is completed, under the Shipping and Payments tab of the listing while it's active, and in the End of Listing e-mail (optional).

- **PayPal and immediate payment:** Fill in this area if you want to require the high bidder to pay through PayPal immediately when using Buy It Now. Add the Immediate Payment option if you know the shipping amount and would like the winner to pay with a click of the mouse (optional).

- **Return policy:** If you are willing to accept returns, indicate it. You can give the customer as few as three days to return the item (that cuts down on spurious returns).

Filling in the Required Blanks

Yes, the Sell an Item form looks daunting, but filling out its many sections doesn't take as long as you may think. Some of the questions you're asked aren't things you even have to think about; just click an answer and off you go. Other questions ask you to type information. Don't sweat a thing; all the answers you need are right here. In this section I describe all the required info; later in this chapter, I talk about optional stuff. After you click your category, you land on the official Sell an Item page.

Selecting a category

Many eBay sellers will tell you that selecting the exact category isn't crucial to achieving the highest price for your item — and they're right. The bulk of buyers (who know what they're looking for) just input search keywords into eBay's search box and look for their items. Others, though, may select a category and, just like when you go to the mall, peruse the items for sale and see if a particular one strikes their fancy.

On the first page of the Sell an Item form, you need to select the main category for your item. Type at least three keywords that best describe your item in the box provided and click Search. Figure 10-1 shows you how the results come up after typing your words, making it easy to select a main category.

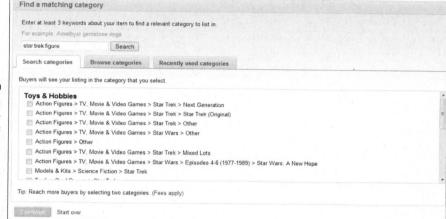

Figure 10-1: Let eBay do some of the work in finding the proper category for your item.

Here's where your creativity can come into play. Who says that a box of Blue Dog (the famous doggie icon painted by Cajun artist George Rodrigue) note cards belongs in *Everything Else: Gifts & Occasions: Greeting Cards: Other Cards.* If you look around, you may find a better category. The Find Categories tool appears the second you open the Sell an Item page. Just click the associated link to browse for categories. Check to see if anyone else is selling the item (and in which category) or just let this tool help you pick a good category.

You can also browse the categories by clicking (surprise!) the Browse Categories tab. This will help you select your main category, and the thousands of subcategories. eBay offers you this wealth of choices in a handy point-and-click way. If you're unfamiliar with the types of items you can actually *find* in those categories, you may want to pore over Chapter 3 before you choose a category to describe *your* item. Figure 10-2 shows you how to manually narrow the subcategory listings on the Sell an Item page.

To select a category, here's the drill:

1. **Click one of the main categories.**

   In the next box, you see a list of subcategories.

2. **Select the most appropriate subcategory.**

3. **Continue selecting subcategories until you have narrowed your item listing as much as possible.**

You know you've come to the last subcategory when you don't see any more right-pointing arrows in the Categories.

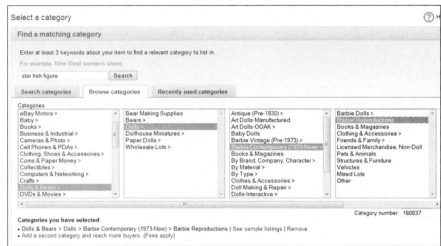

Figure 10-2:
Narrowing
your sub-
categories.

Most bidders scan for specific items in subcategories. For example, if you're selling a Bakelite fruit pin, don't just list it under Jewelry; keep narrowing your choices. In this case, you can put it in a costume jewelry category that is especially for Bakelite. I guarantee that the real Bakelite jewelry collectors out there know where to look to find the jewelry they love. To narrow the category of your item, just keep clicking until you hit the end of the line.

Some subcategories aren't for everyone

If you've chosen to list an item, bid on an item, or even just browse in the Everything Else: Mature Audiences category, you need to follow separate, specific guidelines because that category contains graphic nudity or sexual content that may offend some community members. You must

✔ Be at least 18 years of age (but you already know that all eBay customers must be 18 or older).

✔ Have a valid credit card.

✔ Complete a waiver stating that you're voluntarily choosing to access adults-only materials. For more on how to do this (and a handy primer on privacy issues), see Chapter 15.

If you have Adult/Erotica items that you'd like to sell in a private auction, study the section later in this chapter that details the Private Auction option.

Creating the perfect item title

After you figure out what category you want to list in, eBay wants to get down to the nitty-gritty — what the heck to call that thing you're trying to sell.

Think of your item title as a great newspaper headline. The most valuable real estate on eBay is the 55-character title of your item. *The majority of buyers do title searches, and that's where your item must come up to be sold!* Give the most essential information right away to grab the eye of the reader who's just browsing. Be clear and informative enough to get noticed by eBay's search engine. Figure 10-3 shows examples of good titles. Note how a few of these titles contain subtitles (more info on subtitles further in this chapter).

Tactics Ogre Prima Strategy Guide PS GBA Battle Series
Model Trains Vol 14 No 6 December 1961 Magazine Vintage   Pay Shipping on the first item only - all others free!
Gullwing Poster Mercedes Benz 300SL LARGE 28"x40" Print
New TRUE COLOR Photo Task Lamp LIGHT 13w 5000K w/BULB
White INFINITY Background Backdrop PORTABLE Photo STAGE   Take Perfect eBay pictures anywhere in your home!
100% Egyptian Cotton 3-Packs Tank tops Large size White
2000 Château Montrose Bordeaux WS 96 points Red Wine
SANTA SHOPS ON EBAY Marsha Collier New 2006 Christmas   SHOPPING HINTS FOR THE HOLIDAYS Direct from the Author
MEDIUM 10-13 lbs ~ CAT Soft Claws Paws ~ FREE TOY mice!

Figure 10-3: These item titles are effective because they're clear and concise.

Here are some ideas to help you write your item title:

- Use the most common name for the item.
- If the item is rare, vintage, or hard to find, mention that.
- State the item's condition and whether it's new or old.
- Include the item's special qualities, such as its style, model, or edition.
- Avoid fancy punctuation or unusual characters, such as $, hyphens, and L@@K, because they just clutter up the title — and buyers don't search for them.

When you get into advanced selling mode, you should take a look at one of my other books, coauthored by Patti Louise Ruby, *eBay Listings That Sell For Dummies*. It covers eBay photography and HTML in depth.

Ordinarily, I don't throw out French phrases just for the fun of it. But where making a profit is an issue, I definitely have to agree with the French that choosing or not choosing *le mot juste* can mean the difference between having potential bidders merely see your auction and having an all-out bidding war on your hands. Read on for tips about picking *the best words* to let your listing shine.

Look for a phrase that pays

Here's a crash course in eBay lingo that can help bring you up-to-speed on attracting buyers to your item. The following words are used frequently in eBay listings, and they can do wonders to jump-start your title:

- Mint
- One of a kind (or OOAK — see the abbreviation list in Table 10-1)
- Vintage
- Collectible
- Rare
- Unique
- Primitive
- Well-loved

There's a whole science (called *grading*) to figuring out the value of a collectible. You're ahead of the game if you have a pretty good idea of what most eBay members mean. Do your homework before you assign a grade to your item. If you need more information on what these grades actually mean, Chapter 5 provides a translation.

eBay lingo at a glance

Common grading terms and the phrases in the preceding section aren't the only marketing standards you have at your eBay disposal. As eBay has grown, so has the lingo that members use as shortcuts to describe their merchandise.

Table 10-1 gives you a handy list of common abbreviations and phrases used to describe items. (**Hint:** Mint means "may as well be brand new," not "cool chocolate treat attached.")

Table 10-1		A Quick List of eBay Abbreviations
eBay Code	*What It Abbreviates*	*What It Means*
MIB	Mint in Box	The item is in the original box, in great shape, and just the way you'd expect to find it in a store.
MOC	Mint on Card	The item is mounted on its original display card, attached with the original fastenings, in store-new condition.
NRFB	Never Removed from Box	Just what it says, as in "bought but never opened."
COA	Certificate of Authenticity	Documentation that vouches for the genuineness of an item, such as an autograph or painting.
OEM	Original Equipment Manufacture	You're selling the item and all the equipment that originally came with it, but you don't have the original box, owner's manual, or instructions.
OOAK	One of a Kind	You are selling the only one in existence!
NR	No Reserve Price	A reserve price is the price you can set when you begin your auction. If bids don't meet the reserve, you don't have to sell. Many buyers don't like reserve prices because they don't think that they can get a bargain. (For tips on how to allay these fears and get those bids in reserve-price auctions, see "Writing your description" later in this chapter.) If you're not listing a reserve for your item, let bidders know.
HTF, OOP	Hard to Find, Out of Print	Out of print, only a few ever made, or people grabbed up all there were. (HTF doesn't mean you spent a week looking for it in the attic.)

Often, you can rely on eBay slang to get your point across, but make sure that you mean it and that you're using it accurately. Don't label something MIB (Mint in Box) when it looks like it's been Mashed in Box by a meat grinder. You can find more abbreviations on my Web site, www.cool ebaytools.com.

Don't let your title ruin your auction

Imagine going to a supermarket and asking someone to show you where the stringy stuff that you boil is instead of asking where the spaghetti is. You might end up with mung bean sprouts — delicious to some but hardly what you had in mind. That's why you should check and recheck your spelling. Savvy buyers use the eBay search engine to find merchandise; if the name of your item is spelled wrong, the search engine can't find it. Poor spelling and incomprehensible grammar also reflect badly on you. If you're in competition with another seller, the buyer is likelier to trust the seller *hoo nose gud speling.*

If you've finished writing your item title and you have spaces left over, ***please*** fight the urge to dress it up with lots of asterisks and exclamation points!!!!!!!!!! (See how annoying that is?) No matter how gung-ho you are about your item, the eBay search engine may overlook your item if the title is encrusted with meaningless **** and !!!! symbols. If bidders do see your title, they may become annoyed by the virtual shrillness and ignore it anyway!!!!!!! (It's even more annoying the second time around.)

Another distracting habit is overdoing capital letters. To buyers, seeing everything in caps is LIKE SEEING A CRAZED SALESMAN SCREAMING AT THEM TO BUY NOW! Using all caps is considered *shouting,* which is rude and tough on the eyes. Use capitalization SPARINGLY, and only to finesse a particular point.

Giving the title punch with a subtitle

A new feature on eBay is the availability of subtitles. eBay allows you to buy an additional 55 characters, which will appear under your item title in a search. The fee for this extra promotion is $0.50, and in a few circumstances, it is definitely worth your while. Any text that you input will really make your item stand out in the crowd — but (you knew there would be a *but* didn't you?) these additional 55 characters won't come up in a title search. In other words, if the subtitle includes essential information ("NR MIMB," for example) that isn't in the main title, people searching for *NR MIMB* won't find your listing. So if you have all those words in your description, the words will be found either way with a title and description search. If you choose this option, choose attention-getting info that isn't absolutely needed for the title itself.

Writing your description

After you hook potential bidders with your title, reel 'em in with a fabulous description. Don't think Hemingway here; think infomercial (the classier the better). Figure 10-4 shows a great description of some silver dollars. You can write a magnificent description, as well — all you have to do is click in the box and start typing.

UNCIRCULATED MS63+ 1896 Morgan Silver Dollar

I recently purchased a group of MS63+ Morgan Silver Dollars from a long time collector to sell on ebay. The ones I've already sold have been very well received *(please look at my feedback)*. This is your chance to own a beautiful 1896 Morgan Silver Dollar in Premium Quality Brilliant Uncirculated Condition. Bright and well struck, it has very clean surfaces with very sharp features and details. The picture below doesn't do justice to this striking coin. It will make a lovely addition to any coin collection or a great start towards a new one.

Bid with confidence and bid whatever you feel this coin is worth to you as it is selling with NO RESERVE! Winning bidder to pay shipping & handling of $2.50, and must submit payment within a week of winning the auction. Credit cards are accepted through Paypal.com. Good luck!
Click below to...
Win another of my auctions and Save on shipping!

Figure 10-4:
Writing a good description can mean the difference between success and failure.

Here's a list of suggestions for writing an item description:

- **Accentuate the positive:** Give the buyer a reason to buy your item and be enthusiastic when you list all the reasons everyone should bid on it. Unlike the title, you can use as much space as you want. Even if you use a photo, be precise in your description — its size, color, kind of fabric, design, and so on. Refer to "Creating the perfect item title" earlier in this chapter, as well as Table 10-1, for ideas on what to emphasize and how to word your description.

- **Include the negative:** Don't hide the truth of your item's condition. Trying to conceal flaws costs you in the long run: You'll get tagged with bad feedback. If the item has a scratch, a nick, a dent, a crack, a ding, a tear, a rip, missing pieces, replacement parts, faded color, dirty smudges, or a bad smell (especially if cleaning might damage the item), mention it in the description. If your item has been overhauled, rebuilt, repainted, or hot-rodded (say, a "Pentium computer" that was a 386 until you put in the new motherboard), say so. You don't want the buyer to send back your merchandise because you weren't truthful about imperfections or modifications. This type of omission can lead to a fraud investigation.

- **Be precise about all the logistical details of the post-auction transaction:** Even though you're not required to list any special S&H (shipping and handling) or payment requirements in your item description, the majority of eBay users do. Try to figure out the cost of shipping the item in the United States and add that to your description. If you offer shipping insurance, add it to your item description.

✔ **While you're at it, promote yourself too:** As you accumulate positive feedback, tell potential bidders about your terrific track record. Add statements like "I'm great to deal with. Check out my feedback section." You can even take it a step further by inviting prospective bidders to your About Me page (where you may also include a link to your personal Web site — if you have one). Chapter 14 gives you some tips on how to make your auction seen by a wider audience.

✔ **Wish your potential bidders well:** Communication is the key to a good transaction, and you can set the tone for your auction and post-auction exchanges by including some simple phrases that show your friendly side. Always end your description by wishing bidders good luck, inviting potential bidders to e-mail you with questions, and offering the option of providing additional photos of the item if you have them.

When you input your description, you have the option of jazzing things up with a bit of HTML coding, or you can use eBay's HTML text editor, shown in Figure 10-5. If you know how to use a word processor, you'll have no trouble touching up your text with this tool. Table 10-2 shows you a few additional codes to help you pretty things up.

Figure 10-5:
The HTML text editor shows you the description area with HTML-coded text and free photo inserted.

Table 10-2	A Short List of HTML Codes	
HTML Code	**How to Use It**	**What It Does**
`<b></b>`	`<b>cool collectible</b>`	**cool collectible** (bold type)
`<i></i>`	`<i>cool collectible</i>`	*cool collectible* (italic type)

HTML Code	How to Use It	What It Does
`<b><i></i></b>`	`<b><i>cool collectible</b></i>`	***cool collectible*** (bold and italic type)
`<font color=red></font>`	`<font color=red>cool collectible</font>`	Selected text appears in red. (This book is in black and white so you can't see it.)
`<font size=+1></font>`	`<font size=+3>cool</font> collectible`	cool collectible (font size normal +1 through 4, increases size *x* times)
` `	`cool collectible`	cool collectible (inserts line break)
`<p>`	`cool<p>collectible`	cool collectible (inserts paragraph space)
`<hr>`	`cool collectible<hr>cheap`	cool collectible ――――― cheap (inserts horizontal rule)
`<h1><h1>`	`<h1>cool collectible</h1>`	***cool collectible*** (converts text to headline size)

You can go back and forth from the HTML text editor to regular input and add additional codes here and there by clicking from the Standard form to the HTML entry form tabs. I often prepare all my auctions ahead of time and save them in my computer as plain HTML files — that way they're always retrievable for use (I just copy and paste) — no matter what program or form I'm using to list my auctions. See Chapter 20 for more on software to help you with your auctions.

To insert additional photos in your description (thereby avoiding eBay's additional photo charges), use the following code. (Just insert the URL of your hosted picture, along with the photo file name). My example in Figure 10-5 uses the following code:

```
<img src="http://www.collierad.com/catbed.jpg">
```

Occasionally, sellers offer an item as a *presell,* or an item that the seller doesn't yet have in stock but expects to. If you're offering this kind of item, make sure that you spell out all the details in the description. eBay policy states that you must ship a presell item within 30 days of the auction's end, so be sure you will have the item within that time span. Don't forget to include the actual shipping date. I have found that putting an item up for sale without having it in hand is a practice fraught with risk. The item you're expecting may not arrive in time or may arrive damaged. I've heard of one too many sellers who have had to go out and purchase an item at retail for a buyer to preserve their feedback when caught in this situation.

Listing the number of items for sale

Unless you're planning on holding a Multiple Item listing or Dutch auction, the number of items is always 1, which means you're holding a traditional auction or listing a single item up for sale. If you need to change the quantity number from 1, just type the number in the box.

A matching set of cuff links is considered one item, as is the complete 37-volume set of *The Smith Family Ancestry and Genealogical History since 1270.* If you have more than one of the same item (two sets of cuff links), I suggest that you sell them one at a time. You are much more likely to get higher final bids for your items when you sell them individually. Never try to sell items that belong in a set as separate items.

eBay won't allow you to list the same item in more than 15 auctions at one time.

Setting a starting price — how low can you go?

What do a baseball autographed by JFK, a used walkie-talkie, and a Jaguar sports car all have in common? They all started with a $0.99 starting price. eBay requires you to set a *starting price,* also called a minimum bid — the lowest bid allowed in an auction. You may be surprised to see stuff worth tens of thousands of dollars starting at just a buck. These sellers haven't lost their minds. Neither are they worried someone could be tooling down the highway in a $100,000 sports car they bought for the price of a burger.

Setting an incredibly low minimum (just type it in the box *without* the dollar sign but *with* the decimal point) is a subtle strategy that gives you more bang for your buck. You can use a low starting price to attract more bidders who will, in turn, drive up the price to the item's real value — especially if, after doing your research, you know that the item is particularly hot.

If you're worried about the outcome of the final bid, you can protect your item by using a *reserve price* (the price the bidding needs to reach before the item can be sold). Then you won't have to sell your item for a bargain-basement price because your reserve price protects your investment. The best advice is to set a reserve price that is the lowest amount you'll take for your item and then set a minimum bid that is ridiculously low. Use a reserve only when absolutely necessary because some bidders pass up reserve auctions. (For more info about setting a reserve price, see the section "Your secret safety net — reserve price," later in this chapter.)

Starting with a low starting price is also good for your pocketbook. eBay charges the seller an insertion fee based on your opening bid. If you keep your opening bid low and set no reserve, you get to keep more of your money. (See Chapter 9 for more about eBay fees.)

The more bids you get, the more people who will want to bid on your item because they perceive the item as hot. A hot item with lots of bids draws even more bidders the way a magnet attracts paper clips.

Before you set any starting price, do your homework and make some savvy marketing decisions. If your auction isn't going as you hoped, you *could* end up selling Grandma Ethel's Ming vase for a dollar. Think about your strategy. See "Midcourse Corrections: Fixing Current Auctions" later in this chapter on how you can make changes in your listing if you've made some egregious error.

When entering a starting price, type only the numbers and a decimal point. Don't use dollar signs ($) or cents signs (¢).

Buy It Now

eBay's Buy It Now (*BIN* in eBay-speak) is available for single-item auctions. This feature allows buyers who want to purchase an item *now* to do so. Have you ever wanted an item really badly and didn't want to wait until the end of an auction? If the seller offers Buy It Now, you can purchase that item immediately. If you're the seller, you can entice your bidders to pay just a tad more to have the satisfaction of walking away with the item free and clear. Just specify the amount the item can sell for in the Buy It Now price area — the amount can be whatever you want. If you choose to take advantage of selling a hot item during the holiday rush, for example, you can make the BIN price as high as you think it can go. If you just want the item to move, make your BIN price the average price you see the item go for on eBay.

When your item receives a bid, the BIN option disappears, and the item goes through the normal auction process. If you have a reserve price on your item, the BIN feature doesn't disappear until a bidder meets your reserve price through the normal bidding process. To list an item with Buy It Now, you must have a feedback of 10 or be ID Verified. (See Chapter 16 for more details on ID Verify.)

Setting your auction time

How long do you want to run your auction? eBay gives you a choice — 1, 3, 5, 7, or 10 days. Just click the number you want in the box. If you choose a 10-day auction, you add $0.40 to your listing fee.

My auction-length strategy depends on the time of year and the item I'm selling, and I generally have great success. If you have an item that you think will sell pretty well, run a 7-day auction (be sure it will cover a full weekend) so bidders have time to check it out before they decide to bid. However, if you know that you have a red-hot item that's going to fly off the shelves — like a rare toy or a hard-to-get video game — choose a 3-day auction. Eager bidders tend to bid higher and more often to beat out their competition if the item is hot and going fast. Three days is long enough to give trendy items exposure and ring up bids.

No matter how many days you choose to run your auction, it ends at exactly the same time of day as it starts. A 7-day auction that starts on Thursday at 9:03:02 a.m. ends the following Thursday at 9:03:02 a.m.

Although I know the gang at eBay is a pretty laid back group, they do run on military time. That means they use a 24-hour clock set to Pacific Time. So 3:30 in the afternoon is 15:30, and one minute after midnight is 00:01. Questions about time conversions? Check out www.timezoneconverter.com or look at the table on my Web site in the Tools area, which has a printable conversion chart of eBay times (www.coolebaytools.com). (And so you don't have to keep flipping back to this page, I also include these handy-dandy links on the Cheat Sheet at the front of this book.)

With auctions running 24 hours a day, 7 days a week, you should know when the most bidders are around to take a gander at your wares. Here are some times to think about:

✔ **Saturday/Sunday:** Always run an auction over a weekend. People log on and off eBay all day.

Don't start or end your auction on a Saturday or Sunday — *unless* your completed auction research indicates that you should. Certain types of bidders love sitting at their computers waiting for auctions to end on the weekends, but many bidders are busy having lives, and their schedules are unpredictable. Although a few eager bidders may log on and place a maximum bid on your auction, you can bet that they won't be sitting at a computer making a last-minute flurry of competitive bids if they have something better to do on a Saturday or Sunday.

✔ **Holiday weekends:** If a holiday weekend is coming up around the time you're setting up your auction, run your auction through the weekend and end it a day after the "holiday" Monday. This gives prospective bidders a chance to catch up with the items they perused over the weekend and to plan their bidding strategies.

Don't end an auction on the last day of a three-day holiday. People in the mood to shop are generally at department stores collecting bargains. If eBay members aren't shopping, they're out enjoying an extra day off.

✔ **Time of day:** The best times of day to start and end your auction are during eBay's peak hours of operation, which are 5:00 p.m. to 9:00 p.m. Pacific Time, right after work on the West Coast. Perform your completed auction research, however, to be sure that this strategy applies to your item. Your timing depends on the item you're listing and whether 5:00 p.m. to 9:00 p.m. Pacific Time is the middle of the night where you live.

Unless you're an insomniac or a vampire and want to sell to werewolves, don't let your auctions close in the middle of the night. Not enough bidders are around to cause any last-minute bidding that would bump up the price.

Your secret safety net — reserve price

Here's a little secret: The reason sellers list big-ticket items like Ferraris, grand pianos, and high-tech computer equipment with a starting bid of $1.00 is because they're protected from losing money with a *reserve price.* The reserve price is the lowest price that must be met before the item can be sold. It's not required by eBay but can protect you. eBay charges an additional fee for this feature that varies, depending on how high your reserve is.

For example, say you list a first edition book of John Steinbeck's *The Grapes of Wrath.* You set the starting price at $1.00, and you set a reserve price at $80.00. That means that people can start bidding at $1.00, and if at the end of the auction the bidding hasn't reached the $80.00 reserve, you don't have to sell the book.

As with everything in life, using a reserve price for your auctions has an upside and a downside. Many choosy bidders and bargain hunters blast past reserve-price auctions because they see a reserve price as a sign that proclaims "No bargains here!" Many bidders figure they can get a better deal on the same item with an auction that proudly declares *NR* (for *no reserve*) in its description. As an enticement to those bidders, you see lots of NR listings in auction titles.

If you need to set a reserve on your item, help the bidder out. Many bidders shy away from an auction that has a reserve, but if they're really interested, they will read the item description. To dispel their fears that the item is way too expensive or out of their price range, add a line in your description that states the amount of your reserve price. "I have put a reserve of $75.00 on this item to protect my investment; the highest bid over $75.00 will win the item." A phrase such as this takes away the vagueness of the reserve auction and allows you to place a reserve with a low opening bid. (You want to reel 'em in, remember?)

On lower-priced items, I suggest that you set a higher starting price and set no reserve. Otherwise, if you're not sure about the market, set a low minimum bid but set a high reserve to protect yourself.

If bids don't reach a set reserve price, some sellers e-mail the highest bidder and offer the item at what the seller thinks is a fair price. Sending a Second Chance offer through the eBay system makes much more sense. Two caveats if you try to circumvent eBay fees and contact the bidders:

- ✔ eBay can suspend the seller *and* the buyer if the side deal is reported to Trust & Safety. This activity is strictly prohibited.

- ✔ eBay won't protect buyers or sellers if a side deal goes bad.

I want to be alone: the private auction

In a private auction, bidders' user IDs are kept under wraps. Sellers typically use this option to protect the identities of bidders during auctions for high-priced big-ticket items (say, that restored World War II fighter). Wealthy eBay users may not want the world to know that they have the resources to buy expensive items. Private auctions are also held for items from the Adult/Erotica category. (Gee, there's a shocker.)

The famous sign that was pictured in almost every Disneyland promotion (for the first 40 or so years of Disneyland's existence) was put up for sale on eBay in 2000. Legend has it that the sign was purchased by actor John Stamos for a high bid of $30,700. Unfortunately for John, the Disney auction did not use the private auction feature. After news of the winner's name hit the tabloids, the entire world knew John's eBay user ID! He had to change his ID in a hurry to end the throngs of lovey-dovey e-mail headed to his computer!

In private auctions, the seller's e-mail address is accessible to bidders in case questions arise. Bidders' e-mail addresses remain unseen.

Put me in the Gallery

The Gallery is a legacy term that refers to the single picture you post to accompany your listing. It also causes a postage-stamp-size version of your image to appear next to your listing in the category or search. Many buyers enjoy browsing the Gallery catalog-style, and it's open to all categories. (I explain how to post your pictures in Chapter 14.)

The best things about using a Gallery picture in your listings are that it's *free* and it increases the space your listing takes up on a search or category page. If you don't use a Gallery picture and just have an image in your description, your listing will get very few hits.

Filling out the item location

eBay wants you to list the general area and country where you live. The idea behind telling the bidder where you live is to give him or her a heads-up on what kind of shipping charges to expect. Don't be esoteric (listing where you live as *The Here and Now* isn't a whole lot of help) but don't go crazy with cross-streets, landmarks, or degrees of latitude. Listing your city and state is enough.

If you live in a big area — say, suburban Los Angeles (who, me?), which sprawls for miles — you may want to think about narrowing your region a little. You may find a bidder who lives close to you, which could swing your auction. If you do a face-to-face transaction, doing it in a public place is a good idea. (I picked up an eBay purchase at Starbucks recently.)

A picture is worth a thousand words

Clichés again? Perhaps. But an item on eBay without a picture is almost a waste of time. If you haven't set up photo hosting elsewhere, you can list one picture with eBay's Pictures Service for free. Additional ones cost you $0.15 each. Alternatively, you can put all the pictures you want in your auction description for free. See Chapter 14 for the necessary coding and instructions.

Listing Designer

How many times have you seen an item on eBay laid out on the page all pretty-like with a fancy border around the description? If that sort of thing appeals to you, eBay's Listing Designer will supply you with pretty borders for almost any type of item for $0.10. Selecting your design is as easy as clicking the menu (see Figure 10-6). You can designate where you'd like to place your image on the page relative to the description (left, right, top, or bottom).

Figure 10-6:
Selecting
a graphic
in Listing
Designer is
as simple
as clicking
your mouse.

Will the pretty borders increase the amount of bids your auction will get? It's doubtful. A clean item description with a few good clear pictures of your item is really all you need.

There's a special combination deal called the Value Pack. For $0.65, you can place a subtitle on your listing, add a Gallery Plus picture, and doll things up with Listing Designer. All those features would normally cost $0.95, so the savings is clear if you run several listings a week.

If you don't want to use the Listing Designer graphics to distract from your item, you can still get a discount. Just select the Listing Designer check box, but *don't* choose a graphic pattern. You'll still save $0.30 over the price of a subtitle and Gallery (sneaky, huh?).

Listing the payment methods you'll accept

Yeah, sure, eBay is loads of fun, but the bottom line to selling is the phrase "Show me the money!" eBay allows the following payment options: PayPal, credit or debit card processed through an Internet merchant account, ProPay, Moneybookers, and or Paymate. You make the call on what you're willing to take as money from the buyer of your item.

So as not to confuse you here — just accept PayPal! As a new seller you have enough on your plate without worrying about several payment options. By the way, this advice isn't just for beginners — I accept only PayPal in my listings.

In some cases, you may still accept checks and money orders in certain categories. Since these categories can change per eBay's policy, I suggest you check `http://pages.ebay.com/help/policies/accepted-payments-policy.html` to see if your category is listed.

eBay's rules say that you must clearly state the payment methods you accept and can't make generalized statements or ask buyers to contact you for additional payment methods.

Some sellers who use credit card services try attaching an additional fee (to cover their credit card processing fees) to the final payment. However, that's against the law in California, home of eBay, and therefore against eBay's rules. So forget about it. eBay can end your auction if it catches you.

Setting shipping terms

Ahoy, matey! Hoist the bid! Okay, not quite. Before you run it up the mast, select your shipping options. Here are your choices:

- ✔ **Ship to the United States only:** This option is selected by default; it means you ship only domestically.

- ✔ **Will ship worldwide:** The world is your oyster. But make sure that you can afford the time for the extra processing of customs forms.

- ✔ **Will ship to United States and the following:** If you're comfortable shipping to certain countries but not to others, make your selections here; they show up on your auction page.

When you indicate that you will ship internationally, your auction shows up on the international eBay sites, which is a fantastic way to attract new buyers! eBay has lots of good international users, so you may want to consider selling your items around the world. If you do, be sure to clearly state in the description all extra shipping costs and customs charges. (See Chapter 12 for more information on how to ship to customers abroad.)

Traditionally, the buyer pays for shipping, and this is the point at which you must decide how much to charge. You also have to calculate how much this item will cost you to ship. If it's a small item (weighing under a pound or so), you may decide to charge a flat rate to all buyers. To charge a flat rate, click the Flat Shipping Rates tab and fill in the shipping amount. Before you fill in the amount, be sure to include your costs for packing (see Chapter 12 for more info on how much to add for this task) and how much the insurance charges will be.

If your item weighs 2 pounds or more, you may want to use eBay's versatile shipping calculator. Because UPS and the U.S. Postal Service now charge variable rates for packages of the same weight, based on distance, using the calculator simplifies things for your customers (and you). Be sure you've weighed the item and know how much your handling charge will be. The calculator allows you to input a handling amount and adds it to the overall shipping total but does not break out the amount separately for the customer. The calculator also conveniently calculates the proper insurance amount for the item. Figure 10-7 shows how simple the form is.

Figure 10-7:
The correct shipping amount is automatically posted on the buyer's view of your listing, based on his or her registered zip code.

	Shipping Calculator

Package Description
Package (or thick envelope) (0 lbs. 6 oz.) Change

Seller's ZIP Code
90210 Change

Packaging and Handling Fee
$0.00 Change

Compare services and costs
To calculate Domestic or International rates for various shipping services, select a destination or enter a ZIP code below and click **Show Rates**.

Domestic Rates
Sample Rates ▾   ZIP Code:
Show Rates

International Rates
Worldwide Sample Rates ▾
Show Rates

UNITED STATES POSTAL SERVICE.   ups

To add services to your listing (up to three), use the checkboxes below and click **Offer Services**.
Offer Services   Close

UPS prices based on UPS Retail Rates.

	Chicago	New York City	Los Angeles		Chicago	New York City	Los Angeles
US Postal Service First Class Mail®	$2.02	$2.02	$2.02	UPS Ground	$10.19	$10.37	$9.00
Estimated delivery 2-5 days				Guaranteed in 1-6 days*			
US Postal Service Parcel Post®	$4.55	$4.55	$4.02	UPS 3 Day Select℠	$16.16	$16.56	$9.75
Estimated delivery 2-9 days				Guaranteed in 1-3 days*			
US Postal Service Priority Mail®	$4.95	$4.95	$4.95	UPS 2nd Day Air®	$21.06	$21.36	$14.80
				Guaranteed in 1-2 days*			

The calculator automatically appears on the item page so that prospective buyers can type in their zip code and immediately know how much shipping will be to their location. Check out Chapter 12 for more information on shipping options.

eBay Options: Getting Eyes on Your Item

Although eBay's display options aren't quite as effective as a three-story neon sign in Times Square, they do bring greater attention to your auction. Here are your options:

✔ **Bold:** The eBay fee is $2.00 ($4.00 for a 30-day listing). Bold type does catch your attention but don't bother using it on items that'll bring in less than $25.00. Do use it if you're in hot competition with similar items and you want yours to stand out.

✔ **Highlight:** The eBay fee is $5.00 ($10.00 for a 30-day listing). Yellow highlighter is what I use to point out the high points in books I read. (You're using one now, aren't you?) The eBay highlight feature is lilac, but it can really make your item shine. Check out the category in which you choose to list before selecting this feature. Some categories are overwhelmed with sellers using the highlight option, and the pages look completely shaded in lilac. In these categories, *not* using highlight (and using perhaps a bold title instead) makes your auction stand out more.

✔ **Home Page Featured:** The eBay fee is $59.95 ($179.95 for a 30-day listing). As with expensive real estate, you pay a premium for location, location, location. The $59.95 gives you the highest level of visibility on eBay, and it occasionally appears smack dab in the middle of the eBay home page (although there's no guarantee that it will). Figure 10-8 shows the featured listings on eBay's home page.

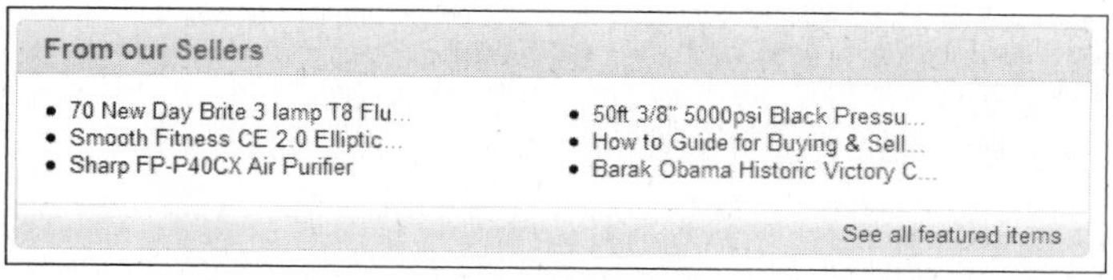

Figure 10-8:
If you're lucky, your Home Page Featured listing will rotate through the home page at a premium time of day.

From our Sellers

- 70 New Day Brite 3 lamp T8 Flu...
- Smooth Fitness CE 2.0 Elliptic...
- Sharp FP-P40CX Air Purifier
- 50ft 3/8" 5000psi Black Pressu...
- How to Guide for Buying & Sell...
- Barak Obama Historic Victory C...

See all featured items

Buyers do browse the Featured Items to see what's there, just as you might head directly to the New Releases section of your video store. But, because the vast majority of items found on eBay are under $25.00, the average seller doesn't use the Featured Items option.

✔ **Featured Plus!** The eBay fee is from $9.95 to $19.95 based on your starting price. You want top billing? You can buy it here. This option puts you on the first page of your item category and search results pages. This is a good option for moving special merchandise. Often, bidders just scan the top items; if you want to be seen, you gotta be there. Ask yourself this: Is it worth $20.00 to have more people see my item? If yes, go for it. Figure 10-9 shows how items are listed in the Featured Plus! listings.

You need a feedback rating of at least 10 to make it to the Featured Items and Featured Plus! listings.

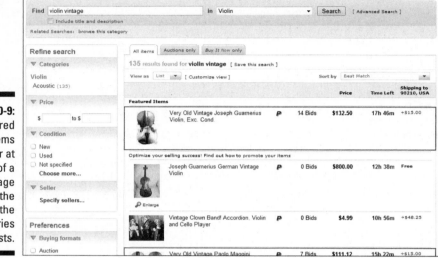

Figure 10-9:
Featured
items
appear at
the top of a
search page
or at the
top of the
Categories
lists.

Checking Your Work and Starting the Auction

After you've filled in all the blanks on the Sell an Item form, you come to the Preview Your Listing page. Scroll down the page and confirm that all the information appears as you intended. If you think you're ready to join the world of e-commerce, follow these steps:

1. **Under the heading titled How Your Listing Will Appear in Search Results, click the Preview Your Listing link.**

   A pop-up page opens showing you exactly how your listing will appear on eBay (see Figure 10-10). This is the place where you can catch mistakes before your item is listed. The bottom of the sell page shows you a condensed version of all your information and tallies how much eBay is charging you in fees and options to run this listing.

   You also may find the preview page helpful as a last-minute chance to get your bearings. You can go back to any of the areas that need correcting by clicking the Edit Listings links on the Preview Your Listing page. Make category changes or any other changes and additions, and then head for the Verification page again.

Figure 10-10:
The Preview
Your Listing
link is the
last place
you can
double-
check
for errors
before
the listing
begins.

2. **Check for mistakes.**

   Nit-pick for common, careless errors; you won't be sorry. I've seen eBay members make goofs such as the wrong category listing, spelling and grammatical errors, and missing information about shipping, handling, insurance, and payment methods.

3. **When you're sure everything's accurate and you're happy with your item listing, click the Submit button.**

   A Confirmation page pops up. At that precise moment, your listing begins, even though it may be a few hours before it appears in eBay's search and listings updates. If you want to see your listing right away and check for bids, your Confirmation page provides a link for that purpose. Click the link, and you're there. You can also keep track of your auctions by using the My eBay page. (To find out how, see Chapter 4.)

All item pages come with this friendly warning: *Seller assumes all responsibility for listing this item. You should contact the seller to resolve any questions before bidding.* Some eBay veterans just gloss over this warning after they've been wheeling and dealing for a while, but it's an important rule to remember. See Chapter 9 for details on the rules sellers must follow and Chapter 12 for tips on your role in closing the deal and receiving good feedback.

For the first 24 hours after your sale is underway, eBay stamps the Item page with a funky sunrise icon next to the listing. This is just a little reminder for buyers to come take a look at the latest items up for sale.

Midcourse Corrections: Fixing Current Listings

Don't worry if you make a mistake filling out the Sell an Item page but don't notice it until after the auction is up and running. Pencils have erasers, and eBay allows revisions. You can make changes at two stages of the game: before the first bid is placed and after the bidding war is underway. The following sections explain what you can and can't correct — and when you have to accept the little imperfections of your Item page.

Making changes before bidding begins

Here's what you can change about your listing before bids have been placed (and when it does not end within 12 hours):

- The title or description of your auction
- The item category
- The item's starting price
- The item's Buy It Now price
- The reserve price (you can add, change, or remove it)
- The duration of your listing
- The URL of the picture you're including with your auction
- A private listing designation (you can add or remove it)
- Accepted payment methods, checkout information, item location, and shipping terms

When you revise a listing, eBay puts a little notation on your auction page that reads: `Description(revised)`. (Think of it as automatic common courtesy.)

To revise a fixed-price listing or any auction before bids have been received, follow these steps:

1. **Go to your My eBay page and find the item you want to revise. Click the Revise link from the drop-down menu on the right side of the item.**

   If the item hasn't received any bids, a message appears on your screen to indicate that you may update the item.

2. **You arrive at the Revise Item page, which looks like the Sell an Item form.**

3. **Make changes to the item information and then click the Save and Continue button at the bottom of the page when you're finished.**

   A summary of your newly revised auction page appears on your screen.

4. **If you're happy with your revisions, click Save Changes.**

   You're taken to your newly revised item page, where you see a disclaimer from eBay that says you've revised the listing before the first bid. If you instead want to make further revisions, click the Back button of your browser and redo the Edit Your Listing page.

Making changes after bidding begins

If your listing is up and running and already receiving bids, you can still make some slight modifications to it. Newly added information is clearly separated from the original text and pictures. In addition, eBay puts a time stamp on the additional info in case questions from early bidders crop up later.

After your item receives bids, eBay allows you to add to your item's description. If you feel you were at a loss for words in writing your item's description, if you discover new information (that vase you thought was a reproduction is actually the real thing!), or if a lot of potential bidders are asking the same questions, go ahead and make all the additions you want. But whatever you put there the first time around stays in the description as well.

Don't let an oversight grow into a failure to communicate and don't ignore iffy communication until the auction is over. Correct any inaccuracies in your auction information now to avoid problems later.

Always check your e-mail to see whether bidders have questions about your item. If a bidder wants to know about flaws, be truthful and courteous when returning e-mails. As you get more familiar with eBay (and with writing auction descriptions), the number of e-mail questions will decrease. If you enjoy good customer service in your day-to-day shopping, here's your chance to give some back.

Chapter 11

Save Gas — Drive Your Mouse to an eBay Store

Sometimes you just don't want to participate in an auction. Sometimes you want to buy your item *now*. The easiest place to go for this type of transaction is to purchase an item from a fixed-price listing or from an eBay store, where you find ready-to-buy items. Visiting the stores can save you money because buying multiple items from one seller allows several items to be shipped in a single box. Even if the items have to be shipped separately, many sellers will discount shipping costs on multiple purchases.

Much of the fine merchandise that you can find on eBay can be found also in the eBay Stores area. Regular eBay sellers run these stores, which are located in a separate area from the regular auctions. eBay Stores is a place where sellers can list as many additional items for sale as they'd like for a reduced insertion fee. Buyers are lured to the store by the small red eBay Stores icon that appears next to the seller's user ID.

Whenever you're looking at an auction and you see that the seller has a store, be sure to click the Stores icon. The seller may have the same (or similar) merchandise in his or her eBay store for a lower buy price.

If sellers have an eBay store, they can list individual items for different sizes of an article of clothing, different variations of items that they sell in regular auctions, or anything that falls within eBay's listing policies. The store items have a listing time of at least 30 days, so sellers can also put up specialty items that may not sell well in a short auction term of only one to ten days.

The requirements to open an eBay store are basic. However, I highly recommend that you transact business (sell) on the site for quite a while before you open a store because you need a solid understanding of how eBay works and how to handle all types of transactions. These are eBay's requirements:

✔ You must be registered as an eBay seller, with a credit card on file.

✔ You must have a feedback rating of 20 or more (or be ID Verified).

✔ You must accept credit card payments, either through PayPal or through a merchant account.

The eBay search engine does not directly search the eBay Stores area. If you perform a search on eBay, be sure to scroll to the bottom of the page to see whether the particular item is available in an eBay store. Store inventory listings appear in the search results when there are 30 or fewer listings for the item on the core eBay site.

To get to the eBay Stores main area, visit the eBay home page and click the Stores link, which is below the search box on the upper portion of the page (see Figure 11-1). Alternatively, you can type **www.ebaystores.com** in the address box of your Web browser.

Figure 11-1:
A quick click on the Stores link takes you to the eBay Stores hub.

Unlimited Shopping from the Stores Page

Okay, you've arrived! You've come to the hub of power shopping online, the eBay Stores home page (see Figure 11-2). Just like the eBay home page, this is your gateway to many incredible bargains. In this section, you find out what you can expect to find in eBay's stores, how to navigate the stores, and how to find the deals.

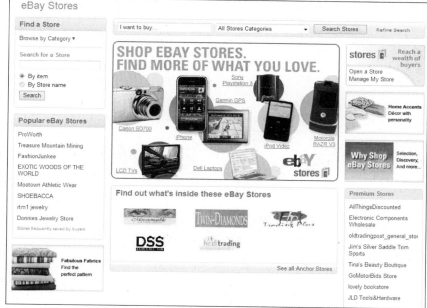

Figure 11-2: The eBay Stores home page, where you can search stores by item or store name.

Conducting an eBay Stores search

On the top-left of the eBay Stores home page is the search engine for eBay Stores. The store search link is available also by clicking the Buy button in the navigation bar. (There's a search box on the resulting page; just below it is an eBay Stores Search link.) You can perform your search in eBay stores on different levels. You can search for Buy It Now items — seems a tad too obvious for me, isn't that why we're here? Anyway, if you type your keyword in the box and stay with the default search, you can find every piece of the fixed-price inventory in the stores that matches your keyword.

eBay Stores don't just list fixed-price items. If sellers have current auctions on eBay, those auctions are listed in their stores as well — only regular auctions won't come up in an eBay Stores item search. So if you find an auction that interests you on eBay, click the item to read the description and the condition of the item. If you want to buy the item, click the Visit My eBay Store link next to the store name on the top of the item page and you go to the seller's eBay store. You just may find some related items that you want. And the seller probably combines shipping so that you save some money!

If you remember a particular seller's store name (or part of it), you can also search eBay Stores by store name. All you have to do is type the store name (or part of the store name) in the Search Stores box and click the Search Store Name and Description button to produce the results shown in Figure 11-3.

Figure 11-3: Results for finding a store by name.

If you can't remember the store name but can remember what it sells, type the keywords in the search box while selecting the Stores with Matching Items option. For example, you can search for *terrier t-shirts*. If the seller has used those words in his or her store description or title, it shows up in the search results listing. In Figure 11-4, I typed the name of one of my books and was transported to my own store.

Browsing the store categories

Browsing store categories is a great idea when you're looking for a specialist — you know, someone who carries a particular type of item that appeals to you. Perhaps you have an affinity for jewelry, art, limited edition books, or needlepoint. Whatever your interest, you'll probably find a store here to suit your needs.

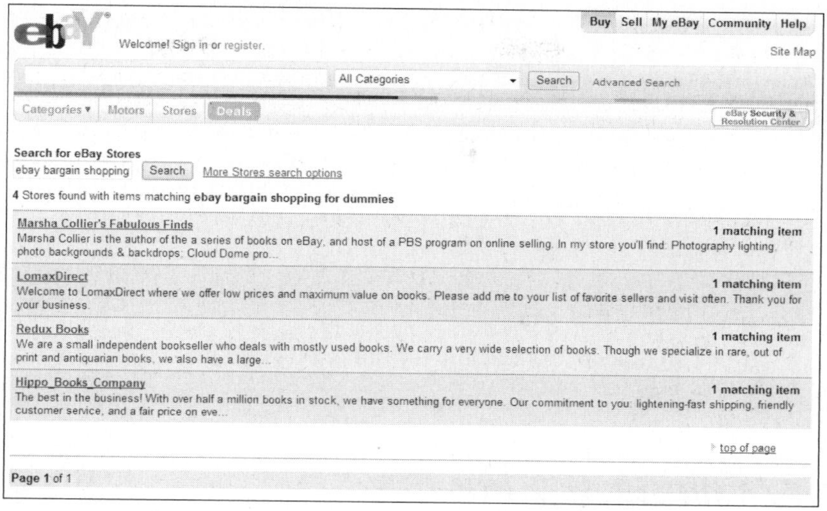

Figure 11-4:
Search
results for
Stores with
Matching
Items in the
store.

To browse eBay Stores, just click Buy in the navigation bar on any eBay page. Near the very bottom of the page on the bottom link area, click the Browse Stores link, and you travel to the eBay Stores hub. Look for a list of categories on the left side of page; click a category that suits your fancy. When you do that, the left side of the page (surprise!) lists subcategories within that category. I clicked the category Coins and then the subcategory U.S. Coins, and got the subcategory hub page.

Browsing eBay Stores categories is like strolling down a mall filled with your favorite items. Note that stores with the highest inventories in the category are listed toward the top.

Just like in the brick-and-mortar world, more "general" stores on eBay carry a wide breadth of merchandise. By browsing individual categories, you may be missing them. Try visiting the Everything Else category, and you'll find, well, everything else.

Selling from Your Own Virtual Storefront

After you've shopped the eBay Stores, you may be thinking that this is a good place to open your own store. There's great news on that end because eBay Stores have the most reasonable rent on the Internet. At an eBay Store, you are not constrained by the auction format of a 1-to-10-day maximum. You can list your fixed-price items in your eBay store on a "good till cancelled" basis.

I don't like to pull punches with my readers, so let me give you a bit of advice. Opening an eBay store without a large stock of items, or many items that you stock in multiples, makes no sense. Opening an eBay store is really for experienced sellers — those who make a business on the eBay site selling merchandise they've bought for the purpose of reselling. Retailers who come to the eBay site to expand their business can be successful with the stores, but certainly it helps to know the e-commerce ropes already. (You can always read my *eBay Business All-In-One Reference,* 2nd edition (Wiley) to catch up on all you need to know).

Too many readers new to eBay e-mail me after reading this book and tell me that they opened a store and have had no sales. You must list a bunch of items on eBay in the auction format (or fixed price) to draw people to your store — simple as that.

Paying the landlord

The rent for an eBay store is as low as $15.95 per month. Featured stores have a rent of $49.95, and anchor stores (just like your local department store) pay $299.95 a month. Featured stores' listings are guaranteed to rotate through the special featured section on the eBay Stores home page. These listings also appear on the top level of their category directory page. Anchor stores get extra promotion, and their logos are showcased in the stores' directory pages. There are also other benefits to owning a store: cost-per-click advertising, sales management tools, and lots of promotional benefits for your merchandise.

The reasonable pricing behind eBay Stores is a remarkable bargain. For as little as $15.95 a month, you have the opportunity to sell your merchandise to over 140 million registered users! See Table 11-1 for eBay Store listing fees.

Table 11-1	eBay Store Listing Fees
Starting Price	*Listing Fee*
$0.01–$24.99	$0.03 per 30 days
$25.00 – $199.99	$0.05 per 30 days
$200.00 and higher	$0.10 per/ 30 days

Listing fees and monthly rent can be just the tip of the iceberg if you choose to get fancy by using all kinds of options. My recommendation? Don't spend too much on them until you're fully entrenched in an eBay business — by that time, you'll have the experience to know what to add and when. Stick with the basics.

The final value fees are charged as a percentage of the sale price and are different in stores than on the regular eBay site. Check them out in Table 11-2.

Table 11-2	eBay Store Final Value Fees
Final Selling Price	*Final Value Fee Calculation*
$0.01–$25.00	**12%**
$25.01–$100.00	**12%** of the first $25.00 and **8%** of the remaining amount, up to $100.00
$100.01–$1,000.00.00	**12%** of the first $25.00, **8%** of the amount from $25.01 to $100.00, and **4%** of the remaining amount up to $1,000.00
$1,000.01 and more	**12%** of the first $25.00, **8%** of the amount from $25.01 to $100.00, **4%** of the amount from $100.01 to $1,000.00 and **2%** of the remaining amount

Opening your eBay store

Because this book is your introduction to eBay, I'll just give you some ideas about opening an eBay store. In my more advanced book, *Starting an eBay Business For Dummies* (Wiley), I take you step-by-step through the basics of opening your store.

Naming your store is your first challenge. Choose a name that describes the type of items your store will carry or one that includes your user ID. Don't choose a name that is so esoteric or overly creative that it doesn't give possible shoppers a clue as to what you carry. A creative store name and logo are pictured in Figure 11-5.

As you can see from my store page, each store can have its own categories. You get to make them up yourself so your customers can find items within your store in an organized manner. You can define up to 300 custom categories up to three levels deep. Each category can have a maximum of 29 characters for each name in your store.

Your eBay store home page has links for your Store Information: Store Policies and About the Seller page. The About the Store Page is the same as your About Me page (which I discuss in Chapter 14).

Spend some serious time on eBay before you open a store. Study some of the successful stores. You need to have enough know-how to make your store a success!

Figure 11-5:
The eBay
Stores page
for my store.

Chapter 12

Closing the Deal and Shipping It Out

The auction's over and you have a winning buyer, who (you hope) is eager to send you money. Sounds perfect, doesn't it? It is if you watch your step, keep on top of things, and communicate like a professional.

In this chapter, I help you figure out how to stay organized by showing you what documents you need to keep and for how long. I also include tips and etiquette on communicating with the buyer so that you're most likely to come out with positive feedback. In addition, you find out how to pack your item, assess costs, and make sure the item reaches the buyer when you say it will (oh, yeah . . . and in one piece).

Bookkeeping and Staying Organized

Although I don't recommend lining your nest with every scrap from every auction you run, you can safely keep some documents without mutating into a giant pack rat. Until you become an eBay expert and are comfortable with other ways to electronically store your information, you should print and file these essentials:

> ✔ **The listing page as it appeared before the auction closed:** This page gives you a record of the item name and number and a lot of other useful information. The page also includes the auction item description (and any revisions you've made to it), which is handy if the buyer argues that an item's disintegrating before his eyes and you honestly described it as just well loved.

Do not use the Print feature on the item page because it will not include all of the seller's description. Print the page directly from your browser.

You may think you don't need this information because you can always look it up, but here practicality rears its head: eBay makes completed listings disappear after 30 days. However, if you use the custom link that appears in your End of Auction e-mail (see the next bullet), you can access the auction online for up to 90 days. Print your auction page *before* you forget about it, file it where you know you can find it, and *then* forget about it.

✔ **The End of Listing e-mail you receive from eBay that notifies you that the auction is over:** If you lose this e-mail, you can't get it back because eBay doesn't keep it.

I set up a separate folder in my Microsoft Outlook e-mail program for my sold item e-mails. When one comes in, I read it and then drag it over to its special folder. That way, I can always check this folder for the information I need.

✔ **E-mail between you and the buyer:** In the virtual world, e-mail is as close to having a face-to-face conversation as most people get. Your e-mail correspondence is a living record of all the things you discuss with the buyer to complete the transaction. Even if you sell just a few items a month on eBay, keep track of who's paid up and who owes you money. And more importantly, if the buyer says, "I told you I'd be out of town," you can look through your e-mail and say, "Nope, it doesn't show up here," or "You're right! How was Tierra del Fuego? Is the payment on the way?" Or something more polite. Be sure to keep that e-mail with the headers and date on it so that you can't be accused of (ahem) creative writing.

✔ **PayPal payment notices:** You get a notice from PayPal when the buyer pays for the item. The notice has the listing information and the buyer's shipping information. (When that e-mail arrives, the clock begins to tick on sending out the item.)

✔ **Any bank statements you receive that reflect a payment that doesn't clear:** Keep anything related to payments, especially payments that didn't go through. That way, if a buyer says he's sure he sent you a check, you can say, "Yes sir, Mr. X, you did send me a check, and it was made of the finest rubber." Or something kinder, especially if you want that payment.

✔ **Any insurance forms:** Until the item has arrived and you're sure the customer is satisfied, be sure to keep those shipping and insurance receipts.

✔ **Refund requests you make:** If you make a request to eBay for a refund from a sale that doesn't go through, hold on to it until you can view the credit on your statement.

✔ **Receipts for items that you buy for the sole purpose of selling on eBay:** This comes in handy as a reference so that you can see if you're making a profit. It can also be helpful at tax time.

Someday, the Internal Revenue Service (or the government agency in your area) may knock on your door. Scary, but true. Like hurricanes and asteroid strikes, audits happen. Any accountant worth his or her salt will tell you that the best way to handle the possibility of an audit is to be prepared for the worst — even if every eBay transaction you conduct runs smooth as silk and you've kept your nose sparkling clean. See Chapter 9 for more tax information.

If you accept online payments by PayPal (PayPal Premier or Business members only), you can download your transaction history for use in QuickBooks, Quicken, or Excel. Additionally, these programs are excellent sources for your documentation.

When you're starting your career as a seller, once a month conduct a By Seller search on yourself so that you can print all the information on the bid histories of your most recent auctions. Do this independently of any auction software you use. Having the listings neatly printed easily helps you see what sold for how much and when. Chapter 5 gives you the lowdown on how to perform this search.

When it comes to printouts of e-mails and documents about transactions, you can dump them as soon as the item arrives at the destination and you get your positive feedback. If you get negative feedback, hang on to your documentation a little longer (say, until you're sure the issues it raises are resolved and everyone's satisfied). If selling on eBay becomes a fairly regular source of income, save all receipts for items you've purchased to sell; for tax purposes, that's inventory.

Tales from the formerly Type A

Confession time. When I first started buying and selling, I used to keep all my paperwork — listings, e-mails, the works. Now I keep the e-mails and receipts sent to me until I know a transaction is complete. Then they go wafting off to the Recycle Bin so that I can still find a file in my Outlook program.

These days, I stay on top of my eBay finances with online auction-management that helps me keep track of who has paid me and who hasn't. These programs also help me figure out my expenses, profit, and other financial calculations, almost painlessly. (See Chapter 20 for more information on these programs.) They can also help spiff up the look of my auctions. Ain't technology grand?

If you sell specialized items, you can keep track of trends and who your frequent buyers are by saving your paperwork. This prudent habit becomes an excellent marketing strategy when you discover that a segment of eBay users faithfully buys your items. An *audience.* Imagine that.

Talking to Buyers: The ABCs of Good Communication

You've heard it countless times — talk is cheap. Compared to what? Granted, empty promises are a dime a dozen, but honest-to-goodness talk and efficient e-mail are worth their weight in gold and good feedback — especially on eBay. Sometimes, *not* talking is costly.

A smooth exchange of money and merchandise starts with you (the seller) and your attitude toward the transaction. Your listing description and then your first e-mail — soon after the sale is made — set the entire transaction in motion and the tone for that transaction. If all goes well, *no more than* a day should elapse between getting paid and sending the item.

I suggest contacting the buyer and sending an invoice even *before* you get eBay's e-mail. Here's how:

1. **Start at your My eBay Summary, Sell: Sold.**

   Locate your newly sold item. *Hint:* It should be at the top of the listings.

2. **Click the down arrow at the end of the listing's line and select Send Invoice.**

   You are presented with a page that summarizes the transaction with a "working version" of the invoice.

3. **Examine the invoice displayed on this page. Make any changes if necessary.**

   If the buyer has purchased more than one item from you, click the link to combine purchases.

4. **Double-check that the shipping amount is correct. When you're satisfied, click the Send Invoice button.**

   If you select the Copy Me check box on this invoice, you'll receive a copy of the invoice. The buyer's copy has a link in the invoice, enabling the buyer to pay directly to PayPal (if you accept PayPal for payment).

Signing in first puts a temporary cookie (a computer file that makes it easier to get around a Web site) in your computer so you don't have to go through this process again. Be sure to select the Keep Me Signed In on This Computer for One Day check box when you sign in to eBay; your password is saved even if you cut off your Internet connection. Your login is saved until you click the Sign Out link. For more yummy info on cookies, see Chapter 15.

Another way to contact your buyer is to go to your My eBay page, scroll down to the Items I've Sold area, find the auction, and click the drop-down menu in the Action column. From there, click the Contact Buyer link.

Thank you — I mean it

What do all the successful big-name department stores have in common? Yes, great prices, good merchandise, and nice displays. But with all things being equal, customer service always wins hands-down. One department store in the United States, Nordstrom, has such a great reputation that the store happily took back a set of snow tires because a customer wasn't happy with them. No big deal, maybe — until you notice that Nordstrom doesn't even *sell* snow tires!

A friend of mine who owns restaurants calls this level of customer satisfaction the Wow! factor. If customers (no matter what they're buying) say, "Wow!" during or after the transaction — admiringly or happily — you've satisfied the customer. A good rule to go by: *Give people the same level of service you expect when you're on the buying end.* The best eBay sellers are regular eBay buyers.

The best way to start satisfying the buyer is with an introductory e-mail. Congratulate the person on winning the item — making him or her feel good about the purchase — and thank the buyer for bidding on your item. A good e-mail provides these important details:

- Item name and item number.

- Winning bid amount.

- Cost of shipping and packing, and any shipping or insurance restrictions. (I give pointers on determining shipping and packaging costs later in this chapter.)

- Payment options.

- The shipping timetable.

You should also include a few vital details in the first e-mail:

- ✔ Include your name and the address to which you want the payment sent should you have arranged for a form of payment other than PayPal.

- ✔ Remind buyers to write the item name, item number, and shipping address on whatever form of payment they send. You'd be surprised how many buyers forget to give you the item number. Also ask buyers to print and send a copy of your e-mail with the payment.

- ✔ If you're using an online payment service, such as PayPal, be sure to give buyers instructions on how they can pay for the auction online.

- ✔ Include your "customer service" phone number if you want.

- ✔ Suggest that if all goes well, you'll be happy to leave positive feedback for the buyer. (See Chapter 4 for more on feedback.)

You can also send an invoice from your My eBay page, Items I've Sold area. Click the drop-down box in the Action column next to the item. Just click the Send Invoice link, verify all the information, and click Send Invoice. Figure 12-1 shows what the invoice e-mail looks like.

Figure 12-1:
An eBay
invoice, as
sent to a
buyer.

Let's keep e-mailing

If you have a good transaction going (and the majority of them are good), the buyer will reply to your e-mail within a few business days. Customarily, most replies come the next day. If your buyer has questions regarding anything you asked in your e-mail, you'll get those inquiries now. Most of the time, all you get back is, "Thanks. I'll send the PayPal Payment when I get paid on Thursday." Hey, that's all I ask.

If any last-minute details need to be worked out, usually the buyer asks to set up a time to call or request further instructions about the transaction. Respond to this communication as soon as possible. If you can't deal with it at the moment, let the buyer know you're working on it and will shoot those answers back ASAP. *Never* let an e-mail go unanswered.

For sample e-mail letters and deeper information, get your hands on a copy of my book on more advanced eBay selling, *Starting an eBay Business For Dummies* (Wiley).

Shipping without Going Postal

Shipping can be the most time-consuming (and most dreaded) task for many eBay sellers. Even if the selling portion of your transaction goes flawlessly, the item has to get to the buyer in one piece. If it doesn't, the deal could be ruined — and so could your reputation.

This section briefs you on shipping etiquette, gives you details about the three most popular shipping options (the U.S. Postal Service, UPS, and FedEx Ground), and offers tips on how to make sure your package is ready to ride.

The best way to avoid shipping problems is to do your homework beforehand, determine which method is likely to work best, and spell out in your item description exactly how you intend to ship the item. Here's how I handle the process:

1. **Before listing, get the package ready to ship.**

   You don't have to seal the package right away, but you should have it ready to seal because the two critical factors in shipping are weight and time. The more a package weighs and the faster it has to be delivered, the higher the charge. (I cover packing materials and tips later in this section.) The time to think about packing and shipping is *before* you put the item up for sale — that way, last-minute surprises are less likely to arise while your buyer waits impatiently for the item!

2. Know your carrier options.

In the United States, the three main shipping options for most eBay transactions are the U.S. Postal Service, UPS, and FedEx. See the section "Shopping for a shipper" (try saying *that* five times fast) for how you can get rate options from each service, painlessly and online. Compare costs and services.

3. Before quoting the shipping fees, make sure that you include all appropriate costs.

I recommend that you charge a nominal handling fee (up to $1.00 isn't out of line) to cover your packing materials, labels, and time, which can add up quickly as you start making multiple transactions. You should also include any insurance costs and any delivery-confirmation costs. See the sidebar "Insuring your peace of mind (and your shipment)" for more information.

Some eBay scam artists inflate shipping and handling costs to make added profit. *Shame, shame, shame on them.* Purposely overcharging is tacky, ugly, and immature. (It's also a violation of eBay policy on circumventing fees and will penalize your listings in Best Match search). The buyer also often figures it out after one look at the postage on the box.

Post a flat shipping amount (or use the eBay online shipping calculator — see Chapter 10 for more on how to use this tool). This way, buyers can include this cost when they consider their bidding strategies. Figure out what the packed item will weigh and then give a good estimate; the online calculators can help.

If the item is heavy and you need to use a shipping service that charges by weight and distance, be sure to say in your auction description that you're just giving an estimate and that the final cost will be determined after the listing is over. Optionally, you can tell the bidder how much the item weighs, where you're shipping from, and what your handling charges are (a few bidders don't mind doing the math).

Occasionally, shipping calculations can be off-target, and you may not know that until after you take the buyer's money. If the mistake is in your favor and is a biggie, notify the buyer and offer a refund. But if shipping ends up costing you a bit more, take your lumps and pay it yourself. Consider it part of the cost of doing business. You can always let the buyer know what happened and that you paid the extra cost. Who knows, it may show up positively on your feedback from the buyer! (Even if it doesn't, spreading goodwill never hurts.)

4. E-mail the buyer and congratulate him or her on winning; reiterate what your shipping choice is and how long you expect delivery will take.

Make sure you're both talking about the same timetable. If the buyer balks at either the price or the shipping time, try working out an option that will make the buyer happy.

5. **Send the package.**

When should you ship the package? Common courtesy says it should go out as soon as the buyer has paid for the item and shipping charges. If the buyer has followed through with his or her side of the bargain, you should do the same. Ship that package no more than a few days after payment (or after the check clears). If you can't, immediately e-mail the buyer and explain the delay. You should e-mail the buyer as soon as you send the package and ask for an e-mail to confirm arrival after the item gets there. (Don't forget to put in a plug for positive feedback.)

Send a prompt follow-up e-mail to let the buyer know the item's on the way. In this e-mail, be sure to include when the item was sent, how long it should take to arrive, any special tracking or delivery confirmation number (if you have one), and a request for a return e-mail confirming arrival after the item gets there. I also include a thank-you note (a receipt would be a business-like addition) in each package I send out. I appreciate when I get one in eBay packages, and it always brings a smile to the recipient's face. It never hurts to take every opportunity to promote goodwill (and future business and positive feedback).

More often than not, you do get an e-mail back from the buyer to let you know the item arrived safely. If you don't (and they haven't received any feedback), it's a good idea to send another e-mail (in about a week) to ask whether the item arrived in good condition. It jogs the buyer's memory and demonstrates your professionalism as a seller. Use this opportunity to gently remind buyers that you'll be leaving positive feedback for them. Ask whether they're satisfied and don't be bashful about suggesting they do the same for you. Leave feedback right away so that you don't forget.

Shopping for a shipper

If only you could transport your item the way they did on *Star Trek* — "Beam up that antique lamp, Scotty!" Alas, it's not so. Priority Mail via the U.S. Postal Service (USPS) is pretty much the eBay standard if you're shipping within the United States and Canada. Many Americans also rely on the USPS to ship internationally as well. FedEx and UPS are global alternatives that work well, too.

Many sellers think that they are unequivocally covered by requiring their buyers to purchase insurance. Even if your buyer opts not to pay for insurance, you are still responsible for making sure that the item arrives at the buyer's door. Federal mail order laws state that when an item is paid for, it must be delivered to the buyer within 30 days unless there has been an agreement between the buyer and the seller for other arrangements.

Insuring your peace of mind (and your shipment)

Sure, "damaged in the mail" is an excuse we've all heard hundreds of times, but despite everyone's best efforts, sometimes things do get damaged or misplaced during shipment. The universe is a dangerous place; that's what insurance is for. I usually offer to get insurance from the shipper if the buyer wants to pay for it, and I always get it on expensive items, one-of-a-kind items, or very fragile items. I spell out in my item description that the buyer pays for the insurance.

The major shippers all offer insurance that's fairly reasonably priced, so check out their rates on their Web sites. But don't forget to read the details. For example, many items on eBay are sold MIMB (Mint in Mint Box). True, the condition of the original box often has a bearing on the final value of the item inside, but the U.S. Postal Service insures only what is *in* the box. So, if you sold a Malibu Barbie mint in a mint box, USPS insures only the doll and not the original box. Pack carefully so that your buyer gets what's been paid for. Be mindful that shippers won't make good on insurance claims if they suspect you of causing the damage by doing a lousy job of packing.

Alternatively, when you're selling on eBay in earnest, you can purchase your own parcel protection policy from a private insurer like U-PIC. When you use this type of insurance, combined with preprinted electronic postage, you no longer have to stand in line at the post office to have your insured package logged in by the clerk at the counter.

Some sellers also offer their own form of *self-insurance*. Realize that I use the term "self-insurance" as a descriptive phrase only. You may not charge your buyer for insurance unless you are actually paying for insurance from a licensed third-party insurance company. Charging and not fulfilling insurance is a violation of state law. Here's what I offer my buyers at no cost to them:

- ✔ On lower-priced items, I am willing to refund the buyer's money if the item is lost or damaged.

- ✔ On some items I sell, I have a *risk reserve*. That means I have more than one of the item I sold. If the item is lost or destroyed, I can send the backup item as a replacement.

Whether you're at the post office, UPS, FedEx, or your doctor's office, be ready, willing, and able to wait in line. There's definitely a "rush hour" at my neighborhood Post Office — everybody's in a rush, so everything moves at a glacial pace. Avoid both the noontime and post-work crunches (easier on the nerves). A good time to ship is around 10:30 a.m., when everyone is still in a good mood. If I have to go in the afternoon, I go about 3:00 p.m., when the clerks are back from their lunch breaks and friendly faces (mine, too — I always smile!) can take the edge off those brusque lunchtime encounters. Why not save yourself the time and stress by requesting a carrier pickup from the Post Office Web site (www.usps.com) if you can ship from home.

Be sure to visit my Web site, www.coolebaytools.com, for introductory offers for much of the software and services that I mention in this book.

U.S. Postal Service

The U.S. Postal Service (USPS) is the butt of many unfair jokes and cheap shots, but when it comes right down to it, I think USPS is still the most efficient and inexpensive way to ship items — eBay or otherwise. It also supplies free boxes and labels for Priority and Express Mail packages. Here are some ways eBay members get their items from here to there via USPS:

- **Priority Mail:** As mentioned earlier, this is the *de facto* standard method of shipping for eBay users. I love the free boxes, and I like the rates. The promised delivery time is two to three days, although I've experienced rare delays of up to a week during peak holiday periods.

  Cost? As of this writing (rates are always subject to change), Priority Mail costs $4.95 for a 1-pound package. Over a pound, the charge is calculated according to weight and distance.

  A $4.95 flat-rate Priority envelope is also available. You can ship as much stuff as you want — as long as you can fit it into the supplied 9½ x 12½ envelope. (You'll be surprised how much stuff you can jam into those envelopes.) You can reinforce the envelope with clear packing tape.

  There are also flat-rate Priority Mail boxes that come in three sizes and allow you to send heavy items for reduced rates. Order them directly from the USPS. Figure 12-2 shows you some of the wide selection!

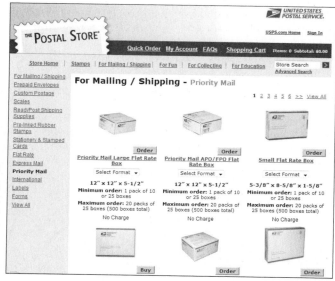

Figure 12-2: USPS Flat Rate Priority boxes ready and waiting for you!

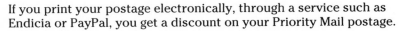

If you print your postage electronically, through a service such as Endicia or PayPal, you get a discount on your Priority Mail postage.

✔ **Express Mail:** If the item needs to be delivered the next day, use Express Mail. The Postal Service promises delivery no later than noon the following afternoon (even on weekends or holidays). And you can get free boxes.

Cost? Express Mail runs $13.05 for packages 8 ounces and under. Express Mail also has a flat-rate envelope, which is the same size as the Priority flat-rate envelope and ships for $17.50. (You get a 5% discount when purchasing your postage electronically).

The Postal Service offers a free special pickup for Priority Mail and Express Mail, no matter how many separate packages are included. If you have several packages, carrier pickup is an excellent option.

Get to know your mail carrier and have your parcels ready and stacked up for him or her for the regular stop at your home. The mail carrier will be happy to take your packages back to the post office at no additional charge. (A bottle of icy-cold water for your letter carrier on hot days will go a long way in your relationship!)

✔ **First-Class Mail:** If your item weighs 13 ounces or less, you can use First-Class Mail. First-Class Mail is considerably cheaper than Priority. I try to ship as much as I can via First Class mail so I can have the edge on other sellers by offering lower shipping prices.

✔ **Media Mail:** This is a popular option among those who sell books on eBay. It's the new name for two older products, Book Rate and Special Standard Mail. Media Mail rates start at $2.23 for the first pound and increase by $0.35 for each additional pound.

✔ **Other options:** The Postal Service offers all sorts of add-ons. I always get the delivery confirmation service that you can add to Priority Mail, as well as with other mailing services such as First Class or Parcel Post. The cost is a mere $0.75 — free on electronic purchases. It buys you the knowledge of when and where your item was delivered. Not only that, but if buyers report to PayPal that they want a refund because they never received an item, the scan on the delivery confirmation code prevents you from getting a chargeback.

You can check on whether the package was delivered (or whether an attempt was made to deliver it). By typing the number online at www. usps.com/shipping/trackandconfirm.htm.

If you're an occasional shipper (you *buy* more than you sell on eBay) and don't use PayPal, you can print bar-coded shipping labels with free delivery confirmation (for Priority Mail only) at the USPS site. No online e-mail functions are available, so you have to do all the e-mailing and record keeping yourself. But hey, the service is free. Just go to www.usps.com and find the Click-N-Ship link.

Delivery confirmation also comes in handy if you try to collect insurance for an item that was never delivered or if the buyer says the item was never delivered. It gives you proof from the Postal Service that the item was sent. (I explain insuring shipments later in this chapter.) But understand that you cannot accurately track your package. Delivery confirmation is merely proof that the package was mailed and delivered. If your package gets lost in the mail for a few weeks, this number rarely acts as a tracking number and won't reveal the location of your package until it's delivered.

The USPS Web site (www.usps.com) gives you an overview of the U.S. Postal Service rates so that you can see all your options. It sure beats standing in that endless line! For a complete explanation of domestic rates, check out www.usps.com/prices/welcome.htm.

Even better, USPS has a page that can help you determine exactly what your item costs to mail (after you've packaged it and weighed it, of course). Start at the Rate Calculator page at postcalc.usps.gov and follow the instructions.

UPS

The folks in the brown UPS trucks love eBay. The options they offer vary, with everything from Overnight service to Ground service. UPS also takes many of the odd-shaped large boxes, such as those for computer equipment, that the U.S. Postal Service won't.

UPS makes pickups, but you have to know the exact weight of your package so that you can pay when the UPS driver shows up. UPS charges for this service unless you have a daily shipper account and ship a minimum number of packages with UPS per week.

The rates for the same UPS shipment can vary based on whether you have a business account with UPS, whether the package goes to or is picked up at a residence, and whether you use the right kind of form. If you're going to use UPS regularly, be sure to set up an account directly with UPS.

Although UPS offers "discounts" to eBay PowerSellers, don't be fooled. If you ship mostly small packages, you'd have to ship truckloads full on a daily basis to compete with USPS rates.

You can find the UPS home page at www.ups.com. For rates, click the Shipping tab and then click Estimate Cost on the left side of the page, which gives you prices based on zip codes and package weights. (Note the ominous "estimate" rates.)

The UPS.com Quick Cost Calculator prices are based on what UPS charges its regular and high-volume users. When you get to the counter, the price may be higher than what you find on the Web.

Sí, oui, ja, yes! Shipping internationally

Money's good no matter what country it comes from. I don't know why, but lots of people seem to be afraid to ship internationally and list "I don't ship overseas" on the auction page. Of course, sending an item that far away may be a burden if you're selling a car or a street-sweeper (they don't fit in boxes too well), but I've found that sending a package across the Atlantic can be just as easy as shipping across state lines. The only downside: My shipper of choice, the U.S. Postal Service, does not insure packages going to certain countries (check with your post office to find out which ones; they seem to change with the headlines), so I use private shipping insurance with U-PIC.

Here are a couple of other timely notes about shipping internationally:

✔ You need to tell what's inside the package. Be truthful when declaring value on customs forms. Use descriptions that customs agents can figure out without knowing eBay shorthand terms. For example, instead of declaring the contents as "MIB Barbie," call it a "small child's doll." Some countries require buyers to pay special duties and taxes, depending on the item and the value. But that's the buyer's headache.

✔ Wherever you send your package (especially if it's going to a country where English is not the native language), write legibly. (Imagine getting a package from Russia and having to decipher a label written in the Cyrillic alphabet. *'Nuff said.*)

My favorite link on the UPS site is the transit map that shows the United States and how long it takes to reach any place in the country (based on the originating zip code). If you're thinking of shipping that compact refrigerator to Maine, you can check out this fun and informative page at www.ups.com/using/services/servicemaps/servicemaps.html.

FedEx

I use FedEx Express Air all the time for rush business, but Express seems rather expensive for my eBay shipping. However, if the buyer wants it fast and is willing to pay, I'll send it by FedEx overnight, you bet.

FedEx Ground service has competitive prices and carries all the best features of FedEx. I use FedEx Ground for items that are heavy (say, antique barbells) or extremely large (such as a 1920s steamer trunk), because FedEx ships anything up to 150 pounds in a single box — 80 more pounds than the U.S. Postal Service takes. FedEx also delivers on Saturdays — which UPS won't. It also charges $4.00 to pick up items from shippers who ship less than $60.00 in weekly package charges.

I also like the FedEx boxes. Like one of my favorite actors, Joe Pesci, from *My Cousin Vinny* and the *Lethal Weapon* movies, these boxes are small but tough. But if you're thinking of reusing these boxes to ship with another service, forget it. The FedEx logo is plastered all over every inch of the freebies, and the company may get seriously peeved about it. You can't use those fancy boxes for its Ground service.

The FedEx Ground Home Delivery service is a major competitor for UPS. The rates are competitive, and FedEx offers a money-back guarantee (if it misses the delivery window) for residential ground delivery. For residential delivery, FedEx charges an additional $2.30 to $2.40 per package. A 2-pound package going from Los Angeles to a residence in New York City takes five days and costs $8.71 including the Home Delivery fee. FedEx includes online package tracking and insurance up to $100.00 in this price. You have to be a business to avail yourself of home delivery — but plenty of home businesses exist.

The same 2-pound U.S. Postal Service Priority Mail package with $100.00 insurance and a delivery confirmation costs you $11.50. (But remember, you know how to get free delivery confirmation forms, and insurance can cost much less with private package insurance!) Granted, the package will arrive within two to three days, but FedEx Ground guarantees a five-day delivery, and I've had a few Priority Mail packages take up to a week. FedEx Ground won't supply boxes for you, so you're on your own there. When you drop off your box at UPS, you can get five-day service for $11.53.

You can find the FedEx home page at www.fedex.com/us. The link for rates is conveniently located at the top of the page.

Getting the right (packing) stuff

You can never think about packing materials too early. If you wait until the last minute, you won't find the right-size box, approved tape, or the labels you need. Start thinking about shipping even before you sell your first item.

Before you pack, give your item the once-over. Here's a checklist of what to consider about your item before you call it a wrap (gotta love Hollywood lingo):

- ✔ **Is your item as you described it?** If the item has been dented or torn somehow, e-mail the winning bidder immediately and come clean. And if you sell an item with its original box or container, don't just check the item, make sure the box is in the same good condition as the item inside. Collectors place a high value on original boxes, so make sure the box lives up to what you described in your listing. Pack to protect it as well.

- ✔ **Is the item dirty or dusty, or does it smell of smoke?** Some buyers may complain if the item they receive is dirty or smelly, especially from cigarette smoke. Make sure the item is fresh and clean, even if it's used or vintage. If something's dirty, check to make sure you know how to clean it properly (you want to take the dirt off, not the paint), and then give it a spritz with an appropriate cleaner or just soap and water. If you can't get rid of the smell or the dirt, say so in your item description. Let the buyer decide whether the item is desirable with aromas and all.

If the item has a faint smell of smoke or is a bit musty, a product called Febreze may help. Just get a plastic bag, give your item a spritz, and keep it in the bag for a short while. *Note:* This is not recommended for cardboard. And, as with any solvent or cleaning agent, read the label before you spray. Or, if you're in a rush to mail the package, cut a 2-by-2-inch piece of sheet fabric softener and place it in a plastic bag with the product.

When the item's ready to go, you're ready to pack it. The following sections give you suggestions on what you should consider using and where to find the right stuff.

Packing material: What to use

This may sound obvious, but you'd be surprised: Any list of packing material should start with a box. But you don't want just any box — you want a heavy cardboard type that's larger than the item. If the item is extremely fragile, I suggest you use two boxes, with the outer box about 3 inches larger on each side than the inner box that holds the item, to allow for extra padding. And if you still have the original shipping container for such things as electronic equipment, consider using the original, especially if it still has the original foam inserts (they were designed for the purpose, and this way they stay out of the environment awhile longer).

As for padding, Table 12-1 compares the most popular types of box-filler material.

Table 12-1	Box-Filler Materials	
Type	*Pros and Cons*	*Suggestions*
Bubble wrap	**Pros:** Lightweight, clean, cushions well **Cons:** Cost	Don't go overboard taping the bubble wrap. If the buyer has to battle to get the tape off, the item may go flying and end up damaged. And for crying out loud, don't pop all the little bubbles, okay?
Newspaper	**Pros:** Cheap, cushions **Cons:** Messy, and adds weight to the package	Seal fairly well. Put your item in a plastic bag to protect it from the ink. I like shredding the newspaper first. It's more manageable and doesn't seem to stain as much as wadded-up paper. I spent about $30.00 at an office-supply store for a shredder. (Or find one on eBay for much less.)

Type	Pros and Cons	Suggestions
Cut-up cardboard	**Pros:** Handy, cheap **Cons:** Transmits some shocks to item, hard to cut up, heavy	If you have some old boxes that aren't sturdy enough to pack in, this is a pretty good use for them.
Styrofoam peanuts	**Pros:** Lightweight, absorb shock well, clean **Cons:** Environmentally unfriendly, annoying	Your item may shift if you don't put enough peanuts in the box, so make sure to fill the box. Also, don't buy these; recycle them from stuff that was shipped to you (plastic trash bags are great for storing them). And never use plastic peanuts when packing electronic equipment, because they can create static electricity. Even a little spark can trash a computer chip.
Air-popped popcorn	**Pros:** Lightweight, environmentally friendly, absorbs shock well, clean (as long as you don't use salt and butter, but you knew that), low in calories **Cons:** Cost, time to pop	You don't want to send it anywhere there may be varmints who like it. The U.S. Postal Service suggests popcorn. Hey, at least you can eat the leftovers!

TIP

Storing those bags of plump packing peanuts

By now, you may have realized that I have commandeered a large chunk of my home for my eBay business, and you might think that I live in a giant swamp of packing materials. Not really. But I do have to store loads of packing peanuts. They're not heavy, but they sure are bulky!

If you have a house with a garage, you're set! Bear with me now, my plan isn't as crazy as it seems. Go to your local store and purchase some large screw-in cup hooks. Then purchase the largest *drawstring* plastic bags you can find. (I'm partial to 39-gallon Glad Lawn & Leaf bags.)

Screw the cup hooks into strategic locations on the ceiling rafters of your garage. Now fill the drawstring bags to capacity with packing peanuts and hang. When you've finished your garage will look like some bizarre art installation, but it gets the packing peanuts off the floor and out of your hair. I even set up a packing-peanuts barricade so I don't hit the end of my garage when I park!

Whatever materials you use, make sure that you pack the item well and that you secure the box. Many shippers will contest insurance claims if they feel you did a lousy job of packing. Do all the little things that you'd want done if you were the buyer — using double boxes for really fragile items, wrapping lids separately from containers, and filling hollow breakables with some kind of padding. Here are a few other items you need:

- **Plastic bags:** Plastic bags protect your item from moisture. I once sent a MIB doll to the Northeast, and the package got caught in a snowstorm. The buyer e-mailed me with words of thanks for the extra plastic bag, which saved the item from being soaked along with the outer box. (Speaking of boxes, if you send an item in an original box, bag it.)

    For any small items, such as stuffed animals, you should always protect them in a lunch baggie. For slightly larger items, go to the 1-quart or 1-gallon size. Be sure to wrap any paper or cloth products, such as clothing and linens, in plastic before you ship.

- **Bubble-padded mailers:** The shipping cost for a package that weighs less than 13 ounces (First-Class mail) is usually considerably cheaper than Priority. Many small items, clothing, books, and so on will fit comfortably into the many available sizes of padded envelopes. You can find them made of Kraft paper or extra sturdy vinyl. A big plus is that they weigh considerably less than boxes — even when using extra padding. See Table 12-2 for standard sizes.

- **Address labels:** You'll need extras because it's always a good idea to toss a duplicate address label inside the box, with the destination address and a return address, in case the outside label falls off or becomes illegible.

- **Shipping tape, 2 or 3 inches:** Make sure that you use a strong shipping tape for the outside of the box. Clear plastic will do just fine. There is also box-color tape that works very well for recycling boxes (taping over old shipping information). Remember not to plaster every inch of box with tape; leave space for those *Fragile* and *Insured* rubber stamps.

- **Hand-held shipping tape dispensers:** It's quite a bit easier to zzzzzip! tape from a tape dispenser than to unwind it and bite it off with your teeth. Have one dispenser for your special shipping tape and one for your clear tape.

- **Lightweight 2-inch clear tape:** For taping the padding around the inside items. I also use a clear strip of tape over the address on the outside of the box so that it won't disappear in the rain.

- **Scissors:** A pair of large, sharp scissors. Having a hobby knife to trim boxes or shred newspaper is also a good idea.

✔ **Handy liquids:** Three that I like are GOO GONE (which is available in the household supply section of most retail stores and is a wonder at removing unwanted stickers and price tags); WD-40 (the unstick-everything standby that works great on getting stickers off plastic); and Un-Du (the best liquid I've found to take labels off cardboard). Lighter fluid also does the trick, but be very careful handling it and be sure to clean up thoroughly to remove any residue.

✔ **Rubber stamps/stickers:** Using custom rubber stamps or stickers can save you a bunch of time when preparing your packages. I purchased some return address self-inking rubber stamps. I use these stamps to stamp all kinds of things that require my identification. I often also use their fluorescent red SCAN NOW stickers next to my Delivery Confirmations.

✔ **Thermal label printer:** Once I thought this was a flagrant waste of money, but now I wouldn't be without one. When you begin shipping several packages a week, you'll find it far more convenient to use a separate label printer for addressing and delivery confirmations. Dymo offers one of the best deals; you can find them on eBay for about $100.00. If you want to get industrial, try one of the Zebra thermal printers (I use the LP2844). These printers can print labels for Fed Ex and UPS as well as USPS (you can also get deals on these on eBay).

✔ **Black permanent marker:** These are handy for writing information ("Please leave on porch behind the planter") and the all-important "Fragile" all over the box or "Do Not Bend" on envelopes. I like the big, fat Sharpie markers.

Table 12-2	Standard Bubble-Padded Mailer Sizes	
Size	*Measurements*	*Suggested items*
#000	4" x 8"	Collector trading cards, jewelry, computer disks, coins
#00	5" x 10"	Postcards, paper ephemera
#0	6" x 10"	CDs, DVDs, Xbox or PS2 games
#1	7¼" x 12"	Cardboard sleeve VHS tapes, jewel-cased CDs and DVDs
#2	8½" x 12"	Clamshell VHS tapes
#3	8½" x 14½"	Toys, clothing, stuffed animals
#4	9½" x 14½"	Small books, trade paperbacks
#5	10½" x 16"	Hardcover books
#6	12½" x 19"	Clothing, soft boxed items
#7	14¼" x 20"	Much larger packaged items, framed items, plaques

If you plan to sell on eBay in earnest, consider adding a 10-pound weight scale (for weighing packages) to your shipping department. I'm using a super-small 13-pound maximum scale, which I bought on eBay for only $29.95.

When it comes to fragile items, dishes, pottery, porcelain, china — anything that can chip, crack, or smash into a thousand pieces — *double box.* The boxes should be about 3 inches different on each side. Make sure that you use enough padding so that the interior box is snug. Just give it a big shake. If nothing rattles, ship away!

Packing material: Where to find it

The place to start looking for packing material is the same place you should start looking for things to sell on eBay: your house. Between us, I've done over a thousand eBay transactions and never once paid for a carton. I buy most of my stuff from catalogs and online companies (I love e-commerce) and save all the boxes, bubble wrap, padding, and packing peanuts I get in the mail. Just empty your boxes of packing peanuts into large plastic trash bags — that way, they don't take up much storage space. If you recently got a mail-order shipment box that was used only once — and it's a good, sturdy box with no dents or dings — there's nothing wrong with using it again. Just be sure to completely cover any old labels so the delivery company doesn't get confused.

Beyond the ol' homestead, here are a few other suggestions for places where you can rustle up some packing stuff:

- ✔ **Your local supermarket, department store, or drugstore:** You won't be the first person pleading with a store manager for boxes. (Ah, fond memories of moving days past.) Stores like giving them away because it saves them the work of compacting the boxes and putting them in the trash or recycling bin.

  I have found that drugstores and beauty supply stores have a better variety of smaller boxes. But make sure that you don't take dirty boxes reeking of food smells.

- ✔ **The inside of your local supermarket, department store, or drugstore:** Places like Kmart, Wal-Mart, Target, and office-supply stores often have good selections of packing supplies.

- ✔ **Shippers such as UPS, FedEx, and the U.S. Postal Service:** These shippers offer all kinds of free supplies as long as you use these supplies to ship things with their service.

  The Postal Service also ships free boxes, packing tape, labels, and shipping forms for Express Mail, Priority Mail, and Global Priority Mail to your house. In the United States, you can order by phone (800-222-1811) or online (shop.usps.com). Here are a few rules for USPS orders:

- Specify the service (Priority Mail, Express Mail, or Global Priority Mail) you're using because the boxes and the labels all come with the service name printed all over them, and you can use them only for that specific service.

- Order in bulk. For example, address labels come in rolls of 500 and boxes in packs of 25.

- The boxes come flat, so you have to assemble them. Hey, don't look a gift box in the mouth — they're free!

✔ **eBay and online sellers:** Many terrific eBay sellers are out to offer you really good deals. (You can't beat eBay sellers for quality goods, low prices, and great service.) I recommend the following family-run eBay stores:

- **Royal Mailers** is where I buy my padded paper envelope mailers for my eBay sales. This company also sells Tyvek envelopes, vinyl bubble mailers, zipper-lock plastic bags, air pillows, box sealing tape, and lots more. They offer *free shipping* and a discount of 5% to my readers if you use this code: COOLEBAY. Visit their Web site at www.royalmailers.com.

- **Bubblefast** — an eBay seller from the Chicago area — sells tons of reasonably priced bubble wrap, mailers, and more.

- **Melrose Stamp** is based in New York (but its items are tiny, so shipping isn't a huge issue). Melrose Stamp mainly sells custom and stock message rubber stamps. They also sell rolls of package identification labels such as Fragile, Scan Me, First Class, Media Mail, and Airmail.

Notice that I mention where these vendors are located. When ordering a large shipment, the distance it has to travel from the vendor's place to yours can tack on quite a bit of cash (and time) to your shipping costs!

Buying Postage Online

Isn't technology great? You no longer have to schlep to the post office every time you need stamps. What's even better, with the new print-it-yourself postage, you can give all your packages directly to your mail carrier. When you install your Internet postage software, you apply for a USPS postal license that allows you to print your own *Information Based Indicia* (IBI) for your postage. IBI is a bar code printed either on labels or directly on an envelope and has both human- and machine-readable information about where it was printed and security-related elements. IBI provides you, and the post office, with a much more secure way of getting your valuable packages through the mail.

You can print postage for First Class, Priority, Express, and Parcel Post, and additional postage for delivery confirmation and insurance. If your printer mangles a sheet of labels or an envelope, you can send the printed piece to your Internet postage provider for a refund. Several vendors of Internet-based postage exist, but Endicia Internet Postage, and Stamps.com are the most popular.

Preparing Postage with Endicia

In the early 90s, a couple of guys came up with new software to enable people to design direct-mail pieces from the desktop. Wow! What an innovation. With the inexpensive software, you could also produce your own bar coding for the Postal Service. I used that software then, like I use DAZzle now. Take a look at the DAZzle software in Figure 12-3.

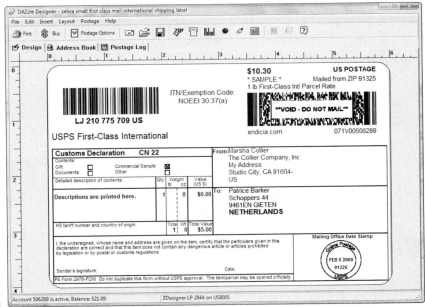

Figure 12-3: DAZzle software all set up to send some International First Class mail.

DAZzle — combined with the patented Dial-A-Zip — became the basis for the software that comes free with the Endicia Internet Postage service. There isn't a more robust mailing program on the market.

Endicia has all the basic features and more:

✔ **Prints postage for all classes of mail, including international:** From Anniston, Alabama, to Bulawayo, Zimbabwe, the DAZzle software not only prints postage but also lists all your shipping options and applicable rates. For international mailing, Endicia advises you about any prohibitions (no prison-made goods can be mailed to Botswana), any restrictions, any necessary customs forms, and areas served within the country.

✔ **Provides free delivery confirmation on Priority Mail:** You can print electronic delivery confirmations for First Class, Parcel Post, and Media Mail for only $0.18 each (a substantial savings from the Postal Service counter purchase).

✔ **Enables you to design mail pieces:** The software enables you to design envelopes, postcards, and labels with color graphics, logos, and text messages. You can print your labels with postage and delivery confirmation on anything from plain paper (tape it on with clear tape) to 4-by-6 labels in a label printer.

✔ **Integrates with U-PIC private insurance:** If you're saving time and money using a private package insurer, you can send your monthly insurance logs electronically to U-PIC at the end of the month.

Endicia offers two levels of service. All the preceding features come with the standard plan for $9.95 a month. The premium plan adds special features, customizable e-mail, enhanced online transaction reports and statistics, business reply mail, return shipping labels (prepaid so your customers won't have to pay for the returns), and stealth indicias for $15.95 a month.

A *stealth indicia* (also known as the postage-paid indicia) is an awesome tool for the eBay seller. By using this feature, your customers can't see the exact amount of postage that you paid for the package. This way, you can add reasonable shipping and handling costs and not inflame buyers when they see the final label.

For a free 60-day trial (30 days longer than offered to anyone else), go to

```
www.endicia.com/coolebaytools
```

Shipping Directly from PayPal

I consider PayPal shipping to be required for all beginning eBay sellers. By using PayPal, a seller can streamline the buyer's shopping experience, making it simple to buy, click, and pay. Those out in the eBay world who haven't used PayPal find the service to be a life-changing experience. Because you don't need to use additional software or sign up with an additional service, shipping with PayPal is a convenient system for those who don't have to ship many packages each week.

When you're ready to deal with shipping, you simply sign on to your PayPal account and handle it right on the site. You can also click the Print Label link from the item's page to start the process. There's no charge for the service and you have a choice of U.S Postal Service or UPS (sorry, no FedEx Ground).

As of this date, PayPal will not print postage for First Class Mail International; it prints postage only for the far more expensive Priority or Express. If you plan on doing business overseas (like I do), be competitive with your shipping costs. It will bring you more business from savvy international buyers.

Chapter 13

Troubleshooting Transactions

. . . .

. . . .

There's no getting around it: The more transactions you conduct on eBay, the more chances you have of facing some potential pitfalls. In this chapter, I give you pointers on how to handle an obnoxious or difficult buyer as if he or she is your new best friend (for a little while anyway). In addition, I explain how to keep an honest misunderstanding from blowing up into a vitriolic e-mail war. You find out how to handle a sale that's (shall I say) on a road to nowhere, how to get some attention, and if it all goes sour, how to sell to the next highest bidder legally and relist the item, and get back the final value fee you paid eBay. There's no way that all of what I mention here will happen to you, but the more you know, the better prepared you'll be.

Dealing with a Buyer Who Doesn't Respond

Most of the time, the post-auction transaction between buyers and sellers goes smoothly. However, if you have difficulty communicating with the winner of your auction or fixed-price sale, you should know the best way to handle the situation.

You've come to the right place if you want help dealing with potential non-paying buyers (more commonly known as *deadbeat bidders,* which is how I refer to them). Of course, you should start with good initial post-auction communication; see Chapter 12 for details. (For more information on how to deal with a fraudulent seller, see Chapter 16.)

Going into nudge mode

Despite my best efforts, sometimes things fall through the cracks. Buyers should pay for the item without delay through PayPal or at least pay within three business days of the close of the sale. Sometimes winners contact sellers immediately, and some use Checkout and pay for the item immediately, which saves you any hassle. However, if you don't hear from the buyer within three business days of your initial contact, my advice is *don't panic.*

People are busy; they travel, they get sick, their computer crashes, or sometimes your item simply slips the winner's mind. After four days of no communication, you can go to your My eBay page and send a payment reminder message. You find the Contact Buyer link on the item's listing on the My eBay Sold page, as shown in Figure 13-1.

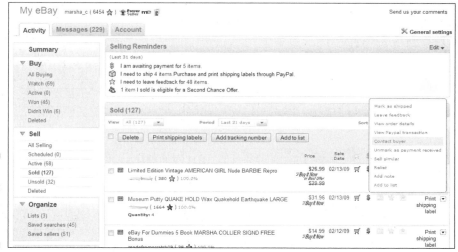

Figure 13-1:
The Contact
Buyer link
on the item
page.

If a few more days pass and you still haven't heard from the winner, you need to get into big-time *nudge-nudge mode* — as in, "Mr. X, remember me and your obligation to buy the Tiffany lamp you purchased on eBay last week?"

Send a polite-but-firm message letting Mr. X know that when he bid and won your auction, he became obligated to pay and complete the transaction. If Mr. X doesn't intend to buy your item for any reason, he needs to let you know immediately.

Don't threaten your buyer. The last thing you want to do is add insult to injury in case the buyer is facing a real problem. Besides, if the high bidder goes to sleep with the fishes, you'll _never_ see your money.

Here's what to include in your nudge-nudge e-mail:

- A gentle admonishment, such as, "Perhaps this slipped your mind," or "You may have missed my e-mail to you," or "I'm sure you didn't mean to ignore my first e-mail."

- A gentle reminder that eBay's policy is that every bid is a binding contract. You can even refer the buyer to eBay's rules and regulations if you want.

- A statement that firmly (but gently) explains that, so far, you've held up your side of the deal and you'd appreciate it if he did the same.

- A date by which you expect to see payment. Gently explain that if the deadline isn't met, you'll have no other choice but to consider the deal invalid.

Technically, you can nullify the transaction if you don't hear from a buyer within three business days. However, eBay members are a forgiving bunch under the right circumstances. I think you should give your buyer a one-week grace period after the listing ends to get in touch with you and set up a payment plan. If, at the end of the grace period, you don't see any real progress toward closing the deal, say goodnight, Gracie. Consider the deal kaput and go directly to the section "Auction Going Badly? Cut Your Losses" (later in this chapter) to find out what recourse you have.

Do a little sleuthing

I'd like to say that history repeats itself, but that would be a cliché. (All right, you caught me, but clichés are memorable because they're so often true.) After you send your polite and gentle nudge-nudge e-mail, but before you decide that the transaction is a lost cause, take a look at the bidder's feedback history. Figure 13-2 shows you what feedback looks like; all this feedback is positive. It's tough (but possible) to be this perfect.

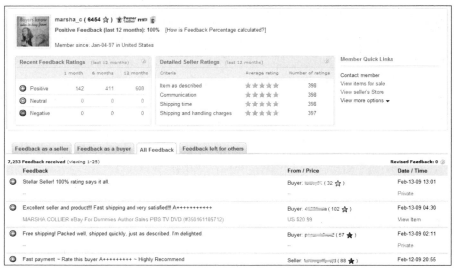

Figure 13-2:
You can get
a good idea
of whether
a buyer will
complete
a sale by
looking at
his or her
feedback
profile.

To check a bidder's feedback (starting at your item page), do the following:

1. **Click the number in parentheses next to your winner's user ID.**

   This action takes you to the member's feedback profile page.

2. **Scroll down the feedback profile page and read the comments.**

   Check to see if the bidder has received negative feedback from previous sellers. Make a note of it in case you need some support and background information (should you be chastised at a later date for blocking an unwanted bid).

3. **Conduct a Bidder search.**

   Click Advanced Search and do an Items by Bidder search to see the buyer's conduct in previous transactions. How many items has the buyer won? Click the item number to see the history of the auction. For more info on Bidder searches, check out Chapter 5.

If you've had a bad experience with a deadbeat buyer and you don't want that person to be able to bid or buy your items in the future, you can set up a bidder block for his or her user ID. If bidders are blocked by you, they can't bid; eBay tells them they have to contact you by e-mail before their bids will be accepted. You can add or delete bidders from your list at any time. eBay has managed to make the page very hard to find; you must go through the Help area or directly to the Buyer/Bidder Management area at `pages.ebay.com/services/buyandsell/biddermanagement.html`.

When all else fails, you may want to double-check with some of the bidder's previous sellers. It's okay to use eBay's Contact Member system to contact previous sellers who've dealt with the bidder. They're often happy to give you details on how well (or badly) the transaction went.

If the buyer's feedback profile provides any indication that the buyer has gone AWOL in the past, start thinking about getting out of the transaction before too much time passes. If the buyer looks to be on the level, continue to give him or her the benefit of the doubt.

Be sure to ask previous sellers that dealt with the bidder the following questions (politely):

- ✔ Did the buyer pay on time?
- ✔ Did his or her check clear? (It could have been an eCheck)
- ✔ Did he or she communicate well?

When e-mailing a third party about any negative feedback he or she has left, choose your words carefully. There's no guarantee that if you trash the bidder, the third party will keep your e-mail private. Make sure that you stick to the facts. Writing false or malicious statements can put you in danger of being sued.

Stepping things up a notch

If you don't hear from the winner after a week, your next course of action is to contact the winner by phone. To get the contact information of an eBay member for transaction purposes only, do the following:

1. **Click the Advanced Search link, which is next to the Search box on the top of most eBay pages.**

    You arrive at the Advanced Search area.

2. **Click the Find Contact Information link, which is under the Members area in the left side link box.**

3. **In the Contact Info box, type the user ID of the person you're trying to contact and the item number of the transaction in question.**

4. **Click the Search button.**

    eBay e-mails you the registered contact information of the person with whom you want to be in touch and *also sends your contact information* to that person.

Wait a day before calling the person. I like sending a last-chance e-mail after seven days that says you want to put the item back up on eBay if the buyer is no longer interested. Also mention that you want to apply for any credits you can get from eBay due to an incomplete transaction. If enough money is involved in the transaction, and you feel it's worth the investment, make the call to the winner. eBay automatically sends your request and your information to the bidder, and that may be enough of a nudge to get some action.

If you do get the person on the phone, keep the conversation like your e-mail — friendly but businesslike. Explain who you are and when the auction closed, and ask if any circumstances have delayed the bidder's reply. Often, the buyer will be so shocked to hear from you that you'll receive payment immediately, or you'll know this person is a complete deadbeat.

Other Possible Auction Problems

I'm not quite sure why, but where money is involved, sometimes people act weird. Buyers may suddenly decide that they can't purchase an item after they've made a commitment, or there may be payment problems or shipping problems. Whatever the problem, look no further than this section to find out how to make things better.

The buyer backs out of the transaction

Every time eBay members place a bid or click Buy It Now, they make a commitment to purchase the item in question — in theory, anyway. In the real world, people have second thoughts, despite the rules. You have every right to be angry that you're losing money and wasting your time. Remind the buyer that making a bid is a binding contract. But, unfortunately, if the winner won't pay up, you can't do much except apply for a final value fee refund and lick your wounds. Jump to Chapter 6 to find out more about buyer's remorse.

Keeping your cool

By all means, if the buyer of your item tells you that the transaction can't be completed, no matter what the reason, remain professional despite your anger. For one thing, at least such a would-be buyer has the heart to break the news to you instead of ignoring your e-mail and phone calls.

A seller's nightmare

I was on Facebook messaging with some other eBay sellers (feel free to find me on Facebook — all my readers are my friends!) and one was bemoaning a recent transaction. A seller always wants to sell a product, and a cooperative buyer makes the entire process pleasant. This particular seller was having a problem receiving payment from a buyer. Here's what she said:

"The buyer first said her boss opened a PayPal account for her under his e-mail address and *she couldn't access it and now her daughter used her credit card so she can't pay me. I tried to tell her she can add another e-mail address to the PayPal account and make it the primary but . . ."*

Is this fair? I recommended to the seller that she offer to mutually close the deal through eBay so she'd be free to resell the item to someone else. A buyer has a responsibility to carry out their part of the transaction as seamlessly as we expect service from the seller.

When Plan A fails, try Plan B, or even C — Second Chance Offer

You have several options if the winner backs out:

- ✔ **You can make a Second Chance offer: Offer the item to another bidder from the auction.** eBay offers a little-known feature called Second Chance offer, which protects buyers just as if they were the winner of the auction. This is a great feature that turned the previously eBay-illegal practice of side deals into fair and approved deals. You can make a Second Chance offer to any underbidder from your auction (at the amount of their high bid) for up to 60 days after the auction's end. The steps that follow this list detail how to make a Second Chance offer.

- ✔ **You can request a full or partial final value fee credit and then relist the item and hope it sells again.** (I give you more information on requesting a final value fee credit and relisting your item later in this chapter.) Who knows? This bidder may actually *earn* you money in the long run if you relist the item and get a higher winning bid.

You can make a Second Chance offer in two ways. Just follow these steps:

1. **Go to the completed auction page.**

2. **On the top of the page, you'll see some transaction-related links, as shown in Figure 13-3. Click the Make a Second Chance Offer link.**

   You're taken to the Second Chance Offer page, which has the auction number already filled in.

3. **Click Continue.**

   A page appears showing all your underbidders and their high bids.

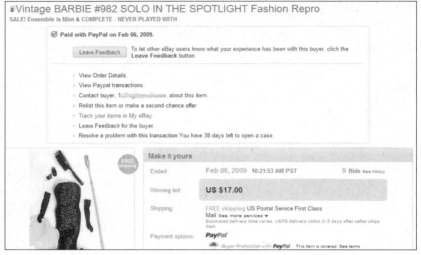

Figure 13-3:
Once an
auction is
completed,
you will find
a bunch of
handy links
on the page.

4. **Select an underbidder (or more than one underbidder if you have multiples of the item) to offer the item to and then click the Review Second Chance Offer link.**

   When you make a Second Chance offer, you can give the recipient one, three, five, or seven days to take you up on the offer. You are not charged a listing fee for the item, but you are responsible for final value fees if the transaction is completed.

5. **Check over the offer and then click Submit to send it to the underbidder.**

   Alternatively, you can go to your My eBay Sold area and click the drop-down menu next to the item listing on the page. Choose Second Chance Offer, as shown in Figure 13-4, and you'll arrive at the decision-making page from there.

Figure 13-4:
Here's
where you
may get out
of a difficult
situation
by offering
your item to
one of the
underbid-
ders in the
unsuccess-
ful auction.

Leaving feedback after an imperfect auction experience

If the buyer never materializes, backs out, bounces a check, or moves slower than a glacier to send your payment (but wants the item sent overnight from Boston to Khartoum at your expense), you need to think about how you want to word your feedback. As a seller, you can no longer leave negative feedback, but you can still write in a comment for other sellers to read. But if you do, remember to stick to the facts and don't get personal. You can always leave no feedback.

Here are a few feedback tips:

✔ If the transaction was shaky but everything turned out all right in the end, go ahead and leave positive feedback, depending on how tough things went.

✔ If a blizzard stopped planes out of Chicago for three days and that's why it took a long time to get online to pay, take a deep breath, blame the fates, and leave positive feedback with a fair comment.

✔ If the buyer was a living nightmare, take a long break before getting nasty — and have someone you love and trust read it before you send something into the virtual world that you can't take back.

For more information on leaving feedback, check out Chapters 4 and 6.

The item you send is busted — and so are you

Uh-oh! Could it be true? Could you have sent the wrong item? Or is it possible that the crystal vase you thought you packed so well is a sad pile of shards at the bottom of a torn box? If so, read Chapter 12 as soon as you take care of this catastrophe so that you can get some hints on packing and insurance.

It's time to do some serious problem solving. If the buyer met his or her end of the deal, you need to do your best to fix the problem. Your communication skills are your number-one asset in this situation, so get to work.

Picking up the pieces

No matter how carefully you pack an item, sometimes it arrives on the buyer's doorstep mangled, broken, or squashed. News of this unfortunate event travels back to you fast. The buyer will let you know in an e-mail in about 30 seconds how unhappy he or she is. (Sometimes they're not very polite, but stay calm.) Tell the buyer to locate the insurance stamp or paper tag that's attached to the package as proof of insurance and then take the whole mangled shebang back to his or her post office.

Here's what happens at the post office:

- ✔ If the item is insured for less than $50.00, the buyer immediately gets a Postal Service money order for the value of the item.

- ✔ If the item is insured for over $50.00, the buyer fills out a claim form, and you're contacted to fill out additional forms. You need to show your insurance receipt to the good people at the post office. You have to wait 60 to 90 days for the paperwork to be processed before you actually get paid.

- ✔ Of course, the post office won't refund the postage. Hey, they delivered the item, didn't they?

If a package is lost, you'll know it because the delivery confirmation never comes through, and the buyer tells you the package is a no-show. You need to go the post office from which you sent the item to file for insurance. Then the Postal Service checks around. If your item isn't located in 30 days, it's declared lost, and there's another round of paperwork and processing before you get your money. And no, you don't get a return on the postage either.

If you have private package insurance the process is much simpler. You don't have to contact the shipper; you merely have to contact the insurance company and place a claim.

Lots of eBay sellers seem to think that if a buyer doesn't pay for insurance and the package gets lost in transit, than it's not the seller's problem. They couldn't be more wrong. The Federal Trade Commission has a strict rule covering mail order merchandise delivery. The short version is that if your item doesn't get to the buyer within 30 days, you must refund the payment. The long version can be found at the FTC Web site:

```
www.ftc.gov/bcp/edu/pubs/business/adv/bus02.shtm
```

Boxed out of a claim

In my experience, neither UPS nor the U.S. Postal Service will pay on an insurance claim if they feel you did a lousy job of packing. Always use good packing products, wrap carefully, and get ready to plead your case.

Every shipping company has its own procedure for complaints. But here's the one thing they do have in common: No procedure is hassle-free. Call your shipper as soon as a problem arises.

You have regrets — seller's remorse

You've undoubtedly heard about buyer's remorse. Here's a new one for you — *seller's remorse*. If you're selling your velvet Elvis footstool because your spouse said, "It's me or that footstool!" and then decide that your spouse should have known how much you revered the King when you went to Graceland on your honeymoon, you can end the listing. Read "Try canceling bids first" and "If all else fails, end your auction early," later in this chapter.

Auction Going Badly? Cut Your Losses

So your auction is cruising along just fine for a couple of days when you notice that the same eBay user who didn't pay on a previous auction is your current high bidder. You don't want to get burned again, do you? Of course not; *cancel* this deadbeat's bid before it's too late. Although canceling bids — or, for that matter, entire auctions — isn't easy (you have a load of explaining to do, pardner), eBay does allow it.

If you feel you have to wash your hands of a listing that's given you nothing but grief, it doesn't mean you have to lose money on the deal. Read on to find out the protocol for dumping untrustworthy bidders or (as a last resort) laying a bad auction to rest and beginning anew.

Many of these functions are also available from the drop-down menus on the right side of the item's listing on the My eBay Selling page.

Try canceling bids first

Face the facts: This auction is fast becoming a big-time loser. You did your very best, and things didn't work out. Before you kill an auction completely, see whether you can improve it by canceling bids first. Canceling a bid removes a bidder from your auction, but the auction continues running.

When you cancel a bid, you need to provide an explanation, which goes on record for all to see. You may have a million reasons for thinking your auction is a bust, but eBay says your explanation had better be good. Here are some eBay-approved reasons for canceling a bid (or even an entire auction):

- ✔ The high bidder informs you that he or she is retracting the bid.

- ✔ Despite your best efforts to determine who your high bidder is, you can't find out — and you get no response to your e-mails or phone calls.

✔ The bidder makes a dollar-amount mistake in the bid. (The bidder bids $100.00 instead of $10.00, for example.)

✔ You decide midauction that you can't sell your item due to the fact that it was sold in an outside venue — or the dog ate it. (You must cancel all bids and end the listing in this instance.)

I can't drive this point home hard enough: *Explain why you're canceling a bid, and your explanation had better be good.* You can cancel any bid for any reason you want, but if you can't give a good explanation of why you did it, you will be sorry. Citing past transaction problems with the current high bidder is okay, but canceling a bidder who lives in Japan because you don't feel like shipping overseas after you said you'd ship internationally could give your feedback history the aroma of week-old sushi.

To cancel a bid (starting from most eBay pages), do the following:

1. **Go to the listing page.**

2. **Click the Bid History link.**

   You're taken to the Bid History page.

3. **Scroll to the bottom of the bidding history and click the Cancel Bids link.**

   You'll be brought to a page outlining eBay's policies on bidding.

4. **Scroll down to the Canceling Bids area and click the Canceling Bids link.**

   You arrive at the Canceling bids page, as shown in Figure 13-5.

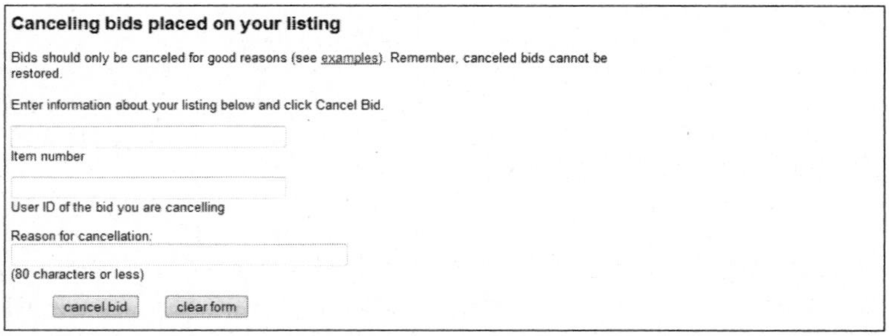

Figure 13-5:
Use this form to remove a bidder from one of your auctions.

Canceling bids placed on your listing

Bids should only be canceled for good reasons (see examples). Remember, canceled bids cannot be restored.

Enter information about your listing below and click Cancel Bid.

Item number

User ID of the bid you are cancelling

Reason for cancellation:

(80 characters or less)

[cancel bid] [clear form]

5. **Type the item number, the user ID for the bid you're canceling, and the reason for canceling the bid.**

6. **Click the Cancel Bid button.**

Be sure that you really want to cancel a bid before you click the Cancel Bid button. Canceled bids can never be reinstated.

Canceling bids means you removed an individual bidder (or several bidders) from your auction, but the auction itself continues running. If you want to end the auction completely, read on.

Blocking bidders

If you have a bidder who just doesn't get the message and continually bids on your auctions despite the fact that you've e-mailed and told him or her not to, you can block the bidder from ever participating in your auctions. You can create a list of bidders to prevent them from bidding temporarily or permanently, and you can edit the list at any time. You can find the page from the same page as described in the preceding section. Click Block Bidders and then create your list. Alternatively, you can go directly to this address:

```
pages.ebay.com/services/buyandsell/biddermanagement.html
```

If all else fails, end your listing early

If you put your auction up for a week and the next day your boss says you have to go to China for a month or your landlord says you have to move out immediately so that he can fumigate for a week, you can end your auction early. But ending an auction early isn't a decision to be taken lightly. You miss all the last-minute bidding action.

eBay makes it clear that ending your auction early does not relieve you of the obligation to sell this item to the highest bidder. To relieve your obligation, you must first cancel all the bids and then end the auction. Of course, if no one has bid, you have nothing to worry about.

When you cancel an auction, you have to write a short explanation (no more than 80 characters) that appears on the bidding history section of your auction page. Anyone who bid on the item may e-mail you for a written explanation. If bidders think your explanation doesn't hold water, don't be surprised if you get some nasty e-mail.

Bidding on your own item is against the rules. Once upon a time, you could cancel an auction by outbidding everyone on your own item and then ending the auction. But some eBay users abused this privilege by bidding on their own items merely to boost the sales price. Shame on them.

To end an auction early, go to your My eBay Active Selling page and in the drop-down menu next to the listing, choose End Item. You will be required to sign in again. Then follow these steps:

1. **Click the appropriate link: either Cancel Bids and End Listing Early or Sell Item to High Bidder and End Listing Early.**

2. **On the next page, select a reason for ending your listing.**

3. **Click the End Your Listing button.**

   An Ended Listing page appears, and eBay sends an End of Listing Confirmation e-mail to you and to the highest bidder.

 If you know when you list the item that you'll be away when an auction ends, in your item description let potential bidders know when you plan to contact them. Bidders who are willing to wait will still be willing to bid. Alerting them to your absence can save you from losing money if you have to cut your auction short.

Filing for a final value fee credit

If closing a successful auction is the thrill of victory, finding out that your buyer is a nonpaying bidder, or deadbeat, is the agony of defeat. Adding insult to injury, eBay still charges you a final value fee even if the high bidder never sends you a cent. But you can do something about it. You can file for a final value fee credit.

To qualify for a final value fee credit, you must prove to eBay that one of the following events occurred:

- ✔ The winning buyer never responded after numerous e-mail contacts.

- ✔ The winning buyer backed out of the sale.

- ✔ The winning buyer's payment did not clear or was never received.

- ✔ The winning buyer returned the item to you, and you refunded the payment.

 If both you and the buyer decide that it's okay not to go through with the transaction, that's okay with eBay, too. eBay will allow you to get back your final value fee by going through the refund process. You'll find an option in the Reason for Refund area that will absolve the buyer of any wrongdoing with eBay's Unpaid Item police.

The instant you file for a Non-Paying Bidder Alert credit, eBay shoots off an e-mail to the winner of your item (copying you on the e-mail) and warns the eBay user of their nonpaying status.

If at least 7 days and no more than 45 days have elapsed since the end of the auction, you can apply for a full final fee credit. First, however, you must file an Unpaid Item Alert:

1. **Go to your My eBay Sold view.**

   Find the transaction in question on the list of sold items.

2. **Click the drop-down menu at the right of the listing and then choose Resolve a Problem.**

   You're taken to the Resolution Center.

3. **Select the I Sold an Item and Haven't Received My Payment Yet option and click Continue.**

4. **Sign in to your account and enter your user ID and password.**

   The Report an Unpaid Item Case form appears.

5. **Type the item number of the listing in question (if it's not already there) and then click the Continue button.**

6. **You'll be asked to select an issue from a drop-down menu that applies to your situation. Once you do, click Continue.**

7. **Review everything you've entered to be sure it's correct, and then click Continue.**

   If you and the buyer mutually agreed not to complete the transaction, when you click Continue, you see the Final Value Fee Credit request page.

After three nonpayment warnings, eBay can boot a deadbeat from the site.

You and your nonpaying buyer now have ten days to work out your problems. If you make no progress after seven days, you may file for your final value fee credit.

You need to wait *at least* seven days after the auction ends to file an Unpaid Item Alert and then seven days before you can apply for a final value fee credit. I think it's jumping the gun to label someone a nonpaying bidder after only seven days — try to contact the bidder again unless the bidder sends you a message about backing out (or you have good cause to believe you have a deadbeat on your hands). If you still want to file for your final value fee credit after seven days, do the following:

1. **On your My eBay page, hover your cursor over the Account tab. When the drop-down menu appears, choose Resolution Center.**

   You're taken to the Resolution Center.

2. **Under the Your Cases heading, find the transaction in question.**

3. **Click the View Dispute link under the status column.**

   You're now in the area where you may respond to any comments the buyer has left regarding why he or she hasn't yet paid for your item.

4. **Enter your response (if any) to the buyer in the messages area and click Submit Response or to get your final value fee refund, click Close Dispute.**

5. **Click the Close Dispute button on the bottom of the page.**

   You're taken to the Credit Request Process Completed page, which confirms that your refund is being processed by eBay, as shown in Figure 13-6.

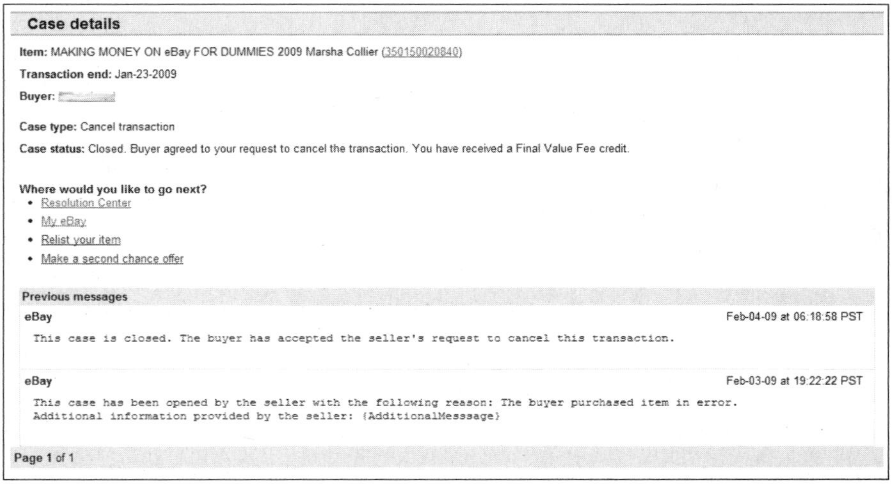

Figure 13-6:
eBay processes your final value fee credit; you can always check the status in the Case History.

> **Case details**
>
> **Item:** MAKING MONEY ON eBay FOR DUMMIES 2009 Marsha Collier (350150020840)
>
> **Transaction end:** Jan-23-2009
>
> **Buyer:**
>
> **Case type:** Cancel transaction
>
> **Case status:** Closed. Buyer agreed to your request to cancel the transaction. You have received a Final Value Fee credit.
>
> **Where would you like to go next?**
> - Resolution Center
> - My eBay
> - Relist your item
> - Make a second chance offer
>
> **Previous messages**
>
> eBay — Feb-04-09 at 06:18:58 PST
>
> This case is closed. The buyer has accepted the seller's request to cancel this transaction.
>
> eBay — Feb-03-09 at 19:22:22 PST
>
> This case has been opened by the seller with the following reason: The buyer purchased item in error. Additional information provided by the seller: {AdditionalMesssage}
>
> Page 1 of 1

When your listing ends, you have up to 45 days after the auction closes to request a credit. After 45 days, kiss your refund goodbye; eBay won't process it.

Anyone caught applying for a refund on a successful item transaction can be suspended or something worse — after all, this is a clear-cut case of fraud.

If you want to verify eBay's accounting, grab your calculator and use Table 9-2 in Chapter 9 to check the math. (Why couldn't I have had one of those in high-school algebra class?)

Always print a copy of any refund and credit requests you make. This paper trail can help bail you out later if eBay asks for documentation.

Déjà vu — relisting your item

Despite all your best efforts, sometimes your auction ends with no bids or bids that are not even close to your reserve price. Or maybe a buyer won your item, but the transaction didn't go through. eBay takes pity on you and offers you the chance to pick yourself up, dust yourself off, and start all over again.

The best way to improve your chances of selling a relisted item is by making changes to the listing. eBay says the majority of the items put up for auction should sell. If you sell your item the second time around (in most cases), eBay rewards you with a refund of your insertion fee. You receive your refund after at least one billing cycle. Accept this refund as a reward for learning the ropes.

In the case of an unpaid item, you may (only in this situation) qualify for an insertion fee credit by relisting the item. If the item sells the second time, eBay will refund the insertion fee for relisting.

You *must* only use eBay's Relist feature to receive the credit. Once the item is filed as a unpaid, you can use the Relist link on the unpaid item page or do the following:

1. **Go to your My eBay page.**

2. **On the left side of the page in the Selling area, click the Sold link.**

   You arrive at the page without Sold Listings. You will be able to find the unpaid item because it's specially marked. See Figure 13-7 for an example.

3. **Click the Relist link from the drop-down menu next to the unpaid item.**

But is she a natural blonde?

Here's an example of an item that would have made the seller a bundle if he or she had performed a little more strategizing up front:

Platinum Mackie Barbie: Beautiful Platinum Bob Mackie Barbie. MIB (removed from box once only to scan). The doll comes with shoes, stand, booklet, and Mackie drawing. The original plastic protects her hair and earrings. Buyer adds $10.00 for shipping and insurance. Payment must be made within 10 days of auction by MO or cashier's check only.

The starting price was $9.99, and even though the bidding went to $256.00, the seller's reserve price was not met, and the item didn't sell. And the Second Chance offer didn't bite.

When relisting this item, the seller should lower the reserve price and add much more to the description about the importance and rarity of the doll (unless, of course, $256.00 was far below what the seller wanted to make on the doll). Offering to accept credit cards through PayPal would have also helped to make the sale.

Figure 13-7:
Finding your unpaid item for relisting on the Sold items page (note I have already relisted this item).

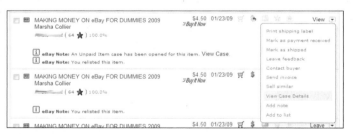

To be eligible for a refund of your insertion fee, here's the scoop:

- ✔ You must relist no more than 90 days after closing the original auction.

- ✔ You can get credit only if you got no bids in your original auction or if the bids you got did not equal the reserve in your reserve-price auction.

- ✔ You can change anything about your auction item description, price, duration, and minimum price, but you can't sell a different item.

- ✔ If you set a reserve price in your original auction, you must set the same reserve, lower it, or cancel the reserve altogether. If you set a higher price or add a reserve, you're not eligible for a relisting credit.

eBay's generosity has exceptions. It doesn't offer refunds for any listing options you paid for, such as the use of Featured Plus! or bold lettering.

Also, fixed-price and store listings aren't covered by this offer. And if you have a deadbeat on your hands, you can relist, but you don't get a return of your insertion fee. More bad news: If you don't sell the item the second time around, you're stuck paying *two* insertion fees. So work a little harder this time and give it your best shot!

If your item doesn't sell after two tries, you need to take a different tack. If you want to be eligible for a new insertion fee refund (once your item hasn't sold twice in a row), you must use the Sell Similar option. This sets up the item in a new cycle for eBay. To get your third shot at selling, do the following (from the Unsold section of your My eBay Selling page):

1. **Click the drop-down menu next to auction item that you want to relist and choose Sell Similar.**

    You're taken to the original listing form with all the information filled in.

2. **Make your changes to the auction (I hope major ones as mentioned further on), launch it, and pray!**

The more specific your item title, the more you improve your odds of being profitable. If you're selling an old Monopoly game, don't just title it **Old Monopoly board game**; call it **Rare 1959 Monopoly Game Complete in Box**. For more information about listing items, see Chapter 10.

Here's a list of ideas that you can use to improve your auction's odds for success:

- ✔ **Change the item category.** See if the item sold better in another category (see Chapter 3).

- ✔ **Add a picture.** If two identical items are up for auction at the same time, the item with a photo gets more and higher bids. Zoom in on Chapter 14.

- ✔ **Spruce up the title and description.** Make it enticing and grab those search engines. Breeze on over to Chapter 10.

- ✔ **Set a lower minimum bid.** The first bidders will think they're getting a bargain, and others will want a hot item. Mosey on over to Chapter 10.

- ✔ **Set a lower reserve price or cancel the reserve.** A reserve price often scares away bidders who fear it's too high. See (yup) Chapter 10 for ways to make your reserve more palatable to prospective bidders.

- ✔ **Change the duration of the auction.** Maybe you need some more time. Go to (you guessed it) Chapter 10.

Long-time eBay veterans say that reducing or canceling your reserve price makes an auction very attractive to buyers.

Chapter 14

Increase Your Profits with Pictures and Other Strategies

You may be enjoying most of what eBay has to offer, and you're probably having some good buying adventures. If you're selling, you're experiencing the excitement of making money. But there's more. Welcome to eBay, the advanced class.

In this chapter, you go to the head of the class by discovering some insider tips on how to enhance your auctions with images and spiffy text. Successful eBay vendors know that pictures (also called *images*) really help sell items. This chapter gives you the basics on how to create great images. I also give you advice on linking pictures to your auctions so that buyers around the world can view them.

Using Images in Your Auctions

Would you buy an item you couldn't see? Most people won't, especially if they're interested in purchasing items that they want to display or clothes they intend to wear. Without a picture, you can't tell whether a seller's idea of good quality is anything like yours — or if the item is exactly what you're looking for.

Welcome to the cyberworld of *imaging*, where pictures are called not pictures but *images,* and your monitor isn't a monitor but a *display*. With a digital camera or a scanner and software, you can manipulate your images — spin, crop, and color-correct — so that they grab viewers by the lapels. Even cooler: When you're happy with your creation, you can add it to your eBay auction for others to see.

Sellers, take heed and read these other reasons why you should use your own well-made digital images in your auction pages:

✔ If you don't have a picture, potential bidders may wonder whether you're deliberately hiding the item from view because you know something is wrong with it. Paranoid? Maybe. Practical? You bet.

✔ Fickle bidders don't even bother reading an item description if they can't see the item. Maybe they were traumatized in English class.

✔ Taking your own pictures shows that you actually have the item in your possession. Many scam artists take images from a manufacturer's Web site to illustrate their bogus sales on eBay. Why risk being suspect? Snap a quick picture!

✔ Everyone's doing it. I hate to pressure you, but digital images are the custom for sellers on eBay, so if you're not using them, you're not reaching the widest possible number of people who would bid on your item. From that point of view, you're not doing the most you can to serve your potential customers' needs. Hey, fads are *driven* by conformity. You may as well use them to your advantage.

So which is better for capturing images: digital cameras or digital scanners? As with all gadgets, here's the classic answer: It depends. For my money, it's hard to beat a digital camera. But before you go snag one, decide what kind of investment (and how big) you plan to make in your eBay auctions.

If you buy a digital SLR, be sure to check with a camera store to see if older, traditional lenses can be used on the camera you buy. It's often the case with the major brands, although digital lenses don't have to be as "good" as the old lenses were — due to all the electronic manipulation that goes on inside the new cameras. Next, go to eBay and see what kind of deals you can find on compatible lenses.

Whether you buy new or used digital equipment on eBay, make sure it comes with a warranty. If you *don't* get a warranty, Murphy's Law practically ensures that your digital equipment will break the second time you use it.

Choosing a digital camera

If price isn't a factor, you should buy the highest-quality digital camera you can afford, especially if you plan to use images for items that vary in size and shape. By *highest-quality,* I don't necessarily mean a camera with vast amounts of megapixels; I mean a camera from a quality manufacturer that has a high optical zoom and has a good (nonplastic) lens.

How I've been shooting on eBay

I've been on eBay since 1996, so I've taken lots of pictures to promote my online sales. I'm pretty happy with the quality of most of my own images. When I've sold paper ephemera, I usually just lay the item on a scanner — and scan away. It's the best way to get a good image of that type of item. I started early on with an Olympus camera, but quickly changed to the Sony Mavica FD-73. The FD-73 was one of the first that had a 10X digital zoom, which helps with intricate close-ups.

Then I upgraded to a used FD-92 with an 8X optical zoom (a newer model that added a memory stick). And a few years ago I purchased a Sony DSC-H1 — a fancy 5-megapixel camera with a 12X zoom. To be perfectly honest, it's way too much camera for my eBay photo shoots. But I like the size — I find my teeny purse-size camera gets lost in my office and I can't find it when I want to take pictures! One excellent improvement on my new camera is the addition of *image stabilization* — it holds the camera steady when I zoom in for ultra macro close-ups. If you've ever taken a picture fully zoomed, you know that the slightest breath can make the resulting image blurry. In the long run, a nice balance between new technological gadgets and familiar, easy-to-use equipment is the way to go.

Sony, Canon, Kodak, and Nikon all make good basic digital cameras. You can find them for about $150.00 (easily found on eBay for even less). Middle-of-the-road new (and quality used) digital cameras sell for between $100.00 and $75.00. Compare prices at computer stores and on the Web.

A great place to buy digital cameras is (surprise!) eBay. Just do a search of some popular manufacturers, such as Canon, Kodak, Sony, and Nikon, and you will find pages of listings of both new and used digital cameras.

When shopping for a digital camera, look at the following features:

- ✔ **Resolution:** Look for a camera that has a resolution of at least 800×600 pixels. This isn't hard to find because new cameras tout their strength in megapixels (millions of pixels). You don't need that high a resolution for eBay because your pictures will ultimately be shown on a 72 dpi monitor, not printed on paper. A *pixel* is a tiny dot of information that, when grouped with other pixels, forms an image. The more pixels an image has, the clearer and sharper the image is; the more memory the image scarfs up, the slower it shows up on-screen. An 800-by-600-pixel resolution may seem paltry next to the 6-million-pixel punch of a high-end digital camera, but trust me: No one bidding on your auctions will ever know the difference. And the picture will load a *lot* faster.

- ✔ **Optical zoom:** Here's where the camera manufacturers try to pull the wool over the consumer's eyes. They sell cameras with an optical and a digital zoom. The *optical zoom* is a true zoom done by the camera, the lens, and its built in CCD (computer chip in cameras that converts light into electronic data) — but a *digital zoom* is virtual; it's *interpolated* through software in the camera. That means it makes up data to fill in any holes it doesn't capture. You've seen this effect if you've ever tried to enlarge a picture from the Web in a software program — it gets all blurry.

If you ever plan on shooting close-ups, look for a high quality optical zoom.

✔ **Storage type:** Smart card? Secure Digital Card? Mini SD card? CompactFlash card? Memory stick? (Whew.) The instructions that come with your camera explain how to transfer images from your media type to your computer. (No instructions? Check the manufacturer's Web site.) Most newer computers have ports into which you can insert your camera's memory card; the computer reads the card like it's a teeny, tiny disk drive.

A versatile way to get the best images of items that require extreme close-ups (such as jewelry, stamps, currency, coins) is to use a super invention called a Cloud Dome. When photographing complex items, no matter how good your camera is, you may find it difficult to capture the item cleanly and exactly (especially the colors and brightness of gems and metals). Your camera mounts to the top of this Cloud Dome, and pictures are taken inside the translucent plastic dome. The dome diffuses the light over the entire surface of the object to reveal all its intricate details. You can purchase Cloud Domes on eBay or from the manufacturer's Web site at `www.clouddome.com`. Even in black and white, you can see the difference that a cloud dome can make when taking pictures of jewelry, as shown Figure 14-1.

Figure 14-1:
Before and after pictures of items shot through a Cloud Dome.

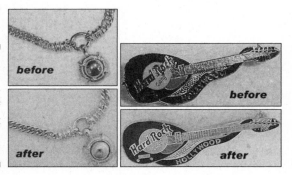

Choosing a scanner

If you plan to sell flat items such as autographs, stamps, books, or documents — or if you need a good piece of business equipment that can double as a photocopier — consider getting a digital scanner. You can pick up a brand new one for a under $100.00 (you can find scanners on eBay).

Here's what you need to look for when you buy a scanner:

- **Resolution:** As with printers and photocopiers, the resolution of digital scanning equipment is measured in *dots per inch* (dpi). The more dpi, the greater the resolution.

  Some scanners can provide resolutions as high as 12,800 dpi, which looks awesome when you print the image, but to dress up your eBay auctions, all you need is (are you ready?) 72 dpi (dots or pixels per inch)! That's it. Your images will look great and won't take up much storage space on your computer's hard drive. Basic scanners can scan images at resolutions of up to 1,200 dpi, so even they are far more powerful than you need for your eBay images.

- **Flatbed:** If you're planning to use your scanner to scan pictures of documents (or even items in boxes), a flatbed scanner is your best bet. Flatbeds work just like photocopiers. You simply lay your item or box on the glass and scan away.

Making Your Picture a Thing of Beauty

The idea behind using images in your auctions is to attract tons of potential buyers. With that goal in mind, you should try to create the best-looking images possible, no matter what kind of technology you're using to capture them.

Get it on camera

Point-and-shoot may be okay for a group shot at some historical monument, but illustrating your auction is a whole different idea. Whether you're using a traditional film camera (so you can scan your developed photographs later) or a digital camera to capture your item, some basic photographic guidelines can give you better results.

Don't forget your camcorder!

The majority of eBay users use either a digital camera or scanner to dress up their auctions with images, but some just use what they already own: their handy-dandy camcorders! Yup, after videotaping your day at the beach, point your lens at that Victorian doll and shoot. With the help of a video-capturing device, you can create a still digital image right from the camera.

For more on using scanners, zoom ahead to the next section, "Use traditional photos? Yes, I scan." Then c'mon back to these do's and don'ts to ensure that your digital image is a genuine enhancement to your auction:

✔ **Do** take the picture of your item outside, in daylight, whenever possible. That way the camera can catch all possible details and color.

✔ **Do** forget about fancy backgrounds; they distract viewers from your item. Put small items on a neutral-colored, nonreflective towel or cloth; put larger items in front of a neutral-colored wall or curtain. You'll cut out almost all the background when you prepare the picture on your computer. (This chapter explains how to prepare your picture.)

✔ **Do** use extra lighting. You can do this with your camera's flash mode or with extra photo lighting on stands. Use extra lighting even when you're taking the picture outside. The extra lighting acts as *fill light* — it adds more light to the item, filling in some of the shadowed spots.

✔ **Don't** get so close to the item that the additional light washes out (over-exposes) the image. The easiest way to figure out the best distance is by trial and error. Start close and keep moving farther away until you get the results you want. This method can get pricey if you use film, but that's where digital cameras really shine: You can see the picture seconds after you shoot it, keep it and modify it, erase it, and start again.

✔ **Do** take two or three acceptable versions of your image; you can choose the best one later on your computer.

✔ **Don't** use incandescent or fluorescent lighting to illuminate the photos you plan to scan. Incandescent lighting tends to make items look yellowish, and fluorescent lights lend a bluish tone to your photos. Some sellers use *GE Reveal* incandescent bulbs; they throw a good-quality light which, when combined with natural daylight, produces an even tone. My favorites are the 5,000 degrees Kelvin full-spectrum bulbs. Yes, at $20.00 apiece they're very expensive, but with a 10,000-hour lifespan, they should have you taking pictures into the next decade. (***Hint:*** you can find 5,000 Kelvin portable lamps on eBay for just a little more.)

✔ If your item relies on detail (for example, an engraved signature or detailed gold trim), **do** take a wide shot of the entire item — and then take a tight close-up or two of the detailed areas that you want buyers to see.

✔ **Do** make sure that you focus the camera; nothing is worse than a blurry picture. If your camera is a fixed-focus model (it can't be adjusted), get only as close as the manufacturer recommends. If you go beyond that distance, the item appears out of focus. (Automatic-focus cameras measure the distance and change the lens setting as needed.)

Taking pictures of your item from different angles gives the prospective buyer more information. When you have several images, use your photo-editing program to put them in one composite image, as shown in Figure 14-2.

Figure 14-2:
Making a composite image of pictures from several angles makes for an attractive auction.

Some eBay creeps, whether out of laziness or deceit, steal images from other eBay members. (They simply make a digital copy of the image and use it in their own auctions. This is so uncool because then the copied image doesn't represent the actual item being sold.) This pilfering has happened to me on several occasions. To prevent picture-snatching, you can watermark your user ID to all your photos. Then, the next time somebody lifts one of your pictures, it has your name on it. Don't forget to report these tools by using the Report Item link at the bottom of their listing — *stealing photos is against eBay rules!*

Use traditional photos? Yes, I scan

If you use a scanner and traditional (that is, nondigital) camera to create images for your eBay auction, you've come to the right place. (Also check out the tips in the preceding section.) If the photo processor will create digital images for you, be sure you get that done. It will save you lots of time in scanning. If that's not possible:

- ✔ Have the photo developer print your photos on glossy paper; it scans best.

- ✔ When you take traditional photos for scanning, get as close to your item as your camera allows. Enlarging photos in the scanner will only result in blurry (or, worse, jagged) images.

- ✔ Scan the box that the item came in, or if there's a photo of the item on the box, scan that portion of the box.

✔ If you're scanning a three-dimensional item (such as a doll, jewelry item, or box) and you can't close the scanner lid, drape a black or white T-shirt over the item after you place it on the scanner's glass plate; that way you get a clean background and good light reflection from the scanner.

✔ If you want to scan an item that's too big to put on your scanner all at once, scan the item in sections and assemble the digital pieces with your image-editing software. The instructions that come with your software should explain how to do this.

Software that adds the artist's touch

After you take the picture (or scan it) and transfer it into your computer according to the manufacturer's instructions, the next step is to edit the picture. Much like a book or magazine editor, you get to cut, fix, resize, and reshape your picture until you think it's good enough to be seen by the public. If you're a non-techie type, don't get nervous; many of the programs have one-button magical corrections that make your pictures look great.

The software program that comes with your digital camera or scanner puts at your disposal an arsenal of editing tools that help you turn a basic image of your item into something special. Although each program has its own collection of features, a few basic tools and techniques are common to all:

✔ **Image quality:** Enables you to enhance or correct colors, sharpen images, remove dust spots, and increase or reduce brightness or contrast.

✔ **Size:** Reduces or increases the size or shape of the image.

✔ **Orientation:** Rotates the image left or right; flips it horizontally or vertically.

✔ **Crop:** Trims your picture to show the item, rather than extraneous background.

✔ **Create an image format:** Gives your edited picture a specific format, such as .JPG, .GIF, or others when you save it. The best format for putting photos on the Web (and thus the preferred format on eBay and the one I strongly recommend) is .JPG (pronounced "JAY-peg").

Every image-editing software program has its own system requirements and capabilities. Study the software that comes with your camera or scanner. If you feel the program is too complicated (or doesn't give you the editing tools you need), investigate some of the other popular programs. A simple-to-use program called Fast Photos was developed by an eBay seller with us in mind. It's incredibly simple to use, and the learning curve is small. I use it and love its simplicity and speed — and it costs only $24.95 (you can get a free 21-day trial at www.pixby.com/marshacollier).

Copying someone else's auction text or images without permission can constitute copyright infringement, which ends your auction and could get you suspended from eBay.

Making Your Images Web-Friendly

Because digital images are made up of pixels — and every pixel has a set of instructions that has to be stored someplace — you have two difficulties facing you right after you take the picture:

- Digital images contain computer instructions, so bigger pictures take up more memory.

- Very large digital images take longer to *build* (appear) on the buyer's screen, and time can be precious in an auction.

To get around both these problems, think small. Here's a checklist of tried-and-true techniques for preparing your elegantly slender, fast-loading images to display on eBay:

- **Set your image resolution at 72 pixels per inch.** You can do this with the settings for your scanner. Although 72 ppi may seem like a low resolution, it only nibbles computer memory (instead of chomping), shows up fast on a buyer's screen, and looks great on eBay.

- **When using a digital camera, set the camera to no higher than the 800×600 format.** That's custom-made for a monitor. You can always crop the picture if it's too large. You can even save the image at 640×480, and it'll display well on eBay — but it will take up less space, and you can add more pictures!

- **Make the finished image no larger than 480 pixels wide.** When you size your picture in your image software, it's best to keep it no larger than 300×300 pixels or 4 inches square, even if it's a snapshot of a classic 4×4 monster truck. These dimensions are big enough for people to see without squinting, and the details of your item show up nicely.

- **Crop any unnecessary areas of the photo.** You need to show your item only; everything else is a waste.

- **Use your software to darken or change the photo's contrast.** When the image looks good on your computer screen, the image looks good on your eBay auction page.

- **Save your image as a .JPG file.** When you finish editing your picture, save it as a .JPG. (To do this, follow the instructions that come with your software.) .JPG is the best format for eBay; it compresses information into a small file that builds fast and reproduces nicely on the Internet.

✔ **Check the total size of your image.** After you save the image, check its total size. If the size hovers around 40K (kilobytes) or smaller, eBay users won't have a hard time seeing the image in a reasonable amount of time.

✔ **Reduce the size of your image if it's larger than 50K.** Small is fast, efficient, and beautiful. Big is slow, sluggish, and dangerous. Impatient eBay users will move on to the next listing if they have to wait to see your image.

The Image Is Perfect — Now What?

Now that your masterpiece is complete, you want to emblazon it on your auction for all the world to see. When most people first get the urge to dazzle prospective buyers with a picture, they poke around the eBay site looking for a place to put it. Trade secret: You're not actually putting pictures on eBay; you're telling eBay's servers where to *find* your picture so that, like a good hunting dog, your auction *points* the buyers' browsers to the exact corner of the virtual universe where your picture is. That's why the picture has to load fast — it's coming in from a different location. (Yeah, it confused me in the beginning too, but now it makes perfect sense. Uh-huh. Sure.)

To help eBay find your image, all you have to do is type its address in the Picture URL box of the Sell Your Item form — so don't forget to write down the Web address (URL) of your image.

If you use eBay's Picture Services, your photo will be on eBay's servers and will upload once, directly from your computer. I talk more about that in just a minute.

You can highlight your image's URL with your cursor, right-click your mouse, and copy it to your computer's clipboard. Then go to the auction page you're filling out on eBay, put your cursor in the Picture URL box, and paste the address into the box.

A typical address (for someone using AOL) looks something like this:

```
members.aol.com/ebay4dummy/rolexwatch.jpg
```

Because your image needs an address, you have to find it a good home online. You have several options:

✔ **Your ISP (Internet service provider):** All the big ISPs — AOL, Comcast, Road Runner, and Earthlink — give you space to store your Internet stuff. You're already paying for an ISP, so you can park pictures there at no extra charge.

✔ **An image-hosting Web site:** Web sites that specialize in hosting pictures are popping up all over the Internet. Some charge a small fee; others are free. The upside here is that they're easy to use.

✔ **Your server:** If you have your own server (those of you who do know who you are), you can store those images right in your own home.

✔ **eBay Picture Services:** You can find out about using eBay's photo-hosting service later in this chapter.

Using an ISP to store your images

Every ISP has its own rules and procedures. Go to the help area of your ISP for directions on how to *access your personal area* (no, I'm not getting naughty — those are authentic computerese phrases!) and how to *upload your images.*

After you've uploaded your images to your ISP, get the Web address of your item's location and type it in the Picture URL box of eBay's Sell Your Item page. Now the picture appears within the item description whenever someone views your auction page. Figure 14-3 shows you an auction description with a picture.

Figure 14-3:
Including pictures in your auctions takes practice, but the results are worth it.

Elegant Frosted & Clear
Floral Stopper Perfume Bottle

This charming and very Lalique style perfume bottle stands approx. 4" tall. The base features alternating swirls of frosted and clear cut glass and has no markings of any kind. The ground frosted stopper has two lovely flowers at the top. A great item for your vanity table, or a wonderful gift. Bid with confidence and bid whatever you feel this bottle is worth to you as he is selling with **NO RESERVE!** *(Feel free to check my feedback!)* I pack all my items carefully. Winning bidder to pay shipping & handling of $4.55 and must submit payment within a week of winning the auction. I will accept credit cards through paypal.com (see below). Good luck on winning!

GOOD LUCK, HAPPY BIDDING!

Click below to...
View my other auctions - Win more than one and SAVE on shipping!

Using image-hosting Web sites to store images

Okay, realistically, many people are combing cyberspace looking for the next great thing. eBay's success has entrepreneurs all over the globe coming up with different kinds of auction-support businesses. As usual, a lot of junk pops up on the Internet in the wake of such trends — but a promising development caught my attention — *image-hosting* Web sites.

Image-hosting Web sites have changed from one-stop shops to mega-markets loaded with tons of services for your auctions. Some image-hosting sites let you post your pictures without requiring you to use their auction-management software. Not that I think such software is a bad thing — it's great! — I just like to choose what I use. (Flip to Chapter 20 for more about auction-management software.)

Here are a few convenient image-hosting sites that allow you to post a few of your images for *free*:

✔ Auctiva (www.Auctiva.com)

✔ FreePictureHosting.com (www.freepicturehosting.com)

✔ ImageShack (www.imageshack.com)

✔ Photobucket (www.photobucket.com)

Using eBay's Picture Services

eBay hosts a single image per auction for free. Additional pictures cost only $0.15. (You can have a maximum of 12 images per auction item.)

If you use this service, your photos appear on your auction in a predesigned template. If you use more than one photo, the first photo shows up in a 400-x-300-pixel format. A miniature of the first image appears to the left of the larger image. The prospective bidder clicks the smaller picture, and it magically appears in the larger photo area.

When you prepare to list an item for auction, a page appears, and you're asked whether you'd like to use the photo service. If you don't want to use it, click the Your Own Web Hosting tab and input the URL of your picture. If you do want to use the service, follow the directions on-screen.

Perfecting your picture in LunaPic

You need to know that I am lazy — sometimes I don't even want to open a program. When it comes to editing my images for eBay, I'm still looking for a magic wand. So I browsed the Internet and found a free online photo-editing Web site, www.lunapic.com.

Although I prefer to use a program on my computer, LunaPic works great for quick, on-the-fly editing that I often need. You can even edit pictures on someone else's computer because

there's no need to install software. It's a Web site that makes photo editing as easy as getting a burger at the drive-through window. Register on the site, and you have full photo-editing capabilities. Upload photos from your computer (or webcam) to the site, perform your touch-up, and then save and download! LunaPic has a full-featured toolset on the site; in it, you find tools to adjust brightness, contrast, color, and sharpness.

To post your photo, click the box, and an Open File dialog box appears. Find your image on your computer and click Open, and the image magically appears in the image box. Add more pictures if you want and click Submit Pictures and Continue. Figure 14-4 shows the upload page — which is where you upload your image from the Sell Your Item page. (If your upload on the Sell Your Item page doesn't look like Figure 14-4, click the link shown on the right to go to Full Featured.)

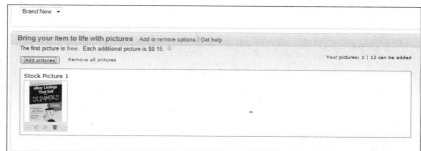

Figure 14-4: Click Add Pictures and you're on your way.

Here are a few things to keep in mind:

✔ eBay keeps an image online for the duration of your listing and for up to 90 days (as long as you have the link available to access the page). After that, the image disappears (unless you relist the same auction).

✔ You can always post the image again if you need it later; be sure to leave a copy of the image on your computer.

✔ This feature doesn't support the MSN TV platform.

eBay's Gallery

Any discussion of images on eBay would be incomplete without a short discussion of eBay's Gallery pictures. Gallery pictures are the small pictures you see next to items in category listings or in your searches. It's obvious that using eBay's Gallery option draws more attention to your sales, but have you ever noticed that not all Gallery images show up crisp and clear? And that some are smaller than others? It's not by chance; eBay reduces the image you uploaded for the Gallery.

The technology that allows eBay's Picture Services to do its magic resizes the seller's picture to fit the allotted space. In the case of the Gallery, a considerable amount of compression is applied to your image. The more compression applied, the fuzzier and more distorted your image gets.

When you use your own photo hosting on eBay, you can use a different photo for your Gallery image. Either use a different picture or reduce your main image to a tiny 110 x 120 pixels. If you reduce the picture yourself, you'll notice a big improvement in the way the Gallery picture looks.

Multiple pictures in your descriptions

Here's the answer to *the most-asked* question when I teach a class on eBay. Many sellers have more than one picture within the auction description area. By putting extra images in the description, they do not have to pay extra for eBay's hosting services. This isn't magic; you can easily do it, too. Just add a tiny bit of HTML code in your auction description. Here is the HTML code to insert one picture in your auction:

```
<img src=http://www.yourserver.com/
        imagename.jpg>
```

Be sure to use the brackets to open and close your code (they're located above the comma and the period on your keyboard). This code reflects the URL of your picture and the coding `img src=` to tell eBay's server to insert a picture.

When you want to insert two pictures, just insert code for each picture, one after the other. If you want one picture to appear below the other, use the HTML code for line break, `<BR>`. Here's how to write that:

```
<img src=http://www.yourserver.com/
        imagenumber1.jpg> <BR>
<img src=http://www.yourserver.com/
        imagenumber2.jpg>
```

Putting on the Hits

Okay, you've got a great auction on eBay and great images to go with it. Now all you need to do is track the number of users peeking at your items and attract even more people to your auction.

Your auction is up and running on eBay, and you're dying to know how many people have stopped by to take a look. To easily monitor your auction's *hits* — the number of times visitors stop to look at the goods — you use a free public *counter* program from an online source. A counter is a useful marketing tool; for example, you can check the number of times people have looked at but not bid on your auctions. If you have lots more lookie-loos than bids, you may have a problem with your auction.

If your counter indicates you're not getting many hits, consider the following potential problems so you can resurrect your auction:

- ✔ Does the picture take too long to load?
- ✔ Is the opening bid too high?
- ✔ Are those neon-orange-and-lime-green bell-bottoms just too funky to sell?

Counters are available when you're listing your item on the eBay Sell Your Item form. You can also find some highly "intelligent" counters elsewhere on the Net, at sites such as Sellathon.com.

Want to know more about the people behind those user IDs? Thousands of eBay members have created their own personal Web pages on eBay (called *About Me pages*). About Me pages are easy to create — and are as unique as each eBay member. eBay users with active About Me pages have a special ME icon next to their user IDs.

Take your time when you create your About Me page. A well-done About Me page improves your sales because people who come across your auctions and check out your About Me page can get a sense of who you are and how serious you are about your eBay activities. They see instantly that you're no fly-by-night seller.

Before you create your About Me page, I suggest that you look at what other users have done. eBay members often include pictures, links to other Web sites (including their personal or business home pages), and links to just about any Web location that reflects their personalities, which is why they're so entertaining. If your purpose is to generate more business, I recommend that you keep your About Me page focused on your auction listings, with a link to your Web site.

Sellers with many auctions running at once often add a message to their About Me pages that indicates that they're willing to reduce shipping charges if bidders also bid on their other auctions. This direct tactic may lack nuance, but it increases the number of people who look at (and bid on) your auctions.

To create your About Me page, do the following:

1. **Go to any eBay user's About Me page, scroll to the very bottom and click the Create My About Me Page link. If you can't find the link, go to: `cgi3.ebay.com/ws/eBayISAPI.dll?AboutMeLogin`.**

   You're taken to About Me: Create Your Own eBay Personal Page.

2. **If you haven't signed in, type your user ID and password in the appropriate boxes.**

3. **Click the Edit Your Page button.**

4. Select the Use Our Easy Step-by-Step Process.

   You're taken to the About Me layout page. You have three layout options, which eBay is kind enough to show you:

   • Newspaper Layout

   • Centered Layout

5. **Click the button that corresponds to the layout option you want.**

   You're taken to a second About Me creation page.

6. **Enter the following information:**

   • **Page Title:** Type the title of your About Me page (for example, *Larry's Lunchboxes*).

   • **Paragraph 1:** Type a personal attention-grabbing headline, such as *Welcome to Larry Lunch's Lunchbox Place.*

   • **Text:** Type a short paragraph that greets your visitors (something like *Hey, I like lunchboxes a lot* only more exciting).

   • **Paragraph 2:** Type another headline for the second paragraph of the page, such as *Vintage, Modern, Ancient,* or *I Collect All Kinds of Lunchboxes.*

   • **Text:** Type another paragraph about yourself or your collection (such as, *I used to stare at lunchboxes in the school cafeteria . . .* only more, you know, *normal*).

   • **Picture:** If you're adding a picture, type a sentence describing it, for example: *This is my wife Loretta with our lunchbox collection.*

- **URL:** Type the Web site address (URL) where people can find your picture. See the section earlier in this chapter that shows you how to upload digital images.

- **Feedback:** Select how many of your feedback postings you want to appear on your About Me page. (You can opt not to show any feedback, but I think you should put in a few comments, especially if they're complimentary, as in, *Larry sent my lunchbox promptly, and it makes lunchtime a blast! Everybody stares at it. . .*)

- **Items for Sale:** Select how many of your current auctions you want to appear on your About Me page. If you don't have any auctions running at the moment, you can select the Show No Items option.

- **Label:** Type a caption to introduce your auctions, for example: *Lunchboxes I'm Currently Selling.*

- **Favorite Links:** Type the names and URLs of any Web links you want visitors to see, for example, a Web site that appraises lunchboxes (*It's in excellent condition except for that petrified ham sandwich. . .*).

  See mine in Figure 14-5.

7. **Click the Back button. (Or, if you don't like your current layout, click the Continue button to go back to Step 1.)**

   You're now looking at your final About Me page.

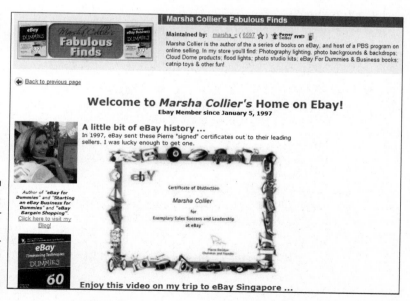

Figure 14-5: Make *your* About Me page *your* home on eBay.

8. **Scroll down to the bottom of the page. You see a group of buttons:**

   • **Edit Some More:** Returns you to Step 2.

   • **Save My Page:** Saves your About Me page so that you're one step closer to publishing it on eBay.

   • **Edit Using HTML:** If you know HTML code, you can customize your About Me page. (For example, you can insert pictures with the code I give you in the "Multiple pictures in your descriptions" sidebar, earlier in this chapter.)

   • **Start Over:** Takes you to a link page where you can delete what you created and begin again.

9. **When you're happy with your masterpiece, click the Save My Page button.**

   Yes, you did it; now anybody in the world with access to the Internet can find your personal About Me page on eBay.

Don't forget to update your About Me page often. A good About Me page makes bidders eager to know more about your auctions. An out-of-date About Me page turns off potential bidders. If you choose to update, you need to edit it using HTML. If you don't use HTML, you have to create a whole new page.

You can link to your About Me page from your Web site or from your e-mail because all About Me pages have their own personal URLs. The address ends with your user ID. For example, here's the URL for my page:

```
members.ebay.com/aboutme/marsha_c
```

Blog on Your My World Page

If blogging is the key to the new Web, your My World page is the hub of your eBay user interaction. Your About Me page is there for customers; the My World page is mostly used by the eBay community. People like to know about other people, and the My World page shows your world, your way.

Although my editors would love for me to give you a long, drawn out, step-by-step list to show you how to get to your My World page, I won't. It's all too simple: Just click your user ID on your My eBay page (or any page for that matter) and you'll arrive at your own (ready-to-fill-out) My World page.

Once you get there, you see a page ready to edit. Here's the lowdown:

✔ **Edit image:** By clicking here, you'll come to a page that allows you to automatically upload a picture from your computer or use one of the handy (but unexciting) eBay-supplied avatars (faux pictures) to appear on your My World page.

- ✔ **Items for sale:** Choose which and how many of the items you have for sale to show on your page.

- ✔ **Add content:** Add things about your eBay life that you'd like everyone to see.

- ✔ **Favorites:** Select if you'd like the page to pick up your favorite searches, sellers, and stores, and show them here.

- ✔ **Bio:** This link takes you to a form where you can write a quick and simple bio.

- ✔ **Neighborhoods:** Once you get going on eBay, you might just want to join a neighborhood, which is a special interest group. I am a member of Coffee Lovers (11,656 members), Photography (3,544 members), and Star Trek (364 members — hey, everybody needs to escape reality now and then).

- ✔ **Reviews and guides:** If you've written reviews of items on the site, or written a guide on how to do something (anything), you can have these reviews appear on your My World page.

- ✔ **Guest Book:** Use this feature to enable people to leave you messages on your page. Visit my My World page at

```
http://myworld.ebay.com/marsha_c
```

to view some of the comments left by other eBay users, as pictured in Figure 14-6.

Figure 14-6: Welcome to My World on eBay!

Part IV

Even More of eBay's Special Features

"He saw your laptop and wants to know if he can check his feedback ratings."

In this part . . .

So you want to protect yourself from bad apples, not just on eBay but all over the Internet? You're not alone. I want to keep safe as well, and that's why I've tipped you off to the information in this part.

This is the place to come if you want to know just what eBay knows about you and is willing to share with other eBay members. I also introduce you to the Security Center (Trust & Safety), the next best thing to a superhero when it comes to protecting you from people who don't qualify for the eBay User of the Year Award.

eBay is a community, so you need to be let in on some of the ways you can commune with other collectors and get into the social scene. In this part, you find out about the special features that make eBay such a unique environment. Where else can you buy an item you really want and also help out a charity, all with the click of a mouse?

Chapter 15

Privacy: To Protect and to Serve

. . . .

. . . .

On the Internet, as in real life, you should never take your personal privacy for granted. Sure, you're ecstatic that you can shop and sell on eBay from the privacy of your home, but remember: Just because your front door is locked doesn't mean that your privacy is being protected. If you're new to the Internet, you may be surprised to find out what you reveal about yourself to the world, no matter how many precautions you take. (Yes, we all know about that neon green exfoliating mask you wear when you're bidding . . . just kidding . . . honest.)

In this chapter, you find out how much eBay knows about you and who eBay shares your information with. I explain what you can do to protect your privacy and tell you some simple steps you can take to increase not only your Internet privacy but also yourpersonal safety.

What eBay Knows about You

The irony of the Internet is that although you think you're sitting at home working anonymously, third parties such as advertisers and marketing companies are secretly getting to know you.

While you're busy collecting Winter Olympic memorabilia and buying that hot new Dooney Burke purse, eBay is busy collecting nuggets of information about you. eBay gets some of this information from you and some of it from your computer. All the data eBay gets is stored in the mammoth eBay memory bank.

What you tell eBay

eBay gets much of what it knows about you *from* you. When you sign up, you voluntarily tell eBay important and personal information about yourself. Right off the bat, you give eBay these juicy tidbits:

- ✔ Name
- ✔ E-mail address
- ✔ Snail-mail address
- ✔ Phone number
- ✔ Your date of birth
- ✔ Password

"Okay, that's no big deal," you say, but if you're using your credit card to settle your eBay fees (or using PayPal), you're also giving out the following personal financial information:

- ✔ Credit card number
- ✔ Expiration date
- ✔ Bank account number
- ✔ Credit card billing address
- ✔ Credit card history

Don't worry about giving this information to eBay or PayPal. The bottom line is that *every time* you pay by check or with a credit card in the real world, you give away personal info about yourself. eBay carefully locks up this information (in a high-tech Alcatraz, of sorts), but other companies or individuals may not be so protective. Before you put a check in the mail, make sure you're comfortable with where it's going.

What cookies gather

Web sites collect information about you by using *cookies*. No, they don't bribe you with oatmeal-raisin goodies. Cookies are nothing more than tiny files that companies (such as eBay) put on your hard drive to store data about your surfing habits.

Most Web site designers install cookies to help you navigate their sites. Sometimes the cookie becomes sort of an "admission ticket" so that you don't need to register every time you log on.

eBay has partnerships with companies that provide page-view and data-tracking technology and advertisers who display advertising banners on eBay pages, whether you want to see the banners or not. If you click a banner, a cookie from that particular advertiser *may* go onto your computer, usually to prevent you from seeing it again.

Cookies can't steal information from other files on your computer. A cookie can access only the information that you provide to its Web site.

DoubleClick, a major player in the cookie-tracking field, says that it uses your information to limit the number of times that you see the same advertisement. DoubleClick also measures the kinds of ads that you respond to and tracks which member Web sites you visit and how often. The bottom line is that DoubleClick is just trying to sell you stuff with ads based on your personal interests. The upside is that you get to see stuff that you may like.

You can find out more about cookies at `www.cookiecentral.com/faq`. This site gives you simple instructions on how to handle cookies on your computer.

If you want to keep your information private, you can remove yourself from the DoubleClick cookie system by going to this Web site:

`http://www.doubleclick.com/privacy/dart_adserving.aspx`

Your eBay sign-in cookie

There are two types of cookies:

- ✔ **End of session:** This cookie type remains on your computer as long as your browser is open or, in the case of eBay, for 24 hours. When you close your Internet browser (Internet Explorer, Firefox, Safari, or Opera) the cookie disappears as if you downed it with icy cold milk.

- ✔ **Permanent:** This flavor is perfect if you don't share your computer with anyone else; it permits your computer to always remain signed in to a particular Web site. (eBay does not use this sort of cookie).

When you visit eBay and sign in, eBay gives you an end-of-session cookie.

eBay's *"keep me signed in"* sign-in cookie is a good thing. It prevents the previously repetitive task of typing your user ID and password at every turn. This cookie simplifies your participation in chats, bidding, watching items, viewing e-mail addresses, and so on. Because you don't have to sign in every moment that you're doing business on eBay, it's a real time-saver.

Web beacons

Web beacons are clear, 1-pixel-by-1-pixel images that are placed in the HTML (or Internet page code) for individual pages. They are also commonly called *pixel tags*. Web beacons, like cookies, are used mainly for collecting marketing information. They track the traffic patterns of users from one page to another.

Web beacons are also often used in e-mails. Ever wonder how someone knows if you've received an e-mail? Or that you may receive an e-mail from a company whose Web site you've just visited? Blame the sneaky but harmless beacons.

Web beacons are invisible as cookies and are incorporated into Web pages without your knowing. Turning off cookies on your browser won't disable beacons, but this action protects your anonymity. Web beacons are not as ominous as they may seem because the information collected is not personally identifiable; they just track your passage along the site.

What Web servers collect

Every time that you log on to the Internet, you leave an electronic trail of information, just like Hansel and Gretel. eBay, like zillions of other Web sites, uses *servers,* which are immense programs that do nothing but collect and transfer bits (and bytes) of information day and night. Your Internet connection has a special address that identifies you to all servers when you surf the Net. This is called an IP (Internet Protocol) address and is often used by law enforcement to track those whose shenanigans wreak havoc on Web sites or other users.

Web servers all over the Internet track some or all of the following information:

- What Web site you came in from
- The ISP (Internet service provider) that you use
- The items that you're selling on eBay
- The Web sites you linked your listings to
- Your favorite Web sites (if you link them to your About Me page)

eBay collects the following information while you visit the eBay site. After you log off, the server discards the data:

- What you do while logged on to the site
- Which categories you tend to browse
- Which items you've viewed recently
- What times you log on and log off

Like incredible Internet archivists, eBay's servers keep a record of everything you bid on, win, and sell, which is great news if you have a problem with a transaction and need eBay to investigate. Also, eBay couldn't display feedback about you and other users if its servers didn't store all the feedback you write and receive. Have you ever sent an e-mail to eBay? eBay's servers record it and keep it in some murky recess of eBay's memory. Remember, we live in the age of electronic commerce, and the people on eBay run a serious business that depends on e-commerce. They have to keep everything in case they need it later.

To see a chart on what personal information is accessible by third parties, check out this address:

```
pages.ebay.com/help/policies/privacy-appendix.html
```

Be sure to visit the page; you may be shocked by the amount of information that exists on the eBay servers about you and your habits.

For current examples of how this type of information can be used against you as you surf the Internet, visit this Web site:

```
www.anonymizer.com/consumer/threat_center/
```

Cookie removal-ware

I got a call from a friend who complained that her laptop computer was getting slower and slower. She brought it over to my house and when I had a look at it, I also noticed that it was opening extra pop-up windows and accessing the Internet spuriously. After checking to see whether she had a virus (no, she didn't), I went to the Internet to get her spyware removal software. Perhaps her problem was that too many people had inserted information-gathering cookies on her computer.

That was certainly the case. After installing and running the software, I found that she had over 350 cookies pulling information from her computer as she surfed. Once deleted, her computer ran much faster.

She certainly didn't give these people permission to spy on her comings and goings on the Internet. These cookies were placed on her computer without her knowledge. If you want to purge these uninvited spies from your computer, download any of the free spyware or malware software from the Internet. Two good free ones are Ad-aware from www.lavasoftusa.com/software/adaware and Spybot Search and Destroy, available from www.safer-networking.org/en/index.html.

If you're apprehensive about all the information that Web servers can collect about you while you innocently roam the Internet, I understand. But before you start looking out for Big Brother watching over your shoulder, consider this: On the Web, everybody's collecting information.

The odds are excellent that all the information that eBay knows about you is already in the hands of many other folks, too — your bank, your grocer, the staff of any magazines you subscribe to, clubs you belong to, any airlines you've flown, and any insurance agencies you use. That's life these days. And if you're thinking, "Just because everybody knows all this stuff about me, that doesn't make it right," all I can say is, "You're right." But maybe you'll sleep better knowing that eBay is one place where folks take the privacy issue seriously. See the next section for details.

eBay's privacy policy

eBay had a privacy policy for all its users before privacy policies were even in vogue. Now eBay maintains the safety standards set forth by the pioneer in online safeguarding: TRUSTe.

TRUSTe (www.truste.org) sets a list of standards that its member Web sites have to follow to earn a "seal of approval." The thousands of Web sites that subscribe to this watchdog group must adhere to its guidelines and set policies to protect privacy. eBay has been a member of TRUSTe since the privacy watchdog group was founded.

Do seals bite back?

Because eBay pays to display the TRUSTe mark, some online critics say that the seal is nothing more than window dressing. These critics wonder whether it would be in the Web watchdog's best financial interest to bite the hand that feeds it all those display fees. Critics complain that the seal offers a false sense of security — and suggest that you view the seal as nothing more than a disclaimer to be careful in your Internet dealings.

Technically, TRUSTe can pull its seal whenever a Web site becomes careless in its handling of privacy issues. However, the critics make a good point: *Always be careful in your Internet dealings,* no matter how much protection a site has. If you ever feel your personal information has been compromised, file a complaint at the TRUSTe Web site: www.truste.org/pvr.php?page=complaint.

Grateful Dead cookie jar

In 1999, an auction description read: "This is one of the grooviest jars I have ever come across — a real find for the die-hard Grateful Dead fan or for the cookie jar collector who has it all. Made by Vandor, this Grateful Dead bus cookie jar looks like something the Dead *would* drive. Beautiful detailing on the peace signs; the roses are running lights. Painted windows. You have just got to see this piece. Only 10,000 made, and I have only seen one other. Comes with box that has Grateful Dead logos on it. Buyer pays all shipping and insurance."

The cookie jar started at $1.00 and sold on eBay for $102.50. When I updated this book in 2002, it sold on eBay for $125.00; when I updated again in 2004, it went for $150.00. The Grateful Dead's bus cookie jar is riding the tracks these days; in 2009 an auction closed with the final bid at $125.00. Perhaps the baby boomer Deadheads are feeling the economic crunch. Still, the price of the original has skyrocketed from the original issue price, so much so that Vandor just came out with a 40th anniversary replica. Buy it now for your Deadhead friends — and buy it quick. Only 1,200 were made, and the price is already edging up to the $100.00 mark.

Oh wow, dude — that's some far-out cookie jar. (Cue the band: *Keep truckin'. . . .*)

To review the policy that's earned eBay the TRUSTe seal of approval, click the Policies link that appears at the bottom of every eBay page.

In addition to setting and displaying a privacy policy, eBay follows these guidelines as well:

- eBay must make its Privacy Policy links easily accessible to users. You can find the logo on eBay's home page. Click the Policies link. On the eBay Policies page, click the Privacy Policy link and you're taken to the Privacy Policies page for more information. Take advantage of this opportunity to find out how your data is being protected.

- eBay must disclose what personal information it collects and how it's using the info.

- Users must have an easy way to review the personal information that eBay has about them.

- Users must have an *opting out* option that lets them decline to share information.

- eBay must follow industry standards to make its Web site and database secure so that hackers and nonmembers have no access to the information. eBay uses Secure Sockets Layer (SSL), which is an encryption program that scrambles data until it gets to eBay. Unfortunately, no Web site, including the CIA's Web site, is completely secure, so you still have to be on your guard while you're online.

What Does eBay Do with Information about Me, Anyway?

Although eBay knows a good chunk of information about you, it puts the information to good use. The fact that it knows so much about you actually helps you in the long run.

Here's what eBay uses personal information for:

- **Upgrading eBay:** Like most e-commerce companies, eBay tracks members' use and habits to improve the Web site. For instance, if a particular item generates a lot of activity, eBay may add a category or a subcategory.

- **Clearing the way for transactions:** If eBay didn't collect personal information such as your e-mail address, your snail-mail address, and your phone number, you couldn't complete the transaction you started after an auction was over. Bummer.

- **Billing:** You think it's important to keep track of your merchandise and money, don't you? So does eBay. It uses your personal information to keep an eye on your account and your paying habits — and on everybody else's. (Call it a gentle encouragement of honest trading habits.)

- **Policing the site:** Never forget that eBay tries to be tough on cybercrime, and that if you break the rules or regulations, eBay will hunt you down and boot you out. Personal information is used to find eBay delinquents, and eBay makes it clear that it cooperates with law enforcement and with third parties whose merchandise you may be selling illegally. For more about this topic, read up on the VeRO program in Chapter 9.

Periodically, eBay runs surveys asking specific questions about your use of the site. It uses your answers to upgrade eBay. In addition, eBay asks whether it can forward your information to a marketing firm. eBay says that it does not forward any personally identifiable information, which means that any info you provide is given to third parties as raw data. However, if you're nervous about privacy, I suggest that you make it clear that you don't want your comments to leave eBay should you decide to participate in eBay surveys. If you don't participate in the surveys, you won't have any hand in creating new eBay features, though, so you can't complain if you don't like how the site looks. Sometimes, eBay advertises surveys that users can take part in on the eBay home page.

What Do Other eBay Members Know about Me?

eBay functions under the premise that eBay's members are buying, selling, working, and playing in an honest and open way. That means that anyone surfing can immediately find out some limited information about you:

- ✔ Your user ID and history
- ✔ Your feedback history
- ✔ All the auctions and eBay store sales you run
- ✔ Your current purchases and any you've made during a 30-day period

eBay clearly states in its policies and guidelines that e-mail addresses should be used only for eBay business. If you abuse this policy, you can be suspended or even kicked off for good.

eBay provides limited eBay member registration information to its users. If another member involved in a transaction with you wants to know the following facts about you, they're available:

- ✔ Your name (and business name if you have provided that information)
- ✔ Your e-mail address
- ✔ The city, state, and country that you provided to eBay
- ✔ The telephone number that you provided to eBay

Following the transaction, buyers and sellers exchange some real-world information. As I explain in Chapters 6 and 12, members initiate the exchange of merchandise and money by e-mail, providing personal addresses for both payments and shipments. Make sure that you're comfortable giving out your home address. If you're not, I explain alternatives in this chapter.

Spam — Not Just a Hawaiian Delicacy

Although you can find plenty of places to socialize and have fun on eBay, when it comes to business, eBay is . . . well, all business. eBay's policy says that requests for registration information can be made only for people with whom you're transacting business on eBay. The contact information request form requires that you type the item number of the transaction you're involved in as well as the user ID of the person whose contact info you want. If you're not involved in a transaction, as a bidder or a seller in the specified item number, you can't access the user information.

Spam I am

Spam, the unwanted electronic junk mail, is named after Spam, the canned meat product. (Spam collectibles on eBay are another matter entirely.) According to the Spam Web site, more than 6 billion cans of Spam have been consumed worldwide. (By the way, Hawaiians eat more Spam than any other state in the union.) Spam is made from a secret recipe of pork shoulder, ham, and special spices. It was first produced in 1937 and got its name from the *SP* for *spice* and the *AM* from *ham.*

It's widely believed that spam (junk e-mail) got its name from the old *Monty Python* sketch because the refrain "Spam-Spam-Spam-Spam" drowned out all other conversation and one of the participants kept saying, "I don't want any Spam. I don't like Spam." Others say that it came from a bunch of computer geeks at USC who thought that junk e-mail was about as satisfying as a Spam sandwich. Perhaps they've never enjoyed a Spam luau in Hawaii under the moonlight — aloha! For more spam fun facts visit www.spam.com.

When it comes to e-mail addresses, your secret is safe. If you bid on an auction, your e-mail is visible only to the seller. The end of listing notice contains your e-mail address so that the person on the other end of the transaction can contact you. After the other user has your e-mail address, eBay rules state that the user can use it only for eBay business.

Here's a list of "business" reasons for e-mail communication, generally accepted by all on eBay:

- Responding to feedback that you left
- Responding to feedback that you received
- Communicating with sellers or buyers during and after transactions
- Suggesting items to friends that they may be interested in via the Share feature (on the item page)
- Leaving chat room comments
- Discussing common interests with other members, such as shared hometowns, interesting collections, and past or current listings.

Sending spam versus eating it

Sending e-mail to other members is a great way to do business and make friends. But don't cross the line into spam. *Spam,* a Hormel canned meat product (I've given Spam its own sidebar), now has an alternate meaning. When you spell it with a small *s, spam* is unsolicited e-mail — most often, advertising — sent to multiple e-mail addresses gleaned from marketing lists.

Eventually, it fills up your inbox the way "Spam, Spam, Spam, and Spam" filled up the menu in an old *Monty Python* restaurant skit.

Think of spam as the electronic version of the junk mail that you get via the U.S. Postal Service. Spam may be okay for eating (if you're into that kind of thing), but sending it can get you banned from eBay.

If you send an e-mail that advertises a product or service to people who haven't agreed (opted in) that they wanted this sort of e-mail, you're guilty of spamming.

Trashing your junk mail

Sometimes spam can come in the form of mail from people you know and expect mail from. Your closest friend's computer may have been abducted by some weird Internet virus and replicated the virus to everyone in his or her e-mail address book. Obviously, this is not a good thing for those who receive and open the e-mail.

Don't open e-mail from anyone you don't know, especially if a file is attached to it. Sometimes, if a spammer is really slick, it's hard to tell that you've received spam. If you receive an e-mail with no subject line, however — or if the e-mail has an addressee name that isn't yours, or is coming from someone you never heard of — delete it. You never know; it could be just annoying spam — or worse, it could contain a computer virus as an attachment, just waiting for you to open and activate it.

Speaking of e-mail, if you're new to the technology, I recommend getting a good antivirus program that can scan e-mail attachments and rid your system of some annoying and increasingly dangerous computer bugs.

For some interesting general anti-spam tips, drop in at `spam.abuse.net`. This Web site offers helpful advice for doing battle with spam artists. Also, I've been using a handy software program for years called MailWasher, which allows me to preview my e-mail before it's downloaded to my computer. It even bounces spam back to the sender on command — as if your e-mail address didn't exist. Best of all, this program is free and available from `www.mailwasher.net`.

E-mail spoofing

E-mail spoofing has become the bane of the online community and can wreak havoc. Spoofing is accomplished when crafty techno-geeks send out e-mail and make it appear to come from someone other than themselves — someone you know and expect e-mail from. Most often, this type of e-mail is programmed to invade your privacy or, even worse, bilk you out of confidential information.

My messages safeguard your privacy

Being the conscientious company it is, eBay has set up a private area, accessible only through one of the three tabs on your My eBay page, called Messages. Messages enables you to communicate with other eBay members without revealing your e-mail address. All your missives with other members, such as Ask the Seller a Question communications, appear in this area. You can answer mail, send new mail, and delete communications from this area, just as if it was your own e-mail software.

This service can protect you from most of the most dangerous forms of spam. For safety's sake, whenever you receive an e-mail sent (in reality or purportedly) from eBay or an eBay member, don't click the e-mail link to Respond Now. Open your Internet browser and go directly to your Messages area. If the e-mail is legitimate, it will appear here. Merely click the e-mail to open it, read it, and reply. Your privacy (in the form of your e-mail address) isn't exposed to the receiving party.

A spate of e-mails have purportedly been sent from eBay, PayPal, and other major e-commerce sites, claiming that your membership has been suspended or that your records need updating. The opportunistic e-mail then asks you to click a link to a page on the site, which then asks you to input your personal information. Don't do it!

Most sites will *never* ask you to provide sensitive information through e-mail, so don't do it. If you receive an e-mail saying your "account has been suspended," close the e-mail and go directly to the site in question — *without* using the supplied link in the e-mail. You'll know soon enough if there is a problem with your account.

If you get this sort of e-mail from eBay and want to confirm whether it is really from eBay, visit this eBay security page:

```
pages.ebay.com/help/account/recognizing-spoof.html
```

To help eBay in its investigation of these information thieves, send a copy of the e-mail (along with all identification headers) to spoof@ebay.com. When forwarding the e-mail, do not alter it in any way.

I Vant to Be Alone — and Vat You Can Do to Stay That Vay

The Internet has a long reach. Don't be surprised if you furnish your personal information freely on one Web site, and it turns up somewhere else. If you don't mind people knowing things about you (your name, your hobbies, where you live, and your phone number, for example), by all means share.

But I personally think you should give only as much information as you need to do business on the site.

Privacy is not secrecy. Don't feel obligated to reveal anything about yourself that isn't absolutely necessary. (Some personal facts are in the same league as body weight — private, even if hardly a secret.)

Although you can't prevent privacy leaks entirely, you can take some precautions to protect yourself. Here are some tips to keep your online information as safe and secure as possible:

- **User ID:** When eBay first started, members used their e-mail addresses to buy and sell. Today, users appear on the site with a *nom de plume* (okay, user ID, but nom de plume sounds oh, so chic). Your first line of defense against everyone who surfs the eBay site is to choose a user ID that doesn't reveal too much about you. Chapter 2 gives you some pointers on how to choose your user ID.

- **Password:** Guard your password as if it were the key to your home. Don't give any buyers or sellers your password. If a window requesting your password pops up in an auction, skip it — it's somebody who is up to no good. Use your password *only* on official eBay screens. (See Chapter 2 for tips on choosing passwords.)

  If you're concerned that someone may have your password, change it immediately:

  1. **Go to your My eBay area and hover your cursor over the Account tab. From the drop-down menu, click Personal Information.**

  2. **On your arrival in the Personal Information area, find the Password line and click the Edit link.**

  3. **Follow the instructions to change your password.**

     Your password is immediately changed.

If your password has been changed by some dastardly evildoer, and you can't sign in to your account, go to the eBay home page. Click the Contact Us link, which is in the upper-right corner. Choose the Chat Online contact option, and you'll be in touch with a live human being who can help you secure your account before damage can be done.

- **Credit card information:** Whenever you use your credit card on eBay, you can make sure that your private information is safe. Look for an SSL (SSL stands for *Security Sockets Layer*) link or check box. Sometimes you may see a link that says You May Also Sign in Securely. SSL is an encryption program that scrambles the information so that hackers have almost no chance of getting your information. (I explain more about SSL in Chapter 2.)

  When buying from a listing that accepts credit cards, check the seller's feedback and carefully weigh the risks of giving your credit card number to someone you don't know versus paying through PayPal. PayPal is the safest way to pay because your credit card number is not released.

Never give anyone your Social Security number online. Guard yours as if it were the key to the Crown Jewels.

✔ **Registration information:** When you first register, eBay requests a phone number and address for billing and contact purposes. I've never had a problem with anyone requesting my registration information and then misusing it. However, many people want an added measure of anonymity. You can give eBay the information it wants in several ways without compromising your privacy:

• Instead of your home phone number, provide eBay with a cell phone number, a work phone number, or a SkypeIn number. (See Chapter 18 for more information on Skype.) Screen your calls with an answering machine.

• Use a post office box instead of your home address.

• Start a bank account solely for eBay transactions. Make it a DBA (doing business as) account so that you can use an alternate name. Your bank can help you with this process.

✔ **Chat rooms:** eBay has a multitude of chat rooms where members exchange information and sometimes heated arguments. (Chat rooms are thoroughly discussed in Chapter 17.) But heed this advice: Be careful what you reveal about yourself in a chat room. Don't expect that "just between us" means that at all. Chat rooms can be viewed by anyone who visits the eBay site, not just eBay members.

Never say anything online that you wouldn't feel comfortable saying to the next person who passed you on the street. Basically, that's who you're talking to. You can find stories of romances blossoming on eBay — and I'm delighted for the happy couples, I swear — but come on, that doesn't mean that you should lose your head. Don't give out any personal information to strangers; too often, that's asking for trouble. Have fun on eBay but hang on to your common sense.

Skim some of the category chat rooms, especially the Discuss eBay's Newest Features room, for warnings about security problems on the chat rooms and boards — and how to avoid 'em. A great bunch of users and eBay staffers frequent that board, and they're sure to give you good information.

✔ **Check feedback:** Yep, I sound like a broken record (in case you don't remember, *records* were the large, black, prone-to-breaking disks used by people to play music on electric turntables before iPods and CDs were invented), but here it is again: *Check feedback.* eBay works because it's policed by its participants. The best way to learn about the folks whom you're dealing with is to see how others felt about them. If you take only one thing away from this book, it's to check feedback *before* you bid or buy!

Fighting back

Robbin was minding her own business, selling software on eBay, when she ran into one of the world's nastiest eBay outlaws. He was a one-stop-shopping outlet of rule-breaking behaviors. First, he ruined her auctions by bidding ridiculously high amounts and then retracting bids at the last legal minute. (This couldn't happen today because eBay changed their bidding policies due to these nefarious practices). He e-mailed her bidders, offering the same item but cheaper. He contacted Robbin's winning bidders to say he was accepting her payments. Then he started leaving messages on her answering machine. When she finally had enough, she contacted Trust & Safety, which suspended him.

But like a bad lunch, he came back up — with a new name. So Robbin fought back on her own. She got his registration information and sent him a letter. She also informed the support area at his ISP about what he was doing, and because he used his work e-mail address, she also contacted his boss.

Her efforts must have done the trick. He finally slipped out of eBay and slithered out of her life. The lesson: Don't rely completely on eBay to pick up the pieces. If you're being abused, stand up for your rights and fight back through the proper channels!

In the virtual world, as in the real world, cyberstalking is scary and illegal. If you think someone is using information from eBay to harass you, contact eBay immediately — as well as your local police. Chapter 16 gives you the ins and outs of contacting eBay's security team.

Chapter 16

Staying Safe and Sane

In This Chapter

▶ Keeping eBay members safe

▶ Staying current with the rules

▶ Filing complaints against eBay bad guys

▶ Knowing your items through authentication

▶ Saving yourself: Where to go when eBay can't help

Millions of people transact business every day on eBay. If you're new to the Internet, however, you may need a reality check. With hundreds of millions of listings worldwide, and close to 30 million new listings every day, the law of averages dictates that you're bound to run into some rough seas eventually. If you do, know that you can get the answers you need from eBay's Trust & Safety department. In this chapter, I take you through the Trust & Safety resources — from reporting abuses to resolving insurance issues. This chapter explains how eBay enforces its rules and regulations, shows how you can use third-party bonding and mediation services, and even points out how to go outside eBay for help if you run into some really big-time problems.

Keeping eBay Safe with Trust & Safety

The Security Center is the eBay area that focuses on protecting eBay buyers and sellers from members who aren't playing by the rules. Through this department, eBay issues warnings and policy changes — and in some cases, it gives eBay bad guys the heave-ho.

You should know about two important safety areas on eBay:

> ✔ **eBay Security Center:** You reach the Security Center from a small link found at the bottom of almost every eBay page. From here you can find and report safety violations. If eBay ever moves this link, just type http://pages.ebay.com/securitycenter/ into your browser and you're there.

✔ **eBay Resolution Center:** From the navigation bar, which is at the top of every eBay page, just cursor over to the Help link and choose Resolution Center from the drop-down menu. This is where you report transactional issues: unpaid items, items received not as described, and more.

The Security Center (as shown in Figure 16-1) is more than just a link to policies and information. It also connects you with a group of eBay staffers who handle complaints, field incoming tips about possible infractions, and dole out warnings and suspensions. These dedicated employees investigate infractions and send out e-mails in response to tips. eBay staffers look at complaints on a case-by-case basis, in the order they receive them. Most complaints they receive are about these problems:

✔ Shill bidders (see the section on "Selling abuses" in this chapter)

✔ Feedback issues and abuses (see the section on "Feedback abuses" in this chapter)

Figure 16-1: The Security & Resolution Center as it appears when you click the Security Center link.

Keep in mind that eBay is a community of people, most of whom have never met each other. No matter what you buy or sell on eBay, don't expect eBay transactions to be any safer than buying or selling from a complete stranger. If you go in with this attitude, you can't be disappointed.

If you've been reading previous chapters in this book, you probably know about eBay's rules and regulations. For a closer online look at them, click the Policies link, which is on the bottom of most eBay pages, and then check the User Agreement. (The agreement is revised regularly, so check it often.)

Another helpful link is the FAQ for the User Agreement, which explains the legalese in clearer English. To find it, go to

```
pages.ebay.com/help/policies/everyone-ov.html
```

Abuses You Should Report to Trust & Safety

Before you even consider blowing the whistle on the guy who (gasp!) gave you negative feedback by reporting him to Trust & Safety, make sure that what you're encountering is actually a misuse of eBay. Some behavior isn't nice (no argument there) but it *also* isn't a violation of eBay rules — in which case, eBay can't do much about it. The following sections list the primary reasons you may start Trust & Safety investigations.

Selling abuses

If you're on eBay long enough, you're bound to find an abuse of the service. It may happen on an auction you're bidding on; or a seller whose listings compete with your auctions may do something really, really wrong. Be a good community member and be on the lookout for the following:

- **Shill bidding:** A seller uses multiple user IDs to bid or has accomplices place bids to boost the price of his or her auction items. eBay investigators look for six telltale signs, including a single bidder putting in a really high bid, a bidder with really low feedback but a really high number of bids on items, a bidder with low feedback who has been an eBay member for a while but who's never won an auction, or excessive bids between two users.

- **Auction interception:** An unscrupulous user, pretending to be the actual seller, contacts the winner to set up terms of payment and shipping in an effort to get the buyer's payment. You can easily avoid this violation by paying directly through the eBay site with PayPal.

- **Fee avoidance:** A user reports a lower-than-actual final price or illegally submits a final value fee credit, or both. Final value fee credits are explained in Chapter 13.

- **Hot bid manipulation:** A user, with the help of accomplices, enters dozens of phony bids to make the auction appear to have a lot of bidding action. Let the experts at eBay decide on this one; but you may wonder if loads of bids come in rapid succession but the price moves very little.

Bidding abuses

If you want to know more about bidding in general, see Chapter 6. Here's a list of bidding abuses that eBay wants to know about:

- **Bid shielding:** Two users working in tandem. User A, with the help of accomplices, intentionally bids an unreasonably high amount and then retracts the bid prior to the 12-hour cancellation deadline of the auction — leaving a lower bid (which the offender or an accomplice places) as the winning bid.

- **Bid siphoning:** Users send e-mail to bidders of a current auction to offer the same merchandise for a lower price elsewhere.

- **Auction interference:** Users warn other bidders through e-mail to stay clear of a seller *during a current auction,* presumably to decrease the number of bids and keep the prices low.

- **Bid manipulation (or invalid bid retraction):** A user bids a ridiculously high amount, raising the next highest bidder to maximum bid. The manipulator then retracts the bid and rebids *slightly* over the previous high bidder's maximum.

- **Nonpaying bidder:** I often call them deadbeats; the bottom line is that these people win auctions but never pay up. Your bid on eBay is a legal contract to buy if you win, it is *not* a game.

- **Unwelcome bidder:** A user bids on a specific seller's auction despite the seller's warning that he or she won't accept that user's bids (as in the case of not selling internationally and receiving international bids). This practice is impolite and obnoxious. If you want to bar specific bidders from your auctions, you can exclude them. See Chapter 13 for the scoop on how to block bidders.

Feedback abuses

All you have on eBay is your reputation, and that reputation is made up of your feedback history. eBay takes any violation of its feedback system very seriously. Because eBay's feedback is transaction-related, unscrupulous eBay members now have less opportunity to take advantage of this system. Here's a checklist of feedback abuses that will get you into trouble. These can all be reported through the Security Center:

- **Feedback extortion:** A member threatens to post reputation-destroying feedback if another eBay member doesn't follow through on some unwarranted demand. Typical extortion attempts include demanding a refund or a generous discount after the bad buyer has won the item.

- ✔ **Personal exposure:** A member leaves feedback for a user that exposes personal information that doesn't relate to transactions on eBay.

- ✔ **Malicious feedback:** Writing malicious feedback is a sick game played by those who have very little to do with their time but upset upstanding eBay sellers. These sickies register on eBay with a new user ID and use the Buy It Now function to buy many items from a seller who has a high positive feedback rating. A few hours later, they leave dastardly negative feedback. The only goal of this action is to ruin the seller's reputation.

- ✔ **–4 Feedback:** Any user reaching a Net Feedback score of –4 is subject to suspension.

Once you post feedback, your words are out there. They become part of cyberspace forever and are there for all to see. Your words are a reflection of your online persona.

Identity abuses

Who you are on eBay is as important as what you sell (or buy). eBay monitors the identities of its members closely — and asks that you report any great pretenders in this area to Trust & Safety. Here's a checklist of identity abuses:

- ✔ **Identity misrepresentation:** A user claims to be an eBay staff member or another eBay user, or he or she registers under the name of another user.

- ✔ **False or missing contact information:** A user deliberately registers with fraudulent contact information or an invalid e-mail address. If you come across someone on eBay who has false information registered on eBay, that member can be suspended.

- ✔ **Under age:** A user falsely claims to be 18 or older. (You must be at least 18 to enter into a legally binding contract.)

- ✔ **Dead/invalid e-mail addresses:** When e-mails bounce *repeatedly* (single bounces are almost a fact of life on the Internet) from a user's registered e-mail address, chances are good that it may be dead — and it's doing nobody any good.

- ✔ **Contact information:** One user publishes another user's contact information on the eBay site.

Operational abuses

If you see someone trying to interfere with eBay's operation, eBay staffers want you to tell them about it. Here are two roguish operational abuses:

- ✔ **Hacking:** A user purposely interferes with eBay's computer operations (for example, by breaking into unauthorized files). If someone attempts to alter any of the eBay-generated information in a listing, such as a feedback rating or user ID, the person is violating important eBay rules.

- ✔ **Spamming:** The user sends unsolicited e-mail to eBay users. Just because you are in a transaction with someone doesn't give you the right to e-mail the person after the auction is over to solicit future business. If you send a newsletter or solicitations, your recipients must have opted in to your list. No one has the right to send you e-mail unrelated to your transaction without your permission.

Miscellaneous abuses

The following are additional problems that you should alert eBay about:

- ✔ A user is threatening physical harm to another eBay member.
- ✔ A person uses racist, obscene, or harassing language in a public area of eBay.

For a complete list of trading offenses and how eBay runs each investigation, go to the following address: `pages.ebay.com/help/buy/report-trading. html`.

Reporting Abuses to Trust & Safety

If you suspect a seller of abusing eBay's rules and regulations, you can report him or her directly on the item page. Look to the Seller Info box of the page of the item in question and click the Report Item link, as shown in Figure 16-2.

When you click that link you'll come to the only area on eBay where you can report listing violations. Select the reason for your report and further information from the drop-down menus. Once you've made your selections, click Continue.

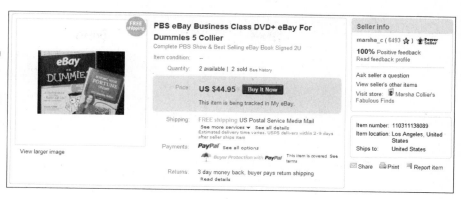

Figure 16-2:
You'll find
the Report
Item link in
the lower-
right corner
of the Seller
Info box.

If your issue is connected to a transaction that you're currently involved in with another eBay member, click the Resolve a Problem link on the Security Center page discussed earlier. You're presented with a page that suggests answers to the various questions you may have. To actually reach eBay, click Contact Us. You'll land on the Contact Us page, which presents you with some of the most basic questions about eBay as well as clickable links to find answers. To *really* (this time I promise) contact eBay, type a short version of your question, find the Get in Touch with Us area, and click the Email Us link on the right of the page, as shown in Figure 16-3.

When you become a PowerSeller or have an eBay store, you see a different page than non-PowerSellers and have considerably more contact options. (More reason to finish this book and get started selling!)

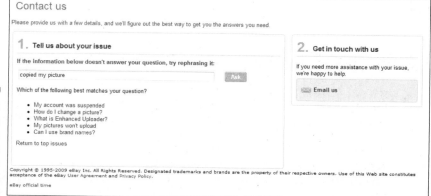

Figure 16-3:
Here's
where you
get to the
heart of the
issue.

If you encounter any of the abuses outlined in this chapter, be sure to report the problem. Community policing is what makes eBay work.

The Security Center offers a wealth of good general information that can help you prevent something from going wrong in a future transaction. Be sure to use these pages regularly as a resource to help prevent problems.

If you're involved in a troubled transaction and need to launch a report, follow these steps:

1. **Read all the information on the Investigations page (`pages.ebay.com/help/buy/report-trading.html`) before filing a new complaint.**

2. **Click any of the many informational links.**

   No matter which link you click, you're taken to an area that instructs you further and provides answers about what offenses eBay can and cannot investigate.

3. **If you've found out that you have a legitimate case that should be investigated, you are supplied a link to the proper reporting area.**

   Alternatively, you can click the Report Item link in the Seller Info box on your transaction page.

If you file a report, make your message clear and concise by including everything that happened — but don't editorialize. (Calling someone a "lowdown mud-sucking cretin" may make you *feel* better, but it doesn't provide any useful info to anyone who can help you; it doesn't make you seem very un-cretin-like, either.) Keep it businesslike — just the facts, ma'am. Do include all pertinent documentation, such as e-mails, receipts, and canceled checks — and don't forget the transaction number.

Here's a checklist of what you should include in your report to Trust & Safety:

- ✔ Write only the facts as you know them.

- ✔ Attach any pertinent e-mails with complete headers if required. (*Headers* contain all the information that precedes an e-mail message.) Trust & Safety uses the headers to verify how the e-mails were sent and to follow the trail back to the originator of the messages. See the sidebar, "Finding the hidden headers in an e-mail message" to decipher this information.

- ✔ Be sure that the subject line of your report precisely names the violation.

After eBay receives your report via the Customer Service form, you usually get an automatic response that your e-mail was received — although in practice, several days may go crawling by before eBay investigates your allegations. (The Customer Service Department must look at a *lot* of transactions.)

Finding the hidden headers in an e-mail message

Most of the time, the headers in an e-mail message are hidden by your e-mail program. If you're using Outlook Express (a free program included with every Windows-enabled personal computer), here's how you find them:

1. **Open an e-mail message by double-clicking the Subject line.**

2. **In the open e-message, choose File⇨ Properties.**

The Properties dialog box appears.

3. **Click the Details tab.**

Bingo! The headers appear. Copy and paste these into the eBay form whenever you need to report any spurious e-mail.

This information is vital not just to eBay, but to any online entity you might need to report an e-mail abuse to.

Depending on the outcome of the probe, eBay may contact you with the results. If your problem becomes a legal matter, eBay may not let you know what's going on. The only indication you may get that some action was taken is that the eBay member you reported is suspended — or NARU *(Not A Registered User)*.

If your complaint doesn't warrant an investigation by the folks at Trust & Safety, they pass it along to someone at the overworked Customer Support staff, who then contacts you. (Don't bawl out the person if the attention you get is tardy.)

Unfortunately, NARU members can show up again on the eBay site. Typically nefarious sorts as these just use a different name and credit card to register back on the site. In fact, this practice is common, so beware! If you suspect that someone who broke the rules once is back under another user ID, alert Trust & Safety. If you're a seller, you can refuse to accept bids from that person. If the person persists, alert Customer Support with e-mail.

As eBay has grown, so has the number of complaints about slow response from Customer Support. I don't doubt that eBay staffers are doing their best. Although slow response can get frustrating, avoid the temptation to initiate a reporting blitzkrieg by sending reports over and over until eBay can't ignore you. This practice is risky at best and inconsiderate at worst, and it just slows the process for everyone — and won't endear the e-mail bombardier to the folks who could help. It's better to just grin and bear it and wait for action to be taken.

Emergency help

For general, all-purpose help, eBay has a Customer Support e-mail response form that will get you an answer within 12 to 36 hours. You can find Customer Support creatively tucked away at `pages.ebay.com/help/contact_us/_base/index_selection.html`

If you're desperate for help and can't get satisfaction, you can post a message with your problem in one of the eBay chat rooms. eBay members participating in chat rooms often share the names of helpful staffers. Often you can find some eBay members who faced the same problem (sometimes with the same member) and can offer advice — or at the very least, compassion and a virtual ear. (Jump to Chapter 17 for more info on discussion boards and chat rooms.)

If you're a PowerSeller, you can easily contact PowerSeller support with your immediate problem.

Make sure that you don't violate any eBay rules by sharing any member's contact information as you share your story in a chat room. In addition, make sure that you don't threaten or libel (that is, say untrue things or spread rumors about) the person in your posting.

Stuff eBay Won't Do Anything About

People are imperfect everywhere, even online. (Ya think?) You probably won't agree with some of the behavior that you run into on eBay (ranging from slightly annoying to just plain rotten). Although much of that conduct is just plain nasty, it can (and does) go on as long as it doesn't break eBay rules.

In some cases, you may need to bite your tongue and chalk up someone's annoying behavior to ignorance of the unwritten rules of eBay etiquette. Just because people have computers and some things to sell or buy doesn't mean that they possess grown-up social skills. (But you knew that.)

Here's a gang of annoying issues that crop up pretty regularly but that *aren't* against eBay's rules and regulations:

✔ **A seller sets astronomical shipping costs:** eBay policy says that shipping costs must be reasonable. Basically, eBay is wagging its finger and saying, "Don't gouge your buyers." When sellers gouge their buyers with high shipping fees, eBay penalizes them in their Best Match search results. Some sellers try to avoid fees or may be disappointed that a sale didn't make enough money, so they think that by jacking up shipping costs they will increase their profit.

Under the rules, eBay will stop someone from charging excessive amounts for shipping. For more information on eBay's Excessive Shipping policy, go to `pages.ebay.com/help/policies/listing-shipping.html`.

Bidders should always check shipping terms in the Item description. Bidders must decide whether to agree to those terms before they bid. The best way to protect yourself from being swindled is to buy only from a seller whose shipping costs feel fair to you.

✔ **A seller or buyer refuses to meet the terms that you mutually set:** eBay has the power only to warn or suspend members. It can't make anyone do anything — even someone who's violating a policy. If you want to make someone fulfill a transaction, you're more or less on your own. I heard one story of a seller who refused to send a product after being paid. The seller said, "Come and get it." The buyer happened to be in town on business and did just that!

But if your item never arrives, you can apply to PayPal for a refund under the Buyer Protection plan. Information on how to file is further on in this chapter.

Often, reluctant eBay buyers just need a nudge from eBay in the form of a warning to comply. So go ahead and file a final value fee credit request (I explain how to do this in Chapter 13) and, if necessary, a fraud report (more on fraud reports later in this chapter).

✔ **An eBay member sends unwanted e-mail messages (spam):** In fact, members can send spam using eBay's own tools. All the user has to do is access the Contact a Member Form by clicking a member's user ID. eBay sees non-transaction–related communication as spam; you need to report any member who abuses this system. (You'll see a reporting link on any e-mail sent through the eBay system). Although the items spammers are selling may be perfectly good, eBay won't offer you any protection if you participate in off-the-site deals. I suggest that you ignore these deals and avoid doing business with them in the future.

New eBay users are often the unwitting perpetrators of annoying behavior, but you're ahead of the pack now that you know what *not* to do. You can afford to cut the other newbies some slack and help them learn the ropes before you report them.

Knowing the Deeds That Can Get You Suspended

Playing by eBay's rules keeps you off the Trust & Safety radar screen. If you start violating eBay policy, the company's going to keep a close eye on you. Depending on the infraction, eBay may be all over you like jelly on peanut butter. Or you may safely lurk in the fringes until your feedback rating is lower than the temperature in Nome in November.

Here's a docket of eBay no-no's that can get a member's permanent record damaged — and possibly *suspended:*

- Feedback rating of –4
- Three instances of deadbeat bidding with three different sellers
- Repeated warning for the same infraction
- Feedback extortion
- Bid shielding
- Unwelcome bidding after a warning from the seller
- Shill bidding
- Auction interception
- Fee avoidance
- Fraudulent selling
- Identity misrepresentation
- Bidding when younger than age 18
- Hacking
- Physical threats

If you get a suspension but think you're innocent, respond directly to the person who suspended you to plead your case. Reversals do occur. Don't broadcast your suspicions on chat boards. If you're wrong, you may regret it. Even if you're right, it's oh-so-gauche.

Be careful about accusing members of cheating. Unless you're involved in a transaction, you don't know all the facts. *Law & Order* moments are great on television, but they're fictional for a reason. In real life, drawing yourself into a possible confrontation is senseless. Start the complaint process, keep it businesslike, and let eBay's staff figure out what's going on.

Getting Buyer Protection

One thing's for sure in this world: Nothing is for sure. That's why insurance companies exist. Several types of insurance are available for eBay users:

- ✔ Insurance that buyers purchase to cover shipping (see Chapter 12)
- ✔ SquareTrade warranties
- ✔ BuySAFE bonds
- ✔ PayPal's Buyer Protection

To cover loss from fraud, eBay buyers can avail themselves of several protection programs. The basic PayPal protection covers money that you pay for an item you never receive (as a result of fraud, not shipping problems) or receive but find to be materially different from the auction item's description.

eBay Motors Vehicle Protection Program

Another beneficial eBay venture is eBay's Vehicle Protection Program, which offers a *free* limited warranty to anyone who purchases a car on eBay. Look for the Vehicle Protection Program Shield at the bottom of the Seller Info box to see whether the vehicle you're interested in is covered. Qualified cars are identified in the listing description in the Item Specifics box, with the words *Vehicle Protection Program up to $50,000.*

Your vehicle purchase is protected for up to $50,000 or the vehicle purchase price, whichever is lower. You can find more information at eBay Motors:

```
pages.motors.ebay.com/buy/purchase-protection/index.html
```

PayPal Buyer Protection

Aside from safety, now PayPal offers an even better reason to pay through its service. If you've purchased your item through a PayPal-verified seller, you're covered for your original purchase price, plus shipping. This protection covers you only for nondelivery of tangible items and tangible items that are received significantly not as described — not if you are disappointed with the item.

If you've paid with a credit card through PayPal, be sure to make a claim with eBay first and *then* with PayPal. Do *not* make a claim with your credit card company. PayPal Buyer Protection is for PayPal purchases, and you're not covered if you've made a claim with your credit card company.

For the latest information on this program, go to

`pages.ebay.com/help/buy/paypal-buyer-protection.html`

Several types of protection are available to eBay buyers, as shown in Table 16-1.

Table 16-1	eBay Shopper's Assurance	
Type	**Who Pays**	**Explanation**
Shipping insurance	Buyer	As the buyer, you must pay the seller the additional charge for package insurance. This will cover your purchase up to the insured amount while the item is in transit through the U. S. Post Office, UPS, or FedEx.
PayPal buyer	No charge	eBay agrees that you've been defrauded if you've paid for your purchase through PayPal up to your purchase price.
BuySAFE bond	Seller	BuySAFE bonds back a preferred seller's performance on the item, up to $25,000.
SquareTrade Seal	Seller	There is no warranty if you have been defrauded by a SquareTrade Seal member. Note that the Seal only assures the buyer that the seller's positive feedback remains constant.

BuySAFE bond

BuySAFE helps make online auctions safer. The "BuySAFE with the Hartford" program offers one of the highest levels of protection available to online auction participants. It's the only program that enables sellers to present a credibility seal and financially protect their online auction transactions with surety bonds.

BuySAFE comprehensively qualifies sellers to display the BuySAFE seal. When a buyer sees the BuySAFE seal on an auction or fixed-price listing, the transaction is 100% guaranteed to be exactly as listed.

SquareTrade warranties

Granted, a SquareTrade warranty is designed to help you *after* you've received the product as described, but that's when most items break for me. You can buy these highly discounted (40% lower than most retailers) warranties from SquareTrade on almost any electronic item you purchase on eBay against breakage. The warranty is simple and straightforward.

To purchase a warranty after you've bought a qualifying product on eBay, go to

```
www.squaretrade.com
```

Launching a Fraud Report

The second that you complain about a seller who's taken money but hasn't delivered the goods, a Trust & Safety investigation automatically starts. The Resolution Center is where you can go to file a formal complaint when you run into trouble with a transaction.

To get to the Resolution Center, click the Help link in the eBay navigation bar and choose Resolution Center, or click the Resolution Center link, which appears at the bottom of most eBay pages. You can get to the Resolution Center also from your listing in My eBay, in which case your item number will be filled in on the form for you:

1. **Go to your My eBay page.**

2. **In the Buy area, click the link to take you to the items you've won.**

3. **Scroll down the page to find the item in question and choose Resolve a Problem from the pull-down menu.**

   The Resolution Center's Resolve a Problem form appears

4. **Choose the problem you are having in your transaction and click Continue.**

   Now you get to the Report an Item Not Received or Not as Described form. If you arrived at the Resolution Center from your item listing, your item number is already filled in. If you got there from the link in the navigation bar, you have to enter the item number.

5. **Click Continue.**

6. **Tell eBay how you paid for this item.**

   If you paid by PayPal you are sent to the Resolution page.

7. **Review your case details, and then click Open Case.**

The Your Case Is Now Open page appears and tells you that your trading partner has been notified and has 10 days to respond. From here on, you can continue your dealings in the Resolution Center.

To file a claim with eBay, you must initiate the complaint process no sooner than 7 days and no later than 45 days after the close of the listing. Be careful not to jump the gun and register a complaint too soon. I suggest waiting about two or three weeks before you register your complaint about an Item Not Received (an item lost in the mail can often take as long as 30 days to arrive); double-check first to make sure that your e-mail is working and that you have the correct contact information of the person with whom you're having difficulties. After all, neither eBay nor your ISP is infallible.

After you register a complaint, eBay informs the other party that you're making a claim. eBay says it will try to contact both parties and help reach a resolution. *Registering* the complaint is not the same thing as *filing* an insurance complaint. Registering starts the process; filing for a refund comes after a month-long grace period if the situation isn't resolved by then.

If you've clearly been ripped off, use the Item Not Received or Significantly Not as Described process to file a complaint. Just scroll to the Links area at the bottom of the page and click the Security & Resolution Center link.

A shortcut to file for an Item Not Received or Significantly Not as Described, go directly to the form at `feedback.ebay.com/ws/eBayISAPI.dll?InrCreateDispute`.

If the accusation you're registering is a clear violation, eBay gives you information on the kind of third-party assistance you can get to help resolve the problem. If eBay deems the problem a violation of the law, it reports the crime to the appropriate law-enforcement agency.

Getting the Real Deal? Authentication and Appraising

Despite eBay's attempts to keep the buying and selling community honest, some people just refuse to play nice. After the New York City Department of Consumer Affairs launched an investigation into counterfeit sports memorabilia sold on the Web site, errant eBay outlaws experienced some anxious moments. I can always hope they mend their ways, while at the same time advising *Don't bet on it*. Fortunately, eBay offers a proactive approach to preventing such occurrences from happening again.

Topmost among the countermeasures is easy member access to several services that can authenticate specific types of merchandise. The good news here is that you know what kind of item you're getting; the bad news is that, as does everything else in life, it costs you money.

Have a good working knowledge of what you're buying or selling. Before you bid, do some homework and get more information. And check the seller's or bidder's feedback. (Does this advice sound familiar?) See Chapters 5 and 9 for more information about conducting research.

Before you spend the money to have your item appraised and authenticated, ask yourself a few practical questions (regardless of whether you're buying or selling):

- ✔ **Is this item quality merchandise?** Am I selling or buying merchandise whose condition is subjective but important to its value — as in, *Is it really well-loved or just busted?* Is this item graded by some professionally accepted standard that I need to know?

- ✔ **Is this item the real thing?** Am I sure that I'm selling or buying a genuine item? Do I need an expert to tell me whether it's the real McCoy?

- ✔ **Do I know the value of the merchandise?** Do I have a good understanding of what this item's worth in the marketplace at this time, considering its condition?

- ✔ **Is the merchandise worth the price?** Is the risk of selling or buying a counterfeit, a fake, or an item I don't completely understand worth the cost of an appraisal?

If you answer "yes" to any of these questions, consider calling in a professional appraiser.

As for *selling* a counterfeit item — otherwise known as a knock-off, phony, or five-finger-discount item — that's a no-brainer: No way. Don't do it.

If you need items appraised, consider using an appraisal agency. You can access several agencies by going to the overview page at pages.ebay.com/ help/buy/authentication.html. eBay offers links to various appraising agencies that offer their services at a discount to eBay members:

- ✔ **The PCGS** (Professional Coin Grading Service) and **NGC** (Numismatic Guaranty Corporation) serve coin collectors. Visit www.pcgs.com/ cobrands/index.chtml?cobrandid=24 and www.ngccoin.com/ ebay_ngcvalue.cfm.

- ✔ **PSA/DNA** (a service of Professional Sports Authenticators) and **Online Authentics.com** authenticate your autographs. Both keep online databases of thousands of certified autographs for you to compare your purchases against. Their respective online addresses are www.psacard.com and www.onlineauthentics.com.

- ✔ **Global Authentication, Inc.** are specialists in authenticating autographs and memorabilia from the sports world. See www.globalauth.com.

- ✔ **PSE** (Professional Stamp Experts) authenticates your postal stamps: www.psestamp.com.

- ✔ **CGC** (Comics Guaranty) grades and restores comic books. Visit www.cgccomics.com/ebay_comic_book_grading.cfm.

- ✔ **IGI** (International Gemological Institute) grades, authenticates, and identifies loose gemstones and jewelry. Visit www.e-igi.com/ebay.

- ✔ **PSA** (Professional Sports Authenticators) and **SGC** (Sportscard Guaranty) help guard against counterfeiting and fraud with sports memorabilia and trading cards. eBay has teamed up with these services to grade and authenticate trading cards. You can visit the respective addresses of these agencies at www.psacard.com and www.sgccard.com/ebay/.

Even if you use an appraiser or an authentication service, do some legwork yourself. Often, two experts can come up with wildly different opinions on the same item. The more you know, the better the questions you can ask.

If a seller isn't sure whether the item he or she is auctioning is authentic, you may find an appropriate comment (such as *Cannot verify authenticity*) in the item description. Knowledgeable eBay gurus always like to share what they know, and I have no doubt that someone on the appropriate chat board may be able to supply you with scads of helpful information. But be careful — some blarney artist (one of *those* is born every minute, too) may try to make a sucker out of you.

ID Verify

During the later years of the Cold War, Ronald Reagan said, "Trust but verify." The President's advice made sense for dealing with the old Soviet Union, and it makes good sense with your dealings on eBay, too! (Even if you're not dealing in nuclear warheads.)

To show other eBay members that you're an honest type — and to get special privileges when you're a newbie on eBay, you can buy a "trust but verify" option, known as *ID Verify,* from eBay for five bucks. The giant credit verification service, VeriSign, verifies your identity by asking for your wallet information, including the following:

- Name
- Address
- Phone number
- Social Security number
- Driver's license information
- Date of birth

VeriSign matches the info you give to what's in its database, and presents you with a list of questions from your credit file that only you should know the answer to. VeriSign may also ask you about any loans you have (for example) or what kinds of credit cards you own (and how many).

Becoming ID-Verified can be a bonus for new users. It allows you to bypass some of eBay's more stringent requirements for participating in higher-level deals. By making sure that the community knows you're really who you say you are, you can get the green light for some higher-level activities:

- **Run auctions with the Buy-It-Now option:** Ordinarily you need a feedback rating of 10 to run a Buy-It-Now auction. This privilege may be worth the price of the verification, but honestly, how hard is it really to get your first 10 feedbacks? Besides, the experience will be priceless.

- **Open an eBay store:** Although eBay requires a feedback rating of only 20 to open a store, I suggest you have much more. An eBay store (see Chapter 11 for more information) requires a bit more eBay savvy than the newbie seller can muster.

- **Run fixed-price sales offering multiple items):** Ordinarily, an eBay seller must have more than a 30 feedback rating to perform this type of sale.

- **Bid on items over $15,000:** Some form of verification is usually even required of eBay's old-timers when bidding this high!

- **Sell items in the Adults Only Category**

VeriSign sends only the results of its Identity Test to eBay (whether you pass the test) and *not* the answers to the private financial questions it asks you. VeriSign doesn't modify or add the information you provide to any of its databases.

VeriSign's questions are meant to protect you against anyone else who may come along and try to steal this information from you and assume your identity. The questions aren't a credit check, and your creditworthiness is never called into question. This info simply verifies that you are who you say you are.

If you pass the test and VeriSign can verify that you are who you say you are (and not your evil twin), you get a cool icon by your name for a year. If, after a year, you like the validation that comes from such verification, you can pay another fee and renew your seal.

Although you can feel secure knowing that a user who's verified is indeed who he or she claims to be, you still have no guarantee that he or she's not going to turn out to be a no-goodnik (or, for that matter, a well-meaning financial airhead) during auction transactions.

Even if an eBay member gets VeriSign verification, what makes this program so controversial is twofold:

- ✔ Many members object to giving out Social Security numbers. They see it as an unwarranted invasion of privacy.

- ✔ Some users also fear that this system creates a two-tiered eBay system, with verified users occupying a sort of upper class and anyone who's not verified stuck in the lower class. They're afraid that sellers may refuse to do business with *un*verified users.

You should consider all of eBay's current and future programs for protecting you from problematic transactions and people, but I think the "undisputed heavyweight champ" for finding out who someone *really is* (and keeping you out of trouble) is the first program eBay created. That's right, folks: *feedback* can show you other eBay members' track records and give you the best information on whether you want to do business with them or take a pass. Feedback is especially effective if you analyze it in conjunction with eBay's other protection programs. I suggest taking the time to read all about feedback in Chapter 4.

If It's Clearly Fraud

After filing either a fraud report or a final value fee credit request, you can do more on your own. If the deal involves the post office in any way — if you mail a check or the seller sends you merchandise that's completely wrong and refuses to make good — file a mail-fraud complaint with the postal inspector.

In the United States, you can call your local post office or dial 800-275-8777 for a form to fill out. After you complete the form, the USPS sends the eBay bad guy a notice that you've filed a fraud complaint. Perhaps that *will* get his or her attention.

In addition to the post office, you can turn to some other agencies for help:

- **The National Fraud Information Center:** NFIC has an online site devoted to combating fraud on the Internet. NFIC works closely with legal authorities. File a claim at `www.fraud.org/info/repoform.htm` or call toll free at 800-876-7060.

- **Law enforcement agencies:** Contact the local district attorney (or state Attorney General's office) and the local and state Consumer Affairs Department in the other person's state and city. (Look online for contact information or try your local agencies for contact numbers.)

- **Federal Trade Commission:** The FTC accepts complaints and investigates repeated cases of fraud. File a claim at `www.ftc.gov/bcp/edu/microsites/idtheft/consumers/filing-a-report.html`.

- **Internet service provider:** Contact the member's ISP. You can get this bit of info from the person's e-mail address, just after the @ symbol. (See? This easy access to information does have its advantages.) Let the ISP know whom you have filed a complaint against, the nature of the problem, and the agencies that you've contacted.

Any time you contact another agency for help, keep Trust & Safety up to date on your progress by writing to its representatives the old-fashioned way. Address your letter to eBay ATTN: Fraud Prevention, 2145 Hamilton Ave., San Jose, CA 95125.

A very thin line separates alerting other members to a particular person's poor behavior and breaking an eBay cardinal rule by interfering with an auction. Don't make unfounded or vitriolic accusations — especially if you were counting on them never getting back to the person they were about (or, for that matter, if you hoped they *would*). Trample the poison out of the gripes of wrath before you have your say. I recommend that you hunt for facts, but don't do any finger-pointing on public message boards or chat rooms. If it turns out that you're wrong, you can be sued for libel.

Communication and compromise are the keys to successful transactions. If you have a difference of opinion, write a polite e-mail outlining your expectations and offer to settle any dispute by phone. See Chapters 12 and 13 for tips on communicating after the auction ends — and solving disputes *before* they turn wicked, aggressive, or unprintable.

Chapter 17

The eBay Community: Joining In with Other eBay Members

*e*Bay is more than just an Internet location for buying and selling great stuff. eBay wants the world to know that it has created (and works hard to maintain) a community. It's not a bad deal — prime real estate in *this* community costs only pennies! As in real-life communities, you participate as much as works for you. You can get involved in all sorts of neighborhood activities, or you can just sit back, mind your own business, and watch the world go by. eBay works exactly the same way.

As you've probably heard by now, one of the main ways to participate in the eBay community is through feedback (which I explain in detail in Chapters 4 and 6). In this chapter, I show you some other ways to become part of the community. You can socialize (making friends who live in your community or who live across the planet), learn from other members, post messages, or just read what everybody's talking about on eBay's discussion boards, groups, chat boards, and the corporate Announcements Board. I include tips on how to use all these places to your benefit, and then give you a change of scenery by surfing through some off-site message boards that can help you with your buying and selling.

On eBay's navigation bar, click the Community link to connect to the happenings on eBay; I use it regularly to check proposed changes to the site on the General Announcements page. But there's a whole lot more to the Community area of eBay. Take a little time to explore it for yourself.

News and Chat, This and That

It's not quite like *The New York Times* ("All the News That's Fit to Print"), but you can find all the news, chat board, group, and discussion board links from the Community Overview page. Figure 17-1 shows you what the page looks like.

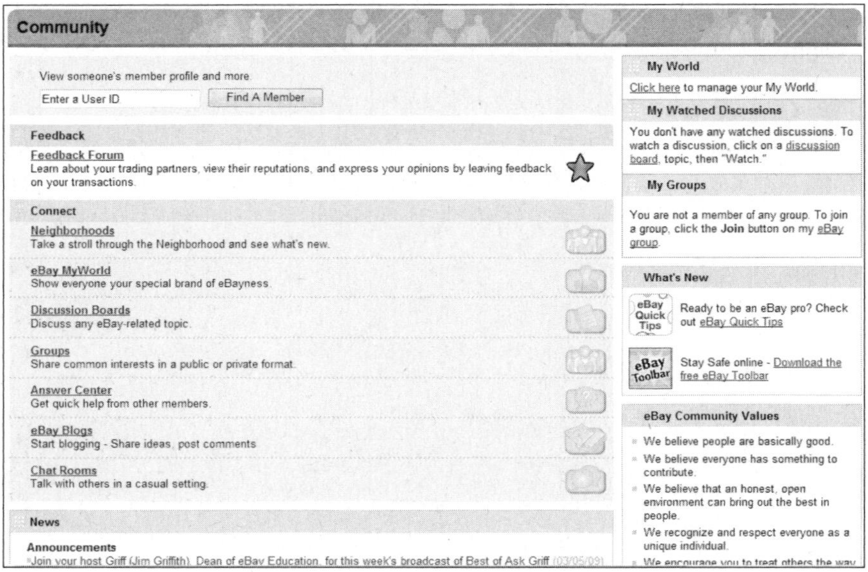

Figure 17-1: The main Community page features links to many informative places on eBay, including areas to chat and post messages.

Here's a list of the core headings of the main Community page. Each heading offers you links to the specific eBay areas:

- ✔ **Feedback:** Find a handy link to the Feedback Forum. (More on feedback in Chapters 4 and 6.)

- ✔ **Connect:** Click the links in this section to be whisked to eBay's discussion boards, groups, chat rooms, blogs, or the Answer Center.

- ✔ **News:** This area contains links to the Announcements page, which covers general news, policy changes, technology updates, system announcements, and more. You can also find links to eBay events, including Town Hall meetings, eBay Radio, and Online Workshops.

Making eBay Your World

Did you know that if you click your user ID on any eBay page, you arrive at your very own My World page? (You also have a link to your My World page on the Community page). Unlike the About Me page, which you have to choose to set up yourself, every eBay member has their own My World page. It's ready and waiting for you to embellish it.

Look at my My World page in Chapter 14 (Figure 14-6). See the link at the top that invites me to customize my page? Yours has it as well. You can customize this page with your favorites, your photo, feedback, a guestbook, your own (short) biography and many of your eBay interests.

Your My World page reflects your many varied interests. From here, eBay gives you other ways to express yourself (links to all these pages are also on the main Community page):

✔ **Neighborhoods:** Have a hobby? Maybe enjoy an old series of TV shows or a movie? (No cracks about my being a member of the Star Trek Neighborhood.) Search eBay's Neighborhoods and see if there's a group you might want to join. The main page (where you can search the various neighborhoods) is at `http://neighborhoods.ebay.com`.

✔ **Reviews:** Wondering what other eBay members think of a particular product, book, or movie? Visit eBay's Reviews to find out. Better yet, contribute one of your own. Reviews show up when a search is made on an item for which eBay users have posted reviews. Figure 17-2 shows a review written by an eBay member on one of my books.

Figure 17-2: eBay members review books. Note the three clickable tabs that will show you the listings, product details, and reviews.

✔ **Guides:** Do you have a special talent? Maybe you're an expert on antique linens and want to share that knowledge? Here's the place. Go to the Reviews & Guides area and post your guide to help other eBay members. Just go to `http://reviews.ebay.com` and you'll see the page shown in Figure 17-3.

Figure 17-3:
The
Reviews
& Guides
home page
(accessed
from the
Community
page) is
where you
can con-
tribute your
knowledge
to the
community.

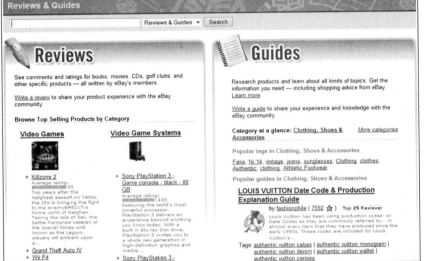

Hear Ye, Hear Ye! eBay's Announcements Boards

If you were living in the 1700s, you'd see a strangely dressed guy in a funny hat ringing a bell and yelling, "Hear ye, hear ye!" every time you opened eBay's announcements boards. (Then again, if you were living in the 1700s, you'd have no electricity, computers, fast food, or anything else you probably consider fun.) In any case, eBay's announcements boards are the most important place to find out what's going on (directly from the home office) on the Web site. And no one even needs to ring a bell.

The General Announcements Board is where eBay lists any new features and policy changes. Visiting this page is like reading your morning eBay newspaper because eBay adds comments to this page almost every day. You find out about upcoming changes in categories, new promotions, and eBay goings-on.

eBay also uses it to help users become aware of critical changes in policies and procedures. Reach this page at www2.ebay.com/aw/marketing.shtml. Figure 17-4 shows you eBay's General Announcements Board with information that could affect your sales.

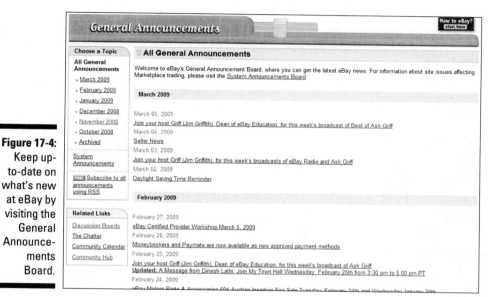

Figure 17-4:
Keep up-
to-date on
what's new
at eBay by
visiting the
General
Announce-
ments
Board.

eBay has over 200 million members — a bigger population than some countries — but it can still have that small-town feel through groups, chat boards, and discussion boards. Start on the main Connect area (refer to Figure 17-1) by clicking Community on the navigation bar. Then click the links below. You can access more than two dozen category-specific chats (although I'm not quite sure what's discussed in the Furbies Board these days), as well as a bunch of general chats, discussion boards, and help discussion boards.

Help! I Need Somebody

If you ever have specific eBay questions to which you need answers, several eBay discussion boards on the Community: Connect page can help you. You can also go directly to the chat rooms to pose your question to the eBay members currently in residence.

Boards work differently than chat rooms. Chat rooms are full of people who are hanging out talking to each other all at the same time, whereas users of discussion boards tend to go in, leave a message or ask a question, and pop out again. Also, in a discussion board, you need to start a thread by asking a question. Title your thread with your question, and you'll no doubt get a swift answer to your query.

Many questions can be answered by going to eBay's Answer Center, which you can get to by clicking the Answer Center link in the Connect area. You then see boards covering almost any topic regarding selling and buying on eBay. Just post your question and some kind eBay member will probably suggest an answer (but remember to take that advice with a grain of salt, just as you would any advice from someone with unknown credentials).

eBay newbies often find that the boards are good places to add to their knowledge of eBay. As you scroll by, read past the postings; your question may already be answered in an earlier posting. You can even ask someone on a chat or discussion board to look at your auction listing and provide an opinion on your descriptions or pictures.

Community Chat Rooms

Because sending e-mail to eBay's Customer Service people can be frustratingly slow if you need an answer right away (they get bombarded with a gazillion questions a day), you may want to try for a faster answer by posting your question on one of the Community chat rooms.

Knowledgeable veteran eBay members generally answer posted questions as best (and as quickly) as they can. The answers are the opinions of members and are certainly not eBay gospel. But you get a fast and honest answer; often you get more than one response. Most questions are answered in about 15 minutes. If not, repost your question. Make sure that you post your question on the appropriate board because each board has a specific topic of discussion.

If a new policy or some sort of big change occurs, the boards are most likely going to quickly fill with discussion about it. On slow days, however, you may need to wade through endless personal messages and "chat" with no connection to eBay. Many of the people who post on these boards are long-time members with histories (as well as feuds) that can rival any soap opera. On a rare occasion, the personal postings can get rather nasty. Getting involved in personality clashes or verbal warfare gains nothing and wastes your valuable time.

One cardinal rule for eBay chat boards and message boards exists: no business. No advertising items for sale! Not now. Not ever. eBay bans any repeat offenders who break this rule from participating on these boards.

Remember that you're visiting eBay and that you're a member. It's not Speakers' Corner — that spot in a London park where protesters are free to stand on a soapbox and scream about the rats in government. If you feel the need to viciously complain about eBay, take it outside, as the bar bouncers say.

User-to-User Discussion Boards

eBay has some other boards that take a different tack on things. They're *discussion* boards as opposed to *chat* boards, which basically means that the topics are deliberately open-ended — just as the topics of discussions in coffee houses tend to vary depending on who happens to be in them at any given time. Check out these areas and read ongoing discussions about eBay's latest buzz. It's a lot of fun and good reading. Post your opinions to the category that suits you. You can find tons of discussion boards on various topics relating to doing business on eBay, but my favorites are in the General Discussion area. Each discussion board carries as many topics as you can imagine. Here are few of my favorites:

- **The eBay Town Square** is a potpourri of various subjects and topics.

- **The Soapbox** is the place to voice your views and suggestions to help build a better eBay.

- **NightOwls Nest** is the fun locale for creatures of the night and their unique postings. (As I'm writing this, for example, there's a thread with spirited advice to a community member who needs help with his "gassy" cat.)

- **eBay Live** is a big eBay user convention. Stop by this board to get a bird's-eye view of the happenings from the previous year's summit. You can also find out what's in store for the upcoming soiree.

- **The Park** is an interesting place where community members join in for fun ideas and threads.

Other Chat Rooms (Message Boards)

About a dozen chat rooms at eBay specialize in everything from pure chat to charity work. The following sections describe a few of these boards.

Café society

The eBay Café (eBay's first chat board from back when they were just selling Pez candy dispensers) and AOL Café message boards attract mostly regulars chatting about eBay gossip. Frequent postings include the sharing of personal milestones and whatever else is on people's minds. You can also find useful information about eBay and warnings about potential scams here.

Holiday Chat Room

Although eBay suggests that this is the place to share your favorite holiday memories and thoughts, it's really a friendly place where people meet and chat about home and family. Stop by for cybermilk and cookies next time you have a few minutes and want to visit with your fellow auction addicts.

Giving Works Board

eBay isn't only about making money. On the Giving Works Board, it's also about making a difference. Members in need post their stories and requests for assistance. Other members with items to donate post offers for everything from school supplies to clothing on this board.

If you feel like doing a good deed and conduct a member benefit auction, click the eBay Giving Works link on the Discussion Board page. For more on charity auctions see Chapter 18.

The eBay Friends from All Over discussion Board

People from all around the world enjoy eBay. If you're considering buying or selling globally, visit the eBay Friends from All Over Board. It's a great place to post questions about shipping and payments for overseas transactions. Along with eBay chat, this board turns up discussions about current events and international politics.

Got a seller or bidder in Italy? Spain? France? Translate your English messages into the appropriate language through the following Web site:

`www.google.com/translate`

Category-Specific Chat Boards

Want to talk about Elvis, Louis XV, Sammy Sosa, or Howard the Duck? Currently over 20 category-specific chat boards enable you to tell eBay members what's on your mind about merchandise and auctions. You reach these boards by clicking Community on the main navigation bar and then clicking Chat in the Connect area.

Of course, you can buy and sell without ever going on a chat board, but you can certainly learn a lot from one. Discussions mainly focus on merchandise and the nuts and bolts of transactions. Category-specific chat boards are great for posting questions on items that you don't know much about.

On eBay, you get all kinds of responses from all kinds of people. Take a portion of the help you get with a grain of salt because some of the folks who help you may be buyers or competitors.

Don't be shy. As your second-grade teacher said, "No questions are dumb." Most eBay members love to share their knowledge of items.

eBay Groups

If you're the friendly type and would like an instant group of new friends, I suggest that you click the link in the Connect area to eBay Groups. Here you can find thousands of user groups, hosted on eBay but run by eBay community members. They may be groups consisting of people from the same geographic area, those with similar hobbies, or those interested in buying or selling in particular categories.

eBay Groups may be public groups (open to all) or private clubs with their own private boards. Only invited members of a private group can access a private board.

Joining a group is easy: Just click any of the links on the main Groups page and you're presented with a dizzying array of groups to join. Your best bet though, is to participate in chats or discussions, and find other members that you'd like to join up with.

Blog It on eBay

A recent addition is eBay's Blogs area. Here's where any eBay member can start his or her own online posting page. You can share your opinions and ideas with the entire Internet universe, directly from eBay. I find reading other members' blogs a fun pastime; plus you get to learn a little more about the faces behind the user IDs. Blogs do not replace the all-important About Me page, but a blog can be a fun pastime and fun for all your friends to read. Keep in mind, I said a pastime. If your plan is to learn to sell on eBay, study this book and lots of PowerSeller listings on the site. Go and list some test items rather than spending precious moments playing here. But if time is not of the essence, have fun.

Chapter 18

eBay's Fun Features

*N*o one can say that eBay isn't fun! The eBay staff is always trying to work with the community by filling needs and finding fun stuff to keep us happy. In this chapter, I show you how eBay members can get great inside deals from manufacturers, and I open the door of The eBay Shop, where you can get T-shirts and coffee cups with the official eBay logo on them. I also show you how you can help your favorite charity earn some well-deserved cash at eBay's charity auctions.

Over and over, eBay members show what big hearts they have. Yes, you actually can pocket some nice-sized profits from selling on the eBay Web site, but (just as in real life) people usually take the time to give a little back for worthy causes. But because we're talking about eBay, giving back means getting something fabulous in return.

Truly Righteous Stuff for Charity

Most of us have donated to charity in one form or another. But here on eBay, charities really rock. Do you need a *Jurassic Park* helmet signed by Steven Spielberg to round out your collection (and deflect the odd dino tooth)? Post a bid on one of the charity auctions. How about a signed original photograph of Jerry Seinfeld from *People* magazine? Yup, you can get that, too. All these and more have turned up in charity auctions. In short, having a big heart for charities has gotten a whole lot easier thanks to eBay.

eBay Giving Works

November 2003 was a lucky time for this country's charities. That's the month that eBay launched the eBay Giving Works Charity auction area. Smartly, the folks on eBay teamed up with one of the finest charity sites on the Internet, MissionFish. MissionFish, a service of the Points of Light Foundation, has been around since early 2000 and has enabled charities to raise hundreds of thousands of dollars by turning in-kind donations into cash. The eBay community has helped raise close to $200 million so far.

If you're involved with a charity, you can register your charity to get on the list of beneficiaries. You can also run your own fundraising events on eBay! Just go to www.ebaygivingworks.com or click the Giving Works link on the left side of the eBay home page and you'll arrive at the Giving Works hub (as in Figure 18-1).

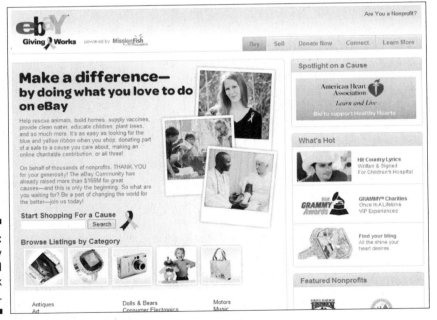

Figure 18-1: Where eBay buyers and sellers work for good.

The best part about this new system is that *you* can run an auction to benefit your favorite charity. eBay sellers can list items for sale and designate those items to benefit a charity from the MissionFish directory of thousands of charities. The seller can also specify what percentage (from as little as 10 up to 100 percent) of the auction proceeds go to the charity. At the end of the sale, MissionFish e-mails a tax receipt to the seller. You can browse to select the charity of your choice on the Giving Works page. When you list your item for sale, you can indicate on the Sell form's Create Your Listing section which charity, and what percentage of the final sale price, you'd like to donate proceeds.

As you visit different areas of eBay, you can recognize the charity auctions by the small blue ribbon icon next to them in searches and the Category list.

Creative charity auctions

New charities are popping up all the time on eBay. To see the auctions that are running, go to the Charity page by starting on eBay's home page and clicking the Giving Works (Charity) link on the left side of the screen. Here are some of the more creative charity auctions that have been held on eBay:

- The highest grossing charity auction occurred in 2008. In an annual eBay fundraising auction run by Kompolt & Company, billionaire Warren Buffet donated a private lunch to benefit the Glide Foundation in New York. The 2008 auction grossed $2,110,100.

- Oprah Winfrey has jumped onto eBay with a bang! To fund her charity, the Angel Network, Oprah auctioned two chairs from her set. These were not just any chairs. Aside from being luxurious leather chairs designed by Ralph Lauren, they housed the behinds of famous names such as John F. Kennedy, Jr., Halle Berry, Tom Hanks, Jim Carrey, and Michael Jordan, to name just a few. The 7-day auction netted the charity an amazing $64,100.

- To celebrate Chivas Regal's 200th year, the company chose eBay for CHIVAS 200, the largest online charity auction in the world. From September 6 to October 31, 2001, the Chivas folks auctioned more than 200 of the world's most-wanted items and experiences — such as an opportunity to become a Russian space station astronaut — all for the benefit of charity partners around the world.

- When I appeared on *The View* with Barbara Walters and Star Jones, all four stars of the show autographed a coffee cup that we auctioned off on eBay to benefit UNICEF. We raised over $1,000 on a single coffee cup! Now that a couple of the hosts have moved on, I wonder what that little cup's worth.

If you go to the About Me page (by clicking the link from the listing page) of any of the charities on the Charity Fundraising page, you can find out exactly where the money that eBay users bid goes.

And Now for Our Feature Presentation

As an eBay member, you're entitled to some features offered on the Web site. The perks aren't quite as high-end as you may receive with, say, a country club membership, but hey, your nonexistent membership dues are a lot less! With about 203 million confirmed registered users, eBay can get outside companies and manufacturers to listen to what it has to say. You know the old saying about power in numbers? On eBay, you find "savings in numbers" on items or services that you can buy outside the Web site, as explained in this section.

Member specials

As eBay gains popularity, more and more outside companies are offering special deals exclusively for members. These deals aren't auctions but are conventional "pay the price and get the item or services" transactions.

To find the member specials, go to the very bottom of eBay's home page and look for the business logos or link boxes at the bottom of the page. eBay also has a page with most of the Power Trading features (special deals) at `pages.ebay.com/services/buyandsell/member-specials.html`.

The special deals change all the time, but here's a small sampling of perks available to you as a member:

- ✔ **eBay gift certificates:** Wow! It doesn't get much better than this. Now I never have to drag myself all over town looking for a gift. You can purchase these certificates in any amount from $5.00 to $200.00. You can print the certificate and give it with a gift (I think my book, *Santa Shops on eBay,* would make an excellent companion for an eBay gift certificate), or you can have it e-mailed to the recipient. You can also find information at the secure site `https://certificates.ebay.com/`.

- ✔ **PayPal:** Online payments integrated directly into your eBay auctions.

- ✔ **Authentication services:** Get a special discount (usually 10 percent) if you authenticate coins through Professional Coin Grading Service (PCGS) or trading cards through Professional Sports Authenticator (PSA). See Chapter 16 for tips on authenticating your items.

As time passes, you can see additional benefits and programs that eBay creates for the community. The folks at eBay are aggressively searching out new and helpful affiliations to help you take care of your auction business. But don't leave the task of maintaining your listings entirely to eBay — take it upon yourself to find new ways to make your listings easier to manage.

A successful seller takes advantage of every program and service he or she can. The less time you spend tied to your computer, the more time you have to plan new auctions and find new items to sell. Investigate these programs and try them out for yourself.

Who's minding The eBay Shop?

eBay's minding The eBay Shop, of course (and freshening up its window-dressing from time to time). If you can't find the perfect item for your favorite eBay member with more than 89 million listings (or so) worldwide running at any given time, go browse around eBay's General Store, The eBay Shop. You don't find any auctions here — just eBay logo items, such as shirts, bags, coffee mugs, and even eBay pick-up sticks!

To get to eBay's online store, start at the home page. Scroll down to the very bottom and click The eBay Shop link (find it directly at `www.theebayshop.com`). Just choose what you like, add it to your shopping cart, and then check out when you're finished. The store will ask you for billing information, so keep your credit card handy.

eBay's Saved Searches e-mail service

If you're too busy to explore the nooks and crannies of eBay on a daily basis (or you're the type who wants to cut to the chase), sign up for eBay's personal shopper through your My eBay Saved Searches.

This service is one of eBay's better ideas. It enables you to find what you're looking for and still have a life, because it sifts through the new listings for you 24 hours a day, looking for the items that meet your description. eBay sniffs 'em out like a bloodhound, and then sends you an e-mail containing a list of items that you may want to bid on, complete with links that take you right to those items. Hey, best of all, the service is free!

To register for the personal shopper e-mail service, begin on the navigation bar, which is at the top of most eBay pages, and follow these steps:

1. **Type keywords and perform a search using the Search box on the top-right side of any eBay page.**

   The results of your search appear.

2. **Click the Save This Search link next to the total number of results.**

   A box pops up, as shown in Figure 18-2.

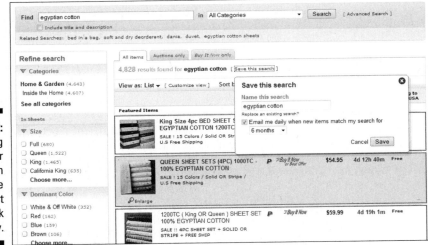

Figure 18-2:
Getting regular reports on your favorite item is just one click away.

3. **Using the drop-down menu, choose how long you want to receive a daily e-mail about the availability of new items that match your search.**

   Select the period of time (from 7 days to 12 months) you'd like to receive the e-mails when new items are listed.

4. **Click the Save box.**

5. **The search is now added to your My eBay Saved Searches page.**

   Go there to see a list of your current searches. You may save up to 100 searches to be notified by e-mail. Yikes, don't do 100! All you'll get is e-mail from eBay!

Getting Free Calls over the Internet with Skype

eBay has purchased a new Internet-based communication service called Skype that enables you to call other Skype users long distance for free. You can bet that in the near future, eBay will be integrating Skype technology with its other services. (Imagine the possibilities!) You need to have a broadband Internet connection to use Skype.

Skype is controlled by software that you download to your computer. It allows you to communicate with the rest of the world at no additional cost (over the expense of your high-speed internet connection). To download the software for PC, Mac, or Linux, just go to www.skype.com and click the Download Skype link.

After you download the software, you can install the program with a click of your mouse. Skype allows you to use your computer (along with a micro-phone and your regular computer speakers) as a telephone. You can contact anyone who is a member of Skype at no charge — wherever in the world they reside or do business. (You can call regular phone numbers for a low, discounted per-minute fee.) All Skype-to-Skype calls are free. As wonderful (and simple) as that is, Skype has other revolutionary features that can really expand your business:

✔ **SkypeIn:** I love this feature. With SkypeIn, you can purchase a special phone number for your Skype computer so that people not set up with Skype can contact you on your Skype account. The super part is that if you live in, say, Atlanta but do a lot of business in London, you can get a local number in London so your London customers only have to make a local call (without incurring long-distance charges) to reach you. Unfortunately, SkypeIn doesn't do anything about the time difference, so you'll still get calls from your British customers in the middle of the night, but this feature does make your business look pretty big time — you have a remote office across the Atlantic! You can get up to ten different SkypeIn numbers.

✔ **Skype voicemail:** If you're not at your computer when another user attempts to call you, your account can receive and store voicemail. Voicemail is free when you purchase a SkypeIn telephone number. If you purchase it separately, the annual cost is minimal.

✔ **SkypeOut:** You can call any number in the United States and Canada (mobile or land line) for $2.95 a month. Skype has reasonable charges for calls made to foreign countries through SkypeOut. For example: London, UK is $.021, Japan $.023, France $.021 per minute. For a complete listing of international per-minute rates go to www.skype.com/price/callrates.

At home I use a Netgear Skype dual-mode phone so that my buyers can reach me with questions whenever they want. The phone carries my office land line as well as my Skype line wirelessly to anywhere I carry the phone. It plugs into my router to pick up my Skype calls, and a phone line wire plugs into the wall jack to access the land line. It also uses a new technology that expands the strength and range of the wireless phone.

My home was built after the Northridge, California, earthquake and it has a good deal of steel in its structure to prevent it from collapsing. This structural element had precluded my using a wireless phone from one end of the house to the other — until I got the Skype phone. Now I can access Skype and get free long distance from anywhere in my home or office. (For more information, check the Web site at www.netgear.com.)

Skype is adding interesting features all the time. The Skype software even allows for free video calls on your computer (assuming you have a Web cam). You can also add a Skype button to your e-mails, allowing your contacts to just click to call you.

Part V
The Part of Tens

The 5th Wave — By Rich Tennant

"Come on Walt — we need a shot of the product to bring in more bids."

In this part . . .

In keeping with a long-standing tradition, this part gives you the short version of the facts, somewhat like downloadable class notes. Check here for the golden rules every eBay user needs to know, whether you buy or sell (or, like most eBay members, do both).

You also get information on a few of the software programs available to help simplify your auction experience — from creating a catchy auction item page to helping you snipe the final bid while you're sleeping, walking Fido, washing your hair, or otherwise occupied. The best thing about some of these programs is that the price is right — you can get started for free.

Following the Part of Tens chapters, you get an appendix that gives eBay fanatics exactly what they've been looking for — tips to help them acquire stock and take their auction habit to the next level by thinking strategically.

Chapter 19

Ten (or So) Golden Rules for eBay Buyers and Sellers

*N*o matter how much experience airplane pilots may have, they always keep multiple checklists to go over. The same is true on eBay (although the only crashing that you need to worry about is on your computer). No matter how many times you buy or sell, the advice in this chapter can help you survive and thrive at eBay.

Although conducting business on eBay is relatively smooth overall, any venture is bound to have a few bumps here and there. A certain etiquette goes along with everything we do in life. If you follow these simple rules, your time on the site will be a whole lot more pleasant for everyone. That said, here are ten (or so) easy, important golden rules for eBay. I note which tips are geared toward buyers or sellers. Happy hunting and gathering!

After a while, posting listings and bidding become rote. You can all too easily forget the basics, so look at this chapter every now and again and remember that, as a successful eBay member, you're part of a very special person-to-person community.

Buyer: Investigate Your Treasure Before You Buy

In the excitement of finding just what you want, you may develop a tendency to leap before you look. Even if the item is closing soon, carefully read the item description. Does the item have any flaws? Can you live with it? Is something missing from the description that should be there? Did you read the terms of payment and shipping?

You can also communicate with the seller of the item that you're longing for. Don't be too shy or embarrassed. If you have any questions, send an e-mail! You're better off covering your bases before you place a bid than facing disappointment after making a purchase. Remember that when you click the Bid or Buy button, you are *legally and morally obligated* to go through with the transaction if you win. Make sure that everything is as you want it and check for a warranty or return policy. Clarify everything upfront. If the seller doesn't answer back, consider that nonresponse an *early warning* that dealing with this person may be a mistake!

Buyer: Check the Seller's Feedback

Never bid without checking the seller's feedback. You need to be able to trust the person you're buying from. Don't just evaluate the Feedback percentage: Investigate the seller's feedback by clicking the number next to his or her user ID. Be sure to read the comments left by other users. Checking some of the seller's other listings, past and present, to get an idea of the seller's history also can't hurt. As badly as you may want something, sending a payment to someone with a high feedback rating but who recently got a bunch of negatives could be risky business.

Buyer: Understand Post-Auction Charges and Payment Methods

Before you bid on an item, make sure that you and the seller have similar ideas on the shipping and handling, insurance, and escrow fees (if applicable — see Chapter 6). Buying a $10 item and finding out that shipping and handling are going to cost more than your winning bid is way bad. Don't forget to look for any "handling charges."

Also, make sure that you and the seller can agree on the form of payment before the deal closes. If you want to pay with a check, is the seller willing to accept one? (You'll have to e-mail them ahead of time to find out.) Are you willing to wait to receive your purchase until a check clears? Is credit card payment available? Stay safe and use a secure method of paying with credit cards like PayPal.

Buyer: Check the Price Tag and Bid Wisely

Before you bid, make sure that you have some knowledge of the item, even if you limit your search to completed auctions to get an idea of how much the item went for in the past.

If a deal sounds too good to be true, it may well be.

I love eBay — but not for every single thing that I buy (okay, almost). Make sure that you can't get the item cheaper at the store or from another online seller.

Beware of getting caught up in the frenzy of last-minute bidding: It's an easy thing to do. Whether you choose proxy bidding or sniping (see Chapter 7 for my discussion on sniping), decide how much you're willing to pay before bidding. If you set a limit, you won't be overcome with the urge to spend more than an item is worth — or, worse, more than you have in your bank account.

Although eBay is lots of fun, it's also serious business. Bidding is a legal and binding contract. Don't get a bad reputation by retracting bids or becoming a deadbeat.

Buyer: Be a Good Buyer Bee

Always leave feedback after you put the finishing touches on a transaction. Leaving feedback, and thereby helping other members, is your responsibility. Remember your manners when making your payment. You like to be paid on time, right? And, speaking practically, the sooner you send the money, the sooner you get your stuff.

Keep in mind that the transaction isn't complete until the buyer receives the merchandise and is happy with the purchase. Don't automatically expect positive feedback because you paid for your item in a timely manner.

Buyer: Cover Your Assets

Remember that just because you're conducting transactions from the privacy of your home doesn't mean that you're doing everything you can to protect your privacy. Legitimate buyers and sellers *never* need to know your password or Social Security number. Do not respond to this sort of e-mail. See Chapter 15 about how to handle this sort of e-mail.

Seller: Know Your Stuff

Do some homework. Know the value of your item. At the very least, get an idea of your item's value by searching completed listings for similar items. If it's a new item, check out other online sites and see what your item is selling for by running a Google/Froogle search at www.google.com/products. Knowing your product also means that you can accurately describe what you have and never, ever pass off a fake as the real McCoy. Make sure that your item isn't prohibited, illegal, questionable, or infringing. It's your responsibility!

Before posting your listing, you should take the following actions:

- ✔ Write an honest description.
- ✔ Take a good, clear photo.
- ✔ Work out your shipping and handling charges.

Add each of the preceding pieces of info to your item's description to avoid any unnecessary disputes later.

Seller: Polish and Shine

Make sure that your title is descriptive enough to catch the eye of someone browsing a category and detailed enough for eBay's search engine to identify. Don't just write *1960s Board Game*. Instead, give some details: *Tiny Tim Vintage '60s Board Game MIB*. That gets 'em tiptoeing to your auction.

Play editor and scrutinize your text for grammar mistakes and misspellings. Typos in either your title or description can cost you money. For example, a search engine will keep skipping over your *Mikky Mouce Choklit Cokie Jare*. Spelling counts — and pays. Double-check your work!

Seller: Picture-Perfect Facts

Photos can be a boon or a bust on eBay. Double-check the photo of your item before you post it. Is the lighting okay? Does the photo paint a flattering image of the item? Crop out unnecessary backgrounds. Would *you* buy this item?

Take your picture as if you didn't have a description; be sure it totally illustrates the item. Also, write your description as if you didn't have a photo. That way if the photo server crashes, the prospective buyer will have a good idea of what you're selling.

Be factual and honest. On eBay, all you have is your reputation, so don't jeopardize it by lying about your item or terms. Tell potential buyers about any flaws. Give as complete a description as possible, with all the facts about the item that you can include.

Seller: Communication Is Key

Respond quickly and honestly to all questions sent via the My eBay Messages page and use the contact to establish a good relationship. Don't let more than 24 hours pass without sending a response. If a bidder makes a reasonable request about payment or shipping, going along with that request is usually worth it to make a sale. *Note:* The customer is always right! (Well, some of the time, anyway.)

Be upfront and fair when charging for sending merchandise to your buyer. You can't make much money by overcharging for shipping and handling. Besides, charging outrageous handling fees will penalize you in eBay search and is a violation of eBay's policies. You could get yourself suspended from the site. After the item arrives, the buyer may realize what it costs to ship. Unreasonable charges inevitably lead to bad feelings, negative feedback, and low DSRs.

Seller: Be a Buyer's Dream

Just because you're transacting through the computer doesn't mean that you can forget your manners. Live by the golden rule: Do unto others as you would have others do unto you. Contact the buyer the day they make their purchase — immediately is even better. (Better yet, why not ship the item that quickly? I try to.) And keep all your correspondence polite.

Ship the goods as soon as you can (in accordance with the shipping terms you outline in the item description, of course). An e-mail stating that the item is on its way is always a nice touch, too. That way, buyers can eagerly anticipate the arrival of their goods.

And, when shipping your items, use quality packing materials and sturdy boxes to prevent disaster. Broken or damaged items can lead to reputation-damaging, negative feedback. Pack as if someone's out to destroy your package (or as if *you* had made this purchase). Your buyers are sure to appreciate the effort.

Seller: Listen to the Music

As I state in the golden rules for buyers, don't underestimate the power of positive feedback. Your reputation is at stake. Always generously dole out feedback when you complete a transaction. Your buyers will appreciate it and should return the favor. What should you do if you get slammed unfairly with negative feedback? Don't freak out! Do, however, post a response to the feedback by using the Respond to Feedback link on your My eBay page. Those who read your feedback can often see past a single disgruntled message.

Keep in mind that many negative feedback reports result from misunderstandings. Contact the buyer the moment you smell a problem arising and see if you can work things out to your satisfaction. Always work to keep your eBay reputation pristine.

Buyers and Sellers: Keep Current, Keep Cool

You'd be surprised at the number of users who get suspended even though they have automatic credit card payments. Maybe they move. Or their e-mail address changes because they change Internet service providers. Regardless, if you don't update your contact and credit card information, and eBay and other users can't contact you as a result, you can be suspended.

If you make any major moves (home address, billing address, ISP), let eBay know this new contact information. Click My eBay on the main navigation bar, scroll down the links on the left side of the page to My eBay Account Preferences, and update the appropriate information.

Chapter 20

Ten (or So) Programs and Services to Ease Your Way on eBay

*R*eady to take your sales to the next level? Are you looking for snappy-looking text or fancy layouts to make your auctions scream, "Buy me!"? Need to slip in a bid in the middle of the night without losing sleep? If so, here's a list of ten (or so) programs and services to help put your auctions ahead of the pack and make your bidding life easier. In this chapter I recommend some reliable companies, and many of them offer free solutions!

As online sales grow in popularity, software developers are constantly upgrading and developing new auction and selling software to meet eBay's changes. Many of these programs even look for new versions of themselves — and update themselves as you start them. (Aladdin never had things so good.)

You absolutely don't *have* to use any of these programs or services to run eBay sales successfully. However, when you're running more than several auctions a week, the addition of a "helper" makes things go ever so much smoother (especially if it's free or very low cost).

A large amount of companies out there are offering online management service and offline programs. (Let's face it, as long as people will pay they will be happy to have something to sell you.) I can't cover each and every one, so the software that I mention in this chapter has been tried and tested by me. You may know of others, and I'd love to hear about them. I do know that these work and are good tools when you choose to expand your eBay sales.

Listed in this chapter are several auction-management Web sites. Each site has its own distinct personality. I also provide the names of some terrific offline software programs you can use to help manage your auctions, make your e-auctions elegant and eye-catching, find the best prices, and snatch up that bargain at the last minute.

Be sure to check my Web site www.coolebaytools.com for updates on software and services pricing, as well as special discounts that are offered to my readers.

Online Services

You're comfortable transacting your auctions online, so why not manage them online as well? The sites in this section offer incredibly useful services that save time in both posting your auctions and wrapping them up.

Auctiva

If you're new on eBay and you'd like to try a little automation to get you started, Auctiva is your entry-level choice. Auctiva has been serving eBay sellers since my first edition of *eBay For Dummies* in 1999. First, let me tell you my favorite part about Auctiva: It's *free*. That's right, FREE (my favorite four-letter word). Now, I always say you get what you pay for, but with Auctiva you get a bit more than that.

Auctiva offers online item-listing software and image hosting for eBay sellers. The easy-to-use site guides you through the process: creating auction listings, posting them on eBay, communicating with buyers, collecting payments, organizing shipments, keeping records of sales, marketing your listings, and much more.

Here are some of the site's features:

✔ **A one-page listing tool:** You can create your professional-looking listings with a complete one-page listing tool — and if you like variety, you can choose from 1500 template options.

✔ **Unlimited image hosting:** Auctiva enables you to upload hundreds of images at a time, and you can keep your account organized by managing your images within Auctiva's online folder structure.

✔ **Auctiva Scrolling Gallery:** You may have noticed that at the bottom of many listing you see on eBay, there is a scrolling gallery showing other items for sale by the seller. This is an excellent tool for selling even more merchandise.

✔ **Profiles:** After you generate your profile information, your Auctiva profile is set to automatically appear in all your listings by default.

For these features and more, visit the Auctiva Web site at www.auctiva.com.

InkFrog

InkFrog is a Web-based service founded by Tomas Salas and Greg Sisung. They've been helping eBay sellers since 1999. In 2006 InkFrog bought out another respected service, SpareDollar. InkFrog represents a super bargain in a Web-based management service. The best part about its service is that you pay a flat monthly fee of only $9.95. With its easy-to-use service, little guys can get the same benefits as large-volume sellers — and pay smaller fees.

You can manage every aspect of your eBay sales, including image hosting, ad design, automated e-mail management, and report tracking. If you want to get fancy, you can design your item listing from any of its templates. Here are some more features:

✔ **Image hosting:** InkFrog hosts your images and has a handy uploader that allows you to insert your images with a click of your mouse.

✔ **One-step lister:** Create your listings (with as many images as you want) using a simple form. InkFrog also lets you schedule your listings to start at a future time at no additional cost.

✔ **Checkout system and tracking:** InkFrog has a checkout system that integrates with eBay's checkout system. You can track which items need to be paid, which items need to be shipped, and which of your customers need feedback left. You can then update these items in bulk. You can also automatically send custom e-mails to your customers.

For more information, and even more features, visit the InkFrog Web site at www.inkfrog.com.

Vendio and Vendio Stores

Vendio was one of eBay's first providers in 1999 and has been serving over a million sellers since. These sellers have sold over $15 billion in merchandise to nearly 300 million buyers. Vendio is a major provider of services that help e-commerce merchants on eBay, Amazon, and many other sites reach consumers, manage transactions, and profitably grow their businesses.

You can buy some or all of Vendio services (kind of like a Chinese restaurant). Here are just a few of their many applications:

- **Buyer appreciation:** This automates the process of personalized customer communication. The first time a customer bids or buys, they send a thank you e-mail. Best of all? This service is free.

- **Counters:** This free service from Vendio will let you see the number of visitors to your item, as well the total number of bids. Er, by the way, this is *also* free.

- **Image hosting:** Store your images on their site. Pricing starts at $3.00 a month for up to 3MB of storage (you really don't need more).

- **Research:** Study what's going on in the market. See what's selling. This service keeps you up with what the competition is doing. Feature analysis and more is available for $20.00 a month.

- **Free stores:** Yes, you read it right, Free! Vendio offers you a free professional online store that's easy to set up. No image fees for stores, no final value fees, no listing fees, no hosting fee. Completely free! (But do yourself a favor, and study my books before you launch a store.)

- **Free Gallery Pro:.** Readers of this book get a great *free* service from Vendio, their Gallery Pro. This service gives you a small bit of text that you add to your listings that displays a scrolling gallery of your items for sale when someone views one of your listings. It is said that it will help increase hits by 50 percent and sell-through by up to 18 percent. You can also specify the order in which specific items appear. To get this free offer, email `ebayfordummies@corp.vendio.com` with your request.

The main Vendio service is a robust listing, inventory, and business management platform. With their site you can manage each step of the online sales cycle: inventory management, marketing, fulfillment, customer communications, and more. This costs only $10.00 a month, plus a percentage of your sales.

To view all their offerings, go to `www.vendio.com`.

Buyitsellit Stores

You want to start small? You can at Buyitsellit. When you're ready to set up your own full-featured Web store, Buyitsellit will give you one for only $9.95 a month. You get 100MB of file storage, custom templates, and a custom domain. They offer a dashboard where you can run your store with real-time traffic statistics. They even offer a starter store, where you can list ten items for free. If you'd like to give it a try, visit `www.buyitsellit.com`.

Fast Photos

If your photos need a touch up to make them Web ready and PhotoShop is too expensive and complex (it really is for eBay purposes), you might be happy giving Fast Photos by Pixby Software a try. It's a simple, all-in-one photo-editing program designed especially for e-commerce and eBay sellers. The developer of the software knew exactly what processes online sellers need for their images and included just those — and nothing else. There are tools for cropping, JPEG compression, sharpening, resizing, enhancing, rotating, and adding watermark text and borders.

The software is a PC application that runs on Vista, Windows XP, 2000, ME, and 98 SE. For a 21-day free trial, visit their Web site at `www.pixby.com/marshacollier`.

BidRobot

As you can tell by reading Chapter 7, I'm a big fan of sniping. It's my favorite way to win an auction. It makes the entire auction experience even more entertaining. Sadly, with the schedule I keep, I am rarely at my computer when the auctions close!

BidRobot to the rescue. When I find an auction that I'm serious about, I simply go to the BidRobot Web site, log in, and place my future snipe bids. All I have to do is type the item number and my high bid, and that's it. I can shut off my computer knowing that BidRobot will do my bidding for me. Nobody on eBay will know what item I'm desperate to have, because the magical BidRobot doesn't place my bid until a few seconds before the auction closes. If I'm the high bidder, no one will have the chance to bid against me!

BidRobot's services are reasonably priced, based on the amount of time that you want to use the service. As of this writing, BidRobot has placed bids for more than 100,000 eBay users since 1998! You pay a flat rate for all the snipes you can handle. You don't pay any extra charges for the service. For a free trial, visit BidRobot's Web site at this special URL for my readers `www.bidrobot.com/cool`.

Software for Offline Use

Software for offline use can handily reside on your computer after a simple download from a Web site. As with online services, this software comes in a variety of flavors, so take a look and decide which program works best for you. Downloadable software may be available from Web sites that offer other services and can be used whether you are online or not. Offline software enables you to handle auctions in your spare time, without the limitations of ISPs or servers.

Auction Wizard 2000

Auction Wizard 2000 is a full-service professional management software package developed by eBay sellers. The software is fairly simple and amazingly powerful. It expedites all the seller functions for running and completing eBay sales, including automating the following tasks:

- Inputting your inventory on the software's HTML templates and uploading auctions in bulk onto eBay.

- Automatically updating the software with the current status of your auctions, including who won, who is a runner-up, and the auction bidding history. The preformatted e-mail and feedback files automatically fill in the values from each auction and send them to the people you do business with directly through the software.

- Tracking income and expenses, as well as creating a full set of reports.

If you choose to become a Trading Assistant — that is, sell items for other people — Auction Wizard 2000 has a separate tracking area where you can keep track of your consignment sales by consignee. It even computes the fees that you're charging for your services. They charge $100.00 for the first year, and $50.00 for annual renewal.

Download a fully functional 60-day test drive with no inactive features and no restrictions from `www.auctionwizard2000.com`.

Finally, for the Mac!

Rejoice! You Mac users out there now have a couple of eBay listing services that will help you expedite your listings on eBay. eLister 2 is a full-powered offline listing program that gives you the freedom to write auctions on your own time and includes a group of good-looking auction templates. It includes an automatic HTML generator and an automatic listing fee calculator. Visit www.blackmagik.com/; the program is updated regularly to conform to any changes in eBay listing procedures and starts at $4.99 a month.

A very robust solution is Auction Genie, which gives you not only listing capabilities but also advanced management software and lots of extras. It also works with your Mac e-mail program and provides FTP services for uploading your photos to your Web site. Check out its services, available for $50.00 a year, at www.luxcentral.com/auctiongenie/.

Shooting Star

A super desktop software from Foodogsoftware, Shooting Star works for sellers on multiple eBay sites: the United States, Canada, Australia, and the United Kingdom. Download the software to your computer, install it, and you're set to perform all listing and management procedures without being online. Check out the e-commerce software, which is available for $120.00, at www.foodogsoftware.com.

eBay's Software and Services

When the users call, eBay answers! As eBay grew, the need for additional services and software also grew. eBay answered the need with Turbo Lister software and its PowerSeller program. Read on to see how these services tailored for the eBay user may benefit you.

eBay's Free Turbo Lister

Turbo Lister is free software that enables you to upload many auctions simultaneously. I use it regularly to set up my listings. After you prepare your auctions offline, the software uploads your auctions to eBay with just the click of a button. You can edit, preview, and (when you're ready) launch all your auctions at once, or schedule them to launch at different times (which costs you $0.10 for each scheduled auction). Your items can include eBay's templates, and the items will remain archived on your computer for later use. The software is convenient and simple to use even if you have only a few items at one time — although Turbo Lister will let you launch thousands of listings at a time! The program is free, and you can download it at `pages.ebay.com/turbo_lister`.

Selling Manager and Selling Manager Pro

I have used Selling Manager Pro for my eBay sales for many years, and I find it to be a convenient way to quickly relist singly (or in bulk), track the progress of my sales, send bulk e-mails, leave feedback, and keep track of what has and hasn't sold.

You also get a nice selection of reports to help you keep track of how your listings are performing. This way you can tell whether your sales are on-target or not. As you can see from Figure 20-1, Selling Manager (or Selling Manager Pro) replaces the All Selling page of My eBay. This thorough data is updated automatically from eBay's servers and PayPal, so you have up-to-the-minute info.

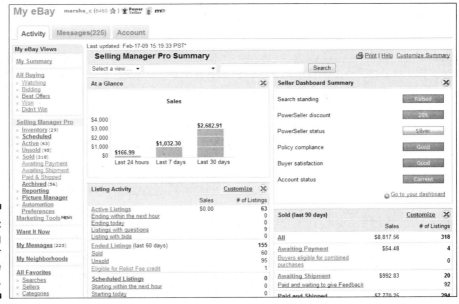

Figure 20-1:
My Selling
Manager
Pro home
page.

Selling Manager is free to all sellers but you must request the feature. The Pro version, which adds inventory management and reporting features, is tailored to high-volume sellers, and costs $15.99 a month. Both versions are available at `pages.ebay.com/selling_manager/`.

eBay PowerSellers program

eBay offers an elite club for PowerSellers who fulfill the following requirements:

- Be an active eBay member for at least 90 days
- Sell a minimum of $1,000 or 100 items per month for 3 consecutive months, or sell a minimum of $12,000 or 1,200 items for the prior 12 months
- Have a minimum overall feedback rating of 100
- Maintain at least a 98 feedback percentage
- Keep your eBay account current
- Comply with all eBay policies
- Maintain a rating of 4.5 or higher for the past 12 months in all four Detailed Seller Ratings (DSRs)
- Run your business by upholding eBay's community values

No, you don't need to wear an ugly tie. PowerSellers get a special icon next to their user IDs on the eBay site, thereby giving potential bidders the assurance that they're dealing with a seller of good repute who stands behind each sale. PowerSellers who meet or exceed eBay's requirements also get the following benefits:

- **Bronze level and higher** ($1,000 in gross monthly sales or 100 items a month) gets you a PowerSeller logo posted on the site next to your user ID. You also have access to a private PowerSeller discussion board and have 24/7 e-mail tech support with a very fast response time.
- **Silver level** ($3,000 average in monthly gross sales or 300 items a month) gets you the benefits of the Bronze level, plus a toll-free phone number for priority support during business hours.
- **Gold level** ($10,000 average in monthly gross sales or 1,000 items a month) gets you the benefits of the Silver level, plus a dedicated account manager and a dedicated support hot line, 24/7!

- ✔ **Platinum level** ($25,000 average month in gross sales or 2,500 items a month) gets you Gold level benefits, plus I'll bet you get quicker callbacks from your account manager than at the Gold level.

- ✔ **Titanium level** ($150,000 average month in gross sales or 15,000 items a month) probably gets you a whole lot of special attention!

- ✔ **Diamond level** ($500,000 average month in gross sales). At this level, I don't think they care how many items you sell, but I'll bet they will be supernice to you.

There are many more benefits to becoming a PowerSeller. It's something important to aim for, but start slow and hone your selling skills. You'll get there soon enough. If you feel that you qualify for eBay's PowerSellers service (eBay knows who you are!), apply at `pages.ebay.com/services/buy andsell/welcome.html`.

Trading Assistant Program

For experienced eBay sellers who have a feedback rating of 97 percent or more, the Trading Assistant program is the place to be! This is where you can register to sell items for others who don't have the time or inclination to learn how to sell on eBay.

People with items to sell go to `pages.ebay.com/tahub/` and search for Trading Assistants by zip or area code. After their search, they're presented with a list of sellers who are ready and willing to sell their goods (that's you, right?). Take a look at some of the sellers in your area who act as Trading Assistants to get an idea of what you should charge for your services. For full information, go to `ebaytradingassistant.com/`.

Appendix

Finding Stuff to Sell

· ·

After you pick clean everything not nailed down in your house, you may want to broaden your horizons. The key to successfully selling items on eBay is to find things people actually want to buy at the right price. (Wow, what an incredible observation.) I know it seems obvious, but having stuff to *sell* isn't always the same as having things people *want to buy*. Using this concept, you can teach yourself all kinds of effective marketing strategies. Finding the item that may be "the next big thing" takes lots of work, timing, and sometimes a dose of good luck.

As an eBay seller, no doubt you'll receive tons of spam (unsolicited e-mails) guaranteeing that the sender has the hottest-selling items for you to sell on eBay. Think about this for a second. If you had the hot ticket to riches, wouldn't you be selling the product on eBay and making the fortune yourself? These people aren't big-hearted millionaires; they make money by preying on those who think there's a magic way to make money on eBay. There isn't. It takes old-fashioned elbow grease and research.

Knowing the Market

Just as successful stockbrokers know about individual companies, they also need to know about the marketplace as a whole. Sure, I know about the top designer purses out there, and so does nearly everyone else. To get a leg up on your competition, you need to know the big picture as well. Here are some questions you should ask yourself as you contemplate making serious buckets of money (well, I hope) by selling items on eBay:

> ✔ **What items are currently hot?** If you see everyone around you rushing to the store to buy a particular item, chances are good that the item will become more valuable as stocks of it diminish. (iPod accessories?) The simple rule of supply and demand says that whoever has something everyone else wants stands to gain major profits. Big-box warehouse stores like Costco usually have a full stock of popular items because their very savvy buyers purchase by the truckload months in advance — how about visiting a warehouse store to find items at discount?

✔ **Do I see a growing interest in a specific item that might make it a big seller?** If you're starting to hear talk about a particular item, or even an era ('80s nostalgia? '60s aluminum Christmas trees? Who knew?), listen carefully and think of what you already own (or can get your hands on) that can help you catch a piece of the trend's action.

✔ **Should I hold on to this item and wait for its value to increase, or should I sell now?** Knowing when to sell an item that you think people may want is a tricky business. Sometimes, you can catch the trend too early and find out that you could have commanded a better price if only you had waited. Other times, you may invest in a fad that's already passé and find that no one's interested anymore. It's best to test the market with a small quantity of your hoard, dribbling items individually into the market until you've made back the money you spent to acquire them. When you have your cash back, the rest will be gravy.

I'm a huge fan of the artist George Rodrigue. When building my collection of his famous "Blue Dog" items years ago, I came across a seller who had liberated some early museum exhibition catalogs from a dumpster. Although the old catalogs had been tossed in the trash, they were boxed and bundled — and in perfect condition. Being a true-blue Rodrigue fan, I thought perhaps these catalogs might make good future eBay items. I asked the seller if he had 30 to sell, he said yes, and he sold them to me for $4 each. I resold them over the next five years for between $15 and $35 each. Spotting the trends and seeing the value in items is what it's all about.

✔ **Is a company discontinuing an item I should stockpile now and sell later?** Pay attention to items that are discontinued, especially toys and novelty items. If you find an item that a manufacturer has a limited supply of, you could make a tidy profit. If the manufacturer ends up reissuing the item, don't forget that the original run is still the most coveted — and valuable. I once bought a case of last season's footless pantyhose at a huge discount — I sold them one at a time, at a 400 percent profit, for three years.

✔ **Was there a recall, an error, or a legal proceeding associated with my item?** If so, how it affects the value of the item takes a backseat to eBay policy: An error item, okay. But items that have been recalled for safety reasons can't be sold on eBay (for details, go to pages.ebay.com/ help/policies/recalled.html). For example, a toy recalled for safety reasons may no longer be appropriate for the kids, but even if it's rare and collectible, you still can't sell it on eBay.

But here's another angle: Consider that shares of (and any paperwork to do with) the now-defunct corporation Enron became highly prized collectibles after the scandal hit.

Some people like to go with their gut feelings about when and what to buy for resale on eBay. By all means, if instinct has worked for you in the past, factor instinct in here, too. If you've done some research that looks optimistic but your gut says, "I'm not sure," listen to it; don't assume you're just hearing that lunchtime burger talking. Try testing the waters by purchasing *one* of the prospective items for resale on eBay. If that sale doesn't work out, you won't have invested a lot of money, and you can credit your gut with saving you some bucks.

Do You Have a Talent?

If you're talented in any way, you can sell your services on eBay. Home artisans, chefs, and even stay-at-home psychics are transacting business daily on the site. (Psychics are doing a land-office business)! What a great way to make money on eBay — make your own product!

Personalized and custom items do well on eBay. There's a demand for personalized invitations, cards, and announcements — and even return address labels (and you thought you had all you needed). Calligraphic work or computer-designed (customized with Fido's picture, awww) items are in big demand today, but no one seems to have the time to make them. Savvy sellers with talent can fill this market niche.

People go to trendy places (when they have the time) like Soho, the Grove, or the Village to find unique custom jewelry. They also go to eBay.

The world is your oyster on eBay, and the sky is the limit. Use your imagination, and you might be surprised at what your new business will be!

Catching Trends in the Media

Catching trends is all about listening and looking. You can find all kinds of inside information from newspapers, magazines, television, and of course, the Internet. Believe it or not, you can even find out what people are interested in these days by bribing a kid. Keep your eyes and ears open. When people say, "That GEICO gecko is *everywhere*," instead of nodding your head vacantly, start getting ideas.

In newspapers

Newspapers are bombarded by press releases and inside information from companies the world over. Pay close attention to the various sections of the newspaper. Look for stories on celebrities and upcoming movies and see if any old fads are making a resurgence (you can sell items as "retro chic" — Lava Lamps, anyone?).

Read the stories about trade conventions, like the New York Toy Fair or the Consumer Electronics show. New products are introduced and given the thumbs-up or -down by journalists. This way you can start to think about the direction your area of expertise is heading.

On television

No matter what you think of television, it has an enormous impact on which trends come and go and which ones stick. Why else would advertisers sink billions of dollars into TV commercials? And look at the impact of Oprah's Book Club. Just one Oprah appearance for an author can turn a book into an overnight bestseller. More and more celebrities (even Homer Simpson) are talking about eBay. The buzz brings people to the site.

Tune in to morning news shows and afternoon talk shows. See what's being featured in the programs. The producers of these shows are on top of pop culture and move fast to be the first to bring you the next big thing. Take what they feature and think of a marketing angle. If you don't, you can be sure somebody else will.

Catch up with youth culture . . .

. . . or at least keep good tabs on it. There seems to be no catching up with it, just as there's no way to say this without sounding over-the-hill: If you remember cranking up The Beatles, James Brown, or The Partridge Family (say what?) until your parents screamed, "Shut that awful noise off," you may be at that awkward time of life when you hardly see the appeal of what young people are doing or listening to. But if you want tips for hot-selling items, tolerate the awful noise of today's music (how *did* that happen?) and listen to the kids around you. (Try to watch a little MTV, too.) Children, especially preteens and teens, may be the best trend-spotters on the planet. See what kind of marketing tips you get when you ask a kid questions like these:

- ✔ **What's cool at the moment?** Or "rad" if you want to sound cool — whoops, that was '80s-speak, wasn't it?

- ✔ **What's totally uncool that was cool two months ago?** Their world moves at warp speed!

- ✔ **What music are you buying?** Kanye West, Kelly Clarkson, Coldplay, and Black-Eyed Peas — yup, all the hot bands with big hits — but maybe *ewww-that's-so-five-minutes-ago* by the time you read this.

- ✔ **What could I buy you that would make you really happy?** *Hint:* If the kid says, "A red BMW Z-3," or "Liposuction," look for a younger kid.

Collecting magazines

Although not quite a plethora, the number of magazines geared to collectors is definitely approaching a slew. Although these magazines won't help you catch a trend (by the time it gets into one of these magazines, somebody's already caught it), they can give you great information on pricing, availability, and general collecting information. And you can follow the course of a trend for a real-life example of how it works. Here's a list of collectors' magazines that I like:

✔ **Antique Trader** has been the bible of the antique collecting industry for over 40 years. Visit its online home at www. antiquetrader.com for more articles and other information.

✔ **Collect.com** is a Web site from Krause publications. It gives you info on over 35 different collector's publications for everything from stamps to toys to muscle cars.

✔ **Barbie Bazaar** has info on everything related to Barbie. Go to www.hautedoll.com.

✔ **Numismatic News** is an old standard that has been around for more than 50 years. The first issue each month includes a pullout guide to retail U.S. coin prices. Every three months, it also includes a U.S. papermoney price guide.

Check out eBay

Another important link goes to the *eBay Pulse*. Visit the Pulse page and you can find an up-to-the-minute snapshot of the most-searched-for items in each category. This is usually pretty amusing reading — you'd be surprised how many people are watching eBay listings for get-rich-quick schemes — right along with expensive real estate! You can also reach this page by going directly to pulse.ebay.com. There's a drop-down menu at the top of the page, so you can see the most-searched-for items in the main categories.

Check out magazines

Magazines geared to the 18-to-34 age group (and sometimes to younger teens — they call them *tweens*) can help you stay on top of what's hot. See what the big companies are pitching to this target audience and whether they're succeeding. If a celebrity's suddenly visible in every other headline or magazine, be on the lookout for merchandise relating to that person. (Are we talking hysteria-plus-cash-flow here, or just hysteria?)

The Hunt for eBay Inventory

If you're not sure what you want to sell for profit on eBay — but you're a shop-till-you-drop person by nature — you have an edge. Incorporate your advanced shopping techniques into your daily routine. If you find a bargain that interests you, chances are you have a knack for spotting stuff that other shoppers would love to get their hands on.

The goods are out there

When you shop to sell on eBay, don't rule out any shopping venue. From the trendiest boutique to the smallest second-hand store, from garage sales to Saks Outlet, keep your eye out for eBay inventory. The items people look for on eBay are out there; you just have to find them.

Check your favorite eBay category and see what the hot-selling items are. Better yet, go to your favorite store and make friends with the manager. Store managers are often privy to this type of information a couple of months in advance of a product release. If you ask, they'll tell you what's going to be the hot new item next month. After you're armed with the information you need, seek out that item for the lowest price you can, and then you can give it a shot on eBay.

Keep these shopping locales in mind when you go on the eBay hunt:

- Upscale department stores, trendy boutiques, outlet stores, or flagship designer stores are good places to do some market research. Check out the newest items — and then head to the clearance area or outlet store and scrutinize the bargain racks for brand-name items.

- Tour some of the discount and dollar stores in your area. Many of the items these places carry are *overruns* (too many of something that didn't sell), *small runs* (too little of something that the big guys weren't interested in stocking), or out-of-date fad items that need a good home on eBay.

- Garage sales, tag sales, and moving sales offer some of the biggest bargains you'll ever come across. Check for vintage kitchen pieces, designer goods, and old toys, and make 'em an offer they can't refuse.

- Thrift stores are packed with used but usually good-quality items. And you can feel good knowing that the money you spend in a nonprofit thrift shop is going to a good cause.

- Find going-out-of-business sales. You can pick up bargains by the case if a shopkeeper just wants to empty the shelves so the store can close.

 ✔ Take advantage of any flea markets or swap meets in your area.

 ✔ Gift shops at museums, monuments, national parks, and theme parks can provide eBay inventory — but think about where to sell the items. Part of your selling success on eBay is *access*. People who can't get to Graceland may pay handsomely for an Elvis mini-guitar with the official logo on the box. *Or maybe not?*

 ✔ Hang on to the freebies you get. If you receive handouts (lapel pins, pencils, pamphlets, books, interesting napkins, flashlights, towels, stuffed toys) from a sporting event, premiere, or historic event — or even a collectible freebie from a fast-food restaurant — any of them could be your ticket to some eBay sales.

Tips for the modest investor

If you're interested in making money in your eBay ventures but you're starting with limited cash, follow this list of eBay inventory do's and don'ts:

 ✔ **Don't** spend more than you can afford to lose. If you shop at boutiques and expensive department stores, buy things that you like to wear yourself (or give as gifts) in case they don't sell.

 ✔ **Do** try to find something local that's unavailable in a wider area. For example, if you live in an out-of-the-way place that has a local specialty, try selling that on eBay.

 ✔ **Don't** go overboard and buy something really cheap just because it's cheap. Figure out who would *want* the item first.

 ✔ **Do** consider buying in bulk, especially if you know the item sells well on eBay or if the item is inexpensive. Chances are good that if you buy one and it sells well on eBay, by the time you try to buy more, the item's sold out. If an item is inexpensive (say, 99 cents), I always buy at least five. If no one bids on the item when you hold your auction, you're only out $5. (Anyone out there need any Bicentennial Commemorative coffee mugs?)

Index

• F •

● **G** ●

● **H** ●

USINESS, CAREERS & PERSONAL FINANCE

ccounting For Dummies, 4th Edition*
8-0-470-24600-9

ookkeeping Workbook For Dummies†
8-0-470-16983-4

mmodities For Dummies
8-0-470-04928-0

ing Business in China For Dummies
8-0-470-04929-7

E-Mail Marketing For Dummies
978-0-470-19087-6

Job Interviews For Dummies, 3rd Edition*†
978-0-470-17748-8

Personal Finance Workbook For Dummies*†
978-0-470-09933-9

Real Estate License Exams For Dummies
978-0-7645-7623-2

Six Sigma For Dummies
978-0-7645-6798-8

Small Business Kit For Dummies, 2nd Edition*†
978-0-7645-5984-6

Telephone Sales For Dummies
978-0-470-16836-3

USINESS PRODUCTIVITY & MICROSOFT OFFICE

cess 2007 For Dummies
8-0-470-03649-5

cel 2007 For Dummies
8-0-470-03737-9

fice 2007 For Dummies
8-0-470-00923-9

tlook 2007 For Dummies
8-0-470-03830-7

PowerPoint 2007 For Dummies
978-0-470-04059-1

Project 2007 For Dummies
978-0-470-03651-8

QuickBooks 2008 For Dummies
978-0-470-18470-7

Quicken 2008 For Dummies
978-0-470-17473-9

Salesforce.com For Dummies, 2nd Edition
978-0-470-04893-1

Word 2007 For Dummies
978-0-470-03658-7

UCATION, HISTORY, REFERENCE & TEST PREPARATION

rican American History For Dummies
8-0-7645-5469-8

gebra For Dummies
8-0-7645-5325-7

gebra Workbook For Dummies
8-0-7645-8467-1

t History For Dummies
8-0-470-09910-0

ASVAB For Dummies, 2nd Edition
978-0-470-10671-6

British Military History For Dummies
978-0-470-03213-8

Calculus For Dummies
978-0-7645-2498-1

Canadian History For Dummies, 2nd Edition
978-0-470-83656-9

Geometry Workbook For Dummies
978-0-471-79940-5

The SAT I For Dummies, 6th Edition
978-0-7645-7193-0

Series 7 Exam For Dummies
978-0-470-09932-2

World History For Dummies
978-0-7645-5242-7

OOD, GARDEN, HOBBIES & HOME

idge For Dummies, 2nd Edition
8-0-471-92426-5

in Collecting For Dummies, 2nd Edition
8-0-470-22275-1

oking Basics For Dummies, 3rd Edition
8-0-7645-7206-7

Drawing For Dummies
978-0-7645-5476-6

Etiquette For Dummies, 2nd Edition
978-0-470-10672-3

Gardening Basics For Dummies*†
978-0-470-03749-2

Knitting Patterns For Dummies
978-0-470-04556-5

Living Gluten-Free For Dummies†
978-0-471-77383-2

Painting Do-It-Yourself For Dummies
978-0-470-17533-0

EALTH, SELF HELP, PARENTING & PETS

ger Management For Dummies
8-0-470-03715-7

xiety & Depression Workbook r Dummies
8-0-7645-9793-0

eting For Dummies, 2nd Edition
8-0-7645-4149-0

g Training For Dummies, 2nd Edition
8-0-7645-8418-3

Horseback Riding For Dummies
978-0-470-09719-9

Infertility For Dummies†
978-0-470-11518-3

Meditation For Dummies with CD-ROM, 2nd Edition
978-0-471-77774-8

Post-Traumatic Stress Disorder For Dummies
978-0-470-04922-8

Puppies For Dummies, 2nd Edition
978-0-470-03717-1

Thyroid For Dummies, 2nd Edition†
978-0-471-78755-6

Type 1 Diabetes For Dummies*†
978-0-470-17811-9

INTERNET & DIGITAL MEDIA

AdWords For Dummies
978-0-470-15252-2

Blogging For Dummies, 2nd Edition
978-0-470-23017-6

Digital Photography All-in-One Desk Reference For Dummies, 3rd Edition
978-0-470-03743-0

Digital Photography For Dummies, 5th Edition
978-0-7645-9802-9

Digital SLR Cameras & Photography For Dummies, 2nd Edition
978-0-470-14927-0

eBay Business All-in-One Desk Reference For Dummies
978-0-7645-8438-1

eBay For Dummies, 5th Edition*
978-0-470-04529-9

eBay Listings That Sell For Dummies
978-0-471-78912-3

Facebook For Dummies
978-0-470-26273-3

The Internet For Dummies, 11th Edition
978-0-470-12174-0

Investing Online For Dummies, 5th Edition
978-0-7645-8456-5

iPod & iTunes For Dummies, 5th Editi
978-0-470-17474-6

MySpace For Dummies
978-0-470-09529-4

Podcasting For Dummies
978-0-471-74898-4

Search Engine Optimization For Dummies, 2nd Edition
978-0-471-97998-2

Second Life For Dummies
978-0-470-18025-9

Starting an eBay Business For Dumm 3rd Edition†
978-0-470-14924-9

GRAPHICS, DESIGN & WEB DEVELOPMENT

Adobe Creative Suite 3 Design Premium All-in-One Desk Reference For Dummies
978-0-470-11724-8

Adobe Web Suite CS3 All-in-One Desk Reference For Dummies
978-0-470-12099-6

AutoCAD 2008 For Dummies
978-0-470-11650-0

Building a Web Site For Dummies, 3rd Edition
978-0-470-14928-7

Creating Web Pages All-in-One Desk Reference For Dummies, 3rd Edition
978-0-470-09629-1

Creating Web Pages For Dummies, 8th Edition
978-0-470-08030-6

Dreamweaver CS3 For Dummies
978-0-470-11490-2

Flash CS3 For Dummies
978-0-470-12100-9

Google SketchUp For Dummies
978-0-470-13744-4

InDesign CS3 For Dummies
978-0-470-11865-8

Photoshop CS3 All-in-One Desk Reference For Dummies
978-0-470-11195-6

Photoshop CS3 For Dummies
978-0-470-11193-2

Photoshop Elements 5 For Dummie
978-0-470-09810-3

SolidWorks For Dummies
978-0-7645-9555-4

Visio 2007 For Dummies
978-0-470-08983-5

Web Design For Dummies, 2nd Edit
978-0-471-78117-2

Web Sites Do-It-Yourself For Dumm
978-0-470-16903-2

Web Stores Do-It-Yourself For Dumm
978-0-470-17443-2

LANGUAGES, RELIGION & SPIRITUALITY

Arabic For Dummies
978-0-471-77270-5

Chinese For Dummies, Audio Set
978-0-470-12766-7

French For Dummies
978-0-7645-5193-2

German For Dummies
978-0-7645-5195-6

Hebrew For Dummies
978-0-7645-5489-6

Ingles Para Dummies
978-0-7645-5427-8

Italian For Dummies, Audio Set
978-0-470-09586-7

Italian Verbs For Dummies
978-0-471-77389-4

Japanese For Dummies
978-0-7645-5429-2

Latin For Dummies
978-0-7645-5431-5

Portuguese For Dummies
978-0-471-78738-9

Russian For Dummies
978-0-471-78001-4

Spanish Phrases For Dummies
978-0-7645-7204-3

Spanish For Dummies
978-0-7645-5194-9

Spanish For Dummies, Audio Set
978-0-470-09585-0

The Bible For Dummies
978-0-7645-5296-0

Catholicism For Dummies
978-0-7645-5391-2

The Historical Jesus For Dummies
978-0-470-16785-4

Islam For Dummies
978-0-7645-5503-9

Spirituality For Dummies, 2nd Edition
978-0-470-19142-2

NETWORKING AND PROGRAMMING

ASP.NET 3.5 For Dummies
978-0-470-19592-5

C# 2008 For Dummies
978-0-470-19109-5

Hacking For Dummies, 2nd Edition
978-0-470-05235-8

Home Networking For Dummies, 4th Edition
978-0-470-11806-1

Java For Dummies, 4th Edition
978-0-470-08716-9

Microsoft® SQL Server™ 2008 All-in-One Desk Reference For Dummies
978-0-470-17954-3

Networking All-in-One Desk Reference For Dummies, 2nd Edition
978-0-7645-9939-2

Networking For Dummies, 8th Edition
978-0-470-05620-2

SharePoint 2007 For Dummies
978-0-470-09941-4

Wireless Home Networking For Dummies, 2nd Edition
978-0-471-74940-0

OPERATING SYSTEMS & COMPUTER BASICS

Mac For Dummies, 5th Edition
978-0-7645-8458-9

Laptops For Dummies, 2nd Edition
978-0-470-05432-1

Linux For Dummies, 8th Edition
978-0-470-11649-4

MacBook For Dummies
978-0-470-04859-7

Mac OS X Leopard All-in-One
Desk Reference For Dummies
978-0-470-05434-5

Mac OS X Leopard For Dummies
978-0-470-05433-8

Macs For Dummies, 9th Edition
978-0-470-04849-8

PCs For Dummies, 11th Edition
978-0-470-13728-4

Windows® Home Server For Dummies
978-0-470-18592-6

Windows Server 2008 For Dummies
978-0-470-18043-3

Windows Vista All-in-One
Desk Reference For Dummies
978-0-471-74941-7

Windows Vista For Dummies
978-0-471-75421-3

Windows Vista Security For Dummies
978-0-470-11805-4

SPORTS, FITNESS & MUSIC

Coaching Hockey For Dummies
978-0-470-83685-9

Coaching Soccer For Dummies
978-0-471-77381-8

Fitness For Dummies, 3rd Edition
978-0-7645-7851-9

Football For Dummies, 3rd Edition
978-0-470-12536-6

GarageBand For Dummies
978-0-7645-7323-1

Golf For Dummies, 3rd Edition
978-0-471-76871-5

Guitar For Dummies, 2nd Edition
978-0-7645-9904-0

Home Recording For Musicians
For Dummies, 2nd Edition
978-0-7645-8884-6

iPod & iTunes For Dummies,
5th Edition
978-0-470-17474-6

Music Theory For Dummies
978-0-7645-7838-0

Stretching For Dummies
978-0-470-06741-3

Get smart @ dummies.com®

- Find a full list of Dummies titles
- Look into loads of FREE on-site articles
- Sign up for FREE eTips e-mailed to you weekly
- See what other products carry the Dummies name
- Shop directly from the Dummies bookstore
- Enter to win new prizes every month!

Separate Canadian edition also available
Separate U.K. edition also available

Available wherever books are sold. For more information or to order direct: U.S. customers visit www.dummies.com or call 1-877-762-2974.
U.K. customers visit www.wileyeurope.com or call (0) 1243 843291. Canadian customers visit www.wiley.ca or call 1-800-567-4797.